Google Blogger For Dummies®

Designing Your Blog

Find Free Blogger Templates to Personalize Your Blog

eBlogTemplates	www.eblogtemplates.com
BTemplates	www.btemplates.com
Blogger Buster	www.bloggerbuster.com
BlogFlux	themes.blogflux.com
Pyzam	www.pyzam.com
Jackbook	www.jackbook.com/category/blogger-templates-gallery

Promoting Your Blog

Find Social Networking and Microblogging Sites

Facebook	www.facebook.com
LinkedIn	www.linkedin.com
MySpace	www.myspace.com
Friendster	www.friendster.com
Ning	www.ning.com
Orkut	www.orkut.com
Xanga	www.xanga.com
Pownce	www.pownce.com
Twitter	www.twitter.com
Plurk	www.plurk.com

Find Social Bookmarking Sites

Digg	www.digg.com
StumbleUpon	www.stumbleupon.com
Reddit	www.reddit.com
Yahoo! Buzz	http://buzz.yahoo.com/
Delicious	www.delicious.com
Fark	www.fark.com
Furl	www.furl.net
Kirtsy	www.kirtsy.com
Magnolia	http://ma.gnolia.com/
Slashdot	www.slashdot.org
Propeller	www.propeller.com
Sphere	www.sphere.com
Newsvine	www.newsvine.com

Making Money from Your Blog

Use Contextual, Text and Impression Ads

Google AdSense	http://adsense.google.com
Kontera	www.kontera.com
AdBrite	www.adbrite.com
Adgenta/Q-Ads	www.adgenta.com
Text Link Ads	www.text-link-ads.com
Text Link Brokers	www.textlinkbrokers.com
Tribal Fusion	www.tribalfusion.com
Value Click	www.valueclick.com

For Dummies: Bestselling Book Series for Beginners

Google Blogger For Dummies®

Cheat Sheet

Join Affiliate Programs

Amazon Associates	https://affiliate program.amazon.com/join
LinkShare	www.linkshare.com
Commission Junction	www.cj.com
eBay Affiliates	affiliates.ebay.com
AllPosters	affiliates.allposters.com/affiliatesnet
Associate Programs	www.associate programs.com
The Affiliate Program Directory	http://affiliates directory.com
Refer-It	http://refer-it.com

Try Paid Posting

PayPerPost	www.payperpost.com
SocialSpark	www.socialspark.com
ReviewMe	www.reviewme.com
PayU2Blog	www.payu2blog.com
Sponsored Reviews	www.sponsored reviews.com

Offer Merchandising and Mini Malls

Chitika's eMiniMalls	www.chitika.com
CafePress	www.cafepress.com
Printfection	www.print fection.com
Zazzle	www.zazzle.com

Getting Help

Blogger Help	http://help.blogger.com
Google Group	http://groups.google.com/group/blogger-help
About.com	http://weblogs.about.com
Blogger Buster	www.blogger buster.com
Blogger Videos	www.recognized expert.com/blogger/
YouTube Help	www.youtube.com/bloggerhelp

For Dummies: Bestselling Book Series for Beginners

ce

Google Blogger™

FOR

D

This book is due for return on or before the last date shown below.

B

Google Blogger™ FOR DUMMIES®

by Susan Gunelius

Wiley Publishing, Inc.

Google Blogger™ For Dummies®

Published by
Wiley Publishing, Inc.
111 River Street
Hoboken, NJ 07030-5774

www.wiley.com

WILEY

About the Author

Susan Gunelius is a marketing expert who added blogging to her skill set as an extension of her career as an author and a freelance writer. Her marketing background and writing experience allowed her to quickly learn and leverage the blogosphere as a tool for personal and professional growth. Today, Susan is a professional blogger authoring several blogs for various small and large companies. Additionally, she writes her company blog at www. KeySplashCreative.com/category/blog and a personal blog at www. WomenOnBusiness.com, and she is the Guide to Web Logs for About.com, a New York Times company (http://weblogs.about.com).

Susan spent the first decade of her career managing and executing marketing programs for some of the largest companies in the world, including divisions of AT&T and HSBC Bank. In 2004, she left the corporate world and, shortly thereafter, began a freelance career as a writer, a copywriter, an author, a professional blogger, and a marketing and branding consultant. In 2008, she opened KeySplash Creative, Inc. (www.KeySplashCreative.com), and as its president, offers marketing and writing services to clients around the world.

Susan's marketing-related articles have appeared on Web sites such as Entrepreneur.com, MSNBC.com, FoxBusiness.com, WashingtonPost.com, TheStreet.com, SmartMoney.com, Yahoo! Small Business, and Yahoo! Finance. Additionally, she is the author of *Harry Potter: The Story of a Global Business Phenomenon* (Palgrave Macmillan) and *Kick-ass Copywriting in 10 Easy Steps* (Entrepreneur Press).

Dedication

To my husband, Scott, who encourages me to pursue my goals and makes countless sacrifices to help me reach them.

Author's Acknowledgments

First, I have to acknowledge my husband, Scott, for making sure our home keeps running while I write, and my children — Brynn, Daniel, and Ryan — for continuing to thrive despite my absence while I write. I also want to thank my parents, Bill and Carol Ann Henry, for their constant support and help while I write.

I want to thank my acquisitions editor at Wiley, Amy Fandrei, for asking me to write this book, and Tiffany Ma, Mark Enochs, and Nicole Sholly at Wiley for helping to make the book a reality. A big thank-you also goes to my technical editor, Roberta Rosenberg.

My agent, Bob Diforio, also deserves a thank-you for staying on top of all the ideas and opportunities I bring to him and working with my best interests in mind.

Finally, I want to acknowledge every person who reads my blogs and say "Thank you" for being interested in reading what I have to say and for joining the conversation.

Publisher's Acknowledgments

We're proud of this book; please send us your comments through our online registration form located at `http://dummies.custhelp.com`. For other comments, please contact our Customer Care Department within the U.S. at 877-762-2974, outside the U.S. at 317-572-3993, or fax 317-572-4002.

Some of the people who helped bring this book to market include the following:

Acquisitions, Editorial

Project Editor: Nicole Sholly

Acquisitions Editor: Amy Fandrei

Copy Editors: Rebecca Whitney, Brian Walls

Technical Editor: Roberta Rosenberg

Editorial Managers: Kevin Kirschner, Jodi Jensen

Editorial Assistant: Amanda Foxworth

Sr. Editorial Assistant: Cherie Case

Cartoons: Rich Tennant (`www.the5thwave.com`)

Composition Services

Project Coordinator: Erin Smith

Layout and Graphics: Reuben W. Davis, Melissa K. Jester, Ronald Terry, Christine Williams

Proofreaders: Evelyn W. Gibson, John Greenough

Indexer: Sharon Shock

Special Help: Colleen Totz-Diamond, Mark Enochs

Publishing and Editorial for Technology Dummies

Richard Swadley, Vice President and Executive Group Publisher

Andy Cummings, Vice President and Publisher

Mary Bednarek, Executive Acquisitions Director

Mary C. Corder, Editorial Director

Publishing for Consumer Dummies

Diane Graves Steele, Vice President and Publisher

Composition Services

Gerry Fahey, Vice President of Production Services

Debbie Stailey, Director of Composition Services

Contents at a Glance

Table of Contents

Introduction

Whether your blogging goals are to flex your creative writing muscles, share photos with friends around the world, make money, or support a growing business, all the tools you need are at your fingertips with Google Blogger. This book shows you how to find those tools and use them successfully.

Blogging can be confusing and intimidating. A perusal of the Internet reveals a wealth of information from people from all walks of life who have varying experiences and opinions. *Google Blogger For Dummies* cuts through the hearsay and opinions to deliver the information you need in order to use the most popular blogging software program now available. Read each chapter as you develop your blog, and you'll soon find that you're no longer a novice but rather, one of the seasoned pros that other bloggers seek out for advice, opinions, and networking.

About Google Blogger For Dummies

Google Blogger For Dummies offers easy-to-follow, step-by-step instructions to help new bloggers get started with Blogger immediately. Here's some of the information you can take in as you read this book — you'll find out how to

- Set up your blog by using Blogger
- Organize your blog so it's positioned for success from the start
- Make sense of blogging terminology
- Become comfortable with the Blogger dashboard (how to use it and what to do with it)
- Publish posts and join the blogosphere
- Design your blog by using layouts and templates
- Incorporate images, videos, and more into your blog
- Explore the many features that are available to enhance your blog
- Manage your blog's performance
- Make money from your blog

✔ Grow your blog through networking, promotion, and search engine optimization

✔ Use various media to blog, such as audio and video

✔ Find help when you need it

Blogger is an excellent blogging platform choice for beginning bloggers. It's easy to use, chock-full of helpful features (and more are added all the time), and — best of all — completely free! Don't be afraid to dive in and start blogging with this book by your side.

Foolish Assumptions

I wrote *Google Blogger For Dummies* with the beginning blogger's knowledge level in mind. Although this book is a beginner's guide, I assume a few things about you before you begin reading:

✔ You have a computer, and you know how to use it. You know at least how to turn it on and access the Internet.

✔ You know how to browse the Web.

✔ You understand what blogging is and have already read (or at least seen) blogs.

✔ You want to start your own blog or you already have a blog and want to find out how to use the features that are available to you in Blogger to enhance your existing blog.

If you aren't familiar with blogging, I suggest that you also read *Blogging For Dummies,* Second Edition, by Susannah Gardner and Shane Birley (Wiley Publishing).

Conventions Used in This Book

Don't get nervous. *Conventions* are simply a set of rules used throughout this book to present information to you consistently. When you see a term *italicized,* for example, look for its definition, which is included so that you know what things mean in the context of blogging. Sometimes, step-by-step instructions included in this book direct you to enter specific text on-screen. In this case, the text you need to type appears in **bold.** Web site addresses (URLs) and e-mail addresses are in `monofont` so that they stand out from regular text.

What You Don't Have to Read

Google Blogger For Dummies is split into six parts. You don't have to read this book sequentially, and you don't even have to read all the sections in any particular chapter. You can use the table of contents and the index to find the information you need and to quickly get answers to help you complete the task at hand.

Keep in mind that you might never need to read some sections of this book. For example, if you have no intention of trying to make money from your blog, you can skip Part III. I have to point out, however, that this book is set up chronologically: A novice blogger who works through each chapter sequentially will have a fully functional and feature-rich blog by the time she reaches the end of the book. How you choose to use this book is up to you, though.

How This Book Is Organized

Google Blogger For Dummies is made up of six parts. Here's a description of what you can find in each part.

Part I: Introducing Google Blogger

Part I provides an introduction to blogging and Blogger. I tell you what blogging is and how to prepare to create your own blog, and then I give you all the basic terminology you need to dive into the blogosphere.

Part II: Using Google Blogger

In Part II, you start to get your feet wet and your hands dirty. In other words, get ready to begin building your blog with Blogger!

You find out how to create your Blogger account, develop your profile, configure your blog's settings and options, and write and publish your first post. You also find out how to enhance your posts with features and personalize your blog design by using unique templates. Because blogging is about more than just publishing content, this part of the book also shows you how to manage and maintain your blog for long-term success. Finally, I tell you about the written and unwritten rules of the blogosphere so that your foray into blogging is successful and problem-free.

Part III: Making Money with Blogger

If you're interested in making money from your blog, you don't want to miss this part of the book. You find out about various blog monetization methods and are introduced in depth to Google AdSense, which integrates directly with Blogger.

Part IV: Growing Your Audience

If you want to grow your blog and attract new visitors to it, be sure to read Part IV, where you find out how to promote your blog by using social networking and social bookmarking. You also find out how to use search engine optimization techniques to boost traffic from search engines to your blog.

Part V: Extending Your Blog

There may come a time when you want to add a blog to your Blogger account or delete a blog. This part teaches you how to do both and how to add users to your existing blog or to join another blogger's blog. You're also introduced to podcasting, vlogging, and moblogging. Finally, if you want to get your own domain name or host your blog by using a third-party host, you can find out how in this part.

Part VI: The Part of Tens

The Part of Tens is a useful feature of all *For Dummies* books. You can read quick lists that provide high level information to help you find Blogger templates and to solve common Blogger problems.

Glossary

The blogosphere and social Web have a language all their own. Use the glossary to make sense of the terms you don't understand that are used throughout this book.

Icons Used in This Book

A unique and incredibly useful feature of all *For Dummies* books is the inclusion of helpful icons that point you in the direction of valuable information, tips, and tricks:

Points out helpful information that's likely to save you time and effort.

Marks a fact that's interesting and useful — something that you might want to remember for later use.

Highlights lurking danger. This icon tells you to pay attention and proceed with caution.

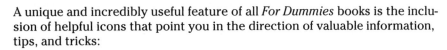

Points to techie-type stuff nearby. If you're not feeling highly technical, you can skip this info, but if you're brave, the information next to the Technical Stuff icons throughout this book can be extremely helpful.

Where to Go from Here

This book can be read in any order you choose. Each chapter stands on its own and can help you tackle specific tasks. For example, if you already have a Blogger account but have yet to set up your blog, go directly to Part II to find how to personalize your blog and start publishing content. If you know how to use Blogger but want to better understand how to use the features that are offered to you, check out Chapter 8. If you have an active blog and want to monetize it, read Part III; to grow your blog, read Part IV. Your first stop is to read the table of contents and find the sections of this book that you need at any time.

Blogging is fun! Don't overthink things. Keep this book handy and refer to it as needed. Now, turn the page and prepare to join the exciting world of blogging.

Part I
Introducing
Google Blogger

The 5th Wave   By Rich Tennant

"No, we're here to introduce Google Bloggers.
Bloggers. Not loggers..."

In this part . . .

Meet Blogger, the most popular free blogging software program. Millions of people just like you started their forays into the blogosphere with little or no knowledge of what to do first or where to find help. You might even be wondering what Blogger is or what Google has to do with this whole blogging thing.

You've come to the right place (or should I say, chosen the right book) to find the answers you need to not just join the blogosphere but also to become an active, contributing member. Starting a blog can be intimidating, so the best place to start is at the beginning.

Part 1 shows you not only what Blogger is but also how to start your own blog by using the Blogger platform. From choosing your blog topic and domain name to understanding the terminology that goes with blogging, you can find all the basics here.

Chapter 1

Choosing Blogger as Your Blogging Software

So you made the decision to start a blog. Blogger is a perfect tool to help you publish your thoughts, ideas, and opinions as part of the growing blogosphere. Blogger not only is user-friendly but also has the power of one of the world's strongest brands behind it: Google. Starting a blog might seem intimidating at first, but blogging is one of the simplest ways to get your voice heard.

Whether you're starting a blog for business or just for fun, Blogger offers the tools, features, and support you need to be a successful blogger. To top it off, Blogger is completely free to use. In this chapter, I tell you what Blogger can do for you to help you make the most of your blogging experience. You might be surprised at just how much this free blogging platform has to offer.

Introducing Blogger

Pyra Labs launched Blogger in 1999 as one of the first programs dedicated completely to blogging. At the time, blogging was in its infancy, and the three Web developers who created Blogger had no idea what their product would grow to become.

Blogger is often credited with helping to boost blogging into the mainstream. By offering an easy-to-use and easily accessible blogging platform, people slowly began to realize how much power blogging could deliver. Terms such as *user-generated content, citizen journalism,* and *social Web* became part of the common vernacular, and people (and businesses) from all walks of life wanted to jump on the blogging bandwagon.

But what exactly is a blogging platform? In the simplest terms, a *blogging platform* (or blogging software) is the computer program that does all the work behind the scenes to publish your content on the Internet. You type the content into your blogging software, such as Blogger, WordPress, or TypePad, and the blogging software creates a Web site where your content resides (see Figure 1-1). The blogging software formats your content, dates it, archives it, and more. Suddenly, having a Web site was no longer a possibility only for businesses with a budget to burn. With the birth of blogging and the popularity of Blogger, anyone could have an online presence, become a *blogger*, and join an online community that would come to be known as the *blogosphere.*

Blogger simply gives your blog a home online. Imagine Blogger as a banquet hall. As host, Blogger offers a location for various people to create and store their blogs just as a banquet hall gives people a place to hold events. What happens on your blog and the success of your blog depends on you.

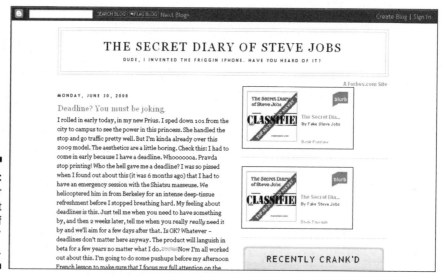

Figure 1-1:
The popular
"The Secret
Diary of
Steve Jobs"
blog.

Unlike a traditional Web site that offers a static message, a blog works more like an online diary with posts published in reverse chronological order. In this way, blogs tell a story, and that story is completely up to the blogger, who has the freedom to write and publish anything he wants. Although blogs started out as very simple online diaries, they grew to be much more. Blogs are still used now by many people simply for fun, but they are also used by people who try to earn an income from them, launch a new career, or build a business, for example. The opportunities that blogs create are seemingly endless. It's all up to the blogger.

Of course, some unwritten rules of the blogosphere and secrets to success exist, such as posting frequency, networking, and creating compelling content. However, a blog is the product of the blogger and evolves the way the blogger desires. At its core, blogging is a simple concept. It requires little to no monetary investment but could potentially demand a great deal of sweat equity.

Understanding the Google Connection

In 2003, Google noticed Blogger and made an offer to purchase the blogging platform from Pyra Labs. Google had been known in the online world as the search engine powerhouse that was extending its reach to include online advertising and more. In fact, Blogger could be considered one of the first in a string of acquisitions made by Google to extend its brand and its strength in the online market.

It turned out that Google's timing was perfect, and Blogger's hundreds of thousands of users quickly turned into millions. Google benefited from new access to millions of customers, and Blogger users benefited from a series of redesigns and upgrades to the software program that made it easier to use and added more functionality than ever. Those upgrades and redesigns would allow the new Blogger to retain its position as the leader in a market that was growing more and more competitive every day. The blogging platform that was once considered the "beginner's tool" continues to attract new users at a staggering rate.

Blogger users can now leverage the power of Google and its many products. Considering the availability of Google applications, users of Blogger can easily incorporate them into their blogs to advertise, publish content from mobile phones, upload and embed videos, and send RSS feeds to their feed readers. Here are several Google applications that users of Blogger can incorporate into their blogs:

✓ **Google Docs:** With Google Docs, users can create documents, spreadsheets, and presentations. Google Docs is particularly helpful when bloggers want to share documents with other people or publish presentations on their blogs.

✓ **Blogger Mobile:** If you use a mobile device in the United States, you may be able to publish content on your blog directly from that device. Take a look at Chapter 15 for details about blogging via your mobile device.

✔ **Google Earth:** Google Earth is a perfect tool for creating maps for your blog.

✔ **Gmail:** Gmail is an excellent free email program that can be accessed from any computer. Read Chapter 9 to see how Gmail works seamlessly with Mail-to-Blogger and makes it easy to publish blog posts from anywhere at any time.

✔ **Google Groups:** You can join Google Groups that interest you in order to network and share information with like-minded people. Alternatively, you can start your own Google Group. Each of these activities can help drive traffic to your blog, as described in Chapter 12.

✔ **Picasa:** When you upload photos to Blogger, they're stored in your Picasa account, which comes free with Blogger. You can also organize and edit your photos by using Picasa. Check out Chapter 6 for details about Picasa.

✔ **Feedburner:** Feedburner is the most popular Web content feed-management program online. You can share your blog's feed using Feedburner for readers to subscribe to using their feed reader of choice, such as Google Reader. Chapter 9 provides more information about blog feeds.

✔ **Google Toolbar:** Using the free Google toolbar helps you save time because redundant tasks are quicker to perform with a click of the mouse. Additionally, the Blogger instant-blogging feature, BlogThis!, appears directly on the Google Toolbar. BlogThis! is covered in Chapter 9.

✔ **Google Reader:** Google Reader allows you to subscribe to blogs and to follow those feeds from any computer or certain mobile devices. More details about Google Reader are in Chapter 9.

✔ **YouTube:** You can upload your own YouTube videos to embed in your blog, or you can use YouTube to find videos by other users that you want to share in your blog. Check out Chapter 15 for more information on adding videos to your blog posts.

✔ **Google Video:** Google Video is a video search engine as well as a site to upload videos that you can link to or embed in your blog.

✔ **Google AdSense:** AdSense is an advertising system you can use to display ads on your blog in order to generate revenue. Read Chapter 11 for all the details about Google AdSense.

✔ **Orkut:** You can use the Orkut social networking site to promote your blog. Find out more about social networking in Chapter 12.

Debunking Blogger Myths

The following Blogger myths can be found circulating the Internet in online conversations, but they hold little to no validity:

✔ **Blogger is too frequently unavailable.** In the past, users complained that the Blogger software would "go down" too frequently, meaning that it was unavailable to users who wanted to update their blogs and to readers who wanted to read those blogs. Since Blogger has moved completely into the Google infrastructure, the system has become more stable and more reliable.

✔ **Blogger deletes blogs haphazardly.** Users also complained about their blogs suddenly disappearing altogether. Many users who suffered this fate discovered their blogs were temporarily or permanently deleted due to potential policy infringements, covered in Chapter 18.

✔ **Blogger offers very few features.** Other blogging software programs, such as WordPress, offer a wide array of added features, which makes them superior to Blogger. Since Google purchased Blogger in 2007, new features are added all the time to make Blogger more competitive with WordPress.

✔ **Blogger is good only for beginner bloggers.** The limited functionality of Blogger created a reputation for the software as inadequate for power bloggers. Google has invested time and money into enhancing Blogger's functionality so it remains easy to use but is more feature-rich. As such, Blogger has become a blogging platform for both beginners and seasoned professionals.

Discovering the Benefits of Blogger

With so many blogging software options, what makes Blogger stand out? Certainly, since Google purchased Blogger, the ease of integration with other Google products and the enhancements that are constantly added to Blogger make it a viable choice for any blogger. Perhaps the most enticing aspects of Blogger are its simple point-and-click usability and its nonexistent price tag. Following are some details about several benefits you'll enjoy when you use Blogger.

It's free!

You can safely assume that a beginner blogger or a casual blogger will be intrigued by the free Blogger platform. Much of the popularity of Blogger can be attributed to the old adage "Why pay for something when you can get it for free?" In other words, why invest in another blogging software program when Blogger can deliver the same features at no cost? To many bloggers, this question is easy to answer, and Blogger is the obvious choice.

Of course, some bloggers prefer the advanced customization options that other blogging platforms provide, but with advanced customization also comes a price tag. You also generally need programming or coding skills that many bloggers don't know or aren't interested in learning. Because blogging applications such as WordPress rely on a variety of third-party plug-ins to add functionality, the customization options are far greater than what Blogger currently offers. However, most of that customization requires that you pay for a domain name, additional disk space, hosting, and more. Each blogger must define his blogging goals and determine whether paying to use a blogging platform is necessary.

It's easy to use

When it comes to blogging software programs, it doesn't get much easier than Blogger. Starting a Blogger account, customizing your blog, and writing and publishing your blog's content are simple tasks, thanks to the basic WYSIWYG (what you see is what you get) editor that requires no technical knowledge to use as long as you're familiar with the functionality of basic word processing software. Although learning to use blogging software might seem intimidating, Blogger takes away much of the challenges, allowing you to become a confident member of the blogosphere!

It has loads of features

Blogger comes jam-packed with features and goodies for users. Unlike other blogging software programs that require users to upload (or pay for) additional features, Blogger has a wealth of built-in tools, such as Google AdSense, feeds, polls, and slideshows. Chapter 8 covers many of these tools.

With the power of Google behind Blogger, new upgrades have been integrated into the program that make blogging easier than ever. You can be certain that Google isn't done yet. More features are sure to be in the pipeline already. You can keep on top of Blogger updates by reading the Blogger Buzz blog at `http://buzz.blogger.com`.

It's versatile

For users who want a more customized experience for their blog readers, Blogger offers versatile domain and hosting options. Users can choose to use their own domain names for their blogs (for example, `MyBlog.com`) rather than traditional Blogspot addresses (for example, `MyBlog.blogspot.com`). This option is popular for business bloggers and power bloggers who want to create a seamless brand experience for their readers and customers.

Additionally, bloggers can choose to host their Blogger blogs through a third-party host rather than through Blogger. Although third-party hosting is an added expense, some bloggers prefer it in order to provide maximum control over their blogs. Read Chapter 16 for more information about third-party hosts and domain names.

It's flexible

Blogger offers options for bloggers of all experience levels and with varying blogging objectives. Whether you understand HTML (hypertext markup language) or not (see Chapter 9 for more information about HTML), you can use Blogger. Users also have a variety of blogging options available to them, such as instant blogging, audio blogging through podcasts, mobile blogging (moblogging), video blogging (vlogging), blogging by e-mail, and voice messaging through their Blogger blogs. In short, Blogger makes it nearly impossible *not* to blog! Get more details about multimedia blogging in Chapter 15.

Blogger also makes it quite easy for multiple authors to write for the same blog. Adding and removing blog authors takes just a few seconds, making it a helpful choice for people who want to start or expand their blogs to a multiuser format. Check out Chapter 14 to find out about multiuser blogging with Blogger.

It can help you make money

Many bloggers are interested in monetizing their blogs. In other words, they want to be able to make money (either passive or active income) through their blogs. Some free blog platforms, such as WordPress.com, don't allow users to monetize their blogs. Blogger not only *allows* monetization — it also encourages it, by making it incredibly easy through Google AdSense, one of the most popular online advertising services.

Because Blogger is owned by Google, the same company that owns Google AdSense, it's not surprising that Google AdSense is integrated directly into the Blogger program. With just a few clicks, Blogger users can insert Google AdSense ads into their blogs and begin making money from them almost immediately.

Blogger users can also monetize their blogs through affiliate advertising, direct advertising, sponsored reviews, and more. Certainly, as Google's online advertising initiatives grow, blog monetization opportunities for Blogger users will also grow. The seamless integration of Google products into Blogger sets it apart from the competition and makes it an excellent blogging choice. Chapters 10 and 11 cover more ways to make money from your blog.

It exposes you to the spirit of community

Blogger users make up a unique online community that shares a passion for blogging and an interest in learning to use all the features and add-ons available through Blogger. As you grow your blog, networking with the Blogger community can be an invaluable resource for you. A search on Technorati (a popular blog search tool) returns numerous blogs that discuss Blogger (visit `http://technorati.com/blogs/tag/google+blogger` for a current list). No matter what problem or question you encounter, the Blogger community is readily available to help you navigate beyond any challenges that might arise throughout your lifetime as a blogger.

Comparing Blogger to Other Blogging Software Options

Blogger has changed significantly in recent years. New functionality is continually added to ensure that Blogger retains its position as market leader. Other blogging software programs have come and gone with several threatening Blogger, but the team behind Blogger continues to improve the product by offering improvements and new technologies. The following list describes some other blogging programs:

- **WordPress:** The biggest rival to Blogger is WordPress, which is known for its wide variety of plug-ins and add-ons, such as contact forms, related posts links, and sitemaps, that allow users to customize their blogs to suit their individual needs. Blogger offers customization, but WordPress wins the race in terms of giving users the most variety. The drawbacks of WordPress are twofold:

    - The free version is far more limited than the version that requires users to pay for their own domain names and web hosting.

    - The free version doesn't allow users to monetize their blogs.

    You can read *WordPress For Dummies,* 2nd Edition, by Lisa Sabin Wilson (Wiley) for more information about WordPress.

- **TypePad:** Although TypePad is easy to use, it isn't free. Users pay a monthly fee to use TypePad. It offers a decent level of customization, such as templates and design (although less than WordPress with paid hosting), but its use comes at a cost.

- **Moveable Type:** The program's biggest drawback is the expensive licenses that users have to pay for in order to use it. The installation process also isn't as simple as in other blogging software programs, and its features aren't as vast. On the flip-side, it is extremely easy to add multiple blogs to the same account with Moveable Type, which made it popular for team blogs in the past (although WordPress is gaining ground in this market).

✔ **LiveJournal:** Users must pay a monthly fee to use LiveJournal, which provides a limited number of features and customization options.

✔ **MySpace:** MySpace offers a blogging option, but it's quite different from Blogger and many of the other available blogging software programs because so much of the success of a MySpace blog comes from the audience of MySpace members who become its "friends". MySpace is more of a social network (see Chapter 12 for more information on MySpace) with a blogging platform included rather than a stand-alone blogging software program such as Blogger.

✔ **Xanga:** Much like MySpace, Xanga is a social networking site with a blogging option integrated into it rather than a stand-alone blogging software program such as Blogger.

You can read more about the various blogging software programs in *Blogging For Dummies,* 2nd Edition, by Susannah Gardner and Shane Birley (Wiley).

Blogging with Blogger

Blogger has been around for a long time — longer than most other blogging software programs. That means people are familiar with it and comfortable with it. Because Blogger works with just about any Web browser, is available in a myriad of languages, and is free to use, the barriers to entry are practically nonexistent.

The first steps

Anyone can start a blog with Blogger *right now* and be a part of the blogosphere in less than five minutes. It's true. To start a blog using Blogger, you only need to visit the Blogger home page, shown in Figure 1-2. Then follow these three simple steps:

1. **Create an account.**

2. **Name your blog.**

3. **Choose a template.**

Naturally, navigating through the above steps and the steps that come after you launch your blog (when you customize it and make it look and act the way you want it to) require a bit more work. This book helps you move through the process smoothly.

Figure 1-2:
The Blogger home page is where your entry into the world of blogging begins.

The right tools

To start a blog with Blogger, you only need a computer and an Internet connection. However, the more you blog, you might find that you want to experiment with different blogging methods and capabilities. For example, you might want to invest in a digital camera so you can take your own pictures to upload in your blog posts. Alternatively, you might want to buy a digital video camera and try your hand at video blogging. You can read Chapter 15 for more about blogging with different media.

The important thing to remember is that your blog will grow with you. Start with the basics. As you become more comfortable with Blogger and with blogging in general, don't be afraid to test the waters and try new things. Creating a podcast might sound impossible to you now, but the more you blog, the more apt you are to jump in and learn something new to take your blogging experience to the next level.

Don't rush in and buy all the cool gadgets on Day One. Take your time to learn and then decide which tools will help you meet your blogging goals. Blogging success doesn't happen overnight. It takes time and patience. None of those tools is going anywhere.

Chapter 2

Welcome to the Blogosphere

After you decide to start a blog, you need to think about some things before you dive into the blogosphere. First, what *is* the blogosphere? Second, what do you do next? This chapter breaks down some of the early steps you need to take and the concepts you need to understand before you can start your new blog. Although starting a blog is easy with Blogger, you have to tackle some upfront considerations first. For example, you need to determine what you're going to blog about, and you need to find out more about how the blogosphere works by finding and reading other blogs, understanding the unwritten rules of blogging, and so on.

Don't worry: These considerations aren't mind-boggling. In fact, they're quite simple. A bit of time spent now making the right choices for you will make your blogging efforts more productive, enjoyable, and successful.

Starting a Blog

From your neighbor next door who shares her joy of knitting to big companies, celebrities, and everyone in between, it seems that every person reads blogs, knows someone who writes a blog, or writes their own blog. As of November 2008, Technorati, the original blog search site, was tracking 112.8 million blogs. That's a lot of blogs, and that means a lot of people are blogging.

Deciding to start a blog is easy enough, but it's important to understand that the decision means more than just writing some posts that you can point your friends to online. Blogging can have far-reaching effects — some good and some bad. Make sure that you fully understand what those effects are before you start writing and publishing content on your blog. Successful bloggers know who else is blogging and what it means to be a member of the blogosphere. Read on to find out more about the phenomenon of blogging.

Joining the blogosphere

Did you know that bloggers who actively publish content to their blogs operate in an online community called the *blogosphere?* When you start your blog, you automatically become a member of the blogosphere community. As a member of the growing social Web, you can express your thoughts and opinions, interact with like-minded people, and more simply by writing your own blog, responding to comments left on your blog, and even leaving comments on other blogs that you enjoy reading.

Truth be told, as a member of the blogosphere, you have the ability to decide what role you want to play in that community. You can play a role in the blogosphere by passively reading blogs, commenting on blogs or writing a blog as a blogger. In fact, bloggers come in all shapes and sizes and with differing views and passions, but it's the blogosphere that allows them to connect easily with each other through the commenting feature found on just about every blog. Blogging is now an integral part of popular culture, with blogs existing to discuss just about any topic you can imagine. You can find out more about how to find blogs of interest to you later in this chapter.

A Who's Who of the blogosphere

The following list is just a small sample of well-known names attached to blogging:

✔ **Celebrities with blogs:** Wil Wheaton, Pamela Anderson, Barbra Streisand, Jennifer Love Hewitt, Rosie O'Donnell, John Mayer, Kanye West, Curt Schilling

✔ **Companies with blogs:** General Motors, Google, Dell, Southwest Airlines, Boeing, Ford, McDonald's, Starbucks, Wal-Mart

✔ **Politicians with blogs:** Barack Obama, Hillary Clinton, John McCain, John Kerry, Ralph Nader, Howard Dean

---

Knowing why people blog

With millions and millions of people blogging, there are many reasons that people choose to blog. There really is no *wrong* reason to start a blog, because the entire purpose of each person's blog is entirely her own choice. With the ease of use of Blogger, it's not surprising that over 14 million Blogger blogs were active as of June 2008. Check out some of the reasons why people blog:

- ✔ **For fun:** Many people write blogs just for fun. Whether they just want to share ideas and thoughts with friends and family or simply want a creative outlet to talk about a subject they love, a large number of bloggers write their blogs as a hobby.

- ✔ **To help people or make a difference:** Many blogs are written with the intention of educating people about a topic or changing the way people think about a topic. Whether these bloggers want to influence political views or share tips for parenting, the possibilities for these types of blogs are endless.

- ✔ **To establish yourself as an expert in a specific field:** Many people write blogs to develop a reputation in their fields as someone with unique expertise. By establishing yourself as an expert or at least as someone who is knowledgeable in a specific field, you can open doors for new opportunities in career advancement and more.

- ✔ **To build a business:** Businesses often start blogs to not only build awareness but also meet customer needs and increase customer loyalty. The goal for business blogs is typically to provide content that makes customers feel valued, which should translate into sales.

- ✔ **To make money:** A large number of people start blogs as simply a way to generate a passive income from blog advertising and other blog monetization efforts.

Understanding the pros and cons of blogging

Your words can live online for a long time. When you publish something on your blog, anyone with Internet access can see it. If you enable comments on your blog, people all over the world can also respond to what you publish, and you might not like what they have to say. Those are just two of the drawbacks of blogging.

Blogging can be a double-edged sword. On one hand, it gives you the opportunity to share your opinions with others and find like-minded people to network with. On the other hand, it exposes you personally to the world. Of course, finding personal information about almost anyone through simple online searches is fairly easy these days, so trying to remain anonymous online is difficult. That's why it's important to be mindful of what you publish online, because you never know who might be reading it now or in the future. For example, that picture of you and your coworkers partying in the boss's office that you publish on your blog today could be found by a future hiring manager five years from now when you're looking for a new job.

Be careful what you publish on your blog. What you publish today can still be found through online searches in the future, and you never know who might be looking.

Blogging can also bring new opportunities to you. As your online presence grows and people within and outside the blogosphere get to know who you are, it's quite possible that new career, volunteer, or interview requests might come your way. However, each of these opportunities brings its own set of pros and cons in terms of the amount of time they require compared to the rewards they bring.

One of the best parts of blogging is developing relationships with your readers and other bloggers. It's possible to connect with people through your blogging efforts who could have a big impact in your personal life or your career.

Establishing Goals for Your Blog

Before your fingers touch your keyboard to enter the Blogger URL and start your first blog, you need to take some time to decide what you want to do with your blog after you start it. Consider the following questions:

- ✔ Why do you want to start a blog?
- ✔ How much time do you have to spend updating your blog each week?
- ✔ Do you want to make money from your blog?
- ✔ Do you want to grow a large audience for your blog?
- ✔ Are you prepared to commit to blogging long term?

By answering these questions, you can start your blogging experience on the right foot. For example, if you simply want to start a blog to share news about your family with your friends and extended relatives, you don't need to consider blog advertising and promotion as you create your blog. However, if your goal is to develop a strong online presence to launch a business, blog promotion should be a top priority. Defining your goals for your blog early allows you to not only prioritize your development efforts but also work efficiently by eliminating unnecessary steps.

Choosing a Topic

What you write about on your blog is 100 percent up to you. No one can tell you what to write about (as long as your content follows the Blogger and Google terms of service). You have complete creative control!

Heather Armstrong gets fired for blogging

In 2001, Heather B. Armstrong (born Heather Hamilton) started the blog Dooce.com, where she wrote honestly and openly about her life, family, and job. A year after Dooce.com was born, she was fired from her job because of her blog's content. In the end, Heather won,

because her blog skyrocketed in popularity after her firing. In fact, her story and blog grew so popular that the site became part of pop culture lexicon. Even now, when a person is fired because of the content on his blog, it is said that he was "dooced."

Popular Blog Topics

Not sure what your blog should be about? Check out these popular blog topics to help spark some ideas.

Animals and pets	Parenting
Art	Personal
Business	Politics
Career development	Reading
Celebrities	Relationships
Crafts	Religion
Education	Sports
Entertainment	Technology
Environment	Travel
Fashion	Video games
Health	Women's issues
Hobbies	Work
Music	Writing
News and current events	

The first thing to remember when you choose your blog topic is that you need to write about that topic *a lot*. If your blogging goals include blogging about your topic for a long time, make sure to pick a topic that you're passionate about. Successful blogs are updated frequently (often several times a day) with fresh content that keeps readers interested. Again, depending on your blogging goals, you need to make sure that you have enough to say to keep your blog going.

Although it's important to pick a topic you're passionate about, it's equally important to avoid topics that you feel *too* strongly about.

Blogging is all about building a community of readers around your blog who will join in the conversation through comments. If you're overly sensitive about your blog's topic, it's difficult to allow your readers to comment freely with differing opinions.

Because blogging requires frequent posting, make sure that you choose a topic you enjoy researching. Coming up with new and entertaining content can be challenging for even the most seasoned bloggers. You need to make time to research other blogs, current events, and more in your blog's subject area to build relationships and find new content when you face blogger's block.

Finding Blogs

As you decide on your blog topic and define your blogging goals, you should take some time to start reading a variety of blogs to not only find others that you like to read but also get a better idea of what works. A number of blog search engines can help you find blogs and blog posts about specific topics, including the blog search function offered by Google or IceRocket. However, the biggest blog search site is Technorati.

Figure 2-1 shows the Technorati advanced search page, where you can search for blogs and blog posts containing certain words, phrases, or tags. Start researching blogs of interest. Visit those blogs and leave comments to start building relationships with those bloggers. These efforts will help you not only develop your own blog and its content but also grow your blog.

Figure 2-1: Use the Technorati search page to find blogs and blog posts.

Growing Your Blog

When you define your blogging goals, you need to determine how big you want your blog to be. In other words, you need to determine how much time you have to commit to blogging in order to write and promote it in such a way as to meet those goals. Blogging with Blogger requires little to no monetary investment, but it does require a time investment that correlates directly with how successful your blog will become.

Blogs don't draw thousands, or even hundreds, of visitors overnight (although that would be nice). If you write compelling content with *search engine optimization* (using tricks to help people find your post through keyword searches on popular search engines like Google, as discussed in Chapter 13) in mind and promote your blog through social networking and relationship building, your blog will grow. Chapters 12 and 13 discuss how to drive traffic to your new Blogger blog. If you want to become a successful blogger, spend some time reading those chapters and experimenting with the techniques they describe.

Making Money from Your Blog

Many people start blogging for one reason — to make money. If you're one of those bloggers whose ultimate goal is to earn money from your blog, you should know upfront that generating a profit takes time. As your blog traffic grows, the opportunities for you to make money will also grow.

Think of your blog as a business. If customers don't come through the door, you won't make any money. The same is true of earning potential on a blog. If visitors don't come to your blog, no one can click on your existing ads. Furthermore, new advertisers won't want to pay to advertise on your blog because no one will see their ads.

Start your blog now, but be patient. As you drive traffic to your blog, more revenue-generating opportunities will arise. In the meantime, read Chapters 10 and 11 to learn about blog monetization options and start putting together a plan that you can implement as your blog traffic increases.

The Secrets to Blogging Success

Suppose that you have plenty of patience and time, and now you need to know how bloggers can turn that patience and time into money. Believe it or not, there isn't a secret recipe for success. Truly, success comes from commitment, time, and possibly a bit of luck. You never know when your blog might get picked up by a major news portal that can attract a lot of attention to it and possibly give your blog a big boost. Sometimes, success is a matter of being in the right place at the right time — the nearby sidebar "Perez Hilton's lucky break" describes one celebrity blogger's rise to stardom. However, for most bloggers, success comes with persistence. Here are some tips:

> ✔ **Pick a topic people are interested in.** The potential size of your blog's audience is directly related to the number of people who are interested in the topic you're writing about. However, you should know that just because you pick a popular topic doesn't mean that your blog will receive a flood of visitors. You also have to pick a blog topic that isn't already covered repeatedly online. If you do pick a topic that has already been overdone, make sure to put a unique spin on your content so that it stands out in the crowded blogosphere.

Perez Hilton's lucky break

Mario Lavandeira started his first celebrity gossip blog in 2004. Within six months, his lucky break came, when his blog was referred to as Hollywood's most hated Web site by the TV show *The Insider*. He adopted the pseudonym Perez Hilton and changed his blog's domain name to www.PerezHilton.com. His blog (shown in the following figure) continues to be one of the most successful celebrity gossip blogs online, and he has found fame outside the blogosphere, through television appearances and more. It all started with a blog topic that people were interested in and a blogger who wasn't afraid to take risks.

✓ **Pick a topic you're passionate about.** Remember that because success-ful blogs are updated frequently, you have to write about your blog's topic *continually* and for a long time. Make sure that you have the stam-ina to stick with it.

✓ **Be social.** This is the biggest key to blogging success. From the tone of your blog posts to your responsiveness to comments posted on your blog and e-mail sent to you based on your blog's content, you need to be friendly and constantly work to build relationships. Those efforts don't stop on your own blog. You also need to visit other blogs and leave rele-vant comments, visit forums, join user groups, and more to get the word out about your blog and build relationships with other bloggers.

✓ **Keep learning.** Successful bloggers never stop learning about new blog-ging tools and concepts, their blog topics, and their audiences. The more knowledge you have, the better equipped you are to take your blog to the next level.

✓ **Take risks.** Don't be afraid to be creative. Try new blogging features and functions, inject some unique content into your blog posts, or change the layout of your home page. You never know what might work. Just make sure to track the results so that you know what works (and what doesn't work) to bring you closer to meeting your goals.

Every blogger has her own definition of blogging success. Before you start your blog, define your success metrics. Do you want to get specific results, such as sales or business contacts? Do you want to attract a certain number of visitors? Do you want to make a certain dollar amount from your blog? Do you want to network and build relationships and create an online pres-ence that leads to other opportunities? Or do you simply want to have fun? Write down your blogging goals and return to them every few months to see whether you're on track to meeting them, whether you need to make some changes to get there, or whether you want to rewrite them completely. Only then can you find and achieve your own blogging success.

Chapter 3

Blogging Basics and Buzzwords

In This Chapter

▶ Identifying basic blog elements

▶ Getting acquainted with Blogger terminology

*W*hen you enter the blogosphere, you enter a world filled with its own jargon and buzzwords. To make matters more confusing, many terms in the blogosphere have multiple meanings or multiple names, depending on the blogging software a person uses. In truth, the nuances in names and meanings are less daunting than they might first appear to be (for example, you say "blogroll," I say "links.") The important thing is to understand basic blogging terminology and the language of Blogger users so that you can start your first blog.

The main features that separate a blog from other types of Web sites are its time-stamped entries, archived entries, and comments. Most blogs incorporate these same basic features and more. Depending on your likes, dislikes, or needs, you can add, delete, or modify features to display on your blog. Chapters 5, 7, and 8 show you how to set up and manage your Blogger blog in detail. In fact, each of the blog images in this chapter is a screen shot taken from the sample blog I created in order to describe the elements presented throughout this book. You hold in your hands, therefore, all the help you need in order to see how to create a blog like the one shown in this chapter.

Picking a Template

When you visit a blog, one of the first things you probably notice is the layout of that blog. The colors, fonts, and design elements of a blog are preconfigured in a *template* (also called a *theme*). Blogger users can choose from a variety of free templates offered directly by Blogger software, or they can upload templates from a third party. A multitude of Web sites and Web designers provide free and paid custom templates to Blogger users, to help make their blogs look distinct and function in a specified way. Figure 3-1 shows a sample of free templates provided by Blogger software.

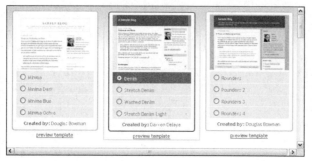

Figure 3-1:
Blogger's
free tem-
plates.

Each template is laid out using one, two, or three columns as well as a header and footer. The header typically includes the title of the blog and a top navigation bar for visitors to access different pages or links. The footer usually displays the template designer's name and any copyright information. The columns are used to hold blog posts, links, ads, and more. Depending on which template you use, you can customize your blog's appearance to meet your needs and goals. Templates are discussed in detail in Chapter 7.

Making a Home Page

A blog's home page is similar to the home page of a Web site — it's the main landing page, or starting point, of the blog. In other words, it's the welcome page for your online presence. Figure 3-2 shows a sample home page from a blog.

Figure 3-2:
A blog home
page.

Your *home page* is the main page of your blog, where your most recent content is usually found. Entries appear on the home page in reverse chronological order — typically, in the largest column of the blog template. On the home page, visitors can easily find links to your blog's other elements, such as your author profile, blog archives, and blog ads. You can read more about the home page in Chapter 5.

A cluttered or poorly designed home page can have a negative effect on your blog and can even drive away visitors. Take some time to create an inviting home page that is easy to navigate and includes elements and features that help your readers.

Creating a Profile

Many bloggers overlook the importance of creating an informative *author profile* (also called an *About page*) on their blogs. When visitors discover your blog, they most likely want to find out who is writing the content. They may wonder what the author's credentials are or what background or experience the author has that leads her to write content that the reader either likes or dislikes.

Because a critical aspect of successful blogging is creating relationships, you should write a thorough profile that helps readers understand why you are *the* person to be writing this blog. Your profile page should include information about the purpose of your blog as well as your experience and contact information. Figure 3-3 shows an example of a well-written profile page. You can find out more about setting up a profile in Chapter 5.

Figure 3-3:
A blog
profile page.

Don't hide your profile page. Make it a prominent part of your blog so that visitors know who you are.

Filling the Sidebar

Depending on your blog template's layout, you might have two or three sidebars flanking or to the right or left of your main blog post column. You can easily fall into the trap of cluttering your sidebars with ads, links, and other elements. Although your sidebar is a useful place to put ads and links to other blogs and Web sites you like, it doesn't add much value to your readers if they can't find anything between the clutter.

Consider what your goals are for the space in your sidebar. If you want to maximize your revenue-generating potential through that space, place just a few ads at a time and then analyze their performance to see which ones deliver the results you require. Publish the best-performing ads and substitute poor performers with new ones until you find the best mix. Use the remaining space on your sidebar to provide *useful* links and information for your readers. You can see a sample sidebar in Figure 3-4.

Don't be afraid to leave much of your sidebar empty. White space provides welcome visual relief on text-heavy blog pages.

Figure 3-4:
A blog
sidebar.

Following are seven of the most common sidebar elements:

- ✔ A link to your About page or a short bio
- ✔ Your picture
- ✔ Your contact information
- ✔ A list of links to other blogs (also called a blogroll)
- ✔ Labels
- ✔ Links to your blog archives
- ✔ Ads

Posting Content

Each entry that you write and publish on your blog is a *post*. Posts are arranged in reverse chronological order, starting with the most recent post at the top of your blog's home page. Older posts are archived (typically by date), so they're easily accessible by readers.

Your posts are the lifeblood of your blog. They not only take up the majority of the space on your blog but also help visitors find your blog. They're also the reason people return to your blog. If you continually update your blog with fresh posts, readers always have something new to see and read.

If your visitors like what you have to say, enjoy your writing style, and feel welcome (for example, they feel comfortable leaving comments, which you respond to in a timely and respectful manner), they return frequently. They're also likely to tell other people about your blog and link to it from their own blog (if they have one), leading to more traffic for you.

Blog posts are made up of these six basic elements, which you can see in action in Figure 3-5:

- ✔ **Title:** The titles of your blog posts serve two purposes. They entice visitors to read the full post, and well-written post titles help people find your blog from keyword searches on search engines such as Google.

- ✔ **Post date:** The date you publish your post to the Internet appears as part of your blog post entry. The date is important to visitors who like to see that a blog is updated frequently. It can also help when someone stumbles on one of your old posts by showing them when the post was originally published.

✔ **Author byline:** The author byline is particularly helpful for blogs written by multiple people. The author byline can link to your About page or profile to provide one-click access to your bio for readers.

✔ **Images or videos:** Images and videos provide visual appeal, as well as interactivity, to a blog. They can further demonstrate a point you make in a post and when named well, can help with search engine optimization.

✔ **Backlinks:** Backlinks provide a virtual shoulder tap to other blogs and Web sites that you link to in your blog posts. They also provide a way for readers to find more information about a topic discussed in your blog post.

✔ **Comments:** Comments are the pulse of a blog. When readers leave comments on your blog posts, conversations start that can be especially powerful. Highly interactive blogs are typically quite successful.

You can find out more about writing your first blog post in Chapter 6.

Title   Post date

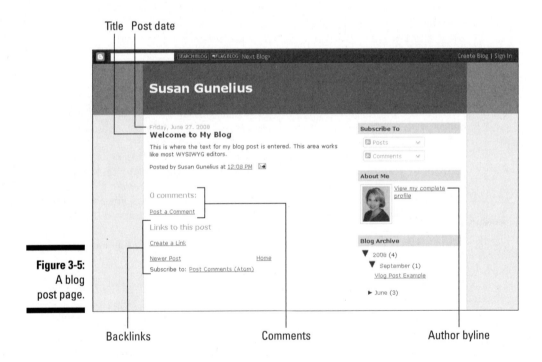

Figure 3-5:
A blog
post page.

Backlinks   Comments   Author byline

Interacting with Comments

Comments are the lifeline of a blog. Because blogging, at its core, is meant to be a social medium, the conversation that happens on a blog shouldn't be one-sided. Comments bring to life the interactivity and relationships that blogging is all about. Figure 3-6 shows how comments look on a blog post.

People like to feel involved. Allowing comments on your blog posts invites visitors to join the conversation and makes them feel like you value their opinions. It also makes them feel like they're part of a larger community of people who enjoy reading your blog and sharing ideas.

Don't ignore your visitors. Take the time to interact with them by responding to their comments.

As your blog grows, visitor comments will increase, as will the conversation and community around it. With reader interaction, though, often comes problems. Remember that it's your blog and that you have the right to moderate comments as you feel it's appropriate. Check out Chapter 9 for details about comment moderation.

Figure 3-6: Comments appear in the order in which they're received.

Comments on a blog post

Publishing Backlinks

A backlink is a virtual tap on the shoulder from another Blogger blog, letting you know that someone else wrote about your blog post and included a link to drive traffic your way. A backlink can be published beneath a blog post when another blog links to that post. Figure 3-7 demonstrates how backlinks look when they're published on a blog post. Blogger doesn't automatically allow backlinks to display on blog posts, but including them is an important way to help you develop relationships with other bloggers and to find out how visitors are finding your blog.

Don't forget to turn on backlinks for your blog! You can find out how in Chapter 5.

Figure 3-7:
Backlinks
appear in
the order
in which
they're
received.

Backlinks on a blog post

Using Labels

Blogger uses labels to categorize blog posts. Your visitors can click on a label of interest to find more posts categorized by using that label. You can also add a list of labels to your blog's sidebar sorted by frequency of use or alphabetically, shown in Figure 3-8, which is a quick and easy way for visitors to find posts about subjects of interest to them. Labels are described in detail in Chapter 6.

Take time to label your posts strategically to help readers find your older blog posts. Think like you're one of your readers. How would you search for a specific blog post? Use intuitive labels so your readers can easily locate related posts.

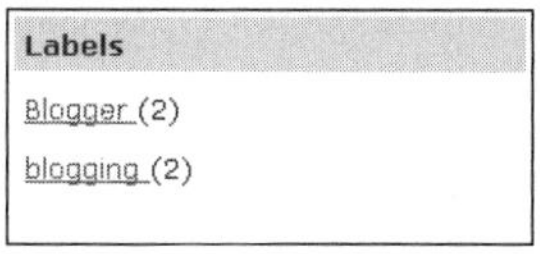

Figure 3-8:
Blog labels.

Labels
Blogger (2)
blogging (2)

Adding a Footer

A blog *footer* typically includes copyright information, a link to the blogger's e-mail address, contact information, and sometimes a link to the blog designer's e-mail or Web site. The footer is located at the bottom of the blog page.

Many bloggers use their blog footers as places to add extra advertising or links to monetize their blogs or provide quick links to posts and Web sites for their readers. You decide which elements you want to add to your blog's footer.

Archiving Content

Archiving is an automatic feature that's inherent to blogs. Each post you write is automatically *archived* (saved) by date by the Blogger software. Archives help to make a blog easier to navigate. The most current content can be read on the home page or by clicking through to the first several pages of content, whereas the archive links can appear in the blog's sidebar for quick access to older content. Figure 3-9 shows how archives can look on a blog's sidebar.

Archives are useful for search engine optimization as well. Because all content published on your blog lives forever (or until you delete it), that equates to many, many possible entry points for people to find your blog on search engines. Chapter 5 discusses archiving in more detail.

Imagine how many entry points some of the most prolific bloggers have. Think of it this way: If you publish one post per day for an entire year, that's 365 entry points for your blog. Multiply that number by five years, and your blog has 1,825 entry points. What if you published a post three times per day for five years? That gives you 5,475 entry points!

Figure 3-9:
Blog
archives.

Building Relationships with Links

Blogger refers to blogrolls as *links*. Many bloggers include blogrolls in their blog sidebars, which display a list of links to other blogs that they like. See Figure 3-10 for a blogroll example. Blogrolls are a helpful way to build relationships with other bloggers because the blogrolls are typically *reciprocal:* If you add a blog to your blogroll, that blog's author is likely to add your blog to his blogroll. The more blogrolls your blog is listed on, the more possible ways visitors can find your blog, which leads to more traffic. You can find out more about links and blogrolls in Chapter 8.

Keep your blogroll current. Check the links every few months to ensure that they still work. A blogroll filled with outdated links isn't useful to your readers or to your blog promotion efforts.

Figure 3-10:
A Blogger
blogroll,
or *links*.

Including Subscriptions and Feeds

Many blogs include a subscription section that says "Subscribe to my feed" (or similar wording) with a link to a page where visitors can sign up to read your blog's feed in a feed reader or receive it by e-mail. Figure 3-11 shows an example of how a subscription link might look on a blog created with Blogger. Blog feeds are syndicated by Atom or RSS (Really Simple Syndication). A blog *feed* is simply a syndicated version of your blog's content, similar to a news feed or stock ticker scrolling on the bottom of a television news screen.

Readers can save time by subscribing to feeds of blogs they enjoy. Rather than visit each blog to find and read new content, a subscriber can simply log in to her preferred feed reader, such as Google Reader, and see — in one place — the most recent posts for all blogs she subscribes to. Alternatively, she can receive the most recent posts by e-mail for each blog she subscribes to. Subscriptions and feeds are covered in detail in Chapter 9.

People who subscribe to your feed are usually extremely loyal visitors.

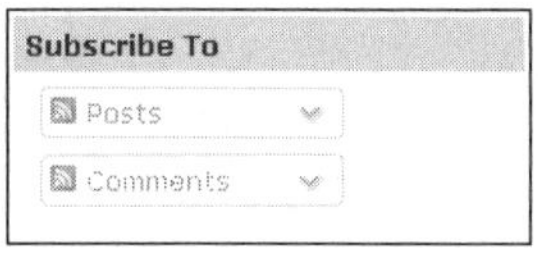

Figure 3-11:
A blog sub-
scription
link.

Subscribe To

Posts

Comments

Part II
Using Google Blogger

The 5th Wave   By Rich Tennant

"My spam filter checks the recipient address, http links, and any writing that panders to postmodern English romanticism with conceits to 20th-century graphic narrative."

In this part . . .

In this part, you find out how to create a Google account and your new blog by using Blogger. Don't be nervous — blogging is easy after you dive in and get started.

Chapters 4 and 5 show you how to create your new blog and configure the settings that should be in place before you start writing a blog post. After you create your new blog, you have to figure out what to do with it. That's where the remaining chapters of Part II come into play.

Chapter 6 shows you how to write and publish blog posts. Next, you find out how to make your blog look good and function just the way you want. Chapters 7, 8, and 9 spell out how to change your blog's template, add useful features, get conversations going with comments, and track your blog's performance.

Chapter 4

Getting Started with Blogger

In This Chapter
▶ Creating an account
▶ Choosing a domain name and a template
▶ Familiarizing yourself with the dashboard
▶ Signing in and out

Starting a free blog with Blogger is easy. There's no need to worry about finding and paying for Web site hosting, downloading or uploading software, and paying to register a domain name. Blogger takes care of all those administrative tasks for you. All you have to do is visit the Blogger Web site, create a Google account, pick a blog name and a template, and you're ready to start blogging!

Taking Your First Steps into the Blogosphere

Turn on your computer, open your Web browser, and get ready because you're about to join the blogosphere!

Creating a Google account

Before you can start a blog with Blogger, you need to create a Google account to access the Blogger software.

To create your Google account (and Blogger blog), follow these simple steps:

1. **Visit the Blogger home page.**

   Enter the URL **www.blogger.com** in your browser.

2. **On the Blogger home page, click the Create Your Blog Now button, shown in Figure 4-1.**

The Create a Google Account page opens, as shown in Figure 4-2.

Figure 4-1:
The Create
Your Blog
Now link.

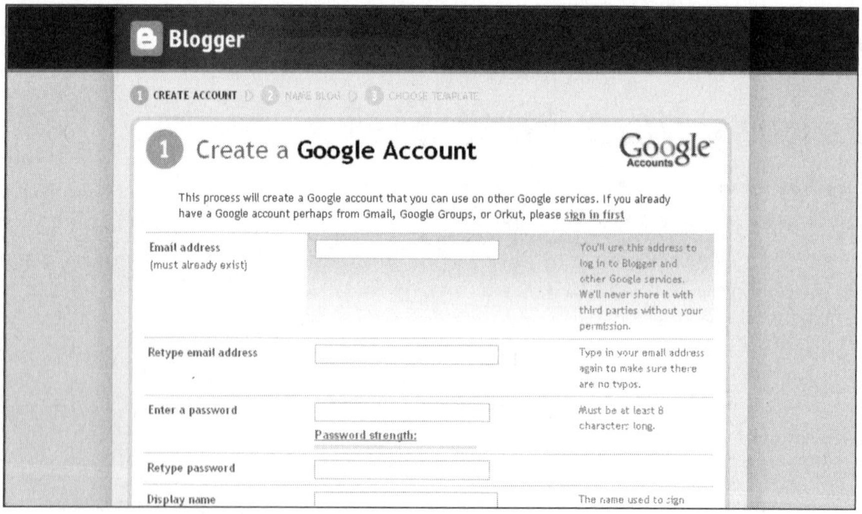

Click here to create a blog.

Figure 4-2:
The Create
a Google
Account
page.

3. **In the Email Address text box, type your e-mail address and then retype it in the Retype Email Address text box.**

   The e-mail address you use doesn't have to be for a Google Gmail account. You can use any e-mail address to create a Google account to access Blogger. The e-mail address you enter is the one you use to log in to Blogger, and it's the one to which Blogger sends your username and password if you forget them.

4. **Enter a password in the Enter a Password text box, and then reenter it in the Retype Password text box.**

   You can change your password later, if you want. Google shows you, just beneath the Enter a Password box, how strong your password is after you enter it.

   Make sure to use a strong password — one that includes letters and numbers or special characters. Also, get into the habit of changing your password periodically.

5. **Enter your display name in the Display Name text box.**

   Your *display name* is shown at the bottom of each of your blog posts, indicating that you're the author of the post.

6. **Type the letters displayed in the Word Verification box.**

   This security procedure ensures that new Google accounts are created by human beings rather than by automated spam systems.

7. **Select the check box in the Acceptance of Terms section to indicate that you accept Blogger's terms of service.**

   You can click the Terms of Service link on your screen to read the complete document.

8. **Click the Continue button.**

   The Name Your Blog page opens on the Blogger Web site, as shown in Figure 4-3.

Figure 4-3:
The Name
Your Blog
page.

What's in a name?

Decide whether you want your domain name to be obvious or creative. Because obvious names are more intuitive, people can more easily find and remember them. Creative names, on the other hand, are unique and can stand out in the overcrowded blogosphere. Here are some tricks for choosing a domain name that works:

✔ Create a list of keywords and then mix them up until you find a combination that you like and that's available.

✔ Make up a word.

✔ Add prefixes or suffixes, such as *est* or *str.*

✔ Add an article, such as *a* or *the.*

✔ Select words that people search for frequently. Research popular keywords by using a keyword-tracking site such as Wordtracker.com.

Choosing a domain name

Free blogs created by using Blogger software are hosted by Blogger's Blogspot hosting service. Therefore, the domain name you select for your blog is followed by the `.blogspot.com` extension to create the complete URL of your blog. When you reach the Name Your Blog page (refer to Figure 4-3), you need to select a title for your blog as well as a domain name to precede the `.blogspot.com` extension. It can be hard to find an available domain name that you like because so many are already taken. Take some time to put words and phrases together that help readers understand what your blog is about and that are easy to remember. Check out the nearby sidebar, "Choosing a domain name."

1. **Enter the title of your blog in the Blog Title text box.**

   Your blog title appears at the top of your blog and gives visitors an idea of what your blog is about. You can change your blog title at any time.

2. **Enter the domain name that you want to precede the `.blogspot.com` segment in the Blog Address (URL) text box, and then click the Check Availability link.**

   Blogger has approximately 14 million blogs, which means that your first blog address choice is likely not to be available. If necessary, try different names until you find one that is available. Your blog name and domain name don't need to match. See the nearby sidebar "Choosing a domain name" for tips on choosing a domain name.

3. **Click the Continue button.**

   Bypass the Advanced Setup section of the Name Your Blog page for now, unless you plan to host your blog through a Web host other than Blogspot.

   The Choose a Template page opens, as shown in Figure 4-4. Third-party hosting and domain names are covered in depth in Chapter 16.

Selecting a basic template

Blogger provides a variety of free templates to its users. When you reach the Choose a Template page during the blog creation process, you're presented with a number of themes to choose from (see Figure 4-4).

To select a basic Blogger template, follow these steps:

1. **On the Choose a Template page, use the scroll bar to view the available Blogger templates.**

   You can preview each template in a larger format by clicking the Preview Template link beneath each template option.

2. **Select the radio button beneath your chosen template.**

   This step tells Blogger which template you want to use for your new blog.

3. **Click the Continue button.**

   The Your Blog Has Been Created page appears, as shown in Figure 4-5. You're now an official member of the blogosphere.

Figure 4-4:
The Choose a Template page.

Figure 4-5:
Welcome to
the blogo-
sphere!

Don't worry too much about choosing just the right template when you're first creating your blog. You can easily change your template later to another free Blogger template or to a third-party template. Learn more about changing templates in Chapter 7.

Joining the blogosphere

Welcome to the world of the social Web. After you're an official member of the blogosphere and you want to publish your first post, all you have to do is click the Start Blogging button. The Create a Post page appears, as shown in Figure 4-6. From this page, you can begin blogging. It's that easy!

Don't go too fast. Before you write your first post, click the Dashboard link in the upper-right corner of your screen and take some time to understand how Blogger works and see what it offers.

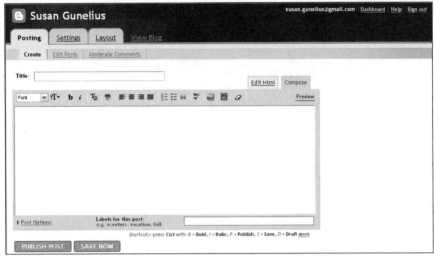

Figure 4-6:
You're ready
to write your
first post.

Getting Familiar with Blogger

As with any new software you want to use, you need to take some time to understand what all the links, buttons, icons, and tools that are offered on your screen can do for you. Most of the features provided by Blogger can be accessed directly from the Blogger dashboard — it's the first page that opens when you sign in to your Blogger account.

Signing in to Blogger

You can access your blog's dashboard at any time after you log into Blogger. Figure 4-7 shows the Blogger home page, where you can sign in to your account.

1. **Visit the Blogger home page.**

   To get there, enter the URL **www.blogger.com** into your browser.

2. **Enter your username and password in the text boxes in the upper-right corner of the page.**

   Use the e-mail address and password you provided when you registered for your Google account and started your Blogger blog.

3. **Click the Sign In button.**

   Your Blogger dashboard automatically opens, as shown in Figure 4-8.

Figure 4-7:
Signing
in to your
Blogger
account.

Enter your username and password to sign in.

Figure 4-8:
The Blogger
dashboard.

If you forget your username or password, you can click the question mark link above the login fields on the Blogger home page or type the URL **www. blogger.com/forgot.g** into your Web browser. This action opens the Forgot Your Username or Password page where you can enter the requested information to recover your username or password. Check out Chapter 18 for more information about recovering your username and password.

Introducing the Blogger dashboard

From your Blogger dashboard, you can access all the controls for your blog, just like the tools to drive your car are located on your car's dashboard. The primary elements of the main Blogger dashboard are described in this list:

- ✔ **Manage Your Blogs:** This section lists your existing blogs with links to each one, where you can write new posts, change the blog's settings, revise the blog's layout, or even view the blog live online. Each of these options is discussed in detail later in this chapter. You can also click the Create a Blog link to start another blog that is then added to the Manage Your Blogs section of the dashboard.

- ✔ **Blogs of Note:** The latest entries from Blogger blogs that you sign up to follow (select the Add button to add blogs you like), the Blogger Buzz blog, and blogs of note according to Blogger appear in the Reading List section of your dashboard so that you can easily see the latest updates and news of interest to you.

- ✔ **View Profile, Edit Profile, and Edit Photo:** These links open your About page, where you can review and revise your bio that appears on your blog. Profiles are discussed in detail in Chapter 5.

- ✔ **My Account:** This link opens your personal account page, where you can modify your account information, such as your e-mail address and password.

- ✔ **Mobile Devices:** Follow the link in this area to begin mobile blogging. Multimedia blogging is covered in depth in Chapter 16.

- ✔ **Tools and Resources:** You can access your Google AdSense and Google Reader accounts directly from the Blogger dashboard. Read more about Google Reader in Chapter 9 and about Google AdSense in Chapter 11.

- ✔ **Help Resources:** The online Help function for Blogger is quite useful. Google Groups dedicated to providing help to Blogger users also exist, which you can access by clicking the links in the Help Resources section of the Blogger dashboard. You can also access help by clicking the link in the Manage Your Blogs section or the link in the upper-right corner of any Blogger account page.

You can also access the controls available from the Blogger dashboard from tabs displayed as a navigation bar along the top of any Blogger page.

Entering and publishing posts

When you click the New Post link from the Blogger dashboard, a page automatically opens where you can enter and publish a new post to your blog, as shown in Figure 4-9.

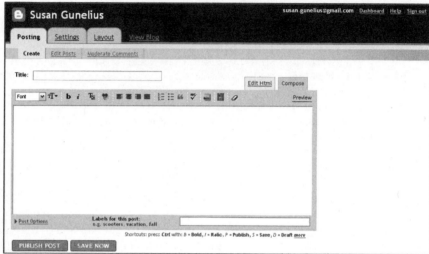

Figure 4-9:
The Posting
tab.

Notice these tabs above the Title text box:

- ✔ **Create:** Write new posts to publish on your blog.
- ✔ **Edit Posts:** Modify posts that you already published on your blog.
- ✔ **Moderate Comments:** Manage the comments that readers leave on your blog.

Read Chapter 6 for more details about writing and editing posts, and see Chapter 9 for information about moderating comments.

Changing Blogger settings

The Settings tab, shown in Figure 4-10, gives you quick access to a variety of tools that allow you to customize your blog to meet your needs.

From decisions about the way your posts are displayed to the way your posts are archived, you can make the modifications you want on the Settings tab and subtabs:

- ✔ **Basic:** Change your blog's title, add a description to display in your blog's header, make your blog public, show quick editing and e-mail links, identify adult content, and more. These features are covered in more detail in Chapter 5.
- ✔ **Publishing:** Modify your publishing settings if you want to switch from Blogspot hosting to a third-party host. Read more about third-party hosting in Chapter 16.

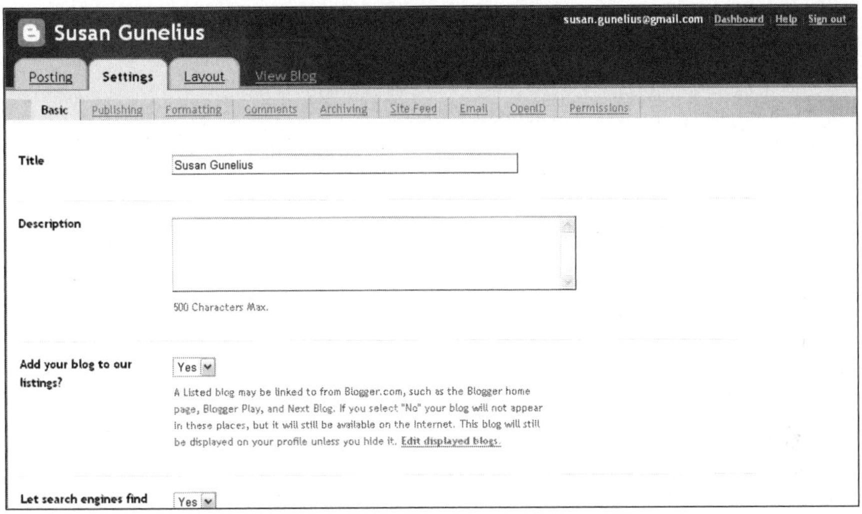

Figure 4-10:
The Settings
tab.

- **Formatting:** Configure date-and-time formats on your blog, time zone, language, and more. Details are in Chapter 5.

- **Comments:** Choose whether you want to show or hide comments on your blogs, determine who can leave comments on your posts, and decide whether you want to display backlinks, enable comment moderation and verification, and more. Chapters 5 and 9 explain these tools.

- **Archiving:** Select how often you want your posts archived and configure post page settings. More information about archiving is in Chapter 5.

- **Site Feed:** Set up your blog feed. Read about feeds in Chapter 9.

What is OpenID?

OpenID is an online identification system. A wide variety of Web sites participate in the OpenID system, which lets you select the OpenID provider of your choice, such as Blogger, and use your username and password associated with that sole account in order to access other participating OpenID sites across the Internet. Rather than have to remember multiple usernames and passwords and spend time registering for numerous accounts at a variety of Web sites, you can simply use your OpenID identity to log in to Web sites participating in OpenID.

When you start your Blogger account, you're automatically given an OpenID identity. You can find your Blogger OpenID identity by selecting the OpenID tab from the Settings section of your Blogger dashboard. Alternatively, you can use the OpenID system to restrict who can leave comments on your blog posts, as described in Chapter 5.

✔ **Email:** Set up Blog Send and Mail-to-Blogger addresses. Details are in Chapter 9.

✔ **OpenID:** Configure OpenID settings for your blog. See the nearby sidebar "What is OpenID?" to find out more about it.

✔ **Permissions:** Add authors and define who can read your blog. Chapter 14 provides information about multiuser blogs, and Chapter 5 explains how to configure privacy settings on your blog.

Customizing your blog

One of the best upgrades to Blogger in recent years has been to the Layout tab, shown in Figure 4-11.

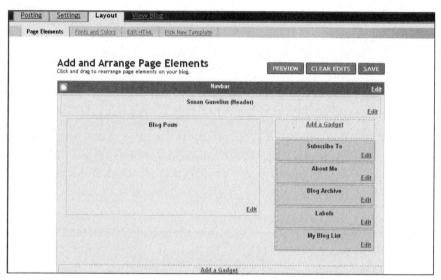

Figure 4-11:
The Layout
tab.

Many tasks that used to require you to insert HTML code can now be completed by using the simple tools provided on the Layout tab, as described in this list:

✔ **Page Elements:** Add, delete, or move the various elements of your page — such as posts, archives, your profile, ads, and more — by using a simple drag-and-drop system.

✔ **Fonts and Colors:** Make your blog your own by selecting the colors and fonts you want to use for each element of your blog.

✔ **Edit HTML:** Back up your existing template, upload a custom template from your hard drive, or restore an old template.

✔ **Pick New Template:** Select a new template from the free templates provided by Blogger.

You can read more about fonts, colors, and templates in Chapter 8.

Signing out of Blogger

When you're ready to leave Blogger and complete your blogging session, all it takes is a click of a button. Figure 4-12 shows the Sign Out link, in the upper-right corner of any page within your Blogger account. Just click the link and you're automatically logged off the Blogger site, and the Blogger home page opens.

Click here to sign out.

Figure 4-12:
Click the
Sign Out link
to end your
Blogger
session.

Always remember to sign out of Blogger when you're done updating your blog, to ensure that your blog and your account stay secure.

Chapter 5

Setting Up Your Blog

· ·

· ·

Before you dive into the blogosphere headfirst by writing your first blog post, it's a good idea to take some time to prepare your blog to make a successful splash right from the start. If you want people to return to your blog after they find it, you need to write interesting blog posts, of course, but you also need to create a comfortable environment for your visitors. You can accomplish this by writing a great profile that helps visitors understand who you are and why you're writing your blog. Additionally, designing a home page that provides easy access to useful tools and information is equally important.

Blogger is loaded with options and settings that you can customize to make your blog perform just the way you want. In this chapter, you'll find out about the many settings and options you should configure before you start writing and publishing blog posts. Taking the time to set up your blog now makes it easier for people to find your blog, and it makes those people more likely to return.

Creating Your Profile

With millions of blogs online and more popping up every day, you have to make sure that your readers know who you are and why you're blogging. Start a relationship with them immediately by sharing your story in your *profile,* or your *About* page. Your profile can highlight information about you, the purpose of your blog, your target audience, and anything else you want visitors to know about you and your place on the Web.

Compare the profiles shown in Figures 5-1 and 5-2. The first shows a blank profile that hasn't been edited in any way since the blog was created. The second shows a comprehensive profile that tells visitors about the blogger's qualifications. Which profile would make you feel more confident as a visitor to read that blog and interact with the author? Hopefully, your answer is the second, detailed profile.

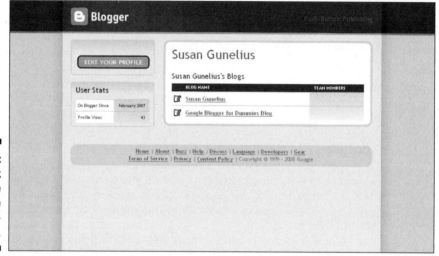

Figure 5-1:
A blank profile page does little to help visitors.

Figure 5-2:
A thorough profile makes visitors feel confident and comfortable.

Be sure to include the following three pieces of information in your blog profile:

- ✔ **Your experience:** Tell readers why you're qualified to write about your blog topic.

- ✔ **Your contact information:** Build a relationship with your readers by making sure that they can contact you easily.

- ✔ **Links to your other blogs or Web sites:** Let readers understand who you are not just on your blog but also as part of the blogosphere and online community overall.

Your profile is your opportunity to sell who you are and what your blog is about. Let your passion for your blog topic shine through in your profile. Include information, links, and other elements to help visitors understand not just who you are and why you're writing your blog but also why your blog is *the place* to visit online to find information about your blog topic.

Adding information to your profile

To create your profile, sign in to Blogger (Chapter 4 shows how), which opens your Blogger account dashboard, shown in Figure 5-3. You can edit your profile at any time, but you benefit greatly if you take the time to complete as much of your profile as possible up front.

Figure 5-3:
Accessing the Edit User Profile page.

Click this link to edit your profile.

Click the Edit Profile link on the left side of your screen, which will take you directly to the Edit User Profile page (see Figure 5-4).

Back To: Dashboard

Edit User Profile

Privacy

Share my profile	☑	
Show my real name	☐	If checked, your first and last name will appear on your profile.
Show my email address	☐	Currently set to susan.gunelius@gmail.com
Show my blogs	Select blogs to display	This list of blogs will only be displayed on your user profile.

Identity

Username	susan.gunelius@gmail.com	Required
Email Address	susan.gunelius@gmail.com	Changing this does not change the e-mail address you use to sign-in

Figure 5-4: Configure privacy and identity settings on the Edit User Profile page.

You don't have to complete every field in the Edit User Profile page. Select the areas that give your blog visitors enough information about you to make your blog have meaning to them and position you as the right person to be writing your blog. Your profile should be a virtual introduction and handshake. You don't have to give your résumé or life story, but you should share enough to spark a relationship with your visitors. In other words, take the time to review each section of the Edit User Profile page and make conscious decisions about which sections you need to complete in order to provide a useful profile of you to your readers.

Your profile appears not only on your blog's Profile page but a snippet of the first few sentences of your profile also appears in your blog's sidebar. Put the most compelling information at the beginning of your profile so it's visible in the sidebar. You should also understand that your profile can help your search engine optimization efforts, which are described in detail in Chapter 13. Search engines *crawl* (review and index for future user searches) your profile text, which can draw more traffic to your blog.

Editing privacy and identity settings

At the top of the Edit User Profile page, you have the option to edit your privacy and identity settings as shown in these steps:

1. **Select the Share My Profile check box to make your profile page public.**

   It's entirely up to you whether you want other users to be able to view your profile. Unless your blog is private, which is described later in this chapter, make your profile public by selecting the Share My Profile check box.

   Be truthful, but not overly modest. Remember that your profile is basically a marketing tool to show readers why you're qualified to write your blog and why they should be interested in reading what you have to say.

2. **Select the Show My Real Name check box to display your real name on your profile page.**

   If you want your real name to be displayed in your profile for visitors to see, select the Show My Real Name check box. Consider the purpose of your blog as well as your audience to help you determine whether it's in your best interest to display your real name in your profile. Using your real name can give your blog more credibility and helps to create a stronger relationship between you and your readers. However, some people prefer to omit their personal information from their blog profiles.

3. **Select the Show My Email Address check box to display your e-mail address on your profile page.**

   If you want other users to be able to see your e-mail address on your profile, select the Show My Email Address check box.

4. **Follow the Select Blogs to Display link after Show My Blogs to choose which of your Blogger blogs you want to display on your profile page.**

   If you have other blogs attached to your Blogger account, you have the option to display links to those other blogs on your profile by clicking the Select Blogs to Display link and choosing which of your blogs you want to show on your profile.

5. **Enter in the Email Address box the e-mail address you want to display on your profile page.**

   The e-mail address you enter to display on your profile page is the address you want visitors to use to contact you. The address doesn't need to be the same as the e-mail address you use to sign into your Blogger account.

   When you display your e-mail address as part of your profile, you publicize it to everyone online, which means that e-mail spammers have access to it. You might want to consider setting up a separate e-mail account to display in your blog profile if you're concerned about receiving spam through your primary e-mail account.

6. **Enter your name in the Display Name box.**

   The name you enter here is the same as the name you use as the author of your blog posts.

7. **Enter your first name in the First Name box.**

   If you selected the Show My Real Name check box (refer to Figure 5-4), the first name you enter in the First Name box is the first name displayed on your profile as part of your real name.

8. **Enter your last name in the Last Name box.**

   If you selected the Show My Real Name check box (refer to Figure 5-4), the last name you enter in the Last Name box is the last name displayed on your profile as part of your real name.

Uploading a photo or an audio clip to your profile

Scroll down the Edit User Profile page to find space where you can upload a photo or an audio clip to display with your profile and to configure more personal information display settings (see Figure 5-5).

Figure 5-5:
Adding a photo and an audio clip to your profile.

1. **Choose one of the following options in the Photo URL area to upload a photo to display on your profile page:**

   • Click the From Your Computer radio button to upload a photo from your local computer hard drive. Use the Browse button to search for the photo you want to use.

• Select From the Web if you want to use a photo that is stored online in an account from a service such as Picasa or Flickr or that has already been uploaded to the Web and has an existing URL.

The photo you upload to your blog profile can be any image you want. Many bloggers upload their own portrait but others prefer to use a wide variety of images from logos to landscapes and everything in between.

2. **In the Audio Clip URL box, enter the URL of an audio clip that you have already uploaded and want to play when your profile page loads.**

Many users don't like blogs or Web sites that use sound and quickly navigate away from blogs that startle them with loud or offensive music. You might want to avoid adding an audio clip entirely. If you choose to use one, consider your audience when you choose the sound for your audio clip.

Creating interest by adding personal information

The next part of the Edit User Profile page gives you various options to add personal information to your profile, such as your location (see Figure 5-6).

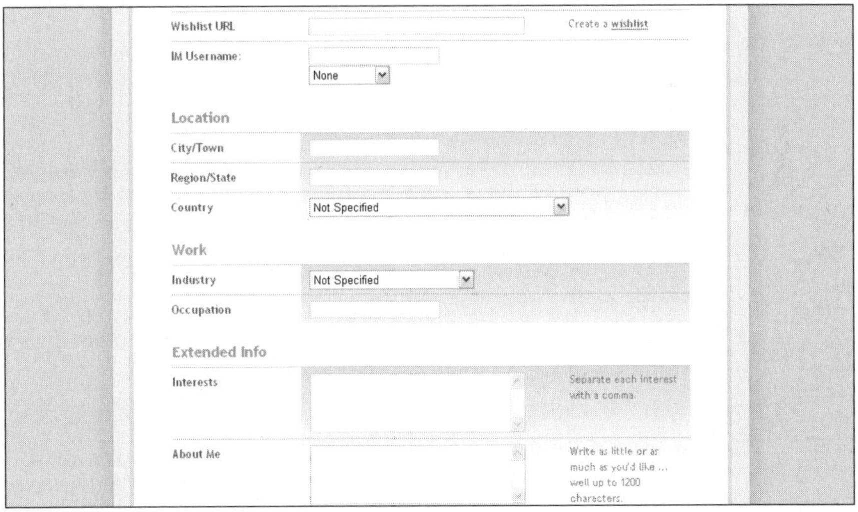

Figure 5-6: Changing your location and other settings.

Wishlist URL	Create a _wishlist_
IM Username:	None
Location	
City/Town	
Region/State	
Country	Not Specified
Work	
Industry	Not Specified
Occupation	
Extended Info	
Interests	Separate each interest with a comma.
About Me	Write as little or as much as you'd like ... well up to 1200 characters.

1. **Click the appropriate radio button to display your gender on your profile page.**

You can choose the Not Specified radio button to keep your gender private.

2. **Enter your birth date in the Birthday fields.**

   You can display your birthday with or without the year, if you choose.

3. **Select the Show Astrological Signs check box if you want your astro-logical sign and Chinese zodiac sign displayed on your profile page.**

   This option works only if you enter your birth date, including your birth year, in the Birthday fields.

4. **Enter your Web site address in the Homepage URL box.**

   If you have another blog or Web site that you want visitors to have easy access to, enter that URL in this box. It's displayed prominently as My Web Page with an active link on your profile page.

Follow these steps to change your location and other settings:

1. **If you have a Google Shopping List, you can enter the URL in the Wishlist URL box.**

   Google Shopping Lists are used to show other people products and items you want or enjoy.

2. **Enter your instant messenger ID in the IM Username text box and click the drop-down box to pick the instant messenger service associ-ated with that username.**

   If you want visitors to be able to send you instant messages, you can enter your instant messaging username and service here.

If you display your instant messenger username in your blog profile, you're publicizing it to everyone with Internet access. That means spam-mers also have access to it. Keep that in mind when you set up your profile.

3. **Enter your hometown in the City/Town text box.**

   If you want visitors to know which city or town you live in, you can enter it in this box to display on your profile.

4. **Enter the area where you live in the Region/State text box.**

   If you want visitors to know which region of the world or country you live in (or your state), you can enter it here, and it's displayed on your profile.

5. **From the Country drop-down box, select the country where you live.**

   If you want visitors to know which country you live in, select it here, and it appears on your profile.

6. **From the Industry drop-down box, select the industry you work in.**

   If you want visitors to know which industry you work in, select it here, and it appears on your profile.

7. **Enter your job in the Occupation text box.**

   Some bloggers like to share their occupation with visitors. If this is something you want your readers to know about you, enter your job information, and it's displayed as part of your profile.

8. **Enter your interests in the Interests text box, separating each one with a comma.**

   You may want to share some of your personal or business interests with your readers. If so, take some time to create a list to display as part of your profile.

9. **Enter information in the About Me text box to describe who you are to your readers.**

   You can enter up to 1,200 characters in the About Me box to tell your readers more about you and why you're qualified to write your blog. This is your chance to shine!

   The About Me box is the area of your profile where you can sell your-self and your blog. Take the time to write something interesting in your About Me box.

Sharing a few of your favorite things

The final section of the Edit User Profile page, shown in Figure 5-7, allows you to enter more personal information to share with readers.

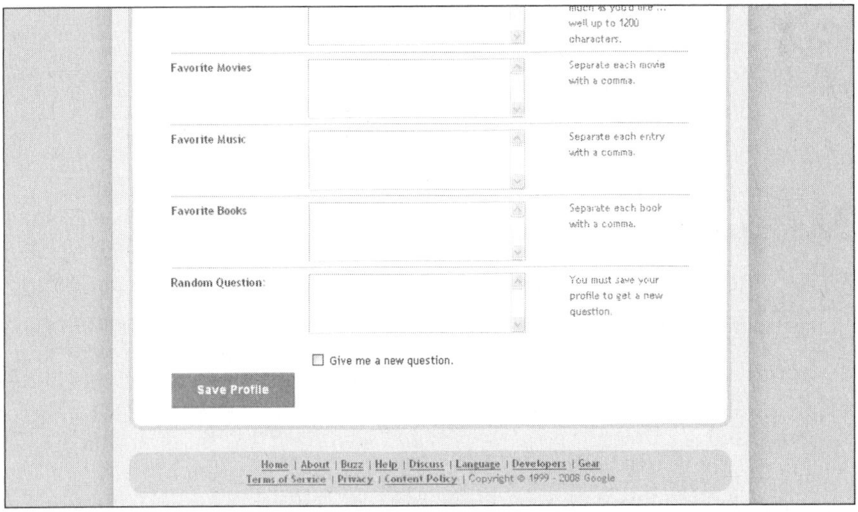

Figure 5-7:
Configure your extended settings and save your profile.

1. **Enter the names of movies you like in the Favorite Movies text box.**

   If you want to share some of your favorite movies with your readers, you can enter the names of those movies in this box, and separate each title with a comma.

2. **Enter the names of bands or songs you like in the Favorite Music text box.**

   If you want to share information about music you enjoy with your readers, you can enter names of bands, CDs, artists, songs, and more in this box, separating each one with a comma.

3. **Enter the names of your favorite books in the Favorite Books text box.**

   If you want to share the names of some of your favorite books with your readers, you can enter book titles in this box, separating each one with a comma.

4. **Enter your response to the Blogger randomly generated question in the Random Question text box.**

   Just for fun, Blogger gives you a question that you can answer to share a random piece of information with your readers, such as "What's the most amount of sand you've ever had in your swimming trunks?" or "You're trapped in a well with a goat and a slinky. Describe how you will escape." To get a new question, select the Give Me a New Question check box and save your profile.

The information entered in the Interests, Favorite Movies, Favorite Music, and Favorite Books text boxes becomes part of a searchable database within Blogger. You can click on each unique entry in a Blogger user's profile to find other users who included the same entry in their profiles. It's a helpful way to find other bloggers with similar interests!

Designing Your Home Page

Your blog's home page is a critical element of your blog. It's your online welcome page and needs to be set up to make visitors feel comfortable as well as give them quick and easy access to the various parts of your blog that they're most interested in and that you want to make sure they see. Before you publish your first blog post, take a few minutes to look at your blog's layout to ensure that all the elements you want visitors to see are easy to find.

Avoid cluttering your home page with too much information and too many elements. Be sure that your design allows your readers to find the most valuable information and links. Follow these steps to pick and choose the page elements you want to display on the home page of your blog:

1. **From the Blogger dashboard, click the Layout link for your blog.**

   This step takes you to the Page Elements page, shown in Figure 5-8.

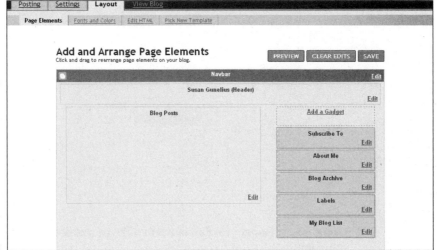

2. **Select the Pick New Template tab from the top navigation bar and choose the template you like from the Templates page, shown in Figure 5-9. Make sure to click the Save Template button if you want to switch to a different theme.**

   This step opens a page where you can view and select a Blogger template for your blog. (The screen shots used in this chapter use the Denim theme.) You can find out more about customizing templates in Chapter 7.

3. **Select the Page Elements tab from the top navigation bar to customize your blog's home page.**

   After your template is chosen, you can return to the Page Elements page (refer to Figure 5-8) to select the elements and gadgets you want visitors to see on your blog.

4. **Click and drag page element boxes to move them around your page.**

   Moving elements on your screen moves them to new locations on your blog.

5. **Click Edit on any of the page element boxes to modify the appearance of each individual page element.**

   For example, you can choose to revise your profile (the About Me page element) directly from the Page Elements page by selecting Edit in the About Me box and choosing the appropriate changes.

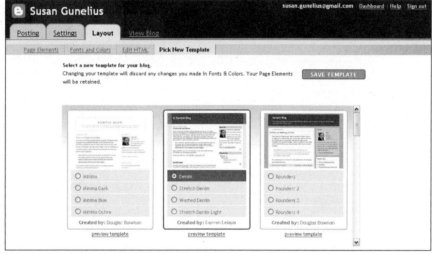

6. Select Add a Gadget to choose from a list of gadgets you can add to your blog.

A new window opens where you can choose from a variety of gadgets to further customize the appearance of your blog's home page, as shown in Figures 5-10 and 5-11. Specific gadgets are described in detail in Chapter 8.

7. **Click the Preview button to see how your changes will look, and choose the Save button to save your changes when you're happy with the layout of your blog's homepage.**

Don't be afraid to test different gadgets. Use the Preview button to see what you like and don't like. Everything can be customized, and nothing can be viewed by visitors until you click the Save button.

Customizing Your Blog

One reason that Blogger is so easy to use is that users can customize their blogs by visiting just a few pages from the Blogger dashboard and then picking and choosing options and saving those choices. To start, just select Settings from your Blogger dashboard. This action takes you to the Basic settings configuration page, shown in Figures 5-12 and 5-13.

Publishing, configuring privacy, editing, and composing

The Basic settings page is a page you shouldn't skip when you start your new Blogger blog. On this page, you can make your blog public or private, add a blog description, change your blog title, and set up editing options. Take some time to review each option shown in Figures 5-12 and 5-13 and configure them as described in the following steps.

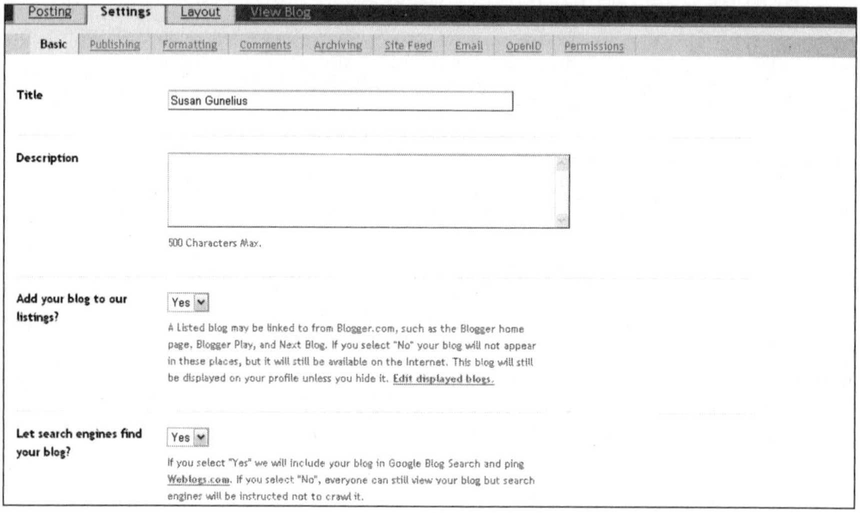

Figure 5-12: Configure your blog description, listing, and pinging options first.

Figure 5-13: Configure editing settings on the Basic Settings tab.

1. Enter a title for your blog in the Title text box.

If you want to change the title of your blog, this box is the place to do it. The title you enter here appears in the header area of your blog.

2. **Enter a description for your blog in the Description box.**

   You can enter a description of as many as 500 characters in the Description text box. Note that whatever you type in the Description box appears beneath your blog title in the blog header area, so take some time to write a useful description that not only describes what your blog is about but also entices visitors to read more.

3. **Select Yes or No from the Add Your Blog to Our Listings drop-down box.**

   When you select Yes, your blog is displayed occasionally on the Blogger home page, on Blogger Play (a slide show of photos published on Blogger blogs) and Next Blog (the navigation bar that appears at the top of all Blogger blogs).

   If you select No to the question Add Your Blog to Our Listings? within your blog's Basic Settings page, your blog is still available on the Internet; however, Blogger rotates blogs in the Blogger listings and displays links to those blogs on the Blogger home page, on Blogger Play, and on Next Blog. If you want to attract additional potential traffic from these Blogger listings, select Yes from the Add Your Blog to Our Listings? drop-down menu.

4. **Select Yes or No from the Let Search Engines Find Your Blog drop-down menu.**

   A helpful Blogger feature is automatic pinging at Weblogs.com (http://weblogs.com) and automatic inclusion in the Google Blog Search (http://blogsearch.google.com) results if you select Yes from the Let Search Engines Find Your Blog drop-down menu. *Pinging* is a behind-the-scenes function that automatically notifies sites such as Google and Technorati whenever a blog is updated. By selecting Yes, every time you update your blog you ensure that Google Blog Search and search engines linked to Weblogs.com are notified that you published new content, and that content is added to those search listings. This strategy provides more traffic and more ways for people to find your blog.

5. **Select Yes or No from the Show Quick Editing on Your Blog drop-down menu.**

   By selecting Yes, you enable one-click blog post editing. When you're signed into Blogger and viewing your blog online, you can select a link directly from each blog post, which automatically opens a page where you can edit that post.

6. **Select Yes or No from the Show Email Post Links drop-down menu.**

   Selecting Yes places an Email Post link on each of your blog posts so that readers can e-mail your posts to other people with one simple click of the mouse.

7. Select Yes or No from the Adult Content drop-down menu.

If your blog contains content that might be considered inappropriate for minors, select Yes from the Adult Content drop-down menu. When people visit a blog that contains adult content, a warning message appears, asking visitors to confirm that they want to proceed before the blog content loads.

8. Select Yes or No from the Show Compose Mode for All Your Blogs drop-down menu.

Unless you know how to use HTML, you should select Yes in the Show Compose Mode for All Your Blogs drop-down menu. Doing so gives you the option to write your blog posts using a What You See Is What You Get (WYSIWYG) editor that acts more like a traditional word processing program than a Web design program.

Formatting posts, times, dates, and languages

You should set several formatting configurations before you start writing and publishing blog posts, such as time, date, and language options. Select the Formatting tab from the Settings navigation bar to display the Formatting page, shown in Figure 5-14.

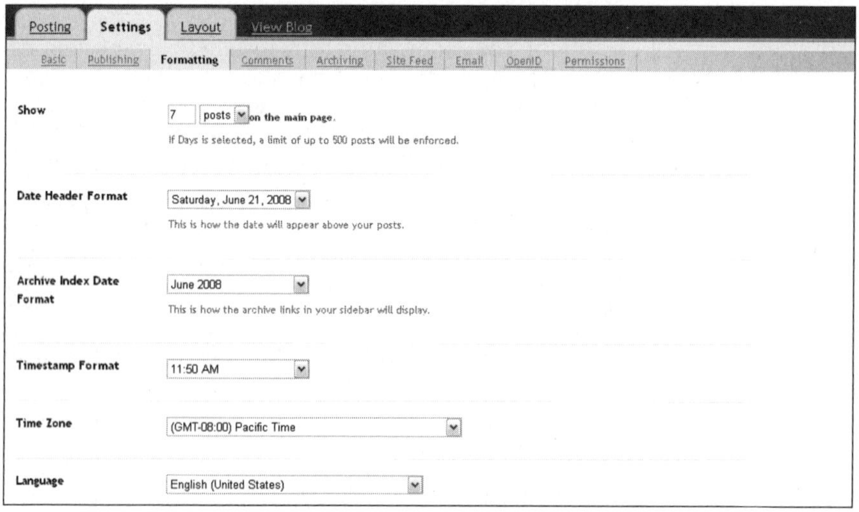

Figure 5-14:
Times,
dates,
languages,
and more
can be set
up on the
Formatting
page.

Then follow these steps to configure how your blog posts are displayed to visitors:

1. **Select the number of posts you want to display on your blog's home page by choosing these options:**

   • From the Show drop-down menu, select Posts or Days to display a designated number of posts on your blog's main page or a designated number of days' worth of posts on your blog's main page.

   • In the Show box, enter the number of posts or days' worth of posts you want to display on your blog's main page based on the setting you selected from the Show drop-down menu.

   The number of posts you show on your blog's home page is entirely up to you, but remember that people don't like to scroll too much. Displaying 5 to 10 posts (depending on post length) on your home page is a common target to keep your blog readable.

2. **From the Date Header Format drop-down menu, select in which format you want the dates to appear on your blog.**

   This date appears at the top of your blog, above your posts, to remind visitors what day it is.

3. **From the Archive Index Date Format drop-down menu, select the format of the dates used in the Archive Links page element on your blog's sidebar.**

   Older posts are automatically archived so they're easily accessible from the Archive Links page element in your blog's sidebar. It's up to you to decide how you want your archived posts to display in your sidebar. Choose the date format that you prefer by configuring the Archive Index Date Format setting.

4. **From the Timestamp Format drop-down menu, select the format you want to use for the publication date for your blog posts.**

   A timestamp appears at the bottom of each blog post that tells readers when each post was published. Changing the Timestamp Format alters how that date appears on each blog post.

5. **Select your time zone from the Time Zone drop-down menu.**

   Selecting the correct time zone ensures that your date header and timestamps synchronize correctly to your location.

6. **Select your language from the Language drop-down menu.**

   Blogger is available in a variety of languages. Make sure that you select the correct language for your blog.

Enabling comments and backlinks

One of the most important elements of a successful blog is the community of readers that grows around it. At the heart of that community is a conversation that occurs by way of comments left on your blog posts. With that in mind, it's essential that you set up the commenting feature on your blog before you publish any content. Figures 5-15 and 5-16 show the Comment configuration page accessed from the Comment tab within the Settings section of the Blogger dashboard.

Figure 5-15:
Set up your blog comments before anyone visits your blog!

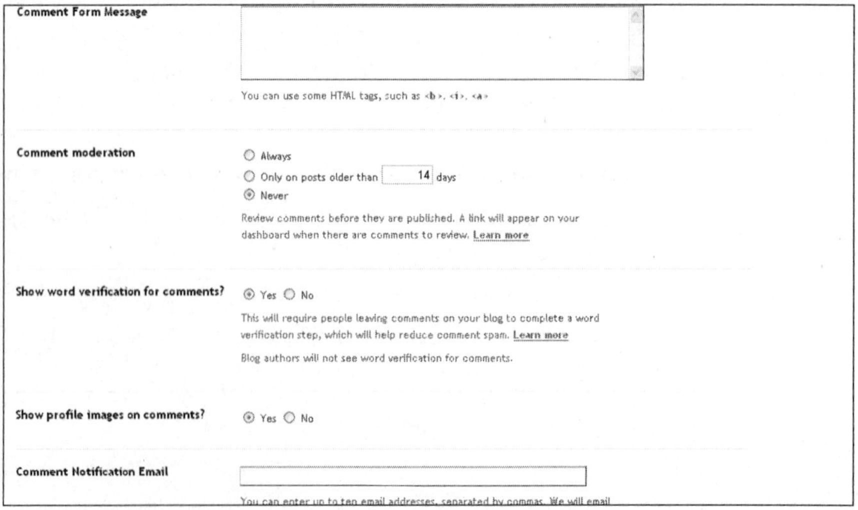

Comments	⦿ Show ◯ Hide
	Note: Selecting "Hide" does not delete existing comments - You can show them at any time by re-selecting "Show".
Who Can Comment?	◯ Anyone - *includes Anonymous Users*
	⦿ Registered Users - *includes OpenID*
	◯ Users with Google Accounts
	◯ Only members of this blog
Comments Default for Posts	[New Posts Have Comments ▾]
Backlinks	◯ Show ⦿ Hide
	Backlinks enable you to keep track of other pages on the web that link to your posts. Learn more
	Note: Selecting "Hide" does not delete backlinks - You can show them at any time by re-selecting "Show".
Backlinks Default for Posts	[New Posts Have Backlinks ▾]
Comments Timestamp Format	[June 21, 2008 11:51 AM ▾]

Figure 5-16:
Don't forget to configure comment security settings.

Comment Form Message	[ ]
	You can use some HTML tags, such as <b>, <i>, <a>
Comment moderation	◯ Always
	◯ Only on posts older than [14] days
	⦿ Never
	Review comments before they are published. A link will appear on your dashboard when there are comments to review. Learn more
Show word verification for comments?	⦿ Yes ◯ No
	This will require people leaving comments on your blog to complete a word verification step, which will help reduce comment spam. Learn more
	Blog authors will not see word verification for comments.
Show profile images on comments?	⦿ Yes ◯ No
Comment Notification Email	[ ]
	You can enter up to ten email addresses, separated by commas. We will email

The following settings should be configured up front:

1. **Select the appropriate radio button to show (or hide, if you prefer) comments on your blog posts.**

   The most popular blogs allows comments, so take some time to think about your blogging goals before you decide whether you want to allow people to comment on your blog posts. See the sidebar to learn more about the importance of blog comments.

2. **Select a radio button to configure the Who Can Comment option on your blog.**

   You can allow anyone to comment on your blog: only registered OpenID users, only users with Google accounts, or only members of your blog (people that you give access to read your blog on the permissions Settings tab described later in this chapter, in the section "Assigning permissions").

3. **Select a Comments Default for Posts setting from the drop-down menu.**

   Choose whether you want new posts to allow comments by default. You can change this setting in the future for specific posts as described in Chapter 6.

4. **Select the appropriate radio button to show (or hide, if you prefer) backlinks within the Comments section of your blog posts.**

   Backlinks appear as comments on Blogger posts and provide a "tap on the shoulder" from another Blogger blog to you, showing that Blogger blog linked to you in a published post. Backlinks are a helpful way to develop relationships with other bloggers and find like-minded bloggers. With that promotional opportunity in mind, most bloggers choose to allow backlinks.

5. **Select a Backlinks Default for Posts setting from the drop-down menu.**

   You can determine whether you want all new posts to allow backlinks within the Comments section by default by configuring this setting. You can change this setting in the future for specific posts as described in Chapter 6.

6. **From the Comments Timestamp Format drop-down menu, select the way you want the time that comments are published on your posts to display on your blog**.

   Each comment left on one of your blog posts is published along with the time it was originally entered. Changing the timestamp format alters how that time appears on your blog.

7. **Enter a message to precede the Comment area in your blog posts in the Comment Form Message box.**

   This message appears above the comment form on all your blog posts. It can be used to invite people to comment on blog posts.

Engaging your readers with blog comments

If blog posts are a blog's heartbeat, blog comments are the veins and arteries that keep blood pumping to and from the heart of a blog. Comments make a blog an interactive and social medium. Show your readers that you value them and their comments by responding promptly to every comment left on your blog. Ask readers to leave comments on your blog posts to invite conversation, and then make an effort to keep that conversation going. By engaging your readers in conversation, you develop a strong blog community of loyal visitors.

8. **Click the Always, Only on Posts Older than 14 Days, or Never radio button to enable Comment Moderation (refer to Figure 5-16).**

   Comment moderation is a helpful way to reduce spam comments on your blog. As new comments are left on your blog posts, they appear on your dashboard for you to review and approve before they're published for others to see. This technique gives you the opportunity to delete spam or offensive comments. Read the later sidebar "Dealing with blog comment spam" to find out more about blog comment spam.

9. **Click the Yes or No radio button to indicate your preference for the Show Word Verification for Comments option.**

   Word verification is an excellent way to block comment spam. Each person who leaves a comment on one of your blog posts is given a word to enter into the comment form in order to be able to submit that comment.

10. **Select whether you want to show profile images on comments by clicking the Yes or No radio button.**

    If you want other Blogger users' profile pictures to be displayed with their comments on your blog posts, select Yes. Otherwise, choose No.

11. **Enter an e-mail address in the Comment Notification Email text box.**

    If you want to be notified by e-mail whenever a new comment is awaiting moderation, simply enter your e-mail address in the Comment Notification Email box, and an e-mail is sent to you automatically when each new comment is submitted. You can enter as many as ten e-mail addresses (separated by commas) in this field.

12. **Click the Save Settings button to save any changes you made on the Comments page.**

Dealing with blog comment spam

Blog comment spam is typically defined as comments left on blog posts for no reason other than to drive traffic to a link provided in that comment. Blog comment spam may include nothing but links, or it can include an irrelevant comment as well as one or more links. Note that many people leave valid links in the comments they publish on your blog posts. Be sure to review each comment to identify which links are valid and which are spam. By deleting spam comments, you create a better user experience for your readers.

Setting up archiving

If you want your readers to be able to access your old posts after the posts are moved off your blog's home page, you need to make sure that you configure your archive settings before you start publishing content on your blog. Figure 5-17 shows the Archiving page on the Settings tab in the Blogger dashboard.

Figure 5-17: Configure your blog archives so visitors can find your old posts.

Configure the following settings to set up your blog archives:

1. **From the Archive Frequency drop-down menu, select how often you want your blog posts to be archived.**

Take a few minutes to decide how you want visitors to be able to access your older blog posts. The setting you choose here affects how your blog archives are displayed in your blog's sidebar. Do you want visitors to find your old posts by month, week, or day? Choose the setting that creates the user experience you want on your blog.

2. **Select Yes or No from the Enable Post Pages drop-down menu depending on whether you want each of your posts to have its own page online.**

   Most bloggers select Yes from this drop-down menu. Giving each blog post its own page means that each post also receives its own *permalink* (permanent link URL). This strategy makes it easy to find and link to older content and gives more entry points for people to find your blog by using search engines. Chapter 13 discusses search engine optimization in more detail.

3. **Select the Save Settings button to save any changes you made on the Archiving page.**

Assigning permissions

You have to decide whether you want anyone with Internet access to be able to read your blog or to allow only a certain group of people, such as friends and family, to see it. This decision affects how you configure your blog permissions settings on the Settings tab of your Blogger dashboard, shown in Figure 5-18.

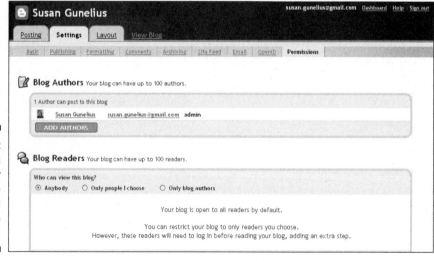

Figure 5-18:
Before you publish your blog, decide whom you want to see it.

You can select from the following options to configure the privacy settings for your blog:

1. **Select the Permissions tab from the Settings navigation bar in your Blogger dashboard.**

2. **Under the Blog Readers heading, choose your privacy settings by selecting the appropriate radio button to determine who can view this blog:**

   - *Anybody:* This setting allows anyone with Internet access to see your blog.

   - *Only people I choose:* Enter e-mail addresses for the specific people you want to invite to read your blog.

   - *Only blog authors:* Only those people who have access to publish content to your blog can view it online. Adding blog authors is discussed in detail in Chapter 14.

The decision to make your blog private or public is up to you and should be a direct result of your goals for your blog. If you want to simply share your thoughts, ideas, or photos with just a few people, creating a private blog is a viable choice. However, if you want to grow your blog, increase traffic, and make money from it, set your blog permission to allow anybody to view it.

Chapter 6

Writing and Publishing Blog Posts

. . . .

In This Chapter

▶ Considering your options before you write

▶ Creating your first blog post

▶ Adding graphics, links, and special formatting to your blog posts

▶ Configuring comments, backlinks, and settings in individual posts

▶ Finding, editing, and deleting old posts

. . . .

After your new Blogger blog is set up, you're ready to start writing your first blog post and truly become a member of the blogosphere. Your foray into the social Web is about to begin. Take a deep breath, put on your creative thinking cap, and get ready to write.

This chapter tells you what to think about before and as you write blog posts. It shows you how to enter your first blog post into the Blogger post editor and publish that post as well as how to add links, photos, and other items to your blog posts to make them visually appealing and easier to read.

Thinking Things Through

Writing blog posts can be as simple or as complex as you want it to be, depending on your goals for your blog. If you write a blog for fun with no long-term goals for driving traffic or making money from your blog, writing blog posts requires little more than translating the thoughts in your head to your keyboard and then online. However, if you want to grow your blog and monetize it, you need to consider several issues before you write and publish content on your blog. Determine your short- and long-term goals for your blog to identify how to apply the following considerations to your writing.

Using different formats for your blog posts

A blog post can be just a few sentences or many paragraphs. Some blog posts include an image and no text, whereas others might contain a complete tutorial or an online lesson teaching readers how to accomplish a task. Think about your audience (or at least the audience you want to have read your blog content) as you write your blog posts and create content that would appeal to them. The variety of blog posts in the following list gives you a starting place to help write your own blog posts.

- ✔ **Current events:** Write about something you heard about in the news.

- ✔ **How-to or tutorials:** Share your expertise in your blog topic by writing a tutorial or instructions to help your readers accomplish a task or an activity.

- ✔ **Interviews:** Contact a prominent person who works in a field related to your blog topic and interview her for a blog post.

- ✔ **Link love:** Find interesting blog posts across the blogosphere that are related to your blog topic and publish a post that provides links to those posts to help your readers find new blogs and to help you connect with other bloggers.

- ✔ **Lists:** Write your top five tips or suggestions or your top ten must-have products to help your blog readers. Alternatively, write a list of don'ts or a similar list of warnings.

- ✔ **Opinion:** Write a post that simply provides your opinion on an issue or event.

- ✔ **Photos:** Post a photo related to your blog topic.

- ✔ **Polls:** Ask your readers for their opinions by publishing a blog post that includes a poll or survey.

- ✔ **Reviews:** Write a review of a product, an event, a book, or anything else related to your blog topic.

Coming up with titles

The first thing visitors to your blog will notice about your blog posts are the titles of those posts. With that in mind, you should consider a few issues as you compose the title for each of your posts. Write titles that

- ✔ **Arouse your readers' curiosity:** Just like an advertising headline, your post title should lure readers in and entice them to want to read further.

- ✔ **Are relevant to your readers:** Web surfers are busy and have little time to read deeply on any page to find content that matters to them. Write headlines that are easy to understand, and make sure the post delivers the content that the title suggests.

- ✔ **Include searchable keywords:** Search engines value blog post titles strongly in terms of prioritizing your content for keyword searches. Be certain to include important keywords in your post titles.

Considering search engine optimization

If you want to grow your blog by attracting new visitors, you should write blog posts with search engine optimization in mind. Search engines such as Google and Yahoo! love blogs simply because the content is updated frequently. With each new blog post comes a new entry point and a new way for a search engine to find your content. Take some time to research keywords that are relevant to your blog topic, and then use those keywords in your blog posts and titles. Each blog post you write should be optimized for a specific keyword phrase, and all your keywords should be relevant to your overall blog topic. You can learn more about search engine optimization in Chapter 13. If you're serious about growing your blog, invest time and effort into finding out how to write for the Web with an eye toward search engine optimization.

Creating a Blog Post

When you sit down to create your first post for your new blog, don't be nervous. Once you dive in and start your first post, you'll find that Blogger is very easy to use. In fact, after you have a few posts written and published, you may even wonder why you didn't start blogging sooner! This section walks you through creating and publishing a new post in Blogger step by step so that you can become an active blogger immediately.

To engage readers, write in a Web-friendly style. Use a personable voice that's welcoming to readers. Use short paragraphs and lists to make your posts easy to skim. Use formatting such as bold and italics sparingly to draw attention to the most important information. It's also effective to mix up the length of your blog posts. Generally, shorter posts are more effective, but that doesn't mean you have to avoid long posts entirely. Offer your readers a variety of content (including post lengths) to keep your blog interesting. To start a new post in Blogger, follow these steps:

1. **Sign in to your Blogger account and click the New Post link from your dashboard.**

   If you created more than one blog, be sure to click the New Post link for the appropriate blog. After you click the link, the Blogger post editor appears (see Figure 6-1).

2. **Think of a title and enter it in the Title text box in the Blogger post editor.**

3. **Enter the body text of your post in the large box under the post editor toolbar.**

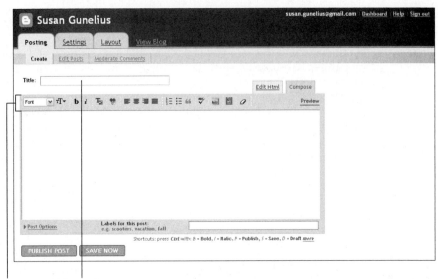

Figure 6-1:
The Blogger
post editor.

Toolbar   Title text box

4. Use the Blogger post editor toolbar icons to add formatting such as bold or italics, alignment, and bullets.

From the Blogger post editor toolbar (refer to Figure 6-1), you can change the font used in the body of your post, change the font size, bold or italicize your text, or change the color of your text. You can also create hyperlinked text, change the alignment of your text, create numbered or bulleted lists, indent text as block quotes, and even check your spelling. The various features of the Blogger post editor toolbar are discussed in greater detail later in this chapter, in the section "Formatting Text Enhancements."

5. Preview your post by clicking the Preview link on the blog post editor toolbar.

As you type your new blog post, you can preview it to get an idea of how it will look online after it's published. Previewing a post is particularly helpful in ensuring that your line breaks look good and image sizes are appropriate, for example. Figure 6-2 shows how a post looks in the post editor when the Preview link is clicked.

6. Click the Publish button to publish your post for the world to see.

A message appears (see Figure 6-3): "Your blog post published successfully!" It means that your blog post is automatically — and immediately — moved from your private account to the World Wide Web and that everyone with Internet access can see it, assuming that you set up your blog to be public, as described in Chapter 5.

Figure 6-2:
Preview
your posts
before you
publish
them.

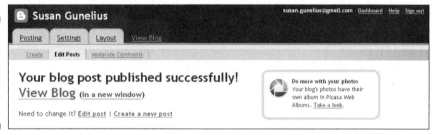

Figure 6-3:
Your blog
post is
published
success-
fully.

When you see the message that your blog post published successfully, a few options are available to you (refer to Figure 6-3). You can view your new blog post as it appears live on your blog by clicking the View Blog link, or click the In a New Window link to open a new browser window to view your live post. Figure 6-4 shows how the new post example used in this chapter looks live online.

If you make a mistake or see something in your blog post that you want to change, you can also do that by simply clicking the Edit Post link. Editing posts is discussed at the end of this chapter, as part of the "Revisiting Old Posts" section.

An easy way to drive visitors away from your blog, never to return, is to publish blog posts filled with spelling errors. Although you might not be an excellent typist or grammarian, it's important to make an effort to proofread your blog posts. Luckily, Blogger has a spell-check feature integrated into its blog post editor. To check the spelling in your blog posts, simply click the Check Spelling icon in the blog post editor. Blogger highlights in yellow any words that are considered misspellings.

Figure 6-4:
Your
new post
appears at
the top of
your blog
as the most
recent
entry.

Saving with Auto Save

Blogger has a helpful Auto Save function that not only automatically saves your blog posts periodically as you're writing them in the blog post editor but also allows you to perform quick saves without leaving the post editor. To save your posts without leaving the post editor, simply click the Save Now button at the bottom of the blog post editor page.

Make sure you save your blog posts periodically as you're working on them in the post editor. You never know when you might lose your Internet connection, and the work you've done could be lost.

Creating a draft post

Sometimes, you might be in the midst of writing a blog post when you're called away from it before it's ready for publishing. Blogger provides an option for you to save an incomplete post as a draft so you can return to it later to finish it and publish it. To save a draft of a post, simply click the Save Now button in the lower-left corner of the blog post editor), and then log out of Blogger. Your post is saved as a draft, as shown in Figure 6-5.

To complete the post, simply click the Edit link next to the post title. The post editor opens with that blog post in the same spot where you left it.

Understanding copyright and fair use

In the simplest terms, copyright laws protect someone's original work, such as written words, photos, videos, and art. Every piece of text on the Internet is protected by copyright laws. However, it's typically too expensive and too time-consuming to sue bloggers for copyright violation, so it's not unusual to see bloggers posting — without permission — text, photos, videos, and other content that they don't own. However, that doesn't mean a day won't come when bloggers will have to answer to a higher power and remove all content on their blogs that violates copyright laws.

Unless you obtain written permission from the original source, don't copy text or use photos, videos, or other materials that don't belong to you. Citing your source or linking back to it isn't enough.

Obtaining permission to copy text or use someone else's material on your blog is the safest route to take if you want to avoid being accused of copyright violation. However, every rule has exceptions. Copyright laws are hazy and often challenged, particularly in the area of copyright law known as fair use. Basically, *fair use* tells publishers (like bloggers) that you can copy an excerpt of previously published text without obtaining permission if the portion of that text you copy is a small excerpt from the original source and you provide attribution or if you're including your own editorial commentary or critique with the text you're copying.

Think of it this way: If your content were copied by another blogger, how would you feel? How much would the other blogger have to copy of your original blog post for you to feel like your content was stolen? Chances are that other bloggers or writers feel the same way when you copy their content for use on your blog.

Copyright laws are meant to protect the person who did the work to produce the original piece. Each time someone else copies the original piece, the original author loses revenue (directly or indirectly). Fair use laws give bloggers some leniency, but they also create a gray area surrounding copyright law that allows bloggers to tread in waters dangerously close to copyright violation territory. Err on the side of caution to protect yourself, your blog, and your readers in the long term.

Copyright laws protect you and your blog, too. Don't forget to include a copyright notice on every page of your blog. If you select a Creative Commons license to apply to your blog, you can obtain the specific license and link directly to the restrictions of use at `www.creativecommons.org`. The nonprofit organization Creative Commons is dedicated to helping content owners protect their work. A perfect place to include a copyright message is in your blog's footer.

Adding Visual Interest

An important part of blogging is not just writing interesting content but also enhancing your posts to make them aesthetically pleasing and easier to read. You can achieve both goals by formatting your posts to be visually appealing and including useful links and images that support your posts or provide additional, helpful information. Formatting your posts and adding images and links also play roles in search engine optimization, which is discussed in detail in Chapter 13. Many of the enhancement features available in the Blogger post editor also make your life as a blogger a lot easier. From autosaving a post to spell checking and postdating it, take some time to test the various tools available to you in the Blogger post editor, as described in this chapter.

Formatting text and layout

The majority of the icons on the Blogger post editor toolbar help you format the text and layout of your blog posts. You can

- ✔ **Choose a font:** Just pick one from the Font drop-down menu.

- ✔ **Choose the size of your text:** Click the icon that has the large and small *T*s and the downward arrow on it.

- ✔ **Make selected text bold:** Click the icon with the *b* on it.

- ✔ **Italicize selected text:** Click the icon with the *i* on it.

- ✔ **Change the color of text:** Click the icon with the *T* and the color grid.

- ✔ **Justify your paragraphs — left, right, center, or full:** Use one of the four alignment icons.

- ✔ **Create numbered lists, bulleted lists, or indented block quotes:** You can easily create them by using the appropriate icons on the blog post editor toolbar.

You can see several of the formatting options that are available in the Blogger post editor in action in Figure 6-6.

Don't overuse text enhancements or else your blog posts become cluttered and difficult to read.

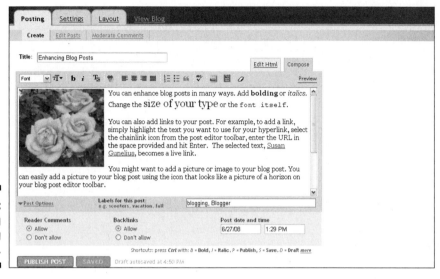

Figure 6-6:
Formatting
your blog
posts.

Adding links to blog posts

Links are a critical part of blogging. When you link to content from other blogs or Web sites within your blog posts, you're not only providing additional valuable information and resources to your readers but also connecting with like-minded bloggers across the Internet. Remember that the strength of blogging comes from the blogger community and the network of people who visit those blogs. Use the power of links within your blog posts to share ideas and information and reach out to other bloggers through backlinks, which are discussed in the next section of this chapter.

Adding a link within a blog post takes just a few steps:

1. **Find the *URL,* or Web address, for the Web page (or blog post) you want to link to.**

   Visit the Web page you want to link to, and copy the URL from your browser by highlighting it, right-clicking it with your mouse, and choosing Copy from the menu that opens (or choose copy from the Edit drop-down menu in your browser). If you want to link to a blog post, check to see whether a Permalink (the permanent URL for the specific page you want to link to that will not change in the future) is included at the end of the post. If so, click that link and then copy the new URL that opens in your browser.

2. **Use your mouse to highlight the text, within your blog post, that you want to use as the anchor for your link.**

   Choose words that might be keywords that people search for on search engines to boost your search engine optimization efforts, as discussed in Chapter 13.

3. **Click the Insert Link icon on the Blogger post editor toolbar.**

   A dialog box opens in which you can enter the URL (such as http://www. WebsiteInfo.com) that you copied earlier, as shown in Figure 6-7.

The Insert Link button

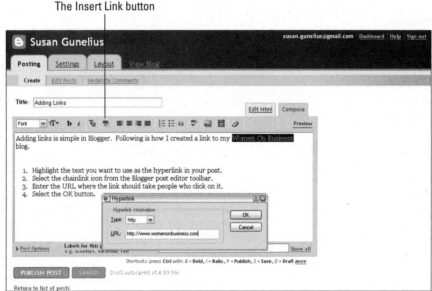

Figure 6-7:
Adding a
hyperlink to
a blog post.

4. **In the URL text box, enter the URL for the Web page (or blog post) you want to link to.**

   Click the Type drop-down menu to change the URL designation, if necessary.

5. **Click the OK button.**

   The dialog box closes, and your selected text is now a different color and underlined, indicating that it's an active hyperlink. When visitors click the hyperlinked text in your blog post, the linked URL opens.

Adding images

Images are an important part of blog posts. Images not only add color and visual appeal to blogs, which are typically text heavy, but also help to further illustrate a point and can boost search engine optimization efforts (see Chapter 13 for details on search engine optimization). Inserting an image into a blog post takes just a few simple steps:

1. **In the Blogger post editor, click the Insert Image icon.**

   This step opens the Upload Images dialog box, shown in Figure 6-8.

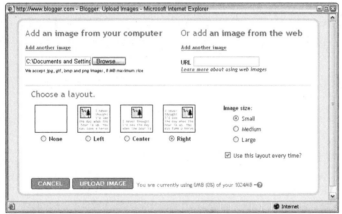

Figure 6-8:
The Blogger
Upload
Images
dialog box.

2. **Determine whether the image you want to upload is located on your computer hard drive or on the Web.**

3. **If the image you want to use is on your hard drive, enter the pathname or click the Browse button to find the image on your computer.**

   After you select the image you want to upload, the pathname appears in the text box.

   Images from your hard drive can be in BMP, GIF, JPG, or PNG format and must be 8 MB or smaller.

4. **If the image you want to use is located online, enter the URL in the URL text box.**

Using images hosted on other Web sites is a gray area in terms of blogging rules and etiquette. Although it isn't illegal to use an image hosted on another Web site on your blog (assuming that the images you're using aren't copyrighted in a manner that doesn't allow you to use them), it's looked at negatively and viewed as stealing bandwidth (online space) from that Web site. In other words, the other Web site is paying for the space to host that image, and by simply linking to it rather than downloading it to your hard drive first and then uploading it to your own account, you're using a portion of their paid bandwidth for free.

5. **In the Choose a Layout section, click the radio button that shows how you want the image aligned in your blog post.**

   You can select left, right, center, or no alignment for your image, depending on how you want your blog post to look. Don't be afraid to try each option to determine which alignment you prefer.

6. **In the Image Size list, select a size for your image.**

   You can select small, medium, or large, depending on how big you want your image to appear in your blog post. Test each size and pick your preference.

7. **Select the Use This Layout Every Time check box if you always want images to appear the same way in your blog posts.**

   You can change this setting at any time.

8. **Click the Upload Image button to upload your image to your Picasa account.**

   A message box opens, telling you that your image has been added (see Figure 6-9).

Figure 6-9: Uploading an image.

Managing your images with Picasa

Blogger is owned by Google, which also owns the online photo-sharing Web site Picasa. When you create a blog with Blogger and upload a photo for your profile or to use in a blog post, that image is stored in a Picasa account that's automatically created for you using your Google account e-mail and password. Google provides this basic Picasa account to you for free.

Your free Picasa account provides only a limited amount of space to upload photos for use on

your blog or blogs (you get one Picasa account per Google account, regardless of the number of blogs you create). After you use up the free space allotted to you, you have to upgrade to a paid Picasa account or find another location online to upload and store your photos for use on your blog.

When you log in to your Picasa account, you can manage your image uploads, share images, create photo albums, and more.

9. Click Done to insert the image into your blog post.

When you're done writing your blog post, click the Publish Post button in the lower left of your blog post editor to see your post live online, including your image, as shown in Figure 6-10.

Figure 6-10: Blog posts with images are visually appealing.

Finding images to use on your blog

Photographs and images are protected under copyright laws, but some photos and images are available for bloggers to use on their blogs. These images are granted Creative Commons licenses, which means that the owner grants permission for other people to use the image with some restrictions. To be able to use an image protected with a Creative Commons license, you need to follow the restrictions related to the specific image.

In order to avoid copyright violations on your blog, be sure to use images that are legally available for you to reproduce on your blog. Following are several sources of free images that you can find online:

- ✓ **StockXchange:** www.sxc.hu
- ✓ **MorgueFile:** www.morguefile.com
- ✓ **Picapp:** www.picapp.com
- ✓ **FreeFoto:** www.freefoto.com
- ✓ **Dreamstime:** www.dreamstime.com

Administering Your Blog Posts

As you write your blog posts, you may notice additional settings that appear at the bottom of the post editor for you to configure. These settings allow you to control the conversation, informal categorization, and publication date of individual posts. Read on to learn how taking the time to configure these settings for each blog post you write can help both you and your blog readers.

Allowing comments

Comments are an essential part of a successful blog. The most popular blogs are typically those that have a strong and vocal community around them. Visitors to blogs like to feel as though they're part of the conversation. Rather than be talked at, blog visitors want to participate in the discussion by leaving comments and interacting with the blogger and other commenters. With that information in mind, it's important to allow visitors to leave comments on your blog posts, as discussed in Chapter 5.

To change your blog's comments setting for an individual blog post, simply start a new post (or open an old post) and click the Post Options link in the lower-left corner of the blog post editor, above the Publish Post button. Doing so opens a new section to the blog post editor (refer to Figure 6-6), where you can click either the Allow or Don't Allow radio button under the Reader Comments heading, depending on whether you want to allow comments on that post.

Adding labels

Labels are helpful for several reasons. First, they help you find old blog posts because you can use labels to quickly sort your posts. Second, labels help readers by allowing them to click a label of interest to find other posts saved with the same label. Labels comprise an informal categorization system that helps in organizing your blog. You can even add a list of your labels in your blog's sidebar to make it easy for readers to find related posts. (This topic is discussed in more detail in Chapter 8.)

To add labels to your blog posts, follow these steps:

1. **Start a new post or open an old post.**

   The blog post editor opens.

2. **Enter the labels you want to use for that specific post in the Labels for This Post text box (see Figure 6-11).**

   Separate each label with a comma.

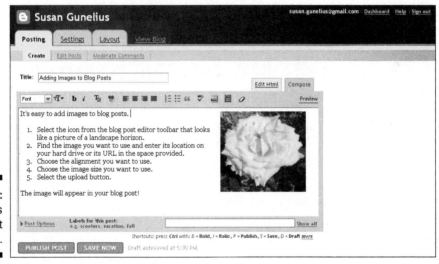

Figure 6-11: The Labels for This Post text box.

 TIP

If you have been writing your blog for an extended period, you should have a long list of labels that you have already used. Rather than continually retype the same labels, you can click the Show All link to the right of the Labels box within the blog post editor to display a list of all labels you have used on your blog. Then simply pick the existing labels you want to apply to the post you're writing.

3. **Click the Publish Post button when you're done writing your post.**

   Your blog post appears live on your blog with the labels you added to your post appearing at the bottom of the post, as shown in Figure 6-12.

Figure 6-12:
Labels
appear
beneath the
blog post.

Using the post date-and-time feature

Sometimes you want to write a blog post now but not publish it until a later date and time. For example, you might be going on vacation and want to pre-post blog entries to ensure that your readers see fresh content while you're away. Changing the date and time that your posts are published is simple in Blogger. Just follow these steps:

1. **In the blog post editor, click the Post Options link on the left side, above the Publish Post button.**

   This step opens a new section of the blog post editor, where you can modify the date and time settings for your blog post (refer to Figure 6-6).

2. **Under the Post Date and Time heading, enter the date and time that you want your blog post to be published, and then click the Publish Post button.**

   Your blog post goes live online at the date and time you specified.

The timestamp of each blog post appears at the bottom of each post. Details for configuring the format of your blog post timestamp are in Chapter 5.

Revisiting Old Posts

The longer you write your blog, the more posts you create. Over time, it can be hard to find old posts that you might want to update or link to from a new post. In fact, at times you might want to delete an old post entirely. Remember that it's your blog, and you can modify your posts as you see fit. However, make sure that the changes you make add value to your readers and don't confuse them.

Finding an archived post

To find old blog posts, simply click the Posts link from the Blogger dashboard to open a list of your blog posts, as shown in Figure 6-13.

Figure 6-13:
A list of your blog posts.

If you've been blogging for a while, this list can be *very* long. To make your search a bit quicker, you can change the number of posts displayed per page by selecting a different number from the Posts Per Page drop-down menu. Luckily, you have a few options to help you find specific posts from this list:

- ✔ Narrow your search by selecting a label from the Labels list on the left side of the Edit Posts page.

- ✔ Enter a search term in the Search text box to narrow your search to posts that include specific words.

- ✔ Click the Drafts, Scheduled, or Published links on the right end of the Your Posts line to narrow your search based on the status of your posts.

Editing a post

After you find the post you want to edit, simply click the Edit link next to the post title on the Edit Posts page, as shown in Figure 6-14, to open the blog post editor, where you can modify and republish that post.

Figure 6-14:
Just click
the Edit link
to revise an
old post.

Deleting a post

To delete a post from your blog, find the post on the Edit Posts page (refer to Figure 6-14). Click the Delete link to the right of that specific post. A new page opens, asking whether you're sure you want to delete the post. Click the Delete It button to delete the post (see Figure 6-15).

Figure 6-15:
Click the
Delete It
button to
remove a
post from
your blog
forever.

Deleted posts are immediately removed from your list of posts. After you click the Delete It button, that blog post is deleted permanently and cannot be retrieved.

Chapter 7

Enhancing Your Blog
with Templates

*O*ne of the easiest ways to personalize your blog is by selecting a unique template (also called a theme) that matches your blog topic, voice, and style. Your blog's template can either invite visitors to stay for a while or scare them away. Take some time up front to consider what you want the layout and design of your blog to say to your visitors. Then choose a template that clearly communicates that message.

This chapter helps you understand what templates are and how to modify your blog's template. It also teaches you where to find templates from Blogger and third parties as well as the pros and cons of paying for a fully customized template.

Reviewing Blogger Layouts

When Blogger was launched, users had to learn how to use hypertext markup language (HTML) or cascading style sheets (CSS) coding to be able to customize their blogs. Luckily, new blogs created by using Blogger these days are automatically set up so that you can use the Blogger Layout feature to quickly and easily manipulate the look and feel of your blog. By selecting the Layout tab on the Blogger dashboard, you can select the specific page elements you want to display on your blog, choose its fonts and colors, and pick your template. Blogger Layouts allows users to perform a variety of tasks without having any HTML or CSS knowledge.

The Page Elements feature, available on the Blogger Layouts tab, works by using a simple drag-and-drop system, which is discussed in greater detail in Chapter 8.

Choosing a Template

A *template* is the skeleton, or map, of a blog: It provides the basic look and feel of a blog through colors and fonts and the basic layout of each element. For example, the template you choose tells Blogger how many sidebars to display and where. It also tells Blogger the font size and type for your post titles. Without a template, Blogger wouldn't know where to display the parts of your blog. In other words, Blogger doesn't know what to do until you give it directions. The template provides those directions by dictating the behind-the-scenes coding that formats the look of your blog. Before you select a template, take some time to visit other blogs and find the layouts and themes that appeal to you. What works well and what doesn't? Determine which type of template will work best for your blog, including the layout and colors that you think will appeal to your visitors. Then find a theme that offers the characteristics you're looking for. You can read more later in this chapter about the types of Blogger templates that are available.

Templates versus headers

Before you select a template for your blog, you need to know the difference between a template and a header. A *header* is the part of your blog's template that appears at the top of your blog pages and typically includes your blog's title, subtitle or description, and graphic. Some headers also include quick links or ads, but the title, subtitle, and graphic are the three most common elements. Figure 7-1 shows a blog using a free template provided by Blogger. A personal image is used in the background of the header to give the blog more of a custom look and feel.

You can customize just about any blog template with a custom header in one of two ways:

- Simply upload a photo or an image to appear in the background.
- Change the font type and size of your blog's title, which is described in more detail later in this chapter.

Figure 7-1:
Using a
photo in
a blog's
header.

Personality

When you're looking for a template to use on your blog, you should choose one that complements your blog's content. In other words, visitors should quickly understand, based on your template, what to expect from your blog's content because your template should consistently communicate your blog's overall personality.

Think of it this way: If you write a blog about baby toys but your blog template has a black background and shows images of cigarettes and beer, your template isn't consistently communicating your blog's personality. Visitors will be confused and be likely to leave your blog quickly — never to return again. However, if your baby toys blog displays pastel colors in the background and shows images of baby bottles and rattles, your template consistently communicates your blog's personality, and visitors will understand what to expect from your blog. They will feel comfortable and be likely to stay for awhile and return later.

Color

The colors you select for your blog affect not just your blog's personality, as described in the preceding section, but also the readability of your blog. When you choose a template for your blog, make sure to take some time to consider the colors used in that template. The following blog elements should use appropriate coloring:

✔ **Background:** Make sure that the color isn't too bright and doesn't hurt visitors' eyes.

✔ **Fonts:** Don't make the color too pale or too bright, which can make the text difficult to read.

✔ **Topic:** Make sure the colors are appropriate for your blog's topic.

✔ **The Complete Picture:** Ensure that all of the colors used in the template complement each other and create an appealing and inviting look overall.

The colors you choose to use in your blog's template are up to you, but keep in mind that certain colors are easier to read and easier on the eyes than others. Also, the colors you choose can be limiting. For example, if you select a black background for your blog, your choices for text color will be quite limited. Although white and yellow are legible on a black background, dark reds, greens, blues, and purples are nearly impossible to read. Another important factor to consider when you select the colors for your blog template is how those colors will look on different computer monitors. Your blog might eventually generate traffic from people all over the world who view your blog from a wide variety of computer monitors. Those monitors can offer variations in resolution as well as in the way colors are displayed. The orange you select for your blog background, for example, might look beautiful to you but be too bright for many visitors.

The best rule to follow when selecting your blog template without the help of a professional Web designer is to keep it simple. Use a light-colored background with dark text (a white background with black text is easiest to read), and use just a few colors rather than a rainbow of colors that can become confusing and difficult to read.

Less is more when it comes to blog design.

Font

The key component to consider when you select the fonts to use in your blog's template is readability. Visitors are unlikely to return to your blog if the text is difficult to read simply because you chose a font that is overly stylized. Keep the following factors in mind when you select fonts for your blog:

✔ **Online readability:** Choose fonts that are easy to read online, such as Verdana or Georgia.

✔ **Availability:** Choose fonts that most people have loaded on their computers already. If you use an uncommon font, people who don't have that font loaded on their computers cannot view it. Instead, the font will automatically default to one that might be unappealing or ugly, such as Courier.

✔ **Number of fonts used:** Stick with two or three fonts. Mixing too many fonts can be confusing and make pages difficult to read.

✔ **Styling:** Save overly stylized fonts for your blog's header graphic and blog title.

Use font enhancements only to call attention to key points. Don't overuse bold, italics, or underlining, or else your blog posts will become cluttered with enhancements, which makes them difficult to read.

Columns and layout

Most blogs are set up using a 2- or 3-column layout. Blog posts appear in reverse chronological order in the widest column, and one or two smaller columns may appear on the left or right side of the blog post column or flanking both sides of the blog post column. Figures 7-2 and 7-3 show how 1- and 2-column blog layouts look, respectively.

Figure 7-2:
One-column
blog layout.

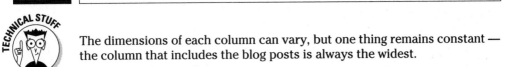

The dimensions of each column can vary, but one thing remains constant — the column that includes the blog posts is always the widest.

The columns to the left and right of the blog post column are *sidebars,* which are used to hold a variety of page elements, such as blogroll links, ads, archive links, profile information and links, and anything else you want to include. The blog post column provides the main content of your blog, and the sidebars lead visitors to all the other areas you want to share with them.

Figure 7-3:
Two-column
blog layout.

Sidebar capacity and placement

Bloggers have the option of placing just about anything they want in the side-bars of their blogs as long as whatever they publish doesn't violate the rules of Blogger and Google. For example, you might want to include a variety of ads on your blog, and the majority of those ads can appear in the sidebars of your blog. If that's the case, selecting a 3-column theme gives you two side-bars in which to place ads.

The placement of sidebars can also affect your blog. For example, a 3-column layout that places both sidebars together, to the right or left of your blog post column, gives you the option to place small button ads as well as larger banner ads that can span the width of both sidebars. After you determine the purpose of your sidebars, select the blog template layout that best helps you achieve those goals.

Future blogging goals

When you start your new blog using Blogger, take some time to establish your short- and long-term objectives for your blog. You can more easily create a plan and develop your blog accordingly now than try to make extreme changes later. Of course, one of the best parts about blogging is that you can grow and change your blog as necessary — although drastic changes might confuse your audience. Choose your blog layout and template with your pie-in-the-sky aspirations for it in mind. Think big, and then work patiently and consistently to meet those goals, knowing that you set up your blog to grow with you in the future.

Knowing Blogger and Google policies

Both Blogger and Google have their own sets of policies and terms of service that apply to you when you register to use Blogger. Terms of service documents are typically long and filled with legal jargon, but you should take the time to read them thoroughly because they contain a number of restrictions related to what you can and cannot publish or do on your blog.

Here are some links to the documents you should read before you start your Blogger blog:

✔ **Google Blogger Terms of Service:** `www.blogger.com/terms`

✔ **Google Blogger Content Policy:** `www.blogger.com/content`

✔ **Google Terms of Service:** `www.google.com/accounts/TOS`

✔ **Google Privacy Policy:** `www.google.com/privacypolicy.html`

Neither Google nor Blogger monitors the information published on users' blogs. If you find a blog that appears to violate the Google or Blogger terms of service or content policy, you can report it to Blogger through the link in the Terms of Service–Report Abuse section of the Blogger online Help system at `www.help.blogger.com`. Other people can report you, too, so make sure that you follow the rules.

Finding templates

A wide variety of free templates is available by using the Templates tab on your Blogger dashboard. You can use and manipulate each of those themes as described later in this chapter. You also can find Web sites that offer unique templates that are compatible with Blogger, as described later in this chapter.

Considering Types of Templates

You can choose from four types of templates to customize your Blogger blog:

1. **Templates from Blogger:** Blogger offers a number of free prebuilt templates that you can access directly from your Blogger dashboard.

2. **Free templates from third parties:** If you want a theme that's unique to your own blog or different from most of the other blog templates you see in the blogosphere, you might want to download a free Blogger template from a third-party Web site.

3. **Premium templates from third parties:** Many Web designers create premium Blogger templates that you can use for a fee. Premium templates are typically sold a certain number of times then retired.

4. **Custom templates from third parties:** You can hire a Web designer to create a complete custom theme that is designed to meet your specifications and can be used only on your blog.

The choice is yours, and this chapter shows you what you need to know to make your decision.

The type of template you select depends on these two factors:

✔ Whether you want a unique look on your blog

✔ Whether you want to spend money on your theme

The weight you give to these two factors will help you decide which type of template you want to use for your blog.

Templates from Blogger

Blogger users can choose from a variety of themes provided by using the Blogger dashboard. Follow these steps to open the Templates page.

1. **Sign in to your Blogger account.**

   This step opens your Blogger dashboard.

2. **From the Blogger dashboard, click the Layout link for your blog.**

   This step opens the Layout configuration page for your blog.

3. **Select the Pick New Template tab from the navigation bar.**

   The Select a New Template for Your Blog page opens, as shown in Figure 7-4.

If you need a refresher on signing in to your Blogger account, opening the Blogger dashboard, or finding the Layout section, you can find detailed steps and information in Chapter 5.

As you scroll through the various themes available from Blogger, notice that each one includes a Preview Template link beneath the template choice box. This link makes it easy to see, without having to save your changes first, what your blog will look like if you select a template. To use the Preview Template feature, follow these steps:

1. **Click the radio button next to the name of the template you want to view.**

2. **Click the Preview Template link beneath the template box.**

   This step opens a new window that displays your existing blog, formatted with the new template, as shown in Figure 7-5.

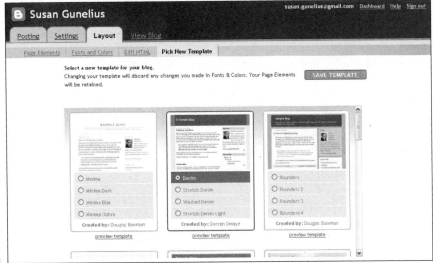

Figure 7-4:
Selecting
a new
template.

Figure 7-5:
Previewing
a template.

3. **Click the Close button in the upper corner of the preview window to close it.**

   This step returns the Select a New Template for Your Blog page to the screen.

4. **Click the Save Template button to save your blog with the new template you chose.**

   You can then click the View Blog link to see your changes live on your blog.

Take your time previewing all the different template options that are available from Blogger, to find the one that works best for your blog. Your changes are not final until you click the Save Template button.

If you made changes to the colors and fonts used in your blog from the Fonts and Colors tab within the Layout configuration settings of the Blogger dashboard, those changes are lost when you choose and save a new template.

Many of the templates available from Blogger are offered in more than one version. For example, the template provided by Jason Sutter (refer to Figure 7-5) is available in two distinctly different versions. Although many of the variations on a single template simply alter the colors that are used, the templates designed by Jason Sutter vary by color, font, and other elements. Compare Figures 7-6 and 7-7 to see the differences between Jason Sutter's template — the Herbert and Jellyfish versions. The Herbert template uses title case (initial caps as in the title of a book) for the headings in the header and sidebar as well as a colored bar in the header and a small font in the blog posts. The Jellyfish template uses lowercase for the headings in the header and sidebar and a large font in the blog posts.

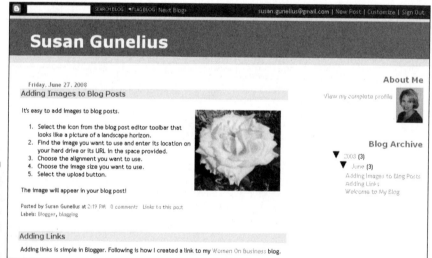

Figure 7-6: Jason Sutter's Herbert template.

Every theme can be modified with HTML or CSS language, but even if you don't know how to use HTML and CSS, you can still make minor changes to your Blogger theme by using the Layouts function in Blogger.

Figure 7-7:
Jason
Sutter's
Jellyfish
template.

The templates available from Blogger are provided by various designers for you to use freely. That's a useful benefit, but because these templates are available for free to every Blogger user, the downside to choosing one is that it doesn't make your blog unique. In other words, your blog might not stand out in the crowded blogosphere. It might not be memorable or distinct from other blogs. Depending on your overall growth goals for your blog, you might want to find a template from another source outside of Blogger.

Free templates from third parties

Many Web designers create Blogger templates and offer them for free downloading from their own blogs or Web sites. Using a free theme from a third party certainly makes your blog a bit different than it would be if you used a free theme provided by Blogger, but because free third-party themes are readily available to anyone who searches for them, the strong possibility exists that many bloggers will use them. In short, a free third-party theme offers two primary benefits:

✔ **Cost:** They cost nothing out of your pocket to use.

✔ **Uniqueness:** They make your blog look different than it is if you use a free theme provided by Blogger.

On the other hand, your blog experiences two key negatives by using a free theme provided by a third party:

- ✔ **Sameness:** Many other blogs will probably use the same free third-party theme that you choose.

- ✔ **Lack of support:** You may not be able to find support or assistance from the template designer if you later have a problem with the free third-party theme you choose.

Chapter 19 provides a number of online resources where you can find free Blogger templates provided by third parties. For example, Figure 7-8 shows a free Blogger template that's available from Eblog Templates (www. eblogtemplates.com). The template is perfect for a family blog, a travel blog, or an environmentally focused blog.

Figure 7-8: The Green Love template suits a variety of purposes.

Make sure that any Blogger templates you download to your computer from a third-party Web site come from a safe source. Avoid downloading viruses or other security breaches by downloading only from trusted sites and by making sure your antivirus software is up-to-date before you download anything. If you do download an infected template, run a virus scan and disinfect your computer immediately.

Premium templates from third parties

Here's another option that's available to you if you're looking for a blog theme that stands out more than the free templates provided by Blogger: Find a premium Blogger template from a third party. Web designers often create premium themes that they offer for a flat fee. The fee is typically much less than you would pay for a completely customized theme, because the template is sold "as is" with no additional customization from the original design. More often than not, designers sell a premium template to only a certain number of users, and then they retire that template. An example of a Web site that offers premium Blogger template designs is Designed by Lara (www.designedbylara.com), which offers a variety of 2-, 3-, and 4-column premade Blogger templates, one of which is shown in Figure 7-9.

Figure 7-9:
The Designed by Lara 2-column Spring Gardening theme.

Before you pay for a premium Blogger template, check to see whether the template will be retired after a specific number of people buy it to ensure you're not paying for a template that thousands of other people can use, too. Also, determine whether the designer offers any kind of support if you have problems using the template.

Custom templates from third parties

If you want your blog to have a one-of-a-kind design that offers a specific layout, consider hiring a designer to create a custom design that you hold the copyright to when it's completed. Of course, a custom design has a steeper price tag on it than a premium Blogger template provided by a third party, because it's created to meet your specifications. Many designers create custom Blogger templates with prices for services ranging from less than $100 to $1,000 or more.

Remember that just because a designer charges a high price tag for her work, it doesn't mean that the designer is the best or offers the most complete service. Before you dive into a contract with a designer to start working on the custom template for your Blogger blog, do some research. Ask other bloggers for recommendations for designers, and be certain to ask for references from the designers you consider working with. Also, take some time to look through other blog templates that designer has created by reviewing his online portfolio or asking for links to his work. Finally, obtain quotes from several designers before you make your selection. Tell each designer to provide an itemized quotation that specifies exactly what she will provide to you, a timeframe for completion, and a description of ongoing support services. You can use the result to compare apples to apples and to determine which quotation is comprehensive and fair and best meets your needs.

Don't accept a bundled price from a designer. Ask each one to provide a detailed breakdown of exactly what services are included in the fee he plans to charge you.

Changing a Template

After you select your template, it's easy to start using it. Blogger offers an easy process to switch between Blogger-provided themes or to upload templates from third parties to use on your blog. You can also easily revert to your old theme, if you need to. You work through the entire process of changing your template by using the Layout link on your Blogger dashboard.

Choosing a different Blogger template

If you select a free template provided by Blogger, simply follow the instructions outlined earlier in this chapter, in the "Templates from Blogger" section, to configure your blog settings properly. You can quite easily experiment with various themes provided by Blogger: Simply click the radio buttons next to each option on the Select a New Template for Your Blog page within your Blogger account, and then click the Preview Template link, as described earlier in this chapter.

You must click the Save Template button in order for your Blogger template choice to take effect and appear live on your blog. After you save your template, a message appears, saying that your changes have been saved. You can click the View Blog link to see your new template live on your blog (see Figure 7-10).

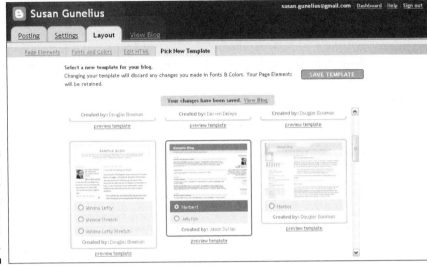

Figure 7-10:
The Your
Changes
Have Been
Saved
message.

Modifying the fonts and colors in your template

No matter which template you choose to use, you can modify the fonts and colors from the Fonts and Colors tab within the Layouts section of your Blogger dashboard, as shown in Figure 7-11.

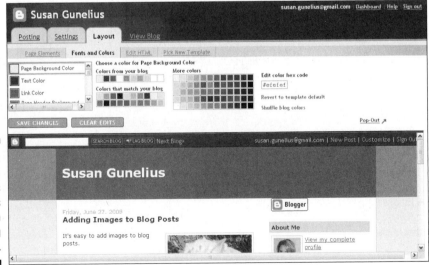

Figure 7-11:
Changing
the colors
and fonts
used in
your blog
template.

Notice the list on the far left side of your screen, as shown in Figure 7-11. Here you can scroll through a list of elements for color and font modifications such as the page background color, link color, header font, and so on. A default list of color or font choices is displayed to the right, depending on the element you select from the list on the left. Any changes made here are made globally meaning an element that you modify here will be changed anywhere it appears on your blog. For example, if you change your link color from blue to orange, all of the links throughout your blog will now appear in orange. Don't be afraid to test different colors and fonts to find which ones you like the most. If you make a change you don't like, simply click the Clear Edits button to erase your changes. Your changes are not final until you click the Save Changes button.

You can also make changes on individual posts through the post editor as described in Chapter 6.

Switching to a custom template

If you decide to use a free template, premium template, or custom template provided by a third party, upload the necessary files to your Blogger account to make the new theme work on your blog. Luckily, most third-party templates are available for downloading. For example, Figure 7-12 shows a post on Blogger Buster (www.bloggerbuster.com), where you can download Amanda Fazani's free Blogger template, BT Dark Green.

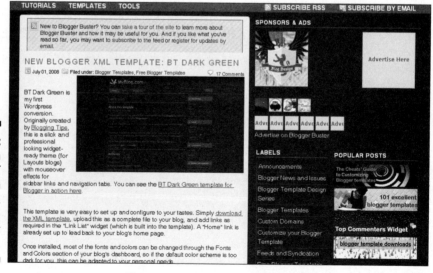

Figure 7-12: Amanda Fazani's BT Dark Green template, available at Blogger Buster.

To download a third-party template for use on your Blogger blog, simply click the download link or button on the third-party Web site. Luckily, designers usually set up the download feature to be easy to use with a zipped folder. After files are saved in a zipped folder on your computer hard drive, just extract the files to your computer's hard drive by using your preferred extraction software, such as Winzip or Stuffit. You need to locate the unzipped file that has the .xml extension in order to upload it to your Blogger account so that the custom template can be applied to your blog. Of course, some free templates might have variations on these steps, so be certain to read the installation instructions for the template you choose.

To save the third-party template to your computer, follow these steps:

1. **Select the Layout tab from the Blogger dashboard.**

   This step opens the Page Elements page within the Layout Configurations section of your Blogger account.

2. **Select the Edit HTML tab from the navigation bar.**

   The Backup/Restore Template and Edit Template page opens (see Figure 7-13).

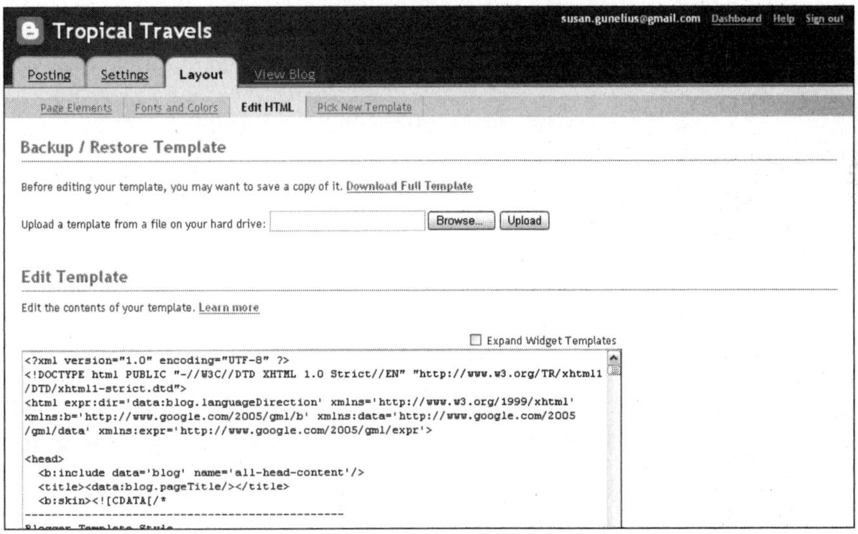

Figure 7-13: Backing up an existing template.

3. **Click the Download Full Template link under the Backup/Restore Template heading.**

   The File Download dialog box appears (see Figure 7-14).

Backing up your template is an essential step if you think that you might want to revert later to the exact template you were using previously .

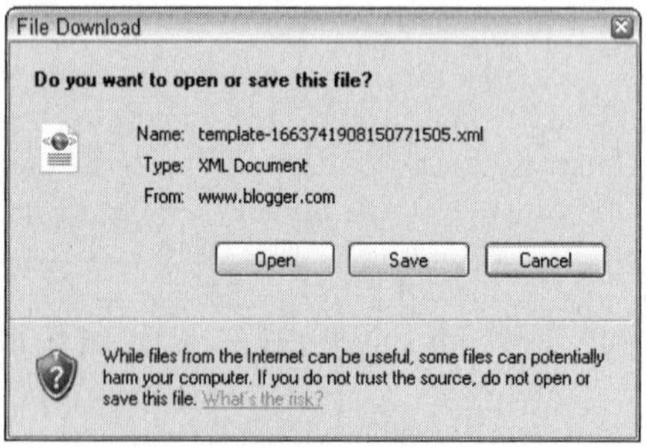

Figure 7-14:
The File
Download
dialog box.

4. Click the Save button.

The Save As dialog box appears.

5. Locate the folder on your hard drive where you want to save a copy of your existing blog template.

Choose a location where you can find the template file if you want to use it again later or create a new folder called My Blog Back-ups. The template backup file is saved in XML format in the folder you choose. It's a good idea to rename the file so you remember what it is if you need it later (for example, TemplateBackup-Jan01-2009.xml).

To upload the third-party template to your Blogger account, open the Backup/Restore Template and Edit Template page, and then follow these steps:

1. Click the Browse button, which appears next to the Upload a Template from a File on Your Hard Drive text box.

The Choose File dialog box appears.

2. Locate the XML file for the new template you just downloaded to your hard drive. Select the file and then click the Open button.

The XML file for your new third-party template is located where you saved it in Step 5 of the preceding step list.

The file path for the XML file you just selected appears in the Upload a Template from a File on Your Hard Drive box (see Figure 7-15).

3. Double-check to ensure that you selected the correct file.

4. Click the Upload button.

Your new template is uploaded to your Blogger account.

Whenever you upload a third-party template to your Blogger account, you're likely to see a warning message: "Widgets are about to be deleted." Be aware that with a new template, you may have to reconfigure some of the page elements and gadgets used on your blog.

5. Click the Confirm & Save button.

The new HTML code for your third-party template now automatically appears in the big box in the Edit Template section of the page, as shown in Figure 7-16.

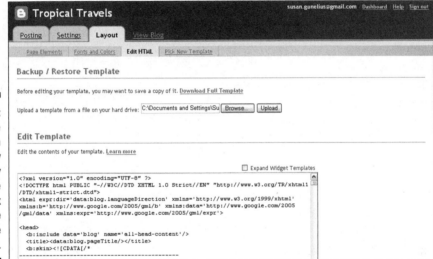

Figure 7-15:
You can see the file path for your new third-party template in the box next to the Browse button.

Figure 7-16:
The HTML for your new third-party template automatically appears in the Edit Template section.

6. **After your new third-party template is uploaded, click the View Blog link to review the look of your blog. Figure 7-17 shows how the new Tropical Travels blog looks using the free BT Dark Green template.**

   You might want to modify your blog's page elements, as described in detail in Chapter 8, after your third-party template is uploaded. For example, you might need to clean up your blog by changing the order of your profile, updating the archives in your sidebar, or adding a graphical image to your header.

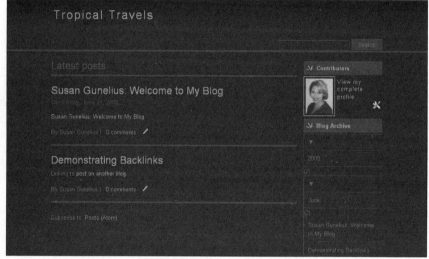

Figure 7-17:
Always review how your blog looks online after you apply a new third-party template.

Knowing what to do after you apply a third-party template

What happens after you select a third-party template, upload it, use it for a while, and then experience a problem with it? That question is important to ask template designers before you purchase design services from them. Changing to a new theme is fairly easy. The more customized your blog is, however (and the longer you blog, the more likely you are to customize its elements), the more difficult it is to switch to a new theme without creating a lot of work for yourself to get things to look and perform the way you want them to.

Changing your blog template can also affect your visitors' expectations for your blog. Take time to warn visitors (particularly loyal readers!) that a template change is coming, so they're not surprised and confused by a sudden design alteration.

Evaluate your goals for your blog before you select a third-party template. Depending on your long-term objectives, it might be in your best interest to select a template from a reliable source that you know will be around for a while. You might want to contact the designer before you make your final decision on a freely available template to ask her whether help is available if you have problems. Don't be afraid to reach out to template designers. Most templates have the designer's name and contact information attached (usually an e-mail address) . If a designer doesn't respond to you, you might not want to use that template. The decisions you make about your template are important. Don't just jump into picking a theme because you like how it looks. Make sure that it offers everything you need to make your blogging experience successful and enjoyable.

Chapter 8

Adding Features and Functionality with Elements and Gadgets

*T*he Blogger platform utilizes a Layout feature that makes changing the look and feel of your blog very easy with a simple drag-and-drop template editor that requires no HTML or CSS knowledge. Using the Layout features, you can change your blog's template (see Chapter 7) in just a few simple steps. You can also modify the colors and fonts used in your blog and customize your blog's header, footer, and sidebar with a variety of pre-defined and easy to use gadgets.

This chapter shows you how to use the Blogger Layout feature, so you can customize your blog to look and perform just how you want it to. I cover what page elements and specialized gadgets are available to you in Blogger so that you can decide which ones you want to include on your blog. You find out how to customize each of your blog's page elements and gadgets and, finally, how to add gadgets created by third parties to your blog.

Throughout this chapter, I reference adding gadgets to your sidebar for consistency but keep in mind it's your blog. You can add gadgets in your sidebar, footer, or wherever else you want (within the parameters of the Blogger platform) to customize your blog exactly how you want.

Editing Basic Page Elements

Every blog has several basic page elements in common. Although these elements might be customized to look differently or appear in different locations, the basic functionality and set up is the same for every blog. These elements include the blog header, posts, archive links, and profile. Of course, including some of these elements (such as archive links and your profile) isn't mandatory, but they help visitors find your published content and learn more about you. That said, including both archive links and a profile is important if you want to grow your blog.

To modify your blog's page elements, select the Layout link from your Blogger dashboard. The Page Elements window opens, as shown in Figure 8-1.

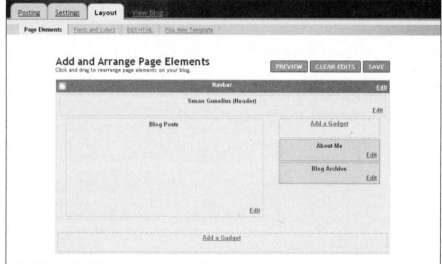

Figure 8-1:
The Page
Elements
window.

Including a header

Your blog's header is one of the most important parts of your blog. At the very least, a header should include your blog's title, but more often than not, blog headers include a graphic and subtitle or description of the blog. Each of these parts of a header helps to tell visitors what your blog is about within seconds. They also help communicate your blog's personality to visitors, which I describe in Chapter 7.

To edit your blog's header, follow these steps:

1. **In the Header box of the Page Elements Window (refer to Figure 8-1), click the Edit link.**

   The Configure Header window opens (see Figure 8-2).

Figure 8-2:
The
Configure
Header
window.

2. **In the Blog Title box, enter the title you want to appear in your blog's header.**

   The title you enter in your blog's header does not need to match the title in your blog's domain name.

3. **In the Blog Description box, enter the text you want to appear with your blog title in your blog's header.**

   The space available in your header isn't very big. Don't clutter it with a long description. Instead, use a subtitle or tagline in the Blog Description box to communicate further what your blog is about to visitors in just a few words.

4. **If you wish to include a graphic in your blog's header, select the radio button next to From Your Computer or next to From the Web depending on where the image you want is saved.**

   Get complete instructions for adding an image to your blog's header in Chapter 7.

5. **Click the Save button when you're done making your edits.**

   You return to the Page Elements window where you can click the View Blog link to see your changes online or continue editing your blog.

Modifying blog posts

You can edit the format and appearance of your blog posts in the Page Elements window. Although you have the option to configure many of these settings when you set up your blog and via the Settings link on the Blogger dashboard, you can also make modifications quickly and easily to your blog post presentation as follows:

1. **In the Page Elements window of your Blogger account, click the Edit link in the Blog Posts box. (Refer to Figure 8-1.)**

   The Configure Blog Posts window opens, as shown in Figure 8-3.

2. **In the Number of Posts on Main Page drop-down menu, choose Posts if you want to display a specific number of posts on your blog's main page at all times or choose Days with Posts to display a specific number of days' worth of posts on your blog's main page.**

   Consider your audience and how often you update your blog with new posts. For example, if you update your blog several times per day, then including a certain number of days' worth of posts might make your main page very long and require users to scroll a lot. Most Web users don't like to scroll excessively, so you might consider including 10 or fewer posts on your blog's main page.

Number of posts on main page: 7   Posts

Select Items

- ☑ Saturday, November 8, 2008
- ☑ Posted by   Susan Gunelius
- ☑ at   11:05 AM
- ☑ 5 comments
- ☑ Links to this post
- ☑ Labels: photos, vacation
- ☑ Show Quick Editing ✎
- ☐ Reactions: funny   interesting   cool   Edit
- ☑ Show Email Post Links ✉
- ☐ Show Ads Between Posts Learn more

Arrange Items

Saturday, November 8, 2008

Post Title

Post Body
Lorem ipsum vim ut utroque mandamus intellegebat, ut eam omittam ancillae sadipscing, per et eius soluta veritus.

Posted by Susan G... | at 11:05 AM | 5 comments | ✎ ✉

Links to this post

Labels: photos, v...

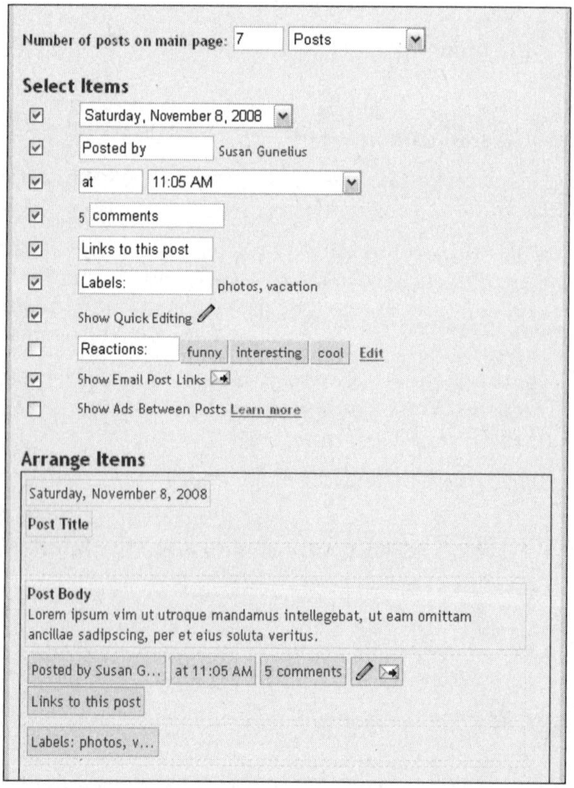

Figure 8-3:
Customizing your blog post settings.

3. **Under the Select Items heading, make sure only the items you want to appear on your blog posts have check marks next to them. Check or uncheck boxes as necessary.**

- The first item is the date when the post is published. If you want the date to appear with your blog posts, check the box and use the drop-down menu to choose the format you want the date to appear in.

- The byline is the second item. If you want a byline, which displays text followed by the blog author's name, on your blog posts, ensure the box is selected. The text that precedes the author's name is your choice; type it in the box provided.

- The third item is the time the post is published. If you want the date to appear with your blog posts, check the box and use the drop-down menu to choose the format the time appears in. The text that precedes the time is your choice; type it in the box provided.

- The fourth item allows you to select whether you want to display comments with your blog posts. If you want to show comments with your blog posts, check the box and modify the text in the box provided. The number that precedes the box is automated and reflects the number of comments left on a post at any given point in time.

- The fifth item allows you to select whether you want to display the links to a blog post. If so, select the check box and modify the text in the box provided.

- The sixth item allows you to select whether you want to display labels with your blog posts. If so, check the box and modify the text if you don't want to use the "Labels" default

- Show Quick Editing is a handy item that allows you to edit a blog post with a simple click of the mouse. If you want to include the Quick Edit icon with your blog posts, ensure the box is selected.

- The Reactions item allows you to add three link buttons beneath each of your blog posts giving readers the ability to provide feedback on your posts. The default settings provide Funny, Interesting and Cool buttons, but you can modify both the title of the feature and the titles of the buttons by typing directly into the text box or selecting the Edit link. When visitors click a reaction button, their feedback is added to a star rating system that appears beneath your blog post.

- Show Email Post Links is a tool that allows visitors to your blog to e-mail a link to one of your posts with a click of the mouse. If you want to include the Email Post Links icon with your blog posts, ensure the box is selected.

- Show Ads Between Posts is a simple way to include Google AdSense ads between your blog posts. If you want to include Google AdSense ads between your blog posts, ensure the box is selected. You need to sign up for a Google AdSense account before ads can appear on your blog. You can find out more about Google AdSense in Chapter 11.

4. **In the Arrange Items section, you can click and drag the various elements you selected to include with your blog posts into the layout you prefer.**

Most bloggers use the same basic layout for the elements of their blog posts, similar to the default layout Blogger puts together when you choose the elements you want to display with your post. It's a good idea not to change the layout of your blog post elements so drastically that it could confuse visitors.

5. **Click the Save button when you finish making changes.**

You return to the Page Elements window where you can click the View Blog link to see your changes online or continue working on your blog.

Editing the About Me box

The About Me box (also called the *profile*) is where you can make quick edits to your blog profile and determine which elements you want to appear on the main page of your blog. Chapter 5 includes detailed information and instructions on creating a compelling profile. To modify the display settings for your profile, follow these steps:

1. **In the Page Elements window of your Blogger account, click the Edit link in the About Me box. (Refer to Figure 8-1.)**

The Edit Profile window opens, as shown in Figure 8-4.

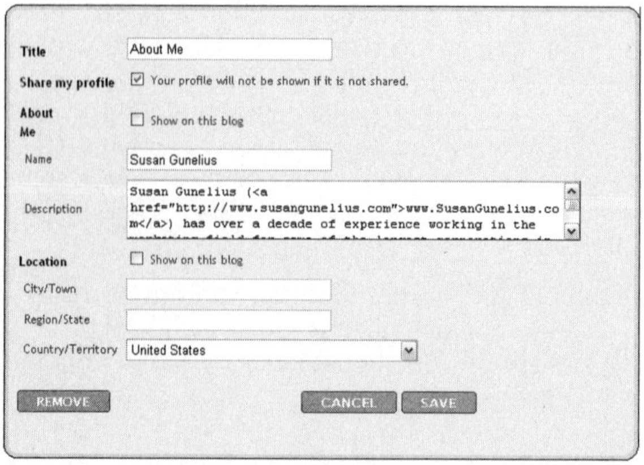

Title	About Me
Share my profile	☑ Your profile will not be shown if it is not shared.
About Me	☐ Show on this blog
Name	Susan Gunelius
Description	Susan Gunelius (<a href="http://www.susangunelius.com">www.SusanGunelius.com</a>) has over a decade of experience working in the
Location	☐ Show on this blog
City/Town	
Region/State	
Country/Territory	United States

REMOVE   CANCEL   SAVE

Figure 8-4:
The Edit Profile window.

2. **In the Title box, enter the heading you want to appear above your profile on your blog.**

   Most bloggers use "About Me," "About," or "About This Blog." The choice is yours!

3. **If you want your profile to be public and appear on your blog in its entirety, select the Share My Profile check box.**

   It's a good idea to share your profile so visitors understand who you are and why you're writing your blog, but be careful what information you publish publicly. There might be some information that you don't want the world to see.

4. **If you want your entire profile to appear on the main page of your blog, select the Show on This Blog check box in the About Me section.**

   If you select this check box, your entire profile appears in the sidebar (or wherever you position the About Me page element) of your blog. If your profile is long, it could take up a lot of space in your sidebar. If that's the case, you might want to deselect this box so your visitors have to follow a View My Complete Profile link to see your profile on a separate page.

5. **In the Name box, enter the name you want to appear in the About Me section of your blog's main page.**

   The name entered here does not need to match your login name or the name you used to open your account.

6. **In the Description box, enter information about you and your blog.**

   Your description should help visitors understand who you are and why your blog is *the* place online to get information about your blog topic.

7. **If you want to show your City/Town, Region/State, or Country/ Territory on your blog, select the Show on This Blog check box in the Location section.**

   As in Step 4 above, showing all of your location information on your blog's main page can make your profile very long. If that's the case, you might want to deselect this box so your visitors have to follow a View My Complete Profile link to see your location information on a separate profile page.

8. **Enter your city or town in the City/Town box.**

   Consider privacy issues as discussed in Chapter 5 before you make the decision to share this information on the main page of your blog.

9. **Enter your region or state in the Region/State box.**

   If you want to share the state that you live in or your region of the country or the world, enter it here.

10. **In the Country/Territory drop-down list, choose the country or territory where you reside.**

   If you don't want to share your country or territory, choose Not Specified from the drop-down list.

11. **Click the Save button when you finish making changes.**

   You return to the Page Elements window where you can click the View Blog link to see your changes online or continue working on your blog.

Adding archives

Archives are an integral part of your blog that offer a place for visitors to find your old blog posts easily. You can configure how your archives are displayed in the Page Elements window of your Blogger account. Chapter 5 describes how to initially set up your Archives when you create your blog. Following are the steps you can take to configure the display settings of your Archives on your main blog page:

1. **In the Page Elements window of your Blogger account, click the Edit link in the Archives box. (Refer to Figure 8-1.)**

   The Configure Blog Archive window opens, as shown in Figure 8-5.

2. **In the Title box, enter the heading you want to appear above your archive links.**

   Most bloggers use a generic title, such as "Archives" here.

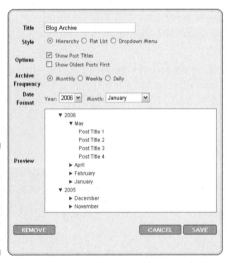

Figure 8-5:
The Configure Blog Archive window.

3. In the Style section, click the Hierarchy, Flat List, or Dropdown Menu radio button to set the appearance of your archive's links.

- The Hierarchy format, shown in the Preview section in Figure 8-5, displays each blog post as a link categorized by year and month of publication.

- The Flat List format, shown in the Preview section in Figure 8-6, displays only months.

- The Dropdown Menu format is the most concise style and displays months by using a traditional drop-down menu, as shown in Figure 8-7.

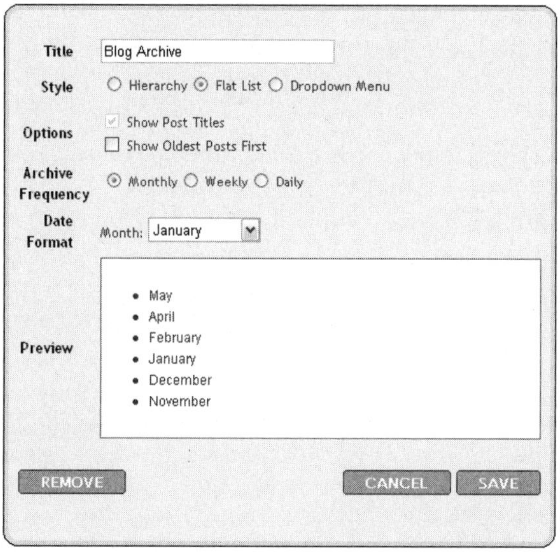

Figure 8-6:
The Flat List format for archives.

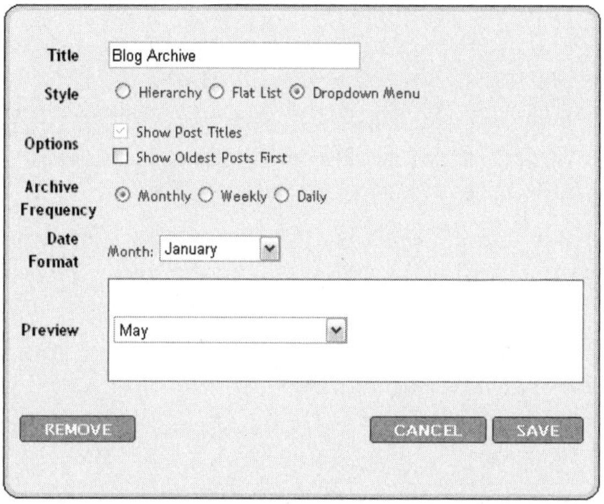

Figure 8-7:
The Dropdown Menu format for archives.

4. **In the Options section, select the Show Post Titles check box to include post titles (refer to Figure 8-5).**

   If you want to consolidate your archives but still use the Hierarchy style, as shown in the Preview section in Figure 8-8, deselect Show Post Titles.

   If you select the Flat List or Dropdown Menu radio button in the Style section of the Configure Blog Archive window, the Show Post Titles check box displays in a gray font and is inactive. In short, the setting doesn't apply to the Flat List or Dropdown Menu styles because neither displays post titles.

5. **In the Options section, select the Show Oldest Posts First check box if you want to display your posts in chronological order.**

   It's uncommon to display archives in chronological order. Blog posts are typically published in reverse chronological order, so most bloggers also display their archives in reverse chronological order. If you wish to do the same, leave the Show Oldest Posts First box unselected.

6. **In the Archive Frequency section, click the Monthly, Weekly, or Daily radio button depending on how you want your old blog posts to display in your archives.**

   • The Monthly Archive Frequency setting shown in the Preview section in Figure 8-5 is the Hierarchy style, Figure 8-6 shows the Flat List style, and Figure 8-7 shows the Dropdown Menu style.

   • The Weekly Archive Frequency setting is shown in the Preview section in Figure 8-9. Rather than group old posts by month, this frequency setting groups old posts by week. The Flat List style and Dropdown Menu style work the same way — instead of months displaying, weeks display. Note the Show End Date check box. Deselecting this check box removes the date after the hyphen for each week displayed so just the first date of each timeframe is shown.

   • The Daily Archive Frequency setting is shown in the Preview section in Figure 8-10. Rather than group old posts by month or week, old posts are shown by day. This setting works the same way in the Flat List style and the Dropdown Menu style.

7. **In the Date Format section, use the drop-down menus to select the date format you want to display for your archives.**

   Depending on the style you choose to display your Archives, the Date Format drop-down menu titles will change to include one or more of the following: Year, Month, and Day.

   You can view all your edits in the Preview section to ensure your archives are configured just how you want.

8. **Click the Save button when you finish making changes.**

You return to the Page Elements window where you can select the View Blog link to see your changes online or continue editing your blog.

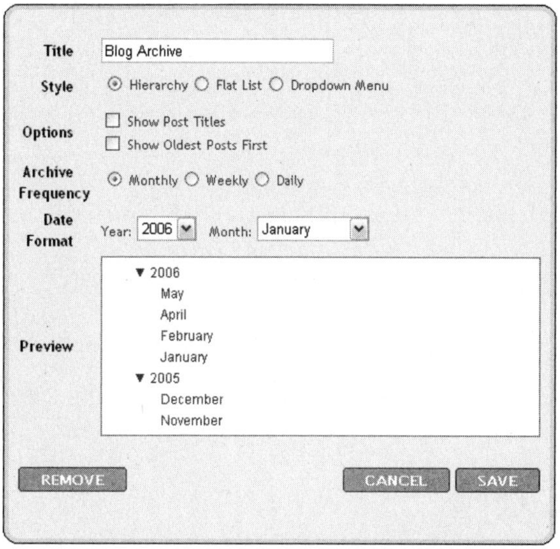

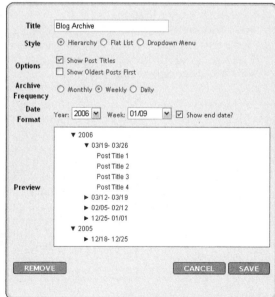

Figure 8-8: Deselect the Show Post Titles check box to consolidate your archive links.

Figure 8-9: Finding old posts.

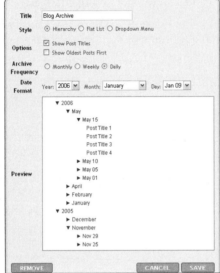

Figure 8-10:
The Daily
Archive
Frequency
used
with the
Hierarchy
style.

Choosing Gadgets

The Blogger platform offers a variety of gadgets that you can add to your blog layout to create the best user experience for your audience. Whether you want to add a blogroll to your sidebar or a list of the labels to categorize your blog posts (or both), you can choose the gadgets that work best for you. Take some time to experiment with the various Blogger gadgets described here. Most importantly, don't be afraid to test the waters with any gadget. Remember, you can always remove a gadget at anytime.

To add a gadget to your blog, simply select the Add a Gadget link on the Page Elements page of your Blogger dashboard (refer to Figure 8-1). The Add a Gadget window opens (see Figure 8-11), where you can scroll through the various gadgets available to add to your blog. Note that on the left side of the window are a variety of links that categorize the gadgets available to choose from directly through this feature window, such as Basic, Featured, News, and so on. The first link is Basic. This is the information that appears when you first open the Add a Gadget window and provides a list of gadgets offered by Blogger to enhance your blog. The other links in the list can include a variety of gadgets created by third parties (described later in this chapter). For now, focus on adding the Basic Blogger gadgets to your blog.

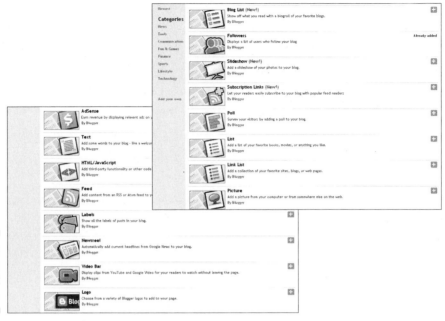

Providing a blog list

The Blog List gadget allows you to add a traditional blogroll to your blog's sidebar. Blogrolls are a great way to network with other bloggers and grow your blog. In simplest terms, when you include links to other blogs you like and you want to share with your audience, each link you add has the potential to drive traffic to that other blog. If the other blogger is interested in growing her blog, it's likely that she monitors where incoming links that are driving traffic come from. She'll see your blog is driving traffic and is likely to add a reciprocal link to your blog on her blogroll. Each additional incoming link to your blog can help in your search engine optimization efforts as well, which I describe in detail in Chapter 13.

With that in mind, monitor where incoming links to your blog generate from. If a link is contained within a post, be certain to acknowledge the blog by leaving a comment or by adding that blog to your blogroll. Furthermore, when you add a blog you like to your blogroll, be sure to send an e-mail to the blogger or leave a comment on one of his blog posts telling him why you like the blog and that you added it to your blogroll.

Adding a blogroll to your blog's sidebar with the Blog List page element is done as follows:

1. **In the Add a Gadget window of your Blogger account, click the + sign to the right of Blog List. (Refer to Figure 8-11).**

   The Configure Blog List window opens, as shown in Figure 8-12.

2. **In the Title box, type the title you want for your blogroll.**

   The Title box populates with "My Blog List" by default. Other options for a title include, "Blogroll," "Blogs I Read," "Recommended Blogs," and so on. The title for your blogroll is entirely up to you, but keep in mind "Blogroll" is the most common.

3. **From the Sort drop-down menu, choose the sort method you want to use to display the links in your blogroll.**

   You can choose to display links in your blogroll in alphabetical order by title or by listing the most recently updated blogs in descending order.

4. **In the Show section, you can configure the settings for how each link within your blogroll will appear in your sidebar.**

   • Select the Icon check box if you want to include an icon next to each link.

   • Select the Title of Most Recent Item check box if you want to include the title of the most recent blog post published for each link in your blogroll.

   • Select the Snippet from Most Recent Item check box if you want to include a short snippet of text from the beginning of the most recent blog post published for each link in your blogroll.

   • Select the Date of Last Update check box if you want to display the date the most recent post was published for each link in your blogroll.

 Your blogroll can clutter quickly if you include too many elements, such as post titles, snippets, and icons. Test each element to ensure your blogroll is readable and useful to your visitors.

5. **Click the Add a Blog to Your List link to add a blog to your blogroll.**

   The Add to Your Blog List window opens, as shown in Figure 8-13. You can select the Add radio button and enter the URL for the blog you want to add, or you can click the Import Subscriptions from Google Reader radio button to add all the blogs you subscribe to through Google Reader to your blogroll. Find out more about Google Reader and blog subscriptions in Chapter 9.

6. **When you finish adding links to your blogroll, click the Save button.**

   You return to the Page Elements window where you can view your changes on your blog, as shown in Figure 8-14, or continue editing your blog.

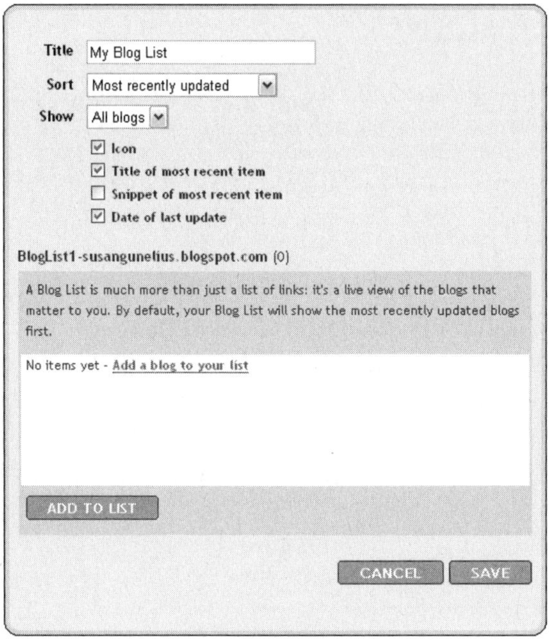

Title   My Blog List

Sort   Most recently updated

Show   All blogs

☑ Icon
☑ Title of most recent item
☐ Snippet of most recent item
☑ Date of last update

BlogList1-susangunelius.blogspot.com (0)

A Blog List is much more than just a list of links: it's a live view of the blogs that matter to you. By default, your Blog List will show the most recently updated blogs first.

No items yet - Add a blog to your list

ADD TO LIST

CANCEL   SAVE

Figure 8-12:
Editing the settings for your blogroll.

Add to your blog list

◉ Add by URL

◯ Import subscriptions from Google Reader

ADD   CANCEL

Figure 8-13:
The Add to Your Blog List window.

Figure 8-14:
A simple blogroll con-figuration.

Inviting followers

Blogger gives you the option to add a link on your blog inviting people to follow your blog. If the Followers gadget is available on your blog, other Blogger users can select a Follow This Blog link on your blog to add it to a list in their Blogger dashboards. Followers see your blog updates directly on their Blogger dashboards when they log into their accounts. Adding a followers link to your blog requires just two steps:

1. **In the Add a Gadget window of your Blogger account, click the + sign to the right of Followers (Refer to Figure 8-11).**

   The Configure Followers window opens as shown in Figure 8-15.

2. **Enter a title for your Followers gadget and select the Save button.**

   You return to the Page Elements window where you can view your changes on your blog, as shown in Figure 8-16, or continue editing your blog.

Figure 8-15:
The
Configure
Followers
window.

Presenting a slideshow

A great way to add a personal touch to your blog is to add a slideshow of photos or images. With Blogger, it's easy to add an automated slideshow using the Slideshow gadget. Here's how:

1. **In the Add a Gadget window of your Blogger account, click the + sign to the right of Slideshow. (Refer to Figure 8-11).**

   The Configure Slideshow window opens, shown in Figure 8-17.

Figure 8-16:
The
Followers
gadget.

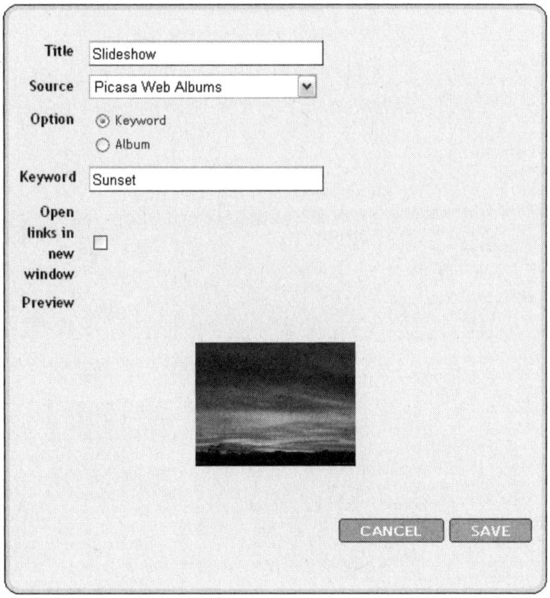

Figure 8-17:
The
Configure
Slideshow
window.

2. **In the Title box, enter the title you want for your slideshow.**

   The title appears above the slideshow on your blog and helps your blog visitors understand the slideshow's content.

3. **In the Source drop-down menu, choose the location where the slide-show you want to display on your blog is saved.**

   You can choose from one of the popular Web sites where people upload, save and share photos, such as Picasa, Flickr, and Photobucket, or you can use a photo feed.

4. **In the Option section, click the Keyword radio button if you want to include photos saved with a specific keyword, or click the Album radio button to display photos from a specific group of photos saved as an album.**

   When you select the Album option, you enter the username for the owner of the album and pick from a list of albums created by that user to find the one you want to display on your blog.

5. **Select the Open Links in New Window check box if you want to give your blog visitors the option to view the slideshow at its original source.**

   This is a useful option to select if you want your blog visitors to have the opportunity to view your slideshow in a larger format than you can offer in your blog's sidebar.

6. **Click the Save button to save your slideshow.**

   You return to the Page Elements window where you can view your changes on your blog, as shown in Figure 8-18, or continue editing your blog.

Figure 8-18:
A slideshow adds color, interactivity, and personality to your blog.

Offering subscription links

If you want to grow your blog, then offering an easy way to subscribe to it in your audience's feed readers is imperative. You can read about subscriptions and feeds in more detail in Chapter 9, including adding the Subscription Links gadget to your blog.

Taking a Poll

Using the Poll gadget is a great way to make your blog interactive. You can add a survey to ask your visitors anything you want by simply adding this gadget to your blog. Polls are fun and a great way to get visitors who may just be lurkers to come out of the woodwork and actively participate in your blog's community. You can create a multiple-choice poll in just a few simple steps as follows:

1. **In the Add a Gadget window of your Blogger account, click the + sign to the right of Poll. (Refer to Figure 8-11).**

   The Create a Poll window opens, shown in Figure 8-19.

2. **In the Question box, type your poll question.**

   Make sure you type a multiple-choice question.

3. **In the Answers boxes, type the various answers you want your blog readers to choose from.**

   If you have fewer answers than boxes provided, click the Remove link next to empty boxes to eliminate them from your poll. Alternately, if you have more answers than boxes, click the Add Another Answer link to add more answer boxes to your poll.

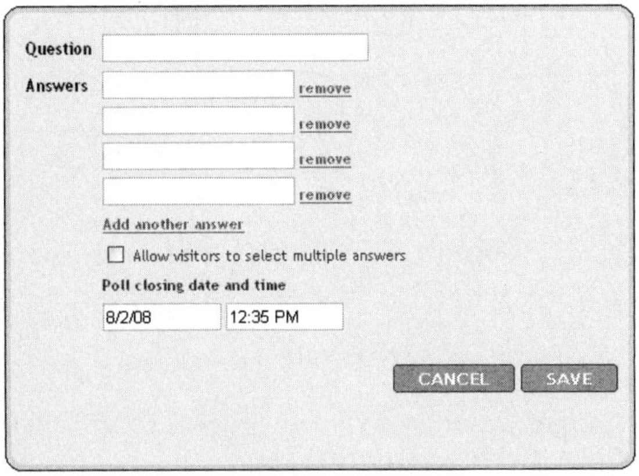

Figure 8-19: Create poll questions and answers in the Create a Poll window.

4. **If you want your blog readers to have the option to select more than one answer to your poll, then select the Allow Visitors to Select Multiple Answers check box.**

   Allowing visitors to select multiple answers is entirely up to you and can change from one poll to another.

5. **In the Poll Closing Date and Time boxes, enter the date and time you want your poll to close to new responses.**

   If you want your poll to have a specific end date, enter it here, so visitors no longer have the ability to cast votes or answer your poll question after the expiration date and time.

6. **Click the Save button to save your poll.**

   You return to the Page Elements window where you can follow the appropriate link to view your poll on your blog, as shown in Figure 8-20, or continue editing your blog.

Figure 8-20: Polls are fun and interactive!

Adding a List

Another simple way to personalize your blog is by adding a list. Using the List gadget in Blogger, you can insert a list of your favorite movies, books, songs, or anything else you want to share with your readers. The choice is yours! Add a list to your blog by following these steps:

1. **In the Add a Gadget window of your Blogger account, click the + sign to the right of List. (Refer to Figure 8-11).**

   The Configure List window opens, shown in Figure 8-21.

2. In the Title box, enter a title for your list.

You can name your list anything you want to help describe it to your readers.

3. In the Number of Items to Show in List box, enter the number of items you want to display in your list.

If you leave this box blank, all the items in your list appear on your blog at all times.

4. From the Sorting drop-down menu, choose how you want your list to sort on your blog.

You can choose to sort your list alphabetically, reverse alphabetically, or not at all.

5. In the Add List Item box, type the item you want to include in your list.

If you want to link your list item to a Web page, click the Create Link icon to the right of the Add List Item box. A dialog box opens where you can enter the complete URL for your list item. When people select the list item on your blog, they're taken directly to that URL. When you finish entering your item, select the Add Item button to add it to your list.

6. When your list is done, click the Save button.

You return to the Page Elements window where you can follow the link to view your changes on your blog, as shown in Figure 8-22, or continue editing your blog.

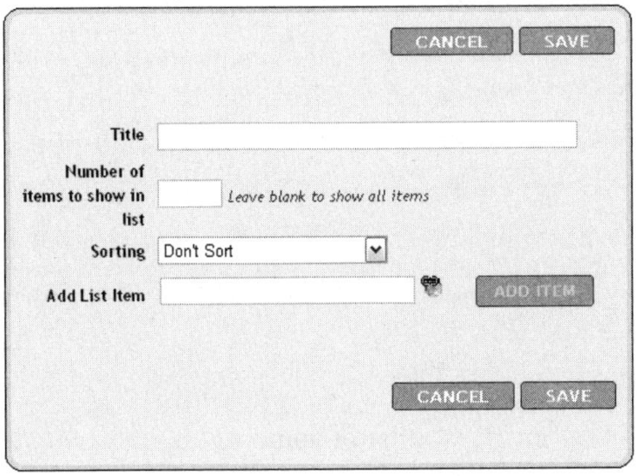

Figure 8-21:
Create a
"favorites"
list using the
List gadget
in Blogger.

Figure 8-22:
Viewing
your
changes.

Including a Link List

A Link List is a simple list of Web sites, blogs, or Web pages that you want to share with your blog's readers. The Link List gadget differs from the Blog List gadget because the Link List gadget doesn't provide an option to include an icon, snippet, or other feature from the Web site you're linking to, which the Blog List gadget does. Instead, a Link List is exactly what its name implies — a list of links to other pages online. You can add a Link List to your blog by following these steps:

1. **In the Add a Gadget window of your Blogger account, click the + sign to the right of Link List. (Refer to Figure 8-11).**

   The Configure Link List window opens, shown in Figure 8-23.

2. **In the Title box, enter a title for your list.**

   Choose a name that quickly tells your readers what the list contains.

3. **In the Number of Links to Show in List box, enter the number of items you want to display in your list.**

   If you leave this box blank, all the items in your list appear on your blog at all times.

4. **From the Sorting drop-down menu, choose how you want your list to sort on your blog.**

   You can choose to sort your list of links alphabetically, reverse alphabetically, or not at all.

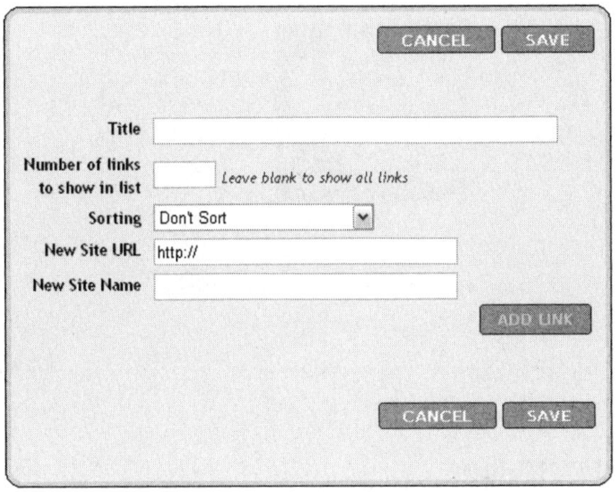

Figure 8-23:
The Link List gadget.

5. **In the New Site URL box, type the complete URL for the Web page you want to add to your Link List.**

   Be certain to include the URL for the specific page you want your blog readers to land on when they select each link in your Link List.

6. **In the New Site Name box, enter the text you want to appear in your Link List to represent the URL you input in Step 6.**

   The site name you enter appears in your Link List on your blog. When visitors select that site name, they're taken to the URL entered in Step 6.

7. **After you enter your New Site URL and New Site Name in the designated boxes, click the Add Link button.**

   The link to your Link List is added. From here, you can add more links to your Link List.

8. **When your list is done, click the Save button.**

   You return to the Page Elements window where you can follow the link to view your changes on your blog, as shown in Figure 8-24, or continue editing your blog.

Adding a picture

A great way to personalize your blog is to add an image. For example, if you write a travel blog, you might want to add a picture of your favorite vacation destination. If you write a business blog, you can add your logo. Alternatively, you can use the picture gadget to insert an ad or sponsored link. It's up to you. Add a picture to your blog as follows:

1. **In the Add a Gadget window of your Blogger account, click the + sign to the right of Picture. (Refer to Figure 8-11).**

   The Configure Image window opens, shown in Figure 8-25.

Figure 8-25:
Adding an
image to
your blog.

2. **In the Title box, enter a title for your picture.**

   If you don't want to include a title above your picture, leave this box blank.

3. **In the Caption box, enter the caption you want to appear beneath your picture on your blog.**

   If you don't want to include a caption with your picture, leave this box blank.

4. **In the Link box, enter the URL you want visitors to go to when they click the picture.**

   If you don't want the picture to link to a Web page, leave this box blank.

5. **In the Image section, click the From Your Computer radio button if the picture you want to add to your blog is saved on your computer hard drive. If the image is stored online, click the From the Web radio button.**

   If the image you're adding is stored on your computer, select the Browse button and locate the image on your hard drive. If it's stored online, enter the URL for the image in the box provided.

6. **Ensure the Shrink to Fit check box is selected if you want the entire image to appear on your blog.**

   Selecting Shrink to Fit reduces the size of your picture to fit in the space provided in your blog's layout.

7. **After you configure your picture settings, click the Save button.**

   You return to the Page Elements window where you can follow the link to view your changes on your blog, as shown in Figure 8-26, or continue editing your blog.

Figure 8-26:
Including
a picture
adds visual
appeal to
your blog.

Using AdSense

Google AdSense is an advertising program that helps bloggers earn money from their blogs. In simplest terms, Google provides a variety of ad types that you can choose from to display on your blog. You simply have to sign up for a Google AdSense account and configure your AdSense settings using the AdSense gadget in Blogger. When visitors click the ads or perform specific actions related to the ads that Google serves on your blog, you earn money.

Monetizing your blog with Google AdSense is discussed in detail in Chapter 11, including configuring the AdSense gadget to work on your blog.

Including text

A simple way to add a block of text that always appears on your blog is by using the Text gadget. For example, if you want to include a favorite quote on your personal blog or a slogan on your business blog, you can do so with the Text gadget as follows:

1. **In the Add a Gadget window of your Blogger account, click the + sign to the right of Text. (Refer to Figure 8-11).**

   The Configure Text window opens, shown in Figure 8-27.

2. **In the Title box, enter the title to appear with your text on your blog.**

   If you don't want to include a title with your text, leave this box blank.

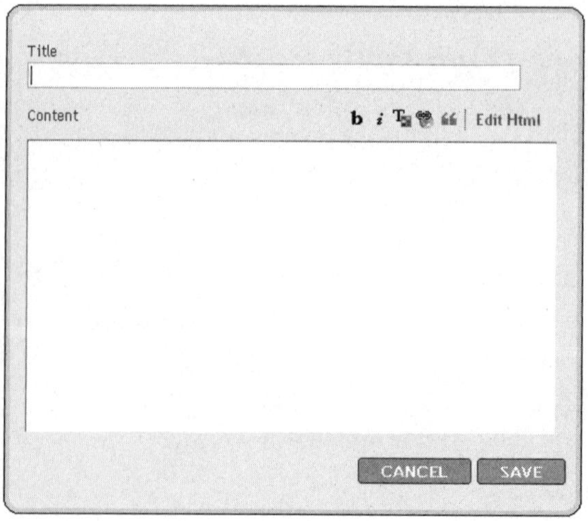

Figure 8-27:
Adding a
block of text
to your blog.

3. **In the Content box, enter the text you want to add to your blog.**

   Use the icons above the Content box to format your text with bold, italics, color, links, or block quotes. You can also edit the HTML by clicking the HTML icon.

4. **When you finish entering text, click the Save button.**

   You return to the Page Elements window where you can follow the link to view your changes on your blog, as shown in Figure 8-28, or continue editing your blog.

Figure 8-28:
Using a Text
gadget.

Using HTML/JavaScript

Blogger is flexible in terms of allowing you to add HTML or JavaScript gadgets provided by third parties. Many Web developers create HTML or JavaScript that allows you to customize your blog further. For example, you could use JavaScript to add audio, music, or video to your blog. When you find JavaScript or HTML that you want to include on your blog, follow these steps to add it:

1. **In the Add a Gadget window of your Blogger account, click the + sign to the right of HTML/JavaScript. (Refer to Figure 8-11).**

   The Configure HTML/JavaScript window opens, shown in Figure 8-29.

Figure 8-29:
Adding
third-party
HTML or
JavaScript.

2. **In the Title box, enter the title you want to appear with your HTML or JavaScript.**

   If you don't want to include a title, leave this box blank.

3. **In the Content box, enter or paste the HTML or JavaScript you want to add to your blog.**

   You can use the icons above the Content box to format your text or edit the HTML.

4. **When you finish adding the HTML or JavaScript, click the Save button.**

   You return to the Page Elements window where you can follow the link to view your changes on your blog or continue editing your blog.

Setting up a feed

Feeds are created through a syndication process where the content of your blog can be viewed through a feed reader or content aggregator. Setting up your blog's feed, adding a feed to your blog, and configuring blog subscriptions are discussed in detail in Chapter 9.

Listing labels

The Labels gadget is very useful to your blog readers because it helps them find content of interest by creating a loose system of categorization. By selecting a label of interest, a person can find all the posts you've ever written on your blog that you saved with that specific label. Labels are a great way to help readers find your old content, keep readers on your blog longer, increase page views, and increase reader loyalty simply because they help visitors find more posts that might be relevant and of interest to them. More page views typically equates to more (and better) advertising opportunities, which is important if you want to make money from your blog. (See Chapter 10.) You can add labels to your blog's sidebar as follows:

1. **In the Add a Gadget window of your Blogger account, click the + sign to the right of Labels. (Refer to Figure 8-11).**

   The Configure Labels window opens, shown in Figure 8-30.

2. **In the Title box, enter the heading you want to give your list of labels.**

   "Labels" is the default title, but you can change it to something else, such as Categories, if you want.

3. **In the Sorting section, click the Alphabetically radio button to sort your labels in alphabetical order or click the By Frequency radio button to sort your labels by how often they're used.**

   Choose the sort method you think is most helpful to your readers.

4. **Look at the Preview section to see how your labels appear on your blog.**

   The number in parentheses next to each label represents the number of posts saved with that specific label.

5. **When you finish configuring your Labels, click the Save button.**

   You return to the Page Elements window where you can follow the link to view your changes on your blog, as shown in Figure 8-31, or continue editing your blog.

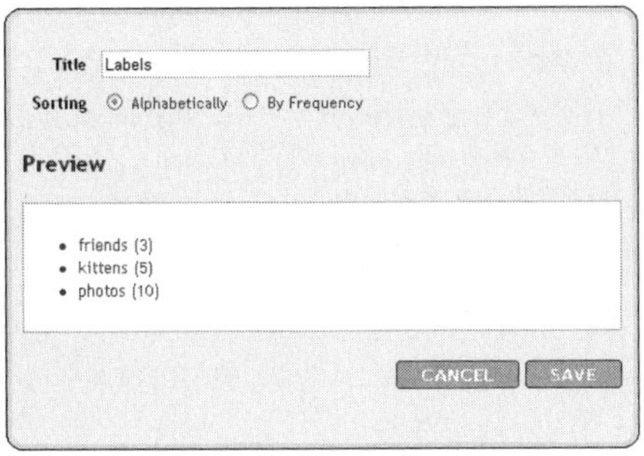

Figure 8-30:
Adding a list of labels.

Figure 8-31:
Labels help
your blog
readers find
content of
interest.

Setting up a newsreel

If you want to share links to current events or news items on your blog, you can do so with the Newsreel gadget in Blogger. For example, if you write a blog about a specific celebrity, you might want to set up a Newsreel gadget that lists Google News links to items about that celebrity to give your readers more information. You can set up your blog's Newsreel gadget to provide links to news stories by using specific keywords as follows:

1. **In the Add a Gadget window of your Blogger account, click the + sign to the right of Newsreel. (Refer to Figure 8-11).**

   The Configure Newsreel window opens, shown in Figure 8-32.

2. **In the Title box, enter the title you want to use for your newsreel.**

   If you don't want to include a title with your newsreel, leave this box blank.

3. **In the Search Expression box, enter the search terms you want to use to find and post relevant news items.**

   Google News uses the search terms entered in this box to deliver relevant news items to your blog. Enter a search phrase or keywords (separated by commas) to identify how you want Google News to find relevant content.

4. **Select the Open Links in New Window check box if you want a new window to open each time a reader selects a link from your Newsreel gadget.**

TIP

It's a good idea to select the Open Links in New Window check box so your visitors aren't taken away from your blog when they click links in your newsreel.

5. **In the Preview section, you can see how your newsreel looks on your blog. When you finish configuring your newsreel, click the Save button.**

You return to the Page Elements window where you can follow the link to view your changes on your blog, as shown in Figure 8-33, or continue editing your blog.

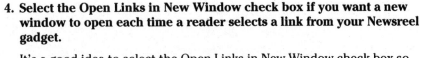

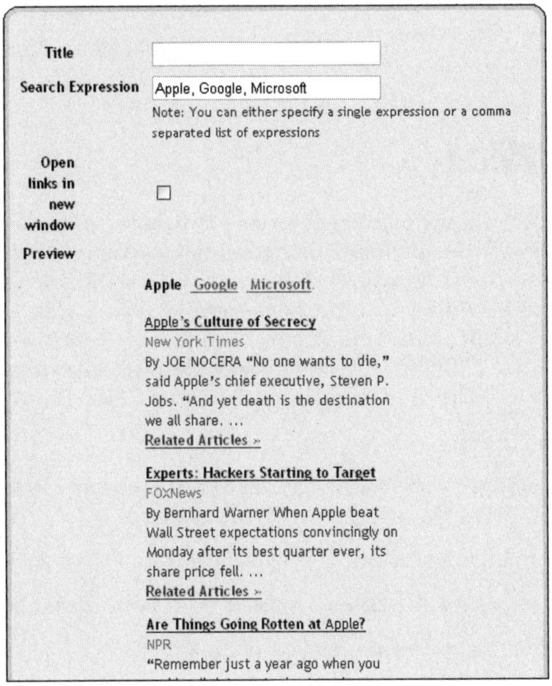

Title	
Search Expression	Apple, Google, Microsoft
	Note: You can either specify a single expression or a comma separated list of expressions
Open links in new window	☐
Preview	

Apple Google Microsoft

Apple's Culture of Secrecy
New York Times
By JOE NOCERA "No one wants to die," said Apple's chief executive, Steven P. Jobs. "And yet death is the destination we all share. ...
Related Articles »

Experts: Hackers Starting to Target
FOXNews
By Bernhard Warner When Apple beat Wall Street expectations convincingly on Monday after its best quarter ever, its share price fell. ...
Related Articles »

Are Things Going Rotten at Apple?
NPR
"Remember just a year ago when you

Figure 8-32:
Adding news items to your blog.

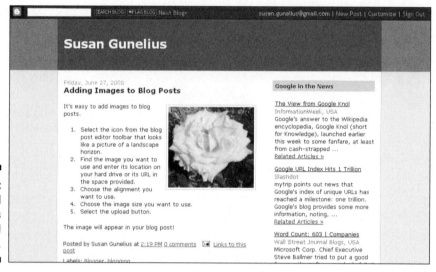

Sharing videos

The Video Bar gadget allows you to share videos from YouTube on your blog. Rather than including links to videos in your sidebar, you can use the Video Bar gadget to embed the videos directly in your sidebar, so your visitors can watch them without leaving your blog. For example, if you write a blog about a specific musician, you can include videos of that artist's performances, or if you write a blog about cooking, you can share videos about cooking gadgets or cooking techniques. The choice is yours! To add a Video Bar to your blog, follow these simple steps:

1. **In the Add a Gadget window of your Blogger account, click the + sign to the right of Video Bar. (Refer to Figure 8-11).**

   The Configure Video Bar window opens, shown in Figure 8-34.

2. **In the Title box, enter the title to appear with your video bar.**

   If you don't want to use a title, leave this box blank.

3. **In the YouTube section, select the check boxes of the video categories you want to include in your video bar.**

   You can choose to include Most Viewed Videos, Top Rated Videos, and Recently Featured Videos as ranked by YouTube.

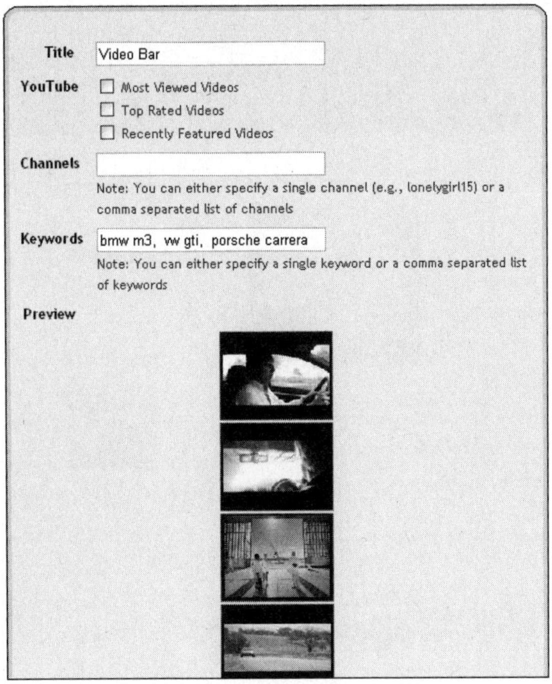

Figure 8-34:
Adding
YouTube
videos.

4. **In the Channels box, enter the YouTube channel you want to pull videos from to show in your video bar.**

   You can enter more than one channel in this box, but you must separate each with a comma.

5. **In the Keywords box, enter the search words to use to find videos on YouTube that you want to show in your video bar.**

   Videos on YouTube typically are saved with keywords to help people searching for videos find relevant content. Enter specific keywords to search YouTube and find content for your video bar in this box. Separate multiple keywords with commas.

6. **Look at the Preview section to see how the videos appear on your blog. When you finish configuring your video bar, click the Save button.**

   You return to the Page Elements window where you can follow the link to view your changes on your blog, as shown in Figure 8-35, or continue editing your blog.

Figure 8-35:
Adding a
video bar.

Including the Blogger logo

If you want to add a Blogger logo to your blog, you can do so easily by using the Logo gadget as follows:

1. **In the Add a Gadget window of your Blogger account, click the + sign to the right of Logo. (Refer to Figure 8-11).**

   The Choose Logo window opens.

2. **Click the radio button next to the Blogger logo you want to add to your blog, as shown in Figure 8-36.**

3. **After you make your selection, click the Save button.**

   You return to the Page Element window where you can follow the link to view your changes on your blog, or you can continue editing your blog.

Figure 8-36:
Add a
Blogger
logo.

Adding Third-Party Gadgets

Earlier in this chapter, I tell you that you can add third-party HTML or JavaScript to your blog using the HTML/JavaScript gadget. Blogger also offers links to a variety of third-party gadgets directly through the Add a Gadget window that you can add to your blog just as you add any of the Basic Blogger gadgets to your blog as discussed throughout this chapter. Alternatively, many third-party developers include a simple +Blogger button, an Add to Your Blog button, or a link that allows you to add a gadget offered on that developer's Web page directly to your blog.

When you select a third-party gadget button on another Web site, you're taken to your Blogger account. If you're not logged in, you're asked to log into your Blogger account. Select the blog you want to add the gadget to and view the information for the new gadget. Simply select the Add a Gadget button, and the code is added to your blog automatically.

Third-party gadgets come from a wide variety of sources. Be sure you're confident that the source providing the third-party gadget is trustworthy. You don't want to add harmful code to your blog!

Arranging Elements and Gadgets

One of the best parts about Blogger is the simple click-and-drag functionality that allows users to move page elements and gadgets around in their blog layouts. To move an individual element or gadget, select it with your mouse and drag it to a new location. (In Figure 8-1, for example, you could drag your Blog Posts element to the right of your sidebar elements.) Click the Preview button to see how your changes look on your blog before you commit to saving them. When you're satisfied with your changes, select the Save button to save them.

Don't be afraid to experiment with your blog's layout by dragging and dropping page elements and gadgets to new locations. You can always click the Cancel button to erase your changes because none of your changes are permanent until you click the Save button.

You can move any page element or gadget used in your blog except for your Navbar, Header, and Blog Posts element in some templates.

Chapter 9

Managing Your Blog

. . . .

In This Chapter

▶ Increasing visibility and accessibility

▶ Maintaining your blog

▶ Managing performance

. . . .

Aside from publishing great content, you need to keep up with a number of other tasks as a blogger, particularly if you want to grow your blog. Remember, a blog is part of the social web where user-generated content is where it's at! What makes blogs unique is their ability to provide two-way conversation between you and your visitors (and amongst your visitors, themselves). The success of your blog depends in part on the community that evolves around it and the relationships you build through it. Much of that conversation occurs through comments left on your blog, which you can learn about in this chapter.

Additionally, you can add functions and features to your blog that can enhance your ability to maintain it and your visitors' abilities to experience it. Some of the most popular features are described in this chapter.

Finally, if you want to grow your blog, you need to track your blog statistics so you can get a clear understanding of what works and what doesn't work on your blog. Blog statistic trackers allow you to learn where traffic is coming from, how visitors find your blog, and much more. This chapter helps you understand how to use blog statistic trackers and how to choose which one is right for you.

Increasing Visibility and Accessibility

Write your blog posts with the understanding that you're publishing the opening of a conversation. The strength of your blog comes from your content and the community that forms around it. The sense of community in relation to your blog is built naturally through commenting. However, with commenting also comes potential problems.

Unfortunately, not every person who visits your blog has something nice to say all the time. Furthermore, people around the world use blog commenting as a method to spread spam. A by-product of blogging is dealing with irrelevant and sometimes hurtful comments. Remember, it's your blog. To create the best possible experience for your audience, you have the power to moderate comments — as you feel appropriate — for your blog. Try to find a happy medium between keeping the conversation going and removing comments that hurt the discussion.

Inviting comments

If your blog posts are the heart of your blog, then the comments left on those posts represent the blood pumping through the veins. In other words, comments are the lifeline that keeps your blog beating. Blog comments make a blog interactive and social.

Think of blog comments the same way you would a face-to-face conversation. Do you prefer it when someone simply speaks *at you* and does all the talking, or do you prefer the conversation to offer a mix between both you and the other person speaking? People feel the same way about conversations via blog posts and comments. They want to feel like they are valuable, contributing members of the conversation, not just bystanders.

Comments separate blogs from traditional Web sites and news articles, which are one-sided and invite readers to participate passively. Comparatively, blogs are two-sided and invite readers to participate actively. Chapter 12 provides details on how you can specifically use comments to drive traffic to your blog. For now, it's important to understand how you can get people talking and leaving comments directly on your blog posts. Here are a few methods that can help generate comments:

- **Ask for them.** Simple enough, but many bloggers don't take a moment to include a question or phrase that directly asks readers what they think about the topic discussed in the post. For example, at the end of your blog posts, include a question, such as, "What do you think?" to invite readers to leave a comment and join the conversation.

- **Write about a controversial topic.** Nothing brings lurkers out of the woodwork faster than controversy. Of course, not every blog is an appropriate place to discuss controversial topics, but if a controversial topic is relevant to your blog, you might want to write a post about it. However, be cautious. Controversial topics can be emotional and might require your strict oversight and moderation to ensure nothing offensive is published.

✔ **Play devil's advocate.** Take a popular topic related to your blog and suggest the opposite point of view rather than the publicly accepted view. For example, if you write a cooking blog and most chefs follow a specific method to complete a culinary task, such as de-boning a chicken, suggest a different method as being superior. You'd be surprised how many people will join the conversation to defend the publicly accepted method or provide their opinions on your alternate point of view.

✔ **Ask your readers to help you make a decision or answer a question you have.** This method of generating comments can help to personalize your blog. For example, if you write a parenting blog and you're having trouble potty training your child, you could write a post about your struggles and ask your readers to help you by leaving comments with their potty-training tips and suggestions.

Most bloggers need months (some even years) to develop a strong and vocal reader following. It's your job to experiment with different methods to get the conversation going and find what works best to get your blog's visitors talking. After a reader leaves a comment, acknowledge that comment by responding with a comment of your own. Doing so shows your readers that you value their opinions, which will make them more likely to comment again.

Don't ignore your readers. If a reader leaves a comment, respond to it. When your audience and comments grow, you'll find that other visitors will respond to each other's comments, meaning you won't be the only other person in the conversation. Instead, group discussions will evolve around your blog posts, and you'll have the opportunity to let them flourish.

Moderating comments

You want to encourage comments on your blog; however, there will come a time when an offensive comment or spam comment is submitted in response to one of your blog posts. When that time comes, it's important that you remove the offensive or spam comment to maintain the integrity of your blog. As the number of comments left on your blog increases, you might want to begin moderating them by using the Comments feature on the Settings tab of your Blogger dashboard.

You find out how to configure comment settings in Chapter 5. The focus here is on the moderation elements found within the Comments feature, as shown in Figure 9-1.

To configure comment moderation settings, follow these steps:

1. **Click the Settings link on your Blogger dashboard.**

   The Settings window opens with the Basic settings window displayed by default.

2. **Select the Comments tab in the navigation bar near the top of your screen.**

   The Comments window opens, as shown in Figure 9-1.

Figure 9-1: The Comments window.

3. **Scroll to the Comment Moderation section of the Comments window, as shown in Figure 9-2.**

   You can configure your comment moderation settings here.

4. **Select the radio button next to Always, Only on Posts Older Than # Days, or Never to configure which comments you want to hold for review before they publish on your blog.**

   Selecting Always means all comments are held for moderation. Selecting Only on Posts Older Than # Days means comments left on posts older than the number of days you enter in the box are held for moderation. Selecting Never means that no comments are held for moderation.

   When comments are held for moderation, a link appears on your Blogger dashboard when comments are in the moderation queue for you to review.

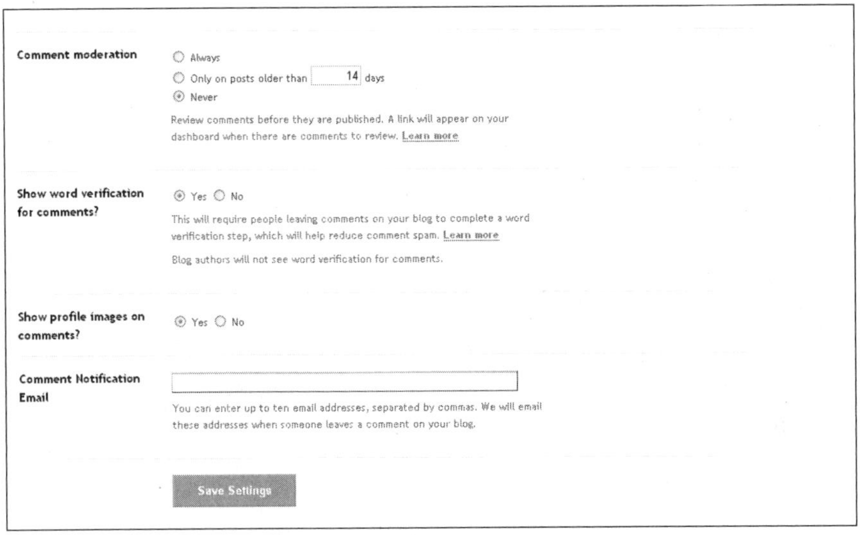

Comment moderation

     ◯ Always
     ◯ Only on posts older than   14   days
     ◉ Never

     Review comments before they are published. A link will appear on your
     dashboard when there are comments to review. Learn more

Show word verification
for comments?

     ◉ Yes ◯ No

     This will require people leaving comments on your blog to complete a word
     verification step, which will help reduce comment spam. Learn more

     Blog authors will not see word verification for comments.

Show profile images on
comments?

     ◉ Yes ◯ No

Comment Notification
Email

     You can enter up to ten email addresses, separated by commas. We will email
     these addresses when someone leaves a comment on your blog.

     Save Settings

Figure 9-2:
Configuring
comment
moderation
settings.

5. **If you select Always or Only on Posts Older Than # Days in the Comment Moderation section, an E-mail Address box automatically appears. Type your e-mail address in this box if you want to be notified via e-mail when a comment is left on your blog and is in the moderation queue.**

An e-mail is sent to the address entered in this box each time a new comment is held for moderation.

People who are already familiar with reading blogs will understand comment moderation. Therefore, they won't be discouraged to find their comments are held for review. In other words, comment moderation is not perceived by the blog-reading community as a negative and doesn't affect your traffic or the conversation that occurs on your blog.

Creating a comment policy

It's important to set expectations and rules for your blog community. Creating a comment policy is an easy way to communicate what is and is not acceptable commenting behavior on your blog. Include information about the types of comments you will delete from blog posts so that visitors understand why certain comments might be deleted or never appear on your blog.

Pinging

An important part of growing your blog is making sure that the World Wide Web knows your blog exists and knows when you publish new content. Blogger helps you achieve this through its automatic pinging service in conjunction with Weblogs.com.

In simplest terms, *pinging* is the process by which a signal is sent to a server (called a ping server) whenever new content is added to a blog (or another online source). Weblogs.com is a ping server that aggregates the pings it receives and makes them available to third parties, such as the search engines Technorati and Google. If you want your blog posts to appear in search engine results, make sure your blog is set up to ping.

Blogger users can easily configure their blogs to ping Weblogs.com, the largest and oldest ping server, as follows:

1. **From the Blogger dashboard, click the Settings link.**

   The Basic configuration window opens, as shown in Figure 9-3.

2. **Choose Yes from the Let Search Engines Find Your Blog? drop-down menu.**

   By selecting yes, your blog will automatically ping Weblogs.com and Google Blog Search (an alternate ping server) every time you publish new content, making it immediately available to search engines.

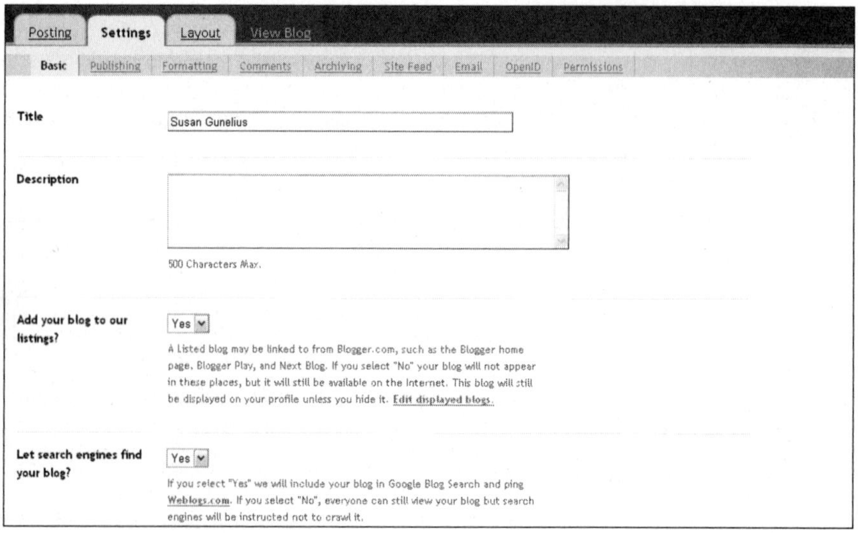

Figure 9-3: Configure your blog to ping Weblogs. com.

When you become more proficient with blogging, you might hear of other ping servers and wonder whether you should manually ping them. Typically, the answer is no. Weblogs.com — the largest ping server — is used by the major search engines. Many other ping servers simply duplicate a portion of what Weblogs.com does. Be sure to research other ping servers before you commit to manually pinging them or add code to your blog to automatically ping them to ensure it's worth your time and effort.

Managing feeds and subscriptions

People who like your blog will want to visit whenever you publish new content. Moreover, if they find the comments on a particular post interesting, they might want to be notified each time a new comment is added to that post. Blog feeds and subscriptions provide an easy way for people to access your new content when it's published and are particularly helpful to people who read many blogs each day.

In short, you can create a feed of your blog's new content that people can subscribe to. Instead of visiting your blog's URL everyday (as well as the URLs of all the other blogs they enjoy reading), subscribers can view all new content for every blog they subscribe to in one location via a feed reader. Many feed readers are available, including Google Reader, which is described in detail later in this chapter.

Setting up your feed

Blogger uses Atom 1.0 language to create and deliver Web feeds. It's very easy to set up your blog to generate a feed and to provide links for visitors to subscribe to your blog's feed in their feed reader of choice. Here's how:

1. **From the Blogger dashboard, click the Settings link.**

   The Settings window opens with the Basic settings window displayed by default.

2. **Select the Site Feed tab from the navigation bar near the top of your screen.**

   The Site Feed window opens, as shown in Figure 9-4.

3. **In the Blog Posts Feed drop-down menu, choose Full to make all your blog posts available in their entirety for subscribers to read in their feed readers.**

   A *blog posts feed* provides the content of your new blog posts to your subscribers to view in their feed reader. If you prefer, choose Short from the drop-down menu to provide only an excerpt of each blog post through your feed. Subscribers need to click through from their feed reader to your blog to read the entire post. Alternatively, choose None from the drop-down menu if you don't want to offer post feed subscriptions to your blog readers.

If you want to grow your blog, it's a good idea to offer all feed and subscription options to your visitors.

4. **In the Blog Comment Feed drop-down menu, choose the Full, Short, or None setting to configure the feed settings for your blog comments.**

   A *blog comment feed* provides all new comments left on all your blog posts to subscribers to view in their feed reader. Each setting works the same as those described in Step 3 above for the Blog Posts Feed setting.

5. **In the Per-Post Comment Feeds drop-down box, choose the Full, Short, or None setting to configure the feed settings for comments on individual blog posts.**

   A *per-post comment feed* provides a person's feed reader all new comments left only on specific posts the viewer subscribes to. Each setting works the same as those described in Step 3 above for the Blog Posts Feed setting.

6. **In the Post Feed Redirect URL box, enter the feed URL from FeedBurner or a third party feed provider.**

   If you want to use a feed provider other than Blogger's Atom 1.0 service, you can create your feed through a third party, such as FeedBurner, and then enter the URL for your blog's new feed in this box. The nearby Using FeedBurner sidebar discusses FeedBurner in greater detail.

Posting	**Settings**	Layout	View Blog

| Basic | Publishing | Formatting | Comments | Archiving | **Site Feed** | Email | OpenID | Permissions |

Switch to: Basic Mode

Blog Posts Feed   Full ▾

Blog Comment Feed   Full ▾

Per-Post Comment Feeds   Full ▾

Post Feed Redirect URL   [   ]

If you have burned your post feed with FeedBurner, or used another service to process your feed, enter the full feed URL here. Blogger will redirect all post feed traffic to this address.

Post Feed Footer

Figure 9-4: The Site Feed window.

7. **In the Post Feed Footer box, enter the text you want to display with your subscription link after each post on your blog.**

   If you're using a third party feed provider such as Feedburner (see the nearby sidebar), enter the post feed code supplied by that provider in this box.

8. **When you finish making edits, click the Save Settings button.**

   Your feed is configured. Next, you need to make it easy for visitors to subscribe to your feed.

9. **Select the Layout tab from the top navigation bar on your screen.**

   The Page Elements window opens, as shown in Figure 9-5.

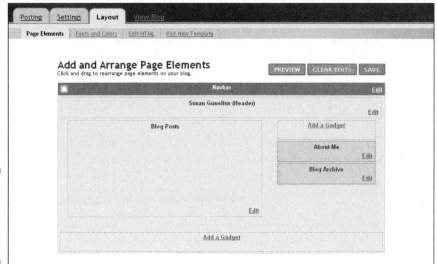

Figure 9-5:
Adding a subscription link to your blog.

10. **Click the Add a Gadget link.**

    The Add a Gadget window opens, as shown in Figure 9-6.

11. **Click the + icon to the right of the Subscription Links gadget.**

    The Configure Subscription Links window opens, as shown in Figure 9-7.

12. **In the Title box, type the text you want to use as a title for your subscription link.**

    You can leave the title's default text, Subscribe To, or choose another phrase.

13. **Click the Save button to save your changes.**

    You return to the Page Elements page where you can follow the link to view your changes on your blog, as shown in Figure 9-8.

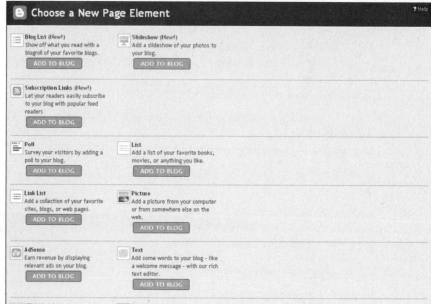

Figure 9-6:
Accessing
the
Subscription
Links
element.

Figure 9-7:
Add a title to
make it easy
for your
readers to
subscribe to
your blog.

Subscribing to blogs

The longer you blog, the more blogs you're apt to read on a daily basis. Instead of opening all of those blogs each day to see what people are talking about, you can subscribe to your favorite blogs and read all the updates in a single location. Feed readers save you time and effort.

Many feed readers are available, including Google Reader. When you start your Google Blogger blog, you create a Google account, as I describe in Chapter 4. You can use that Google Account username and password to log into Google Reader and begin subscribing to blog feeds.

To subscribe to a blog's feed, simply select the subscribe icon or link found on that blog. Typically, a window or list will open showing the various feed readers you can choose from to subscribe to that feed, as shown in Figure 9-9. Select Google Reader from the list. You're prompted to log into Google Reader to complete your subscription. The next time you want to see the new content from that blog (and others that you subscribe to), you can simply log into Google Reader and view that content in a single location.

You can learn more about feeds and subscriptions in *Syndicating Web Sites with RSS Feeds For Dummies* by Ellen Finkelstein (Wiley, 2005).

Using FeedBurner

Two different feed formats are used primarily — Atom 1.0 and RSS 2.0. Most feed readers can handle both languages, but there may come a time when you decide you want to offer an RSS subscription option on your blog. If that's the case, FeedBurner is one of the most popular choices for burning an RSS feed. You can visit www.FeedBurner.com, register for an account, and go through the simple steps provided to burn your blog's feed. When you're done configuring your blog's RSS feed, simply copy the code provided by FeedBurner into a new HTML/JavaScript gadget on your blog as described in Chapter 8, and you're done.

You can also include an option to subscribe to your blog via e-mail through FeedBurner. Rather than using a feed reader, e-mail subscribers receive an e-mail when new content is published on your blog. That's just one more way you can enhance your visitors' experiences on your blog.

Figure 9-9:
Blogs syn-
dicated by
FeedBurner
provide a
subscription
window.

Adding More Features to Your Blog

When you become an experienced blogger, you may want to try new tools and features that can make your life as a blogger easier. Although getting stuck in a rut of using the same, comfortable tools every day is easy, don't be afraid to seek more advanced tools and options. Some of the most popular advanced tools are described here.

Instant blogging with BlogThis!

Sometimes you might find an article, a video, or other content online that you want to write about on your blog. Rather than taking the time to open a new browser window and log into your Blogger account to write your new post, you can use BlogThis! to blog instantly.

BlogThis! is a tool that can be added to your Web browser's toolbar. When you see something of interest online that you want to write about, simply select the BlogThis! icon from your browser's toolbar. A stripped-down Blogger post editor window opens where you can type your post and publish it directly from the BlogThis! window, as shown in Figure 9-10. To make things even easier, if you highlight text on the Web site you're visiting before you select the BlogThis! icon from your browser toolbar, the BlogThis! window opens with the selected text already inserted into the post editor. You can't blog much faster than that!

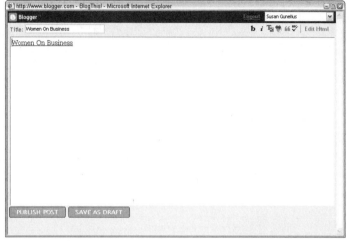

Figure 9-10:
The
BlogThis!
post editor.

If you use Internet Explorer from a Windows-based computer, you can access the BlogThis! icon from the Send To link on the Google toolbar. If you use Mozilla Firefox as your Web browser, an add-on is available through the Firefox Web site that adds the BlogThis! link to your right-click menu. If you use a different browser, you can drag the BlogThis! link to your browser's link toolbar from Blogger's online help site (`http://help.blogger.com`).

Sending posts with BlogSend

Blogger gives you the option to automatically send each new post that you publish on your blog to a specific e-mail address via BlogSend. To configure the BlogSend feature, follow these steps:

1. **From the Blogger dashboard, click the Settings link.**

   The Settings window from your Blogger account opens with the Basic settings window displayed by default.

2. **Select the Email tab from the navigation bar near the top of your screen.**

   The Email window opens, as shown in Figure 9-11.

3. **In the BlogSend Address box, type the e-mail address that you want your new blog posts to be sent to.**

   In this box, you can enter ten e-mail addresses separated with commas.

4. **Select the Save Settings button to save your changes.**

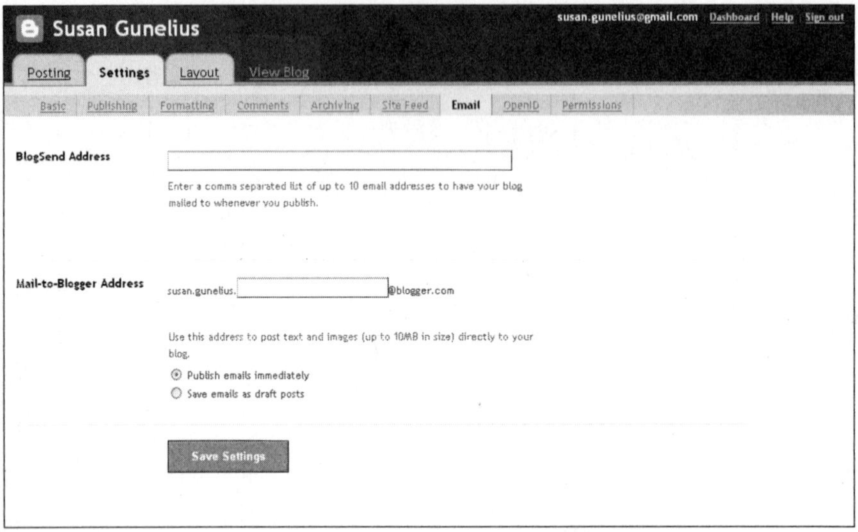

Susan Gunelius

susan.gunelius@gmail.com   Dashboard   Help   Sign out

Posting   **Settings**   Layout   View Blog

Basic   Publishing   Formatting   Comments   Archiving   Site Feed   **Email**   OpenID   Permissions

BlogSend Address

Enter a comma separated list of up to 10 email addresses to have your blog mailed to whenever you publish.

Mail-to-Blogger Address   susan.gunelius.[   ]@blogger.com

Use this address to post text and images (up to 10MB in size) directly to your blog.

◉ Publish emails immediately
○ Save emails as draft posts

[Save Settings]

Figure 9-11:
Automatically sending new posts to a specific person.

Publishing posts with Mail-to-Blogger

With Mail-to-Blogger, you can publish blog posts through any e-mail program without logging into Blogger. To use this functionality, you need to configure the e-mail address and settings for Mail-to-Blogger as follows:

1. **In the Email window shown in Figure 9-11, enter a secret word of your choice in the box provided to create your private Mail-to-Blogger e-mail address.**

   You send blog posts directly to this address via e-mail to publish to your blog.

   Do not share your Mail-to-Blogger e-mail address. If it gets into the wrong hands, a malicious person could post on your blog pretending to be you.

2. **Select the radio button next to either Publish Emails Immediately or Save Emails as Draft Posts.**

   If you select Publish Emails Immediately, any posts you send to your Mail-to-Blogger e-mail address automatically publish on your blog. If you select the Save Emails as Draft Posts option, the posts you send to your Mail-to-Blogger e-mail address sit in the draft queue within your Blogger account until you log into Blogger and manually publish them.

3. **Select the Save Settings button to save your changes.**

Before you send posts using Mail-to-Blogger, understanding how your e-mail client handles text formatting is important. For example, if your e-mail client uses plain-text formatting, then any formatting you apply to your text, such as bold, italics, and so on (even if you do so using HTML coding), won't appear in your post when it publishes on your blog. However, if your e-mail client uses HTML formatting, then any formatting you apply should appear in your post when it publishes on your blog.

When you write posts using Mail-to-Blogger, the title of the e-mail message publishes as the title of your blog post, and the content of your e-mail message publishes as the content of your blog post. You can also include an image with your post by attaching it to your e-mail message.

To determine how your e-mail client works with the Mail-to-Blogger functionality, try publishing some test posts with Mail-to-Blogger that you can delete after they publish.

If your e-mail program automatically adds a signature or copyright message to the end of your e-mail messages, insert *#end* at the end of your post to ensure that the additional text does not publish with your blog post.

Understanding basic HTML

HTML is an acronym for Hypertext Markup Language, which is the primary programming language used to write Web pages. While Blogger provides a simple WYSIWYG (What You See Is What You Get) post editor interface that allows you to publish blog posts without any knowledge of HTML, learning some HTML can only help you succeed as a blogger.

Understanding just a few HTML commands can help you enhance the formatting of your blog posts, your sidebar, and more. Although it's not necessary to become an HTML expert, every piece of HTML that you learn helps you grow as a blogger.

In simplest terms, HTML uses tags to provide instructions to your Web browser about how to display text and other elements. For example, if you want a specific word to appear in bold, you need to tell the Web browser to do so with HTML tags. Each instruction is provided by using an opening and closing HTML tag. In other words, if you want to tell your Web browser to display a word in bold, you type the opening HTML tag followed by the word you want bolded and the closing HTML tag. HTML tags are always enclosed in brackets, and the closing tag is always preceded with a slash.

For example, if you want the sentence "The sun is yellow" to display online as "The sun is **yellow**," you tell your Web browser to do so as follows:

The sun is `<start bold>`yellow`<end bold>`

Of course, the example above uses laymen's terms within the HTML coding brackets to demonstrate how the HTML coding communicates to your Web browser. The actual HTML coding would appear as follows:

The sun is `<b>`yellow`</b>`

Looking at the coding example above, you can determine that the HTML tag `<b>` tells your Web browser to bold the text that follows the tag. The HTML tag `</b>` tells your Web browser to stop bold.

To help you get started, following are some of the most common HTML tags that bloggers use. You can learn more about HTML in *HTML, XHTML & CSS, 6th Edition For Dummies* by Ed Tittel and Jeff Noble (Wiley, 2008).

- ✔ Bold: `<b>` and `</b>`
- ✔ Italics: `<i>` and `</i>`
- ✔ Underline: `<u>` and `</u>`
- ✔ Paragraph: `<p>` and `</p>`
- ✔ Line break: `<br>`
- ✔ Hyperlink: `<a href="ENTER URL HERE">text you want to appear as the link</a>`
- ✔ Font size: `<font size=2>` and `</font>`
- ✔ Font color: `<font color=green>` and `</font>`
- ✔ Numbered list: `<ol>` to start the list, `<li>` before each line item, `</ol>` to end the list
- ✔ Bulleted list: `<ul>` to start the list, `<li>` before each line item, `</ul>` to end the list

Managing Performance

An important part of growing your blog is understanding where visitors are coming from, what content they find and like, and what they do when they're on your blog. This is where Web analytics are useful. Luckily, a number of free blog statistic trackers are available to use on your blog.

When you begin to analyze your blog statistics, do so with realistic short-term and long-term goals in mind. Don't expect to receive thousands of visitors within a month or two of launching your blog. In time, traffic to your blog will grow, particularly when you begin promoting your blog, which I discuss in Chapter 12. By analyzing your blog's traffic, you can find what efforts are (and aren't) working, so you can concentrate your time on activities that truly boost traffic and make your blog more valuable and enjoyable to everyone who visits.

Tracking your stats

Now that you know it's important to track your blog's statistics, you're probably wondering why. In short, blog statistics can help you understand:

- ✔ Where visitors to your blog are coming from. What Web sites, blogs, or search engines are helping them find your blog.
- ✔ What keywords people enter into search engines that lead them to your blog.
- ✔ How many posts visitors look at before they leave your blog.
- ✔ How many new visitors come to your blog each day versus repeat visitors.
- ✔ The length of time that people spend on your blog.
- ✔ The most frequently viewed posts on your blog.

These are just a few of the statistics you can track on your blog. How can these statistics help you grow your blog? Take a look at the following explanations:

- ✔ **Where visitors to your blog are coming from.** When you know which Web sites and blogs are sending traffic your way, you can concentrate your marketing efforts on those sites. For example, you can leave comments on those blogs or mention their posts with links to the original post on your blog. It's a proven traffic generator that you can exploit and grow further.
- ✔ **What keywords people enter.** When you know which keywords people use to find your blog, you can further optimize your blog posts to get more search results by using those popular keywords or keyword phrases.
- ✔ **How many posts visitors look at.** If you see that most visitors look at more than one post on your blog, you can feel confident that you're publishing compelling content and building a loyal readership.

✔ **How many new visitors come to your blog versus repeat visitors.** Ultimately, you want a mix of loyal, repeat visitors and new visitors to find your blog each day.

✔ **The length of time people spend on your blog.** If people arrive at your blog and leave immediately, they're not the type of traffic you want, and you need to adjust your efforts to find qualified traffic or enhance your content to be more compelling.

✔ **The most frequently viewed posts on your blog.** When you know your most popular posts, you can exploit that knowledge by linking to those posts from new posts, promoting those posts through your marketing efforts, and writing similar posts in the future.

You have countless ways to use your blog statistics to learn about your blog's audience and what they want from your blog. Review your blog's statistics to see if there are any trends or patterns. Try different writing and promotional techniques, and then analyze your blog statistics to see how those techniques affect your blog's traffic and performance.

Choosing a statistic tracker

Many Web analytics tools are available to bloggers. Some are provided free whereas others have a cost. Take some time to research the various Web analytics providers to find the one that offers you the functionality you want at the price you're willing to pay.

Most Web analytics tools integrate with your blog through a simple copy-and-paste procedure. You register for an account, enter information about your blog, and a snippet of code automatically generates that you copy and paste into a new HTML/JavaScript gadget (as described in Chapter 8) on your blog. It's a simple process but one that helps your blog to grow immensely.

Several free Web analytics tools provide sufficient data and functionality for typical bloggers. Following is an introduction to several popular Web analytics providers that offer a variety of free blog statistic tracking services.

✔ **Google Analytics.** Google Analytics integrates seamlessly with Google Blogger, as you'd expect. It's considered one of the best blog statistic trackers because it provides comprehensive information to users at no charge. You can create custom reports and even track advertising and promotional campaigns.

✔ **StatCounter.** StatCounter delivers basic blog statistics to users for free. However, the free version of StatCounter displays only the last 100 visitors to your blog in its statistics. This may or may not be adequate for you depending on your goals for your blog and the level of tracking detail you want. StatCounter also offers a package that delivers additional data and functionality for a fee.

✔ **FreeStats.** FreeStats provides a variety of reports for bloggers to analyze their blog traffic patterns. As the name implies, FreeStats is available for free.

✔ **SiteMeter.** SiteMeter offers a basic amount of blog statistics for free, but only displays information about the last 100 visitors to your blog (similar to StatCounter). Depending on your requirements, this might not be enough for you. SiteMeter also offers a package that provides more information and data for a fee.

Some of the blog statistic trackers and tools available to you online are not compatible with blogs hosted through Blogger (meaning they have a Blogspot extension in the URL). Hosting your blog on a third-party server gives you maximum control and provides access to the widest array of blogging tools, including blog statistic trackers. You can read more about third-party blog hosting in Chapter 16.

The Web analytics tool you choose is entirely up to you. In fact, you might want to test the free versions from multiple providers to compare their offerings and find the one that works best for you. If you require more robust statistics, you might want to consider upgrading to a package that provides more features and functionality for a fee. However, most bloggers find the free tools adequate.

Deciding what to track

When you first open your blog statistic reports, you probably won't know where to begin. Don't feel overwhelmed. Begin by focusing on the "big ticket" stats, such as page views, referrers, and keywords. In time, you'll learn to use the various reports and data available through your blog statistic tracker. You'll even learn how to analyze those numbers and apply your learning to your blog. For a complete education about Web analytics, check out *Web Analytics For Dummies* by Pedro Sostre and Jennifer LeClaire (Wiley, 2007).

For now, take a few moments to familiarize yourself with some of the most commonly analyzed blog statistics.

Always make sure you set the time period you want to analyze before you begin to review your blog stats.

✔ **Hits:** Your blog statistic tracker counts a hit every time a file downloads from your blog. Each page on your blog can have multiple files on it. When a person accesses a page on your blog, every file on that page downloads and counts as a hit. For example, if your page includes a blog post with multiple images in it, each of those images downloads when a visitor accesses that page, which gives an inflated view of the popularity of your blog. Therefore, hits aren't typically used to determine Web traffic trends.

✔ **Visits:** Each time your Web site is accessed (any page), a visit is counted in your blog statistic tracker. This means a person who visits more than once is counted multiple times. Therefore, visits give an inflated view of your blog's popularity and aren't typically used to determine Web traffic trends.

✔ **Visitors:** Accurately tracking the number of visitors who enter your blog is challenging for blog statistic trackers. Unless visitors register and sign in to access pages on your blog, it's close to impossible to ensure repeat visitors are counted only once. Stat trackers often use cookies to reduce the number of visitors who are counted twice, but if people clear their cookies, there's no way for the stat tracker to identify them. That is, if visitors return after clearing their cookies, they're counted as a new visitor. Therefore, tracking visitors is more accurate than tracking visits in terms of determining the true metrics related to your blog.

Some blog statistic trackers break this stat into unique visitors (those who visit one time only) and repeat visitors (those who visit more than once), but these numbers can never be 100 percent accurate. Use them for guidance but do so with caution. Some of the high-level visitor information provided by Google Analytics is shown in Figure 9-12.

✔ **Page Views:** Page Views is the most commonly used statistic that bloggers track because it provides the clearest picture of how popular a blog is. Each page viewed on your blog regardless of who views it counts as a page view. Online advertisers use page views as the standard of measurement to calculate advertising rates. More page views equals more people seeing the ad and potentially clicking it or acting on it. Figure 9-13 shows visits versus page views data provided by SiteMeter.

Figure 9-12: Google Analytics.

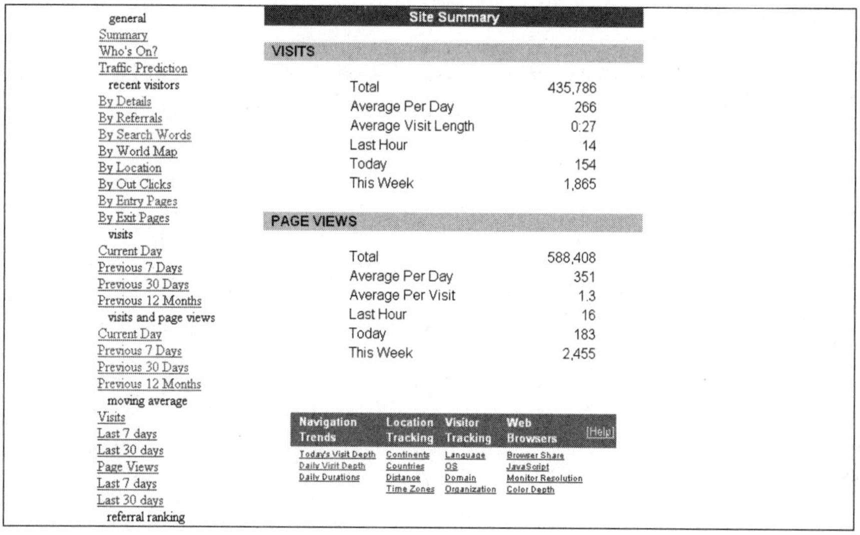

Figure 9-13: SiteMeter.

✔ **Top Pages Viewed:** Blog statistic trackers typically provide a report that shows your blog's most viewed pages (which correlate to specific posts if you choose Enable Post Pages in your blog settings, as I describe in Chapter 5). Monitoring Top Pages Viewed can help you focus your content creation and marketing efforts.

✔ **Top Paths Taken:** Paths represent the way visitors travel through your blog — the links they follow, the content that's most interesting to them, and the features that keep them on your blog longer.

✔ **Top Entry Pages:** Top Entry Pages represent the pages that people most frequently land on when they visit your blog. This statistic is helpful in terms of finding where visitors are coming from. Using the Top Paths Taken statistic with the Top Entry Pages statistic can provide valuable information.

✔ **Top Exit Pages:** Top Exit Pages represent the last pages that people view before leaving your blog. This statistic can help you identify content that is underperforming.

✔ **Bounce Rate:** Bounce rate is a useful statistic that shows you the percentage of people who leave your blog immediately after finding it. The bounce rate represents people who didn't find what they were looking for when they were led to your blog. The lower this number, the more effective your marketing and search engine optimization efforts are; meaning the people who are finding your blog are the ones that you want to find it. In other words, your search engine optimization and marketing efforts are reaching your blog's target audience.

✔ **Referrers:** One of the most powerful statistics you can access through your Web analytics, referrers are the Web sites, blogs, and search engines that lead visitors to your blog. Often the Referrers statistic is broken down further into a category for search engines only and another for non-search engines. You can find where traffic is coming from and determine where to focus your marketing efforts going forward.

✔ **Keywords and Keyword Phrases:** Another powerful statistic you can access through your Web analytics is Keywords and Keyword Phrases. Search engines have the potential to drive large numbers of visitors to your blog. By analyzing the keywords and keyword phrases that people type into search engines, which lead them to find your blog, you can focus your future search engine optimization efforts and content creation efforts to target those keywords.

Don't think you'll be a master at blog statistic analysis overnight. It takes time to understand how to read your blog's statistics and then effectively apply them to your blog plan to meet your blogging goals. Keep in mind that there are no regulations or rules related to Web analytics; the statistics one provider delivers could be very different from those delivered by another provider. With that in mind, you might want to try a few different stat trackers and compare the results delivered by each until you find the one that works best for you and appears to offer the most accurate data.

Part III
Making Money with Blogger

The 5th Wave   By Rich Tennant

"Look-what if we just increase the size of the charts?"

In this part . . .

The name of the game is blog monetization, and you have many ways to take part in it. The main issue is figuring out which moneymaking programs are best for you and your blog, and you can find answers in Chapter 10, which shows you some of the most popular options.

In the area of quick and easy monetization, Google AdSense is in a class all its own, so Chapter 11 is devoted to that topic. Find out how to start your own Google AdSense account and add advertisements to your blog so you can start making money.

Chapter 10

The Business of Blogging

In This Chapter

▶ Finding ways to make money from your blog

▶ Determining which moneymaking options you should try

*A*dvertising is the most common form of blog monetization, and you can quite easily integrate advertising into your Blogger blog. Including online ads in your blog is a simple way to earn a passive income from your blogging efforts. In many cases, you simply need to register for an account with an ad network or affiliate marketing program, copy some code provided to you into a new gadget in your blog, and you're done. Ads are automatically displayed to your visitors based on the criteria you selected during the registration process in each specific advertising program.

Blog advertising is growing in popularity not just among bloggers looking for ways to earn extra money but also among companies and advertisers that recognize the power of the blogosphere and the broad reach many blogs provide. As your blog traffic grows, more and more opportunities will open to you to attract bigger advertisers with bigger budgets. You'll also have more opportunities to join ad networks and affiliate programs that have minimum participation restrictions based on page views or subscribers, for example. In other words, the bigger your blog becomes, the more money you can make from it through advertising.

The key to making money from your blog is understanding the moneymaking options available to you and experimenting with those opportunities until you find the right mix for your blog. Much of your moneymaking success lies in finding the right balance of ads that your visitors appreciate and act on. This chapter breaks down some of the most popular blog monetization options so you can begin experimenting on your own blog.

Making Money from Your Blog

Making money from your blog, or *blog monetization,* doesn't happen over-night. You won't place an ad on your blog today and find money rolling in tomorrow. Instead, blog monetization takes time, practice, experimentation, and patience to flourish. Much of your moneymaking success comes from your blog visitors' reactions to your efforts, so it takes time to figure out what your readers respond to best. Just as people respond differently to tele-vision or magazine ads, they also respond differently to ads that appear on blogs. If your goal is to make money from blog advertising, you need to be prepared to test ads and track the results to find the right mix to maximize your earnings.

It's equally important to understand that different advertising opportunities might perform better on your blog than others strictly because of the nature of your blog's topic. For example, some blog topics are perfectly suited for affiliate advertising with a directly related affiliate program. Consider a blog about pregnancy that uses affiliate advertising from a top baby store. Naturally, this ad program would work better on that blog than an affiliate program that sells unrelated products, such as humidors and tobacco prod-ucts. Some blog topics are perfect for blog advertising and offer a wealth of opportunities for the blogger to choose from, and other blog topics are a bit more challenging to monetize. The challenge for the blogger is always the same: Find the best ad opportunities that deliver the best results.

Understanding monetization options

You can add advertisements to your blog in a variety of ways to derive a pas-sive income. Each one requires a different amount of real estate (or space) on your blog, and each one brings in a different amount of money, depending on your blog's topic and readers. Most blog advertising opportunities offer one of three primary payment methods for bloggers:

- **Pay-per-click:** The advertiser pays the blogger every time someone clicks the ad placed on the blog.
- **Pay-per-impression:** The advertiser pays the blogger every time the ad appears on the blog — or every time a visitor views the page where the ad is placed. Typically, pay-per-impression ads are paid using a "per 1,000 impressions" model or a similar pay structure rather than pay on individual impressions.
- **Pay-per-action:** The advertiser pays the blogger every time a person clicks the ad and performs an action, such as making a purchase or registering for an account.

Examining the pros and cons of monetization options

With each advertising opportunity comes different guidelines and restrictions. Make sure that you read all the terms and conditions of each online advertising network or affiliate program you join. Also ensure that those programs are in line with the Google and Blogger terms and conditions you agreed to when you created your blogging accounts, as described in Chapter 4.

Additionally, listen to the online buzz to hear current information about the pros and cons of different advertising opportunities. For example, bloggers and search engine optimization experts warn against writing sponsored reviews (described later in this chapter) of products or Web sites without fully disclosing that you're being paid to write those reviews. If you write them, you run the risk of having Google drop your blog from its search results, making your blog's traffic drop significantly. It's these types of conversations that can help you make decisions about the types of advertising you want to include on your blog. Spend time on the Blogger Buzz blog (`http://buzz.blogger.com`) and the Blogger Google Group (`http://groups.google.com/group/blogger-help`) to hear the discussions around blog advertising, and then pick and choose the moneymaking opportunities that meet your current and future needs and goals.

It's your content, not your ads, that makes visitors return to your blog. Don't cover your blog in so many ads that visitors have difficulty finding your content.

Knowing what to look for in a monetization option

Each blog monetization option that you consider offers different payments and different rules. Make sure that you understand both before you dive in to joining a new advertising program. When you choose a new money-making option to experiment with on your blog, make sure that it offers these features:

- ✔ **Acceptable payment rates:** Some advertising opportunities pay much more than others, but if your visitors aren't interested in those ads, those high rates might not help you earn more money. Balance the payment rate with the usefulness of the ad for your audience to find the best opportunities for your blog.

✔ **Clear payment terms:** Avoid advertisers that don't offer clear and acceptable payment terms. Make sure that you know when you'll be paid and how. For example, some advertisers don't pay bloggers until they earn $100. It can take some bloggers quite a long time to reach the $100 threshold for payout. Additionally, some advertisers pay only by way of PayPal (www.PayPal.com). If you don't want to have a PayPal account and don't want to open one, look for alternate advertising opportunities.

✔ **Free and effective reporting tools:** Be certain that the advertising programs you join offer free reporting tools and that the tools provide you with a real-time picture of your earnings and performance.

✔ **Detailed tracking tools:** Reporting tools must allow you to track your detailed performance, including earnings per ad unit and earnings by day. Don't settle for high-level information. The only way you can truly create a long-term, targeted advertising plan for your blog is to analyze the results of each program in detail.

✔ **Easy-to-understand terms and conditions:** Read the terms and conditions to ensure that you understand them and that they answer all your questions. Don't be afraid to do a Google search on a new advertising opportunity to see what other bloggers have to say about it before you make your decision to join.

✔ **Support:** If you have a problem with an ad unit or a tool, you have to be able to find help when you need it. Make sure that the advertising programs you sign up with offer support by e-mail or telephone.

Choosing Blogger Monetization Options

After you decide to include advertising on your blog, you need to begin reviewing advertising and moneymaking options to find the ones you want to try. Most bloggers begin with monetization programs that are

✔ Easy to add to their blogs

✔ Open to all bloggers regardless of traffic

As a Blogger user, you can sign up for a wide variety of blog monetization programs. This chapter highlights some of the most popular programs that bloggers typically try first.

Your blog monetization efforts don't have to stop with the programs discussed in this chapter. You can find out more about blog monetization from a variety of Web sites and blogs, including the About.com Guide to Web Logs (`http://weblogs.about.com`). Additionally, you can read *Blogging For Dummies,* by Susannah Gardner and Shane Birley (Wiley), which includes information about several blog monetization programs.

Not all blog monetization options are equal. Take the time to research a new opportunity before you apply or implement it on your blog. The rules and requirements for different blog monetization options change frequently, and a program that might not work on your blog today may work perfectly tomorrow. For example, some moneymaking programs aren't compatible with Blogger blogs now, but they might be compatible later. Always check the restrictions and ensure that your blog qualifies to participate in a blog monetization program before you spend time applying.

Contextual link ads

Contextual link ads can consist of text or images and are displayed to visitors based on the content on the page where they appear. Because these ads are by definition contextually relevant to the content of the page, visitors are quite likely to be interested in them and click on them. Contextual ads are typically pay-per-click ads, so the blogger is paid when a person clicks the ad. Advertisers generally bid on keywords in pay-per-click contextual link ad programs, so bloggers who write about topics with popular keywords (that is, keywords that many advertisers bid on, driving the price for those keywords up, similar to an auction) are likely to earn more than bloggers who write about topics with less popular keywords. Of course, showing ads based on higher-value keywords is helpful to increase your earning potential, but that money doesn't come in unless visitors click those ads. The remedy: Experimentation. To find the best contextual link ad strategy, you need to test ad placement, keywords, and ad types to determine which ads are driving the most interest and revenue.

Google AdSense

Google AdSense is the most popular contextual link, pay-per-click ad program available to bloggers. Because Google owns both AdSense and Blogger, adding Google AdSense ads to your Blogger blog is extremely easy. Chapter 11 describes Google AdSense and explains in detail how to add it to your blog.

Kontera

```
www.Kontera.com
```

Kontera is another popular contextual link advertising program. When you sign up to serve Kontera ads on your blog, its ContentLink function automatically links contextually relevant keywords in your blog posts to ads. Those keywords appear with a double underline within your existing blog post. Figure 10-1 shows how Kontera ads look on a blog. When a visitor hovers the mouse cursor over the Kontera linked text, a small bubble box appears and displays an advertisement served by one of Kontera's advertisers. When a visitor to your blog clicks that advertisement, the advertiser's Web site opens in the browser. Kontera works harmoniously with Google AdSense and is open to bloggers whose blogs meet the current requirements outlined on the Kontera Web site.

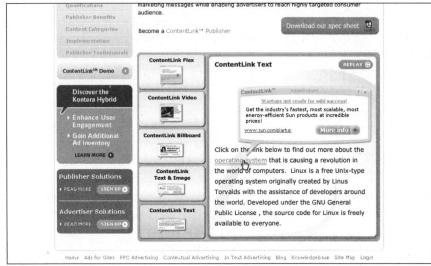

Figure 10-1:
Kontera
in-text ads
are offset
by a double
underline.

One of the best features about Kontera is its virtual lack of a footprint on your blog. Rather than use space in your sidebar or header or between your blog posts, Kontera in-text ads appear within your blog posts and link relevant ads to the words that are already used in your posts. It's a simple way to add a moneymaking option with some upfront effort but little ongoing work to keep it going. You can customize the look of your ContentLink ads, create filtering instructions to define the number of ads and advertisers allowed and customize other factors, too. Of course, for optimum results, you should monitor keyword performance and write your blog posts with high-performing keywords in mind.

The key to a successful blog is quality content. Don't write with keywords as your priority. If you write for ads, your visitors will know it. Ads should *enhance* people's visits on your blog, not overpower them or detract from them.

To add Kontera contextual link ads to your blog, follow these steps:

1. **Visit www.Kontera.com and sign up for an account.**

   Complete the online application to request a Kontera publisher account.

2. **After your application is accepted, simply sign in to your account and click the ContentLink Setup tab that allows you to add Kontera in-text ads to your Blogger blog, as shown in Figure 10-2.**

After you add Kontera in-text ads to your blog, analyze the ads that are served based on your content to ensure that they're relevant and helpful to your visitors. Also, review your Kontera-provided reports to ensure that the ads are driving revenue. Some people find Kontera ads to be obtrusive. You must analyze your results and your blog traffic statistics to ensure that the amount of money you make from Kontera ads is positive in relation to the effect of those ads on your blog's traffic.

Figure 10-2: The Kontera It widget.

Text link ads

Text link ads appear as simple text links on your blog based on the content of your pages. In short, when you join a text link advertising network, you submit specific pages of your blog into the network's inventory. Advertisers look for inventory pages that are likely to attract visitors who will be interested in their products and then purchase text link ad space on those pages. When space is purchased on your blog, a text link ad from that advertiser automatically appears in that space.

Text link ad rates, which are typically set by the advertising network, are usually based on a blog's Google page rank and Alexa rank. Although these two metrics aren't perfect, they comprise the standard that most text link brokers use to determine the amount of traffic to your blog and attach an advertising rate to it. Be sure, therefore, to submit your most popular blog pages to be included in a broker's inventory.

Text-Link-Ads

www.Text-Link-Ads.com

The popular text link broker Text-Link-Ads helps bloggers get paid for publishing text link ads, as shown in Figure 10-3. Ad publishers receive 50 percent of the sale price for each text link sold on your blog, and Text-Link-Ads integrate seamlessly with other advertising programs, such as Google AdSense. As a Text-Link-Ad publisher, you can approve or deny all ads that are purchased to display on your blog. The payout threshold is low, at just $25, and payment is sent by way of check or PayPal on the first day of every month.

Even though the payout threshold is low, which makes Text-Link-Ads attractive to bloggers with lower traffic levels, smaller bloggers find it difficult to get accepted as a Text-Link-Ads publisher. Blogs with a Google page rank of 4 or higher are automatically accepted; blogs with a rank lower than 4 are manually reviewed and typically aren't accepted. The price of ads shown on your blog is set by Text-Link-Ads using a proprietary algorithm that first considers your blog's traffic and page rank statistics.

To become a Text-Link-Ads publisher, follow these simple steps:

1. **Visit `www.Text-Link-Ads.com` and complete the online publisher application.**

   When your application is approved, you receive an e-mail providing you with your account information.

2. **Sign in to your Text-Link-Ads account and follow the instructions to install the ad code on your blog in the Get Ad Code section of your account.**

   You can find here the ad code to copy and paste into your blog, and instructions for doing so. After the code is pasted into your blog, ads begin appearing on your blog as they're purchased.

Figure 10-3:
This site offers a simple way to monetize your blog.

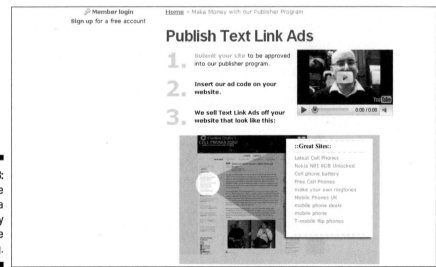

TextLinkBrokers

`www.TextLinkBrokers.com`

The popular text link ad broker TextLinkBrokers accepts applications from blogs with a Google page rank of 1 or higher. This site sets the ad rate for text link ads that appear on your blog based on your Google page rank and an evaluation of your blog. The ad publisher can approve or deny ads, and the payout threshold is $100. Overall, the process works similarly to Text-Link-Ads (see the earlier section "Text-Link-Ads").

To become a TextLinkBrokers publisher, visit `www.TextLinkBrokers.com` and complete the Publisher sign-up form, as shown in Figure 10-4. When you submit your sign-up form, TextLinkBrokers reviews your application and e-mails you with an acceptance or rejection. It also notifies you of the amount you'll be paid for links if your application is accepted and sends you a list of questions to answer in order to add your site to the TextLinkBrokers inventory.

When your site is added to the TextLinkBrokers inventory, an e-mail is sent to you with the information you need to create an account in the Partner's Console section of the TextLinkBrokers Web site.

After your partner's console account is created, you receive a link to activate the account.

When an advertiser selects your blog to place a text link ad, you receive an e-mail directing you to log in to your account to view details of the request.

The publisher's terms of service with TextLinkBrokers says that you agree to place ad requests (or deny them) on your blog within two business days.

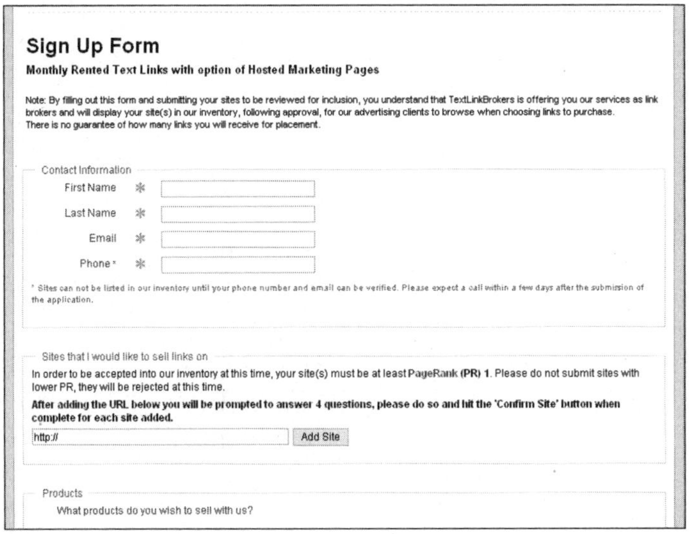

Figure 10-4: A simple application at an online publishing site.

Sign Up Form

Monthly Rented Text Links with option of Hosted Marketing Pages

Note: By filling out this form and submitting your sites to be reviewed for inclusion, you understand that TextLinkBrokers is offering you our services as link brokers and will display your site(s) in our inventory, following approval, for our advertising clients to browse when choosing links to purchase. There is no guarantee of how many links you will receive for placement.

Contact Information

First Name *

Last Name *

Email *

Phone *

* Sites can not be listed in our inventory until your phone number and email can be verified. Please expect a call within a few days after the submission of the application.

Sites that I would like to sell links on

In order to be accepted into our inventory at this time, your site(s) must be at least PageRank (PR) 1. Please do not submit sites with lower PR, they will be rejected at this time.

After adding the URL below you will be prompted to answer 4 questions, please do so and hit the 'Confirm Site' button when complete for each site added.

http://   [Add Site]

Products

What products do you wish to sell with us?

Text link ad warnings

Text link ads are an easy and unobtrusive blog monetization option, but they have some drawbacks. First and foremost, text link ads are often linked with a drop in Google search rankings. In short, many search engine optimization experts believe that Google downgrades sites that publish text link ads. The reason for the downgrade comes from Google's attempt to weed out Web sites that try to "buy" top search rankings. Having more incoming links from popular blogs and Web sites equates to receiving a higher Google ranking. However, when those links are paid for, the popularity of that Web site is unnaturally inflated. Google penalizes Web sites that pay for links and those that publish them,

according to many online experts, by lowering their Google search rankings.

It has been suggested that bloggers can mitigate Google penalties and still monetize their blogs with text ads by incorporating the NoFollow HTML tag with text ad links. However, doing so isn't beneficial to the advertisers paying for those links, which may lead to fewer text link ad buyers on your blog or your blog's removal from text link ad programs that rely on search engine recognition of those links. You can read more about the NoFollow tag in *Search Engine Optimization For Dummies,* by Peter Kent (Wiley Publishing).

Impression-based ads

Impression-based ads pay you as the publisher based on the number of times an ad is shown on your blog. With each page view where the ad is placed, that ad is delivered to a visitor, which counts as an impression. Cost-per-impression ads typically pay bloggers a small fee, such as ten cents per 1,000 impressions, so you're not likely to make a lot of money from these ads unless your site generates a lot of traffic each day. However, the ads are easy to set up and work particularly well below the fold (the area of the page that isn't visible unless you scroll down the page).

ValueClick

```
www.ValueClickMedia.com
```

ValueClick is an easy-to-use, impression-based advertising program that offers banner ads, pop-unders, videos, and rich-media ads, as shown in Figure 10-5. As the publisher, you can set the minimum cost per impression (CPM) that you're willing to accept on your blog. The minimum traffic level to become a ValueClick publisher is 3,000 impressions per month, and you can pick and choose which types of ads you want to run on your site.

Figure 10-5:
This program's
ads come in
a variety of
shapes and
sizes.

Take the time to read the complete ValueClick terms of service before you apply. The site has a wide variety of restrictions related to the types of blogs (for example, you must host your blog on your own domain, as discussed in Chapter 16) and blog content (no non-English pages or excessive advertising) that are accepted into the ValueClick ad program.

To sign up to become part of the ValueClick ad network, follow these steps:

1. **Visit www.ValueClickMedia.com and click the Join button in the Publishers section of the Web site.**

   This step opens the online application.

2. **Complete and submit the online application.**

   You receive, within 24 to 48 hours, an e-mail notifying you whether your application was accepted with additional instructions to set up your new account.

TribalFusion

```
www.TribalFusion.com
```

The popular impression-based advertising network TribalFusion operates globally. The site offers a variety of ad formats to publishers that receive a minimum of 2,000 unique users per day. Additionally, the blog must be active and updated frequently and must have a professional design. Tribal Fusion pays publishers 50 percent of all revenue made from their blogs. The payout threshold is $50 with payment made by check.

You can control the types of ads delivered on your blog by Tribal Fusion by blocking ad categories or specific advertisers. The site includes Flash ads and pop-up ads, which might be viewed as intrusive to your visitors. Be sure to monitor your Tribal Fusion revenue as well as any traffic changes to ensure that your efforts help you meet your overall goals for your blog.

To apply to become a Tribal Fusion ad publisher, simply complete the online application on the Tribal Fusion Web site, as shown in Figure 10-6. A representative from Tribal Fusion reviews your blog and responds to your application within one business week. If your application is accepted, instructions to establish your account are provided so that you can begin publishing ads on your blog.

Figure 10-6: Complete this application to become an ad publisher.

Affiliate ads

Affiliate ads help you generate an income based on your blog visitors' actions, similar to a sales commission business model. Most often, a visitor clicks an ad placed on your blog through your affiliate ad network membership, and you're paid when that visitor makes a purchase. Affiliate advertising comes in a wide variety of formats, allowing you to generate revenue from a myriad of products and services related to your blog.

In fact, affiliate ads perform best when the products offered by the ads appearing on your blog are directly related to your blog's topic. The reason is simple: People who visit your blog are likely to be interested in products and services related to your blog's topic. By visiting your blog, they've already demonstrated their interest in your blog topic, so offering products that might appeal to them based on that interest is a natural fit.

With so many programs to choose from, you must be sure to research each one, and test several, to find the ones that are the best match for your blog and your audience. The success of your affiliate advertising efforts comes directly from your efforts in finding the most suitable program to help you meet your blogging goals.

Amazon Associates

www.affiliate-program.amazon.com

Amazon.com is one of the most popular Web sites now online, so it makes sense that Amazon Associates is one of the most popular affiliate advertising programs available to bloggers. Amazon.com not only offers an incredibly wide variety of products to choose from to advertise with your affiliate link on your blog, but it also makes it extremely easy to set up your Amazon Associates account. Additionally, you face almost no barriers to entry.

To become an Amazon associate, simply visit the Amazon Associates Web site and click the Join Now link to fill out the online registration form. Doing so gives you immediate access to Associates Central, where you can build ad links and start earning money.

The Amazon Associates program also offers a great deal of flexibility and customization. You can choose from a wide variety of ad formats, as shown in Figure 10-7, and you can choose the specific products and links used in your Amazon Affiliate ads. You can even set up an Amazon store and link it directly to your blog to increase exponentially your Amazon Associates revenue-generating potential.

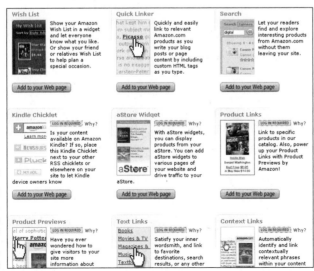

Figure 10-7:
Amazon
Associates
offers lots of
ad formats.

Because Amazon is a well-known brand, your blog visitors are likely to be comfortable clicking Amazon links and purchasing products from Amazon. However, the commission earned from Amazon Associates ads is typically small and varies greatly among bloggers. The bottom line: It takes time, experimentation, and patience to figure out how best to use Amazon Associates ads to monetize your blog, but the potential does exist to bring in revenue.

eBay Partner Network

`www.ebaypartnernetwork.com`

The eBay Partner Network is an excellent way to use the popularity of online auctions to generate revenue from your blog. The concept of the eBay Partner Network is similar to the Amazon Associates affiliate program in that you can create banners and links to products on eBay or an eBay storefront. When visitors to your blog click those links and make a purchase or win an auction, you earn a percentage of the revenue received by eBay. Additionally, as in the Amazon Associates program, you need to experiment with the eBay Partner Network to find the best products and ads that convert clicks from your blog visitors into sales and thus generate earnings for you.

Each eBay Partner Network program has different payment structures and ads, so be sure to read about the programs you're interested in before applying to make sure that they match your needs and goals.

To join the eBay Partner Network, simply complete the online application by clicking the Join Now link on the eBay Partner Network home page, as shown in Figure 10-8.

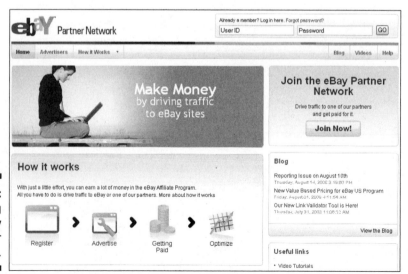

Figure 10-8: Joining the eBay Partner Network.

AllPosters

www.affiliates.allposters.com/affiliatesnet

AllPosters is a profitable affiliate program for blogs related to celebrities, sports, music, art, or other topics where visitors are likely to be interested in related posters or art. AllPosters sells posters, art, photography, magnets, apparel, and more with images from celebrities, travel, animals, movies, musicians, and education. Using the wide variety of ad formats offered by the AllPosters affiliate program, shown in Figure 10-9, you can include ads for specific products on your blog or create a storefront.

The AllPosters affiliate program pays a commission of 25 to 30 percent, with a payout threshold of just $20 paid monthly. You can imagine the potential income a niche site can generate if it ties nicely to the products offered on AllPosters. Think Britney Spears or Paris Hilton!

To join the AllPosters affiliate network, simply click the Join Now button on the Allposters affiliate program Web site and fill out the online application.

Figure 10-9:
Ads at this site revel in pop culture.

LinkShare

www.LinkShare.com

LinkShare, a large affiliate advertising network, works with hundreds of advertisers to provide ad inventory to publishers such as bloggers. Some of those advertisers are shown in Figure 10-10. When you become a LinkShare affiliate, you have access to revenue-generating opportunities from some of the most well-known brands in the world, such as Wal-Mart, American Express, LEGO, and others. You select the ads you want to display on your blog that you expect will meet your revenue criteria. Of course, selecting ads from advertisers whose products match the wants and needs of your blog visitors is the key to success.

Not all advertisers in the LinkShare network pay the same amounts, and not all pay based only on conversions. Take the time to research the various advertising options and choose the ones that work best for you, your blog, and your audience. Of course, take the time to experiment with different ads, advertisers, and other elements to find the best mix for your blog in order to generate the highest returns.

LinkShare is popular for many reasons:

✔ The program is open to just about anyone with few barriers to entry.

✔ People feel comfortable following links to Web sites (and buying products from) well-known brands and companies.

✔ The payout threshold is only $1 with payments made monthly.

Figure 10-10:
These advertisers include many well-known brand names.

To sign up with LinkShare, simply follow the Join link in the upper-right corner of the LinkShare home page and complete the online registration form. An e-mail is sent to you with instructions to complete your registration and begin selecting affiliate advertisements to display on your blog.

Commission Junction

www.CommissionJunction.com

Commission Junction is a well-known affiliate advertising program with a wide variety of advertisers in its CJ Marketingplace network. The site is owned by ValueClick Media (discussed earlier in this chapter, in the section "Impression-based ads"). Commission Junction works primarily with large companies and well-known brands, which typically appeal to consumers and blog visitors, particularly when the ads align closely with your blog topic. The minimum payout threshold is just $25 with payments made monthly.

On the negative side, in order to earn money through Commission Junction, you need to go through a multistep approval process. First, you sign up to become a Commission Junction publisher by using the online form, shown in Figure 10-11. After your application is accepted, you apply to each advertiser's program that you want to participate in, which can make the process to monetize your blog through Commission Junction a long one. Another drawback to Commission Junction is the user account center, which is more challenging to navigate than the interfaces offered by other affiliate programs.

Figure 10-11:
Fill out the form and get approved to join this well-known ad program.

Merchandising and mini-malls

Selling merchandise from your blog is a helpful way to bring in money. No matter what topic you blog about, you can likely find a way to link merchandise to it, whether you create a logo and sell T-shirts or imprint a quote on a magnet or button. If creating your own designs for merchandise doesn't work for you, some programs let you simply sell popular products, from iPods to baby gear and everything in between, from a wide variety of merchants.

CafePress

www.CafePress.com

CafePress is one of the most popular online merchandising Web sites, where people can upload custom designs to appear on products such as clothing, posters, calendars, and mugs. You can then sell those products from your own CafePress storefront, which can link directly to your blog by using a unique URL.

Each product is produced on-demand when an order is placed and shipped directly to the customer. CafePress also manages all exchanges and returns and offers customer service. You receive a check each month with your earnings from each sale, which come from the markup you choose to place on the base price of each item. You can open an unlimited number of basic shops for free and sell as many as 80 items per shop, or you can open a premium shop for as little as $4.99 per month and offer an unlimited amount of merchandise, which also gives you the most customization options. A premium shop tour is shown in Figure 10-12 to give you an idea of what a custom storefront provides.

Figure 10-12:
CafePress premium shop.

To create a CafePress store of your own, simply click the Sell Stuff link from the top navigation bar on the CafePress home page and then click the Start Selling Now button in the sidebar on the right to create your account. Follow the instructions to create your storefront, upload images, and perform other tasks. Simply link your blog to your store and you're done. Of course, promoting your store by blogging about it helps, too!

Make sure you own the copyright for (or get permission to use) any images or artwork you use on merchandise you sell.

Chitika eMiniMalls

`www.chitika.com`

Chitika eMiniMalls offer an interactive product merchandising service where ads for merchandise are shown based on the content of the page in which the ad code is placed. In other words, Chitika displays ads based on the keywords found on your blog page. The ads are unique in that they include a picture of the product and several tabs offering a product description and comparative shopping information, as shown in Figure 10-13.

Chitika eMiniMall ads are based on pay-per-click, and you earn 60 percent of Chitika's revenue each time someone clicks an ad on your blog. The payment threshold is just $10 for accounts paid by way of PayPal and $50 for accounts paid by check. You can easily sign up for the Chitika eMiniMall program by visiting the Chitika home page, clicking the Publishers link in the top navigation bar, and then clicking the Apply Now button to fill out the online application. A response is e-mailed to you as soon as your application is manually reviewed.

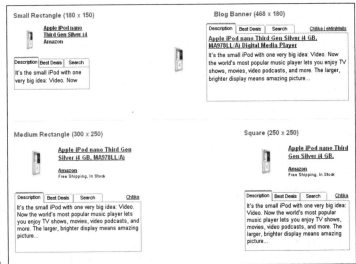

Figure 10-13: Compare shopping info at the Chitika site.

Chitika eMiniMalls work best on sites that are related to tangible products, receive a significant amount of traffic each month, and use highly targeted keywords. Chitika offers tools to help users choose keywords and maximize their earning potential, but it can take time and patience to figure out how to make Chitika eMiniMalls perform well on your blog. The potential exists to make a significant revenue stream after Chitika eMiniMalls are optimized on your blog.

Feed ads

Many bloggers use feed ads to monetize their blogs' RSS feeds. With more and more blog visitors using RSS feed readers to view their favorite blogs, bloggers have found that they lose money from lost page views. One way to combat that lost revenue is to add advertisements to your blog's feed. If you have an RSS feed set up for your blog, as described in Chapter 10, you might want to consider monetizing it with one of the following feed advertising programs.

Feedburner ads

As discussed in Chapter 9, FeedBurner is one of the most popular tools that bloggers use to create their blog feeds (called burning a feed). Because Google owns both Blogger and FeedBurner, you can easily add Google AdSense ads to your FeedBurner feed. Google AdSense is described in detail in Chapter 11.

Pheedo

```
www.pheedo.com
```

Pheedo offers RSS feed advertising from a wide variety of well-known brands and companies, including Microsoft, Ford, and ESPN. Ads are placed between, beside, or within your RSS articles or as stand-alone items. The position and format choices are up to you. Figure 10-14 shows how several Pheedo ad formats look online.

Your earnings from Pheedo are contingent on your feed traffic, the frequency with which you update your blog, your blog topic, and your blog's popularity. Advertisers determine how much they're willing to pay to reach your readers. Popular, highly trafficked, and frequently updated blogs typically generate significantly higher revenues from Pheedo RSS ads than smaller blogs do.

If you try Pheedo RSS feed advertising, make sure that you take the time to analyze your results in terms of the revenue generated from those ads as well as the impact on your overall traffic patterns. Some people find RSS feed ads to be intrusive. The last thing you want to do is turn away visitors because they don't like your RSS feed ads.

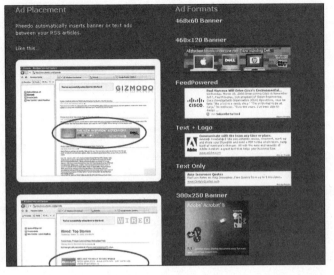

Figure 10-14:
Pheedo
ads are
available
in several
formats.

To join the Pheedo syndicated content advertising network, simply visit the Pheedo home page and click the Get Started button in the Publishers section on the right side of the screen. Complete and submit the online application, and a Pheedo publisher services professional contacts you for follow up.

Direct ads

Rather than rely on ad networks and third parties to provide advertising content for your blog, you can sell ad space directly. You can sell a variety of types of ads on your blog by setting up a page on your blog and announcing that you're accepting ads and inviting interested advertisers to send an e-mail for details. Selling ad space can be difficult until your blog grows to a minimum of at least 1,000 visitors per day, but it's certainly not impossible, particularly for niche topic blogs. Your Google page rank and Technorati authority ranking can also help you (or hurt you) in your direct advertising sales efforts.

Basically, an advertiser doesn't pay to place an ad on your blog unless the amount of exposure and number of click-throughs and conversions (such as leads or sales) bring in a higher return than does the initial advertising investment. Your goal in selling ads directly is to make your blog attractive to advertisers by offering appropriate rates based on the return they're likely to get.

Distinguishing between types of ads

Bloggers can sell just about any kind of ad they want directly on their blogs. The only limitation is what you can handle technically when you configure ads to appear on your blog. In other words, don't offer more than you're capable of delivering. If you're only comfortable copying code or images from the advertiser into a page element in your blog's sidebar, offer only that type of ad on your blog.

The following list describes some of the most common types of ads that bloggers sell directly:

- ✓ **Sidebar button, skyscraper, or other image-based ad:** Your sidebar is an excellent place for ads. You can place 125x125 pixel button ads, larger skyscraper ads, or an image ad of any size that fits in your sidebar to use that area in the best way to meet your goals.

- ✓ **Sidebar text link ads:** Your sidebar can contain a multitude of text links. Of course, too many text links become cluttered and make your blog unreadable, but adding a small number of text link ads is a great way to monetize your blog.

- ✓ **Graphical ads between posts:** Just as you can insert image-based ads in your sidebar, you can also insert them between blog posts.

- ✓ **Text link ads between posts:** Just as you can insert text link ads in your sidebar, you can add them between your blog posts.

- ✓ **Text link ads within posts:** Advertisers might want to purchase a specific keyword and ask you to use it in an upcoming post.

- ✓ **Banner ads in the header:** If your header has room to fit a banner ad, you can monetize that space and sell advertising there.

Selling and negotiating

After you decide to sell ads on your blog directly, you need to create an Advertise Here page or section on your blog. Include your contact information for details, and then you can negotiate each ad with buyers individually. After your blog grows big enough and interest in advertising on your blog increases, you can publish your acceptable ad rates and formats on your Advertise Here page. By that time, you'll have a good idea of what types of ads work on your blog and which rates are appropriate to charge.

Have your site statistics ready (refer to Chapter 9), because advertisers will ask for them. Be prepared to share your rankings, subscriber numbers, page views, and number of visitors and unique visitors, and have access to other stats in case they're requested. Additionally, advertisers may ask for demographic information about your readers. You might know some of that information from communicating with your readers. For more specific information, you can use a service such as www.Quantcast.com to find out more about your audience or survey your audience using a free survey service, such as SurveyGizmo (www.surveygizmo.com) or SurveyMonkey (www.surveymonkey.com).

The most important thing about selling ads on your blog directly is to ensure that you don't exaggerate your blog's traffic or reach. Be honest in what you believe you can deliver for advertisers and charge your rates accordingly.

Sponsored reviews

Sponsored reviews help you get paid for writing and publishing posts. Advertisers search for bloggers to write posts and reviews, for example, about their brands, products, and Web sites to create an online buzz, increase Web site traffic, and boost sales. A number of companies run sponsored review networks, and the three most popular are discussed in this chapter.

Each sponsored review network operates similarly in that you submit your blog for inclusion in the network's marketplace. If your blog is approved, you can either search for sponsored review opportunities that your blog qualifies for, or advertisers can search for your blog based on the criteria they establish for each opportunity. When you accept a sponsored review opportunity, you're given the requirements of the opportunity and a time-frame within which the sponsored post must be published. The payment amount is agreed on upfront and is typically based on the specific opportunity as well as on the Google, Technorati, and Alexa rankings of your blog.

Be sure to read the specific rules for each sponsored review network you consider joining. Each network has individual nuances that make it unique.

Sponsored reviews are a useful way for smaller bloggers to make some extra money, but they can also hurt your blog in the long run. Unfortunately, Google and other search engines don't like paid links, and the links in a sponsored review are exactly that. If the sponsored review network you join doesn't use the NoFollow HTML tag, discussed earlier in this chapter, and doesn't allow you to fully disclose sponsored reviews on your blog, Google is likely to downgrade your page rank or remove your blog from its searches entirely, which can lead to a significant decline in search-related traffic to your blog. With that in mind, you should consider avoiding sponsored review programs that don't use the NoFollow HTML tag, don't allow you to disclose your posts as paid for by sponsors and don't allow you to write honest reviews.

PayPerPost

www.payperpost.com

PayPerPost is the pioneer of sponsored reviews. Bloggers who join the PayPerPost marketplace submit an application by clicking the Sign Up Now button on the PayPerPost home page, shown in Figure 10-15. After your application is accepted, you can set up your blog's profile, select your blog's category, and begin looking for opportunities.

Figure 10-15: The pioneer of sponsored reviews.

PayPerPost bloggers have six hours to complete an assignment after accepting an opportunity and are paid 30 days after the sponsored review post is published. Opportunities begin at $5 and can increase to thousands of dollars, but those high-paying opportunities are typically available only to blogs with very high amounts of traffic.

ReviewMe

www.reviewme.com

At ReviewMe, another popular sponsored-review network, bloggers can click the Signup Now button on the home page, as shown in Figure 10-16. When your application is approved, you can set up your blog information for advertisers to find you. Rather than search for opportunities as you do on PayPerPost, advertisers search for bloggers with ReviewMe.

Figure 10-16:
Joining
ReviewMe.

When an advertiser sends an opportunity to you, you can approve or reject it. Completed reviews typically pay between $20 and $200, but higher-paying reviews are usually reserved for highly trafficked blogs.

SponsoredReviews

www.SponsoredReviews.com

SponsoredReviews works a bit like both PayPerPost and ReviewMe, in that bloggers can search for opportunities and bid on jobs, which allows for rate negotiation directly with the advertisers, and they can create a blog profile and let advertisers bring offers to them, which they can accept or reject.

If you accept an opportunity through SponsoredReviews, you're given three days to complete the assignment. Your post is reviewed to ensure that it meets specified guidelines, and you're paid by way of PayPal every two weeks. SponsoredReviews opportunities are available from $10 to $1,000, but the higher-paying reviews are usually available only to extremely popular blogs.

You can sign up for SponsoredReviews by clicking the Free Sign Up button on its home page, shown in Figure 10-17.

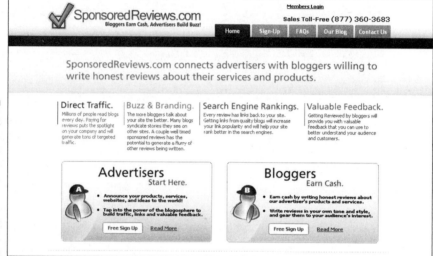

Figure 10-17:
Connecting
advertisers
with
bloggers
willing
to write
honest
reviews.

Other monetization options

Advertising and merchandise sales are common, but you're not limited to those moneymaking options on your blog. Don't be afraid to be creative and think "out of the box." What would your blog readers enjoy? Find ways to provide the content, links, and information your readers want, and then create ways to monetize them.

You can even extend your monetization opportunities outside your blog. For example, as your blog grows in popularity and your online presence becomes stronger, you can seek out opportunities to write paid articles for online publications and magazines, for example, or pursue paid speaking engagements as an expert in your blog's topic. The opportunities are available with creative thinking, effort, and commitment. Check out the monetization options in the following sections for some ideas to get you started.

Donations

As your blog and your audience grow, you can ask visitors to donate money to help keep the blog going. You can use that money toward hosting costs, contest prizes, design costs, and other costs. To make the process of asking for donations simple, you can add a PayPal (www.PayPal.com) donation button to your blog, which automates the process by electronically transferring the money from the donor's account to yours. An example of a PayPal donation button is shown in Figure 10-18.

Figure 10-18: A PayPal donation button.

Setting up a PayPal account takes only a few minutes and can be quite helpful as your blog grows to accept advertising payments, pay hosting fees, and much more. After your PayPal account is up and running, you can simply use the tools provided on the PayPal Web site to create your Donation button and upload it to your blog by adding a new gadget to your sidebar, as described in Chapter 8.

Guest blogging

Guest blogging is a simple process of writing a post to be published on another blogger's blog. Guest blogging works well as a promotional tool, particularly when you write a guest post that appears on a blog that's more popular than your own. To get started as a guest blogger, contact other bloggers whom you admire or whose audience is similar to your own and pitch a guest post idea. If the other blogger accepts your guest post, you can simply write it (always include a link to your own blog in your guest posts) and provide it to the other blogger for publishing. The goal of guest blogging for free is to get your name out there across the blogosphere and build an online reputation as well as generate traffic to your blog.

After your blog is established and you're well known online, you can begin offering your guest blogging services for a fee. Some of the most popular bloggers charge several hundred dollars to write a guest post. You have to start with lower fees, of course, but the potential exists to make some extra money from paid guest blogging. Advertise your service on your blog, social networks, and other outlets to spread the word and generate interest. To make the process easy, you can use your PayPal account to accept payment.

Chapter 11

Maximizing Revenue with Google AdSense

Google AdSense is the most popular moneymaking method available to bloggers. With its ease of integration into your Blogger blog, AdSense is usually one of the first moneymaking methods that bloggers try. Although you aren't likely to get rich by using AdSense (at least not right away), it's a widely accepted and fairly unobtrusive option.

In fact, your success with AdSense depends on a number of factors discussed in this chapter. However, you have no way of knowing how AdSense ads will perform on your blog until you register for an account and start displaying ads. This chapter teaches you how to create an AdSense account, insert Google AdSense ads into your blog, and track your success with AdSense.

Making Sense of AdSense

Google AdSense is a contextual link advertising program. Advertisers bid on keywords related to their products, brands, Web sites, and other elements by using the Google AdWords program. You can get more information about the Google AdWords program by reading *Google AdWords For Dummies,* by Howie Jacobson (Wiley).

Bloggers and Web site owners sign up as publishers on the Google AdSense program and allow Google to serve ads related to the content of their blog or Web site pages. Relevant ads are chosen using a set of secret rules created by Google which is based on keywords found on blog or Web site pages where ads are to be served. When a person clicks on an AdSense ad, the publisher (the blogger or Web site publisher), receives a portion of the revenue earned from those ads. The rates that publishers are paid vary significantly depending on the popularity of the keywords that advertisers bid on for the ads served on their blogs or Web sites.

To maintain the integrity of your blog, you should review the ads served on your blog and filter out any specific advertisers whose ads you don't want to display. Although all ads undergo the Google editorial review process, you shouldn't rely on it to block ads that don't match your readers' expectations for your blog. Instead, review the ads your visitors are seeing and ensure that they're appropriate for your blog and your audience. You can set ad filters and restrictions to block inappropriate ads from the Google AdSense dashboard, discussed in more detail later in this chapter.

Exploring the available ads

Google AdSense ads come in two popular formats for bloggers:

- ✔ **AdSense for content:** Ads are displayed based on the content of your page. Ads can be in text or graphical format and link to a separate page determined by the advertiser. You're paid when a visitor clicks on the ad.

- ✔ **AdSense for search:** A search box is displayed on your blog where visitors can enter search terms to find more information. You're paid when the visitor clicks a link that's returned in the search results, making it a two-step process before you generate earnings.

You can customize the appearance of the AdSense ads displayed on your blog, including the colors of the border, title, background, text, and URL. You can also choose from a wide variety of ad formats, including text ads, image ads, video ads, link units, and themed units. These features are discussed later in this chapter, in the section "Setting Up AdSense on Your Blog."

Finding your way around Google AdSense

Google AdSense does all the work for you to help you earn money from your blog. You simply need to create an account and configure your blog settings in order to start making money. The success of your Google AdSense ads comes from your efforts to maximize return. The following list describes several ways you can help boost your AdSense earning potential:

- ✔ **Write focused content.** Google AdSense ads are served based on the content found on the page of your blog where those ads appear. Make sure that your content is focused on a single topic to ensure that related ads are displayed.

- ✔ **Do your keyword research.** To maximize your AdSense income, take some time to research keyword popularity. Open your own Google AdWords account and analyze the going rates for keywords related to your blog's niche. Use tools such as the ones available at www. wordtracker.com to further research keyword popularity. The more popular a keyword is, the higher advertisers have to bid to serve ads related to it. Try to write content that is relevant to your blog's topic and that maximizes popular keywords.

- ✔ **Increase traffic to your blog.** With more visitors comes the potential for more clicks on your AdSense ads, and that means increased earnings for you. Chapters 12 and 13 discuss how you can grow your blog's audience in detail.

- ✔ **Test, test, and test again.** Much of your AdSense success comes from experimentation and finding out what works best. Test ad types, ad placement, and keywords to determine how to maximize your AdSense earning potential.

- ✔ **Avoid covering your blog in Google AdSense ads.** Too many ads make your blog cluttered. Rather than click your ads and help you earn money, visitors click away from your blog entirely if they can't find useful content amid the many ads. The quality (the *relevancy*) of the ads you display on your blog is more useful than the quantity.

Understanding Google AdSense policies

Before you start your AdSense account, read the Google AdSense program policies. Publishers have to adhere to a variety of restrictions and requirements in order to participate in the AdSense program. If you're caught violating the AdSense policies, your account is disabled, and you're removed from the program. The AdSense policies in the following list give you an idea of what you are *not* allowed to do as an AdSense publisher:

- ✔ **Click ads that appear on your own blog.** Avoid click fraud of any kind. Don't click your own ads or allow any kind of automated robot to click your ads.

- ✔ **Display too many AdSense ads.** Google has specific restrictions related to how many AdSense ads can appear on a page in your blog at any time. Check the most recent version of the program policies to ensure that you're adhering to the rules.

- ✔ **Ask people to click your AdSense ads.** Again, avoid click fraud of any kind. Even a small suggestion to someone about clicking the AdSense ads that appear on your blog can be deemed click fraud.

- ✔ **Publish pages that include AdSense ads but no other useful or original content.** Google considers pages that include AdSense ads but no other original, useful content to be spam. Sites that simply copy content from other sites or publish nothing but ads on their pages are removed from the AdSense program if they're caught.

- ✔ **Publish ads that look like AdSense ads but aren't AdSense ads.** Check the AdSense program policies to confirm the most current restrictions related to the other types of ads you're allowed to display on your blog along with AdSense ads. Don't publish any other ads that can be confused with AdSense ads.

- ✔ **Publish unacceptable content.** The AdSense program policies list a myriad of site content restrictions, including pornography, gambling, and excessive profanity. Be sure to read the restrictions before you sign up for an AdSense account.

- ✔ **Reveal your earnings per click.** Although you can give a general idea on your blog of how much money you make from AdSense (for example, $1,000 per month), it's a violation of AdSense policies to reveal how much you're paid per click for specific ads.

Three pages of restrictions are listed in the Google AdSense program policies. Be sure to read them and adhere to them, or else you stand a strong chance of having your AdSense account deactivated. Getting back into the AdSense program after your account has been deactivated is no small feat.

Getting help

Many blogs and Web sites are dedicated to unraveling the mysteries of AdSense success. If you're serious about maximizing your earning potential with Google AdSense, read *Google AdSense For Dummies,* by Jerri Ledford (Wiley) for extensive instructions and tips. Help is also available on these Web sites:

✔ **Google AdSense blog:** www.Adsense.blogspot.com

✔ **Google AdSense Help Center:** www.Google.com/AdSense/Support

✔ **Google AdSense Help Group:** www.groups.google.com/group/adsense-help

Registering with AdSense

Before you can include AdSense ads on your blog, you have to sign up to become an AdSense publisher and Google has to approve your blog for the program. Google AdSense is free to publishers, and ads are available in numerous languages to match appropriate ads with publishers from around the world.

To sign up for Google AdSense, follow these steps:

1. **Visit the AdSense home page at www.google.com/adsense and click the Sign Up Now button.**

   The button is on the right side of the page, as shown in Figure 11-1. This step opens the online application.

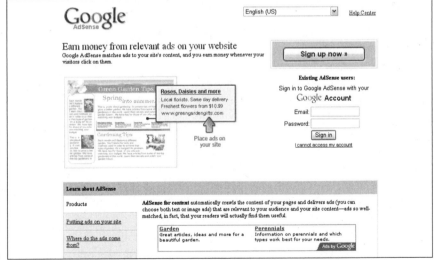

Figure 11-1: The Sign Up Now button on the Google AdSense home page.

2. **Enter the requested information in the appropriate fields of the online application.**

   Be sure to complete all fields shown in Figures 11-2 and 11-3 to ensure that your application is approved in a timely manner.

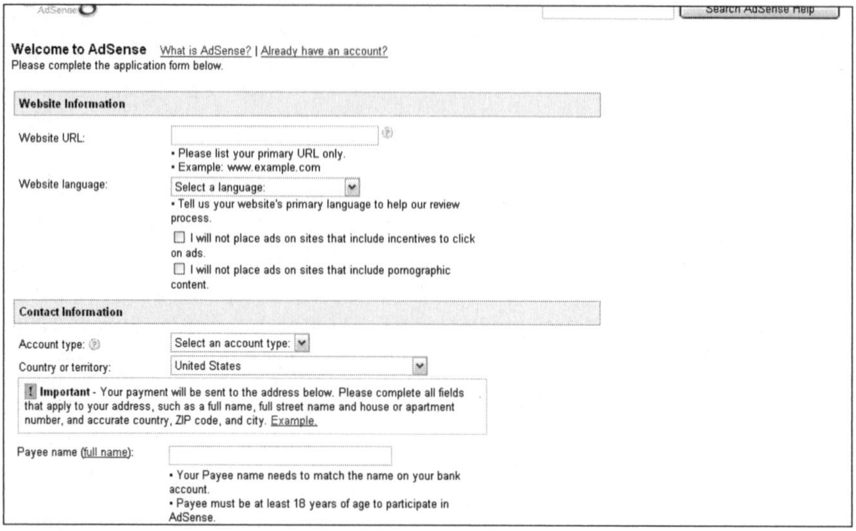

Welcome to AdSense   What is AdSense? | Already have an account?
Please complete the application form below.

Website Information

Website URL:
• Please list your primary URL only.
• Example: www.example.com

Website language: Select a language:
• Tell us your website's primary language to help our review process.

☐ I will not place ads on sites that include incentives to click on ads.

☐ I will not place ads on sites that include pornographic content.

Contact Information

Account type: Select an account type:

Country or territory: United States

⚠ **Important** - Your payment will be sent to the address below. Please complete all fields that apply to your address, such as a full name, full street name and house or apartment number, and accurate country, ZIP code, and city. Example.

Payee name (full name):
• Your Payee name needs to match the name on your bank account.
• Payee must be at least 18 years of age to participate in AdSense.

Figure 11-2:
The Google AdSense application.

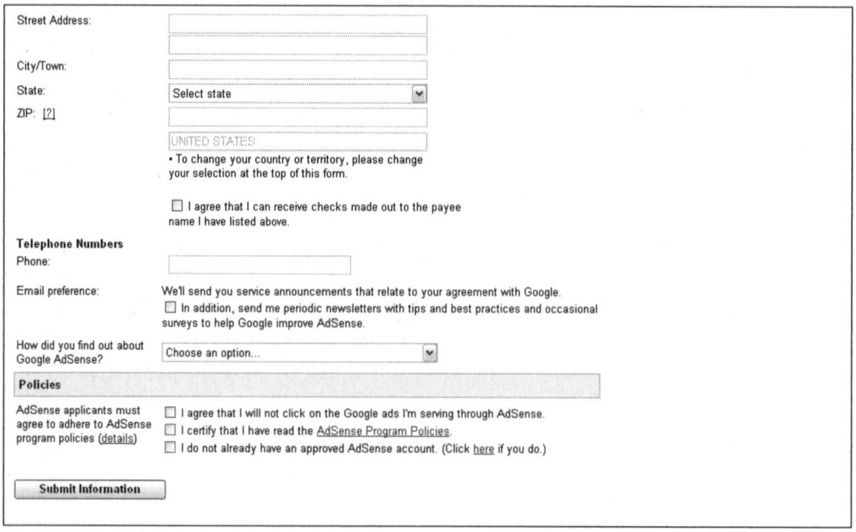

Street Address:

City/Town:

State: Select state

ZIP: [?]

UNITED STATES
• To change your country or territory, please change your selection at the top of this form.

☐ I agree that I can receive checks made out to the payee name I have listed above.

Telephone Numbers
Phone:

Email preference: We'll send you service announcements that relate to your agreement with Google.
☐ In addition, send me periodic newsletters with tips and best practices and occasional surveys to help Google improve AdSense.

How did you find out about Google AdSense?   Choose an option...

Policies

AdSense applicants must agree to adhere to AdSense program policies (details)
☐ I agree that I will not click on the Google ads I'm serving through AdSense.
☐ I certify that I have read the AdSense Program Policies.
☐ I do not already have an approved AdSense account. (Click here if you do.)

[Submit Information]

Figure 11-3:
Google policies appear in the bottom half of the AdSense application.

Your payments are sent to the address included in your application unless you change your payment method after your account is set up as described later in this chapter. Be certain to enter the correct address.

 3. **Click the Submit Information button when your application is complete.**

Google reviews your application and notifies you by e-mail when your application is accepted or rejected.

Be certain to read the AdSense program policies in the Policies section of the online application to ensure that you understand what you can and cannot do as a Google AdSense publisher.

4. After your application is approved, log in to your AdSense account and familiarize yourself with the AdSense dashboard.

Using the navigation bar at the top of the page after you log in, notice the area to view and create reports, set up your ads, review and change your account settings, and find additional resources and help.

5. Select the AdSense Setup tab from the top navigation bar to configure your ad settings.

You can use the tabs in the top navigation bar of the AdSense Setup page (shown in Figure 11-4) to set up your ads, color palette, filters, and allowed sites, or you can make these configurations from the Blogger dashboard, as discussed in detail later in this chapter.

Figure 11-4:
Configure your AdSense ads from the AdSense Setup page.

Setting Up AdSense on Your Blog

As a Blogger user, you benefit from the fact that Google owns both AdSense and Blogger. Rather than set up your ads by using the Google AdSense dashboard, you can set them up directly in Blogger, making it that much easier to monetize your blog with AdSense after you have an approved and activated Google AdSense account.

Before you start placing AdSense ads on your blog, take some time to understand which ad formats are available to you and how you can best integrate those ads into your blog to maximize revenue without sacrificing traffic. Also, keep in mind that you can customize the color palette of the ad units you choose to display on your blog to either blend the ads into your blog's design or contrast them against that design. These options are discussed later in this chapter.

Too many ads on a page make your blog cluttered and drive away traffic. Visitors are looking for compelling content, not ads. The ads you include on your blog should complement the page and help visitors, not distract and confuse them.

Choosing an ad format

Google AdSense ads come in five primary formats: text ads, image ads, video ads, link units, and themed units. Each one is explained in more detail in the following sections.

Text

Text ads typically include a link, a short marketing message, and a URL. You can choose the size and number of ads displayed on your blog based on the text ad format you choose. Figure 11-5 shows how several text link ad-format options look. You can choose from 12 different text ad formats to find the best options for your blog.

If you add Google AdSense ads to your blog directly by using Blogger, fewer ad format choices are available to you. To place ads in additional formats, you need to place them by using your Google AdSense dashboard, where you can select ads, copy the necessary code, and place the code in a new gadget on your blog.

Images

Image ads include a graphical image and a URL. They're available in eight sizes, and you can select the size that works best on your blog. You can see four size option examples in Figure 11-6.

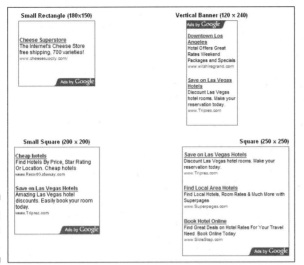

Figure 11-5: AdSense text ads.

Figure 11-6: Image ads are colorful and eye-catching.

Video

Video ads come in seven sizes and include an animated Play button that plays a short video advertisement when clicked. A URL is also displayed in a video ad. When a visitor plays the video, the URL displays as an active link button at the end of the ad. You can see four size option examples in Figure 11-7.

Figure 11-7:
Google
AdSense
video ads
come in four
size options.

Link units

Link units are basically lists of topic links. Each link leads a visitor to a list of links related to that topic from advertisers. If one of those links is clicked, the advertiser's Web page opens and you earn money. With that in mind, remember that it's a two-step process to earn money from link units. However, link units are the least intrusive ad format simply because they include the least amount of extraneous text and no graphical images. That means they can blend easily into any blog. Figure 11-8 shows examples of link unit ad formats.

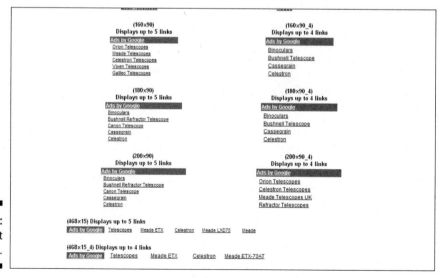

Figure 11-8:
Link unit
ads.

Themed units

Themed units change depending on the time of year. Themed units have the potential to perform well on blogs directly related to a seasonal holiday or an event matching the ads served. Figure 11-9 shows examples of themed units.

Figure 11-9:
Themed
units.

Choosing the appropriate ad size

Ad sizes are always communicated in pixels as width by height. AdSense ad sizes can vary from small, 120 x 90 link units to large, 728 x 90 leader boards. The following list describes different ad sizes and where they might work well on your blog:

- ✔ **Leader board:** Typically wide and short. Google AdSense leader board ads are 728 x 90 and fit well in a blog's header or footer.

- ✔ **Skyscraper:** Typically narrow and long. Google AdSense skyscraper ads are 120 x 600, and wide skyscraper ads are 160 x 600. Skyscraper ads fit well in sidebars.

- ✔ **Banner and half banner:** Come in a variety of sizes and are typically wide and short, but can also be produced as vertical banners, where the ads are long and narrow. Banner ads work well in a variety of places, including the header, footer, sidebar, and between posts, depending on the selected size.

✔ **Button:** Increasingly the most popular blog sidebar advertising format is the button ad. You commonly see button ads, which measure 125 x 125, placed side by side and in groups of two, four, six, or eight in a blog's sidebar.

✔ **Square and rectangle:** Come in a variety of sizes and typically work well in sidebars and in between blog posts.

Choosing the appropriate ad size for your blog is basically a process of balancing the intrusiveness of the ad with your monetization goals. Naturally, larger ads are more noticeable, but if those ads are bothersome to your visitors, your traffic can decrease as a result. Don't be afraid to experiment and find the right ad format and size choices for your blog.

Placing AdSense ads on your blog

Your blog's sidebar is a perfect place to ad Google AdSense ads. By simply adding a Google AdSense gadget to your blog layout, ads automatically appear on your blog, assuming that you already set up your Google AdSense account. Follow these steps to ad a Google AdSense unit to your blog:

1. Select the Layout tab from your Blogger dashboard.

The Page Elements page opens, shown in Figure 11-10.

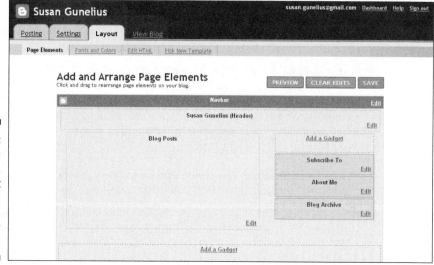

Figure 11-10:
Click the
Add a
Gadget
link to add
AdSense
ads to your
blog.

2. **From the Page Elements page, click the Add a Gadget link on the right side of the page to add a new gadget to your blog's sidebar.**

   The Add a Gadget window opens.

3. **Scroll down within the Add a Gadget window until you see the AdSense element and then click the AdSense link, as shown in Figure 11-11.**

   This step opens the Configure AdSense window.

Figure 11-11: AdSense is listed in the Add a Gadget window.

4. **Using the Format drop-down menu in the Configure AdSense window, shown in Figure 11-12, choose the ad size you want to display on your blog.**

   Click the radio button next to Text and Image if you want to show both ad formats or the radio button next to Text Only to display only text ads.

5. **Using the Colors drop-down menu, choose a color scheme or select individual colors to format your AdSense ads.**

   You can view your changes in the Preview area before you accept them.

6. Under the Advanced heading, ensure that the correct AdSense publisher ID is shown.

This ID is for the account that's paid when visitors click the ads on your blog.

This step is particularly important if you have more than one AdSense publisher ID.

7. Click the Save button.

This step reopens the Page Elements window.

8. Click the View Blog link after the `Page Element Added` message beneath the top navigation bars, shown in Figure 11-13, to see your changes.

AdSense ads begin displaying on your blog automatically, as shown in Figure 11-14.

You can add multiple Google AdSense gadgets to your blog's sidebars, footer, and other elements. Be sure to check the current Google AdSense policies to ensure that you don't add more units than allowed.

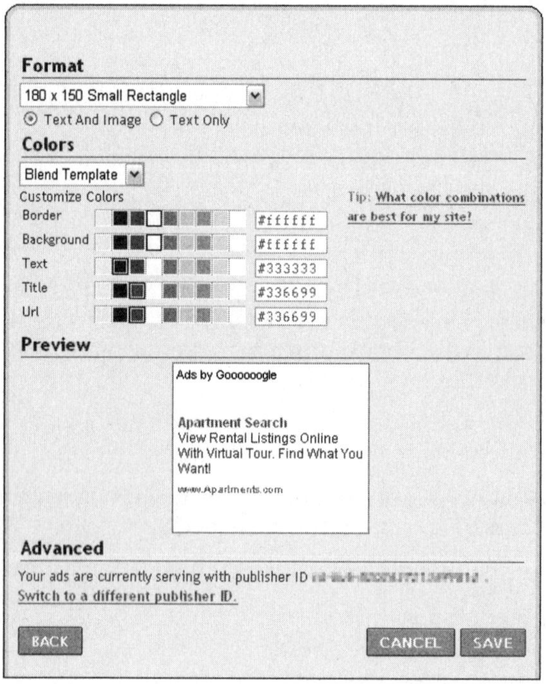

Figure 11-12:
Choosing formatting options for your ad.

The View Blog link

Figure 11-13:
The View
Blog link.

Figure 11-14:
Google text
ads fit well
in a blog's
sidebar.

Adding AdSense ads between blog posts

Ads placed between blog posts typically perform well; however, they can be intrusive. Use your own judgment related to your moneymaking goals and your visitors' preferences to help you decide whether to include AdSense ads between your blog posts. If you decide to include them, follow these steps to get started:

1. **From the Blogger dashboard, click the Layout link.**

   This step opens the Page Elements page, shown in Figure 11-15.

2. **Click the Edit link in the lower right corner of the Blog Posts element box.**

The Edit link

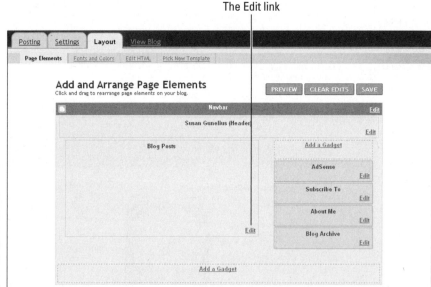

Figure 11-15:
The Edit link within the Blog Post element.

The Configure Blog Posts window opens, as shown in Figure 11-16.

3. **Select the Show Ads Between Posts check box.**

   When this check box is selected, the window expands to display the Configure Inline Ads section, shown in Figure 11-17.

4. **In the Configure Inline Ads Section, choose the color scheme you want to use for your ads by either using the Colors drop-down box or selecting individual colors from the palette.**

   Preview your changes in the Preview section.

5. **Click the Save button when you're done.**

   This step reopens the Page Elements page, where you can click the View Blog link to see your changes live on your blog, as shown in Figure 11-18.

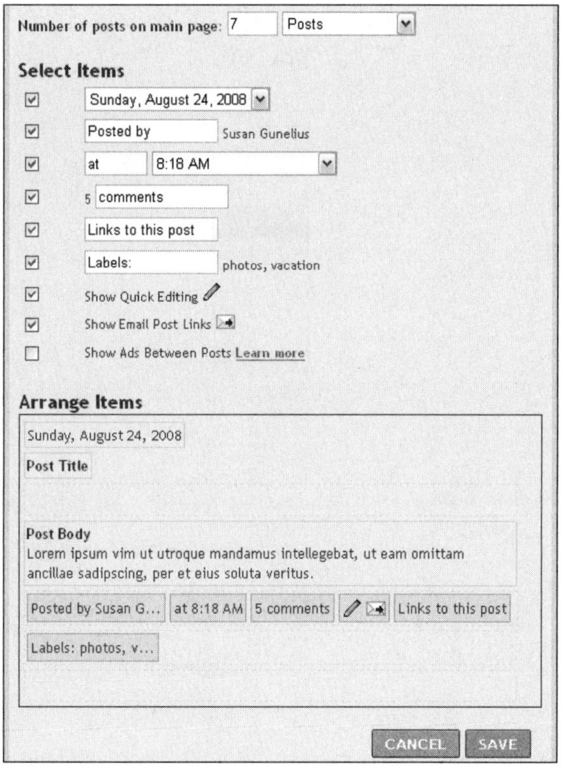

Figure 11-16:
The
Configure
Blog Posts
window.

☑ Show Quick Editing ✎

☑ Show Email Post Links ✉

☑ Show Ads Between Posts Learn more

Configure Inline Ads

Show after every 1 ⌄ posts (up to 3 times on a page).

Format

300 x 250 Rectangle ⌄

⦿ Text And Image ○ Text Only

Colors

Blend Template ⌄

Customize Colors

Border		#ffffff
Background		#ffffff
Text		#333333
Title		#336699
Url		#999999

Tip: What color combinations are best for my site?

Preview

Ads by Goooooogle

Apartment Search
Search here for Apartment Search
zimply.com

Apartments for rent
Quickly search online listings & submit a lead via email. aff
www.apartments.com

Need a place to live?
apartment search Stop searching - find out how now!
Apartments.Near.You.TrueLocal.com

Apartments For Rent
Search By Location And Price View Photos Plus Floorplans
www.Faster-Results.com

Advanced

Figure 11-17:
Configuring
AdSense
ads that
appear
between
blog posts.

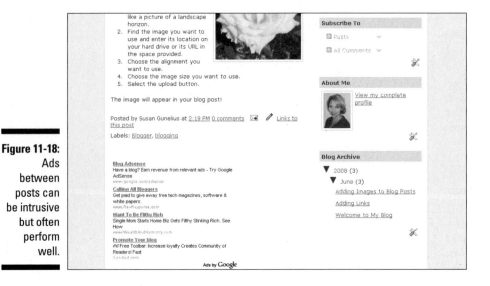

Figure 11-18:
Ads
between
posts can
be intrusive
but often
perform
well.

Configuring AdSense for Feeds

Adding Google AdSense ads to your blog's feed takes several steps, but luckily, they are not difficult. As discussed in Chapter 9, feeds are a popular way for people to read content from multiple blogs in a single location called a feed reader. Rather than visit each blog to see whether any new content has been published, people can subscribe to a blog's feed. All the feeds a person is subscribed to are collected together and delivered by using a single feed reader, such as Google Reader.

With the growing popularity of viewing blogs by way of a feed reader rather than visiting numerous blogs, bloggers were faced with decreasing page views and a loss in revenue from advertising. For example, if your blog has no visitors, it also has no one to click your AdSense ads. Because Google owns Blogger, AdSense, and FeedBurner (the most popular tool to create, or "burn", your blog's feed, as described in Chapter 9), it isn't surprising that it has become quite easy to add Google AdSense ads to your Blogger blog's feed through FeedBurner.

Follow these steps to configure AdSense ads to appear in your blog's RSS feed by using FeedBurner.

1. **Visit the FeedBurner home page at `www.feedburner.com`, shown in Figure 11-19.**

Figure 11-19:
Burning
your feed.

   2. **In the long text box in the middle of the page, enter your blog's domain name and click the Next button.**

      This step opens the Identify Feed Source window, shown in Figure 11-20.

Figure 11-20:
Use your
blog's RSS
feed to
burn your
FeedBurner
feed.

   3. **Click the radio button next to the RSS feed and click the Next button.**

      This step opens the feed verification window, shown in Figure 11-21.

   4. **Click the Sign In link if you already have a FeedBurner account, or enter the necessary information in the appropriate fields to start a new FeedBurner account. Then click the Next button.**

      The Congratulations window opens and displays your FeedBurner feed URL, as shown in Figure 11-22.

   5. **Copy the new FeedBurner feed URL for your blog. In a different browser window, open your Blogger account and click the Settings link from your Blogger dashboard.**

      The Basic Settings page opens.

   6. **Click the Site Feed link from the navigation bar to open the Site Feed page, and paste the FeedBurner feed URL that you just copied for your blog into the Post Feed Redirect URL text box, shown in Figure 11-23.**

      This step redirects your RSS feed to your FeedBurner account.

   7. **Click the Save button. Next, return to the browser window where you have FeedBurner open and you just copied your feed URL. Click the link at the bottom of the page that says Skip Directly to Feed Management.**

      This step opens a page where you can begin configuring settings for your feed, as shown in Figure 11-24.

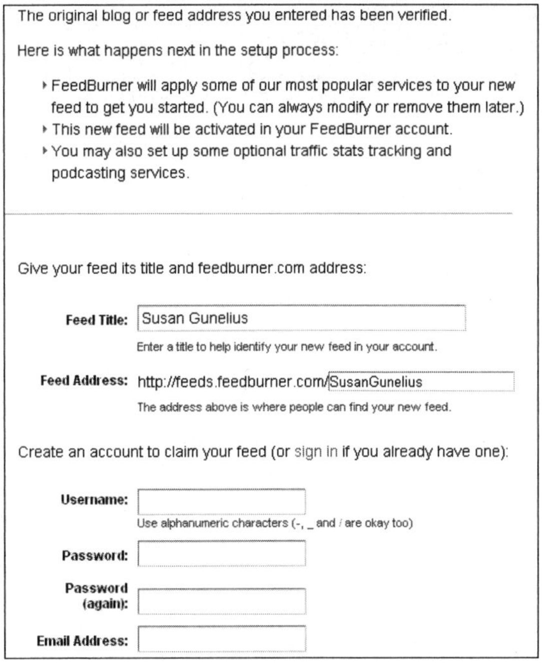

The original blog or feed address you entered has been verified.

Here is what happens next in the setup process:

▸ FeedBurner will apply some of our most popular services to your new feed to get you started. (You can always modify or remove them later.)
▸ This new feed will be activated in your FeedBurner account.
▸ You may also set up some optional traffic stats tracking and podcasting services.

Give your feed its title and feedburner.com address:

Feed Title: Susan Gunelius

Enter a title to help identify your new feed in your account.

Feed Address: http://feeds.feedburner.com/SusanGunelius

The address above is where people can find your new feed.

Create an account to claim your feed (or sign in if you already have one):

Username:

Use alphanumeric characters (-, _ and / are okay too)

Password:

Password (again):

Email Address:

Figure 11-21:
After your feed is verified, complete the activation process by signing in to FeedBurner or creating a new account.

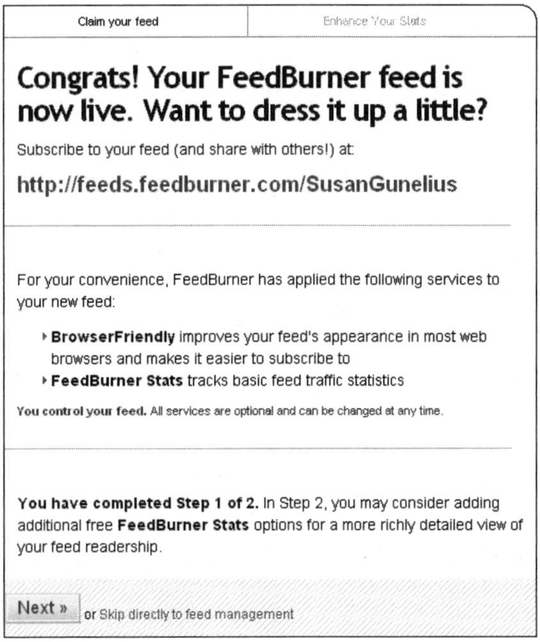

Claim your feed	Enhance Your Stats

Congrats! Your FeedBurner feed is now live. Want to dress it up a little?

Subscribe to your feed (and share with others!) at:

http://feeds.feedburner.com/SusanGunelius

For your convenience, FeedBurner has applied the following services to your new feed:

▸ **BrowserFriendly** improves your feed's appearance in most web browsers and makes it easier to subscribe to
▸ **FeedBurner Stats** tracks basic feed traffic statistics

You control your feed. All services are optional and can be changed at any time.

You have completed Step 1 of 2. In Step 2, you may consider adding additional free **FeedBurner Stats** options for a more richly detailed view of your feed readership.

Next » or Skip directly to feed management

Figure 11-22:
The Congratulations window.

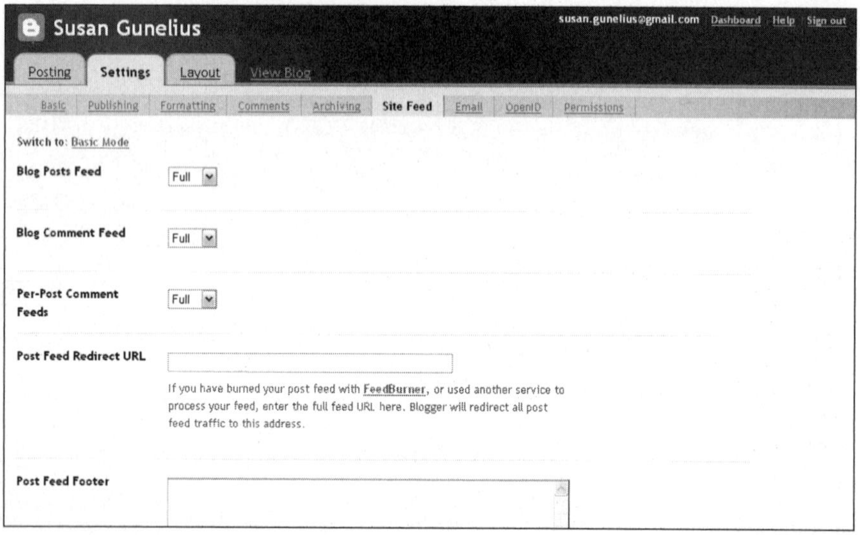

Figure 11-23:
The Post
Feed
Redirect
URL text
box.

Figure 11-24:
Configuring
AdSense for
your blog's
feed.

8. **Select the Monetize tab from the navigation bar.**

   The Configure Ads page opens, as shown in Figure 11-25.

9. **Click the Sign In to AdSense link to sign in to your AdSense account.**

   Enter the username and password for your AdSense account.

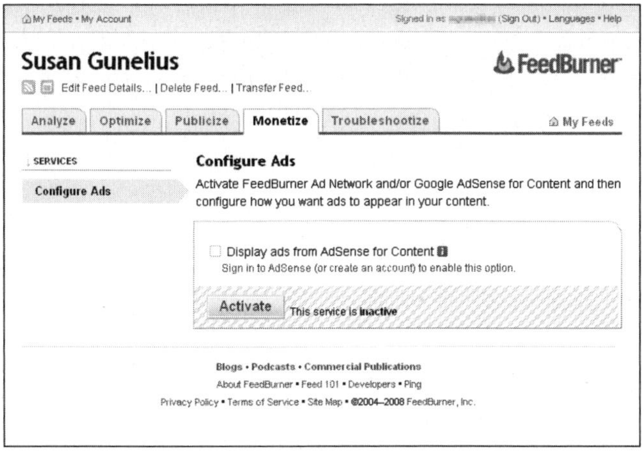

Figure 11-25:
The
Configure
Ads page in
FeedBurner.

10. Return to the Configure Ads page and click the Activate button.

When you return to the Configure Ads page after signing in to your AdSense account, the page expands to include options for you to customize the appearance of AdSense ads in your blog as shown in Figure 11-26.

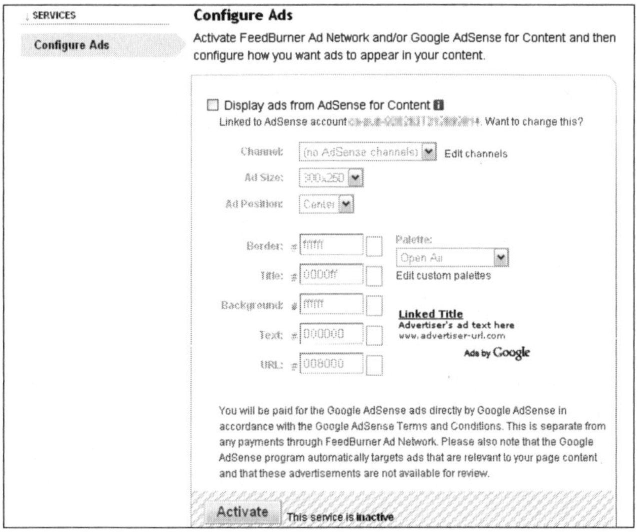

Figure 11-26:
An
expanded
Configure
Ads page in
FeedBurner.

11. Click the Display Ads from AdSense for Content radio button and then click the Activate button.

Near the bottom of the page, a new section of the Configure Ads page opens, titled Get the HTML Code to Put Ads on Your Site, as shown in Figure 11-27.

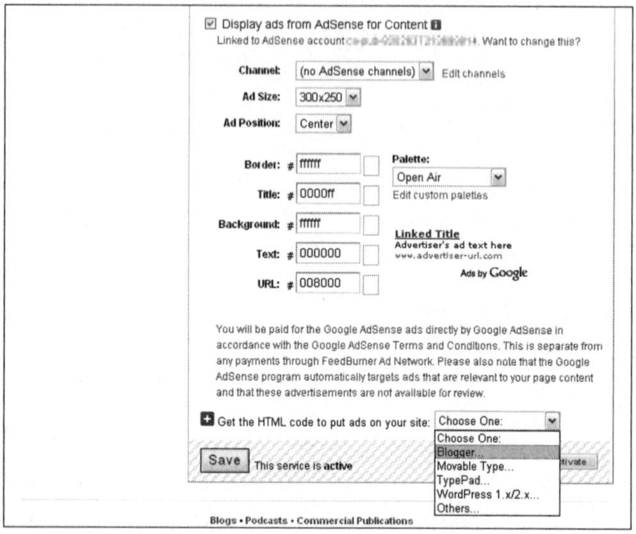

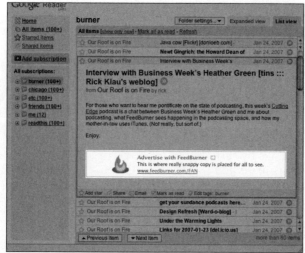

Figure 11-27:
Getting the
HTML code
to display
Google
AdSense
ads in your
blog's feed.

12. **Choose Blogger from the drop-down menu.**

    A new window opens with instructions for adding FeedFlare to Your Blogger blog. FeedFlare works behind the scenes to display AdSense ads on your blog's FeedBurner feed.

13. **Follow the instructions and copy the supplied code into your blog's template as directed.**

    After the code is properly added to your blog's template, AdSense ads appear in your blog's feed by way of FeedBurner. An example is shown in Figure 11-28.

Figure 11-28:
AdSense
ads appear
in your
blog's feed
as text ads,
text ads
with logos,
or banners.

Getting Paid

The payment process for Google AdSense publishers is simple: You're paid whenever someone clicks one of the AdSense ads that appear on your blog. Your earnings depend on several factors, including how much traffic your blog receives, how relevant the ads are to your blog visitors, and how much the advertiser had to bid to serve the ad based on specific keywords triggered by your blog content. Much of your earning potential through Google AdSense comes from trial and error and determining which combination of ads performs best on your blog without hurting your traffic levels.

AdSense publishers must reach a threshold of $100 in order to get paid. Earnings roll over from one month to the next until you earn a minimum total of $100. After you reach that threshold, you're paid by check or electronic transfer to your bank account, depending on your settings in the My Account section of the AdSense dashboard. Payment is typically made within approximately 30 days of the end of the month in which you reach the $100 payout threshold. In other words, if you reach the $100 threshold in June, you should receive payment by the end of July. You can access your payment history from the Google AdSense dashboard.

You cannot change your payment method or enter required tax details into your account until you reach $10 in earnings. At that point, a personal identification number (PIN) is mailed by snail mail to the payment address listed in your account. (Make sure that it's accurate.) You must enter the PIN into your account before any payments are sent to you. The PIN can take two to three weeks to arrive. You may also be required to verify your telephone number. If so, you're called at a predetermined time and asked to enter a verification number that's provided within your AdSense account. Google notifies you if this step is required.

Tracking Your Success

An important component of your AdSense success is tracking your results. Don't limit your analysis to earnings. Be certain to compare earnings by ad unit, ad format, and ad placement to find which ones are bringing in the most revenue. Also, analyze the performance of your AdSense ads against your blog's traffic statistics, as described in Chapter 9, to ensure that your ads aren't negatively affecting your traffic levels. You can track the performance of your AdSense ads by selecting the Reports tab within the Google AdSense dashboard, which leads you to the Overview page, shown in Figure 11-29. By selecting the Advanced Reports tab from the navigation bar, you can create a wide variety of customized reports, as shown in Figure 11-30.

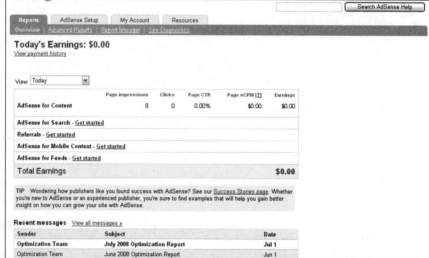

Figure 11-29:
The
AdSense
Reports
Overview
page.

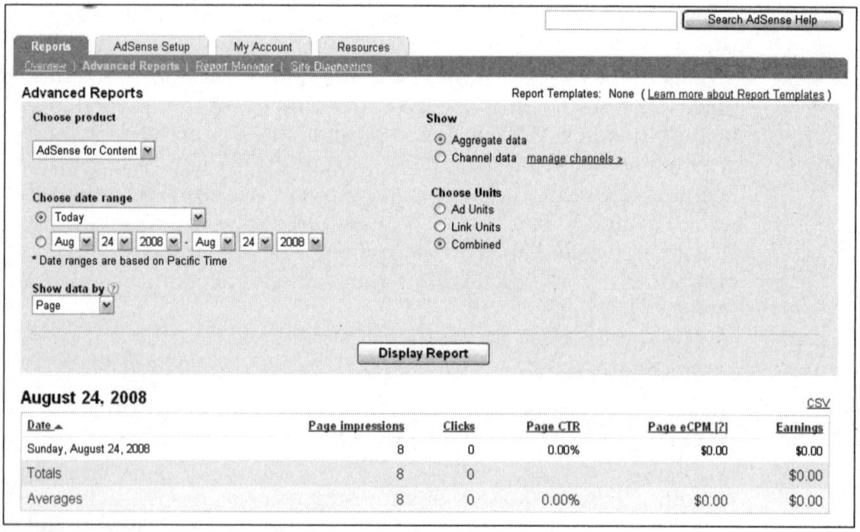

Figure 11-30:
Google
AdSense
Advanced
Reports.

Much of your success with Google AdSense or any advertising program comes from the amount of traffic your blog receives. Chapters 12 and 13 provide a variety of ideas and information about growing your blog and attracting visitors to it by way of networking and relationship building, promotion, and search engine optimization.

Part IV
Growing Your Audience

The 5th Wave   By Rich Tennant

Serch Injin
Optamazashun

Kee Werd
Stratageez

1. Top

"How long has he been programming our META tags?"

In this part . . .

*I*f you want your blog to grow and attract more visitors (leading to more moneymaking opportunities), make sure that you read Part IV. Chapter 12 shows you how to use the tools available to you on the social Web to build an audience, including social networking and social bookmarking.

You can also grow your blog by using organic search. Every time a person enters keywords into a search engine, it can translate into traffic to your blog. Chapter 13 shows you the basic search engine optimization concepts to help you grow your blog from search engine traffic.

Chapter 12

The Power of Networking and Relationship Building

In This Chapter

▶ Making your blog entries show up in search engines

▶ Finding your way around the social Web

▶ Discovering social networking

▶ Getting the hang of social bookmarking

▶ Using microblogging

*M*uch of your success as a blogger comes as a result of hard work and patience, but you can help move things along more quickly by using the tools available to you to promote your blog. A world of people search online every day, and helping them find your blog is the best route to building your blog's traffic. How do you reach all those people?

This chapter starts you on the path to raising awareness of your blog and driving traffic to it. You also find out how to become an active member of the social Web both on and off your blog and to develop relationships that are the key to your ultimate blogging success. Remember that your blog becomes whatever you want it to be, so your job is to invest the time and effort required to take it there.

Submitting Your Blog to Search Engines

Although many search engines find your blog eventually, you should make sure that *eventually* happens sooner rather than later by submitting your blog to popular search engines. Doing so ensures that your blog is on each search engine's radar screen and that your blog posts begin appearing in user searches. If you optimize your posts for search, as discussed in detail in Chapter 13, and acquire more and more incoming links, your rankings in search engine keyword queries should rise.

The higher your content appears in search engine rankings, the greater the possibility that someone clicks your link and finds your blog. If you write outstanding content and post consistently and frequently, your traffic should increase over time. The following sections describe how to submit your blog to some of the most popular search engines.

Don't waste time submitting every page of your blog. Just submit your blog's main page to each search engine, and they find the rest automatically.

Google

www.google.com/addurl/?continue=/addurl

To submit your blog to Google, simply go to the online submission form, shown in Figure 12-1, and enter your blog's main URL. It's usually your blog's home page, and you should include the `http://` part of your blog's URL (for example, `http://www.myblogdomain.com`). You can enter any additional information or keywords that you want to provide, but they don't affect your submission or appear with it after your page is indexed. Then type, in the text box, the spam-blocker text that appears on your screen and click the Add URL button. It's that easy!

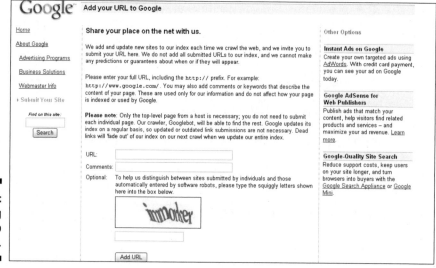

Figure 12-1: Submitting your blog to Google.

Yahoo!

```
https://siteexplorer.search.yahoo.com/submit
```

You can submit your blog to Yahoo by visiting the online submission form. Enter your blog's URL in the first text box and click the Submit URL button, shown in Figure 12-2. You can also enter your blog's feed URL in the second text box. Instructions for creating your blog's feed by using FeedBurner are in Chapter 11.

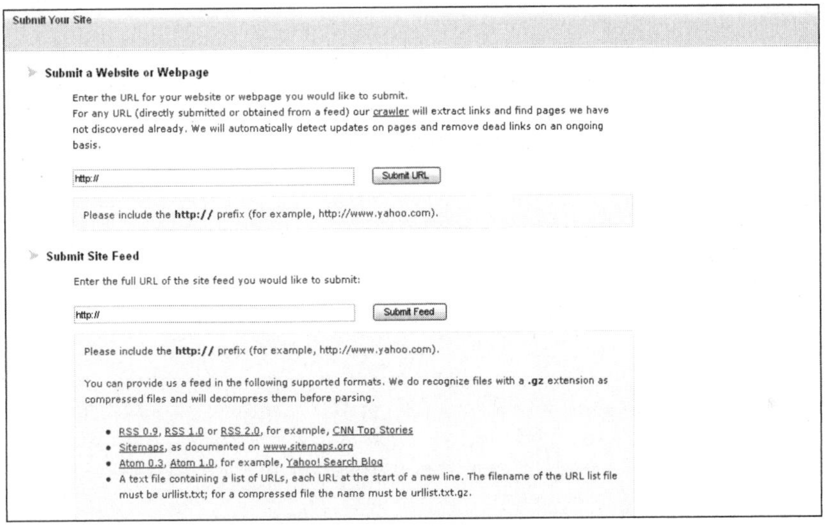

Figure 12-2: Submitting your blog to Yahoo.

MSN Live Search

```
http://search.msn.com/docs/submit.aspx
```

Visit the MSN Live Search submission page, shown in Figure 12-3. Simply type into the appropriate box the spam-blocker text that's displayed, and enter your blog's URL in the text box. Click the Submit URL button and you're done.

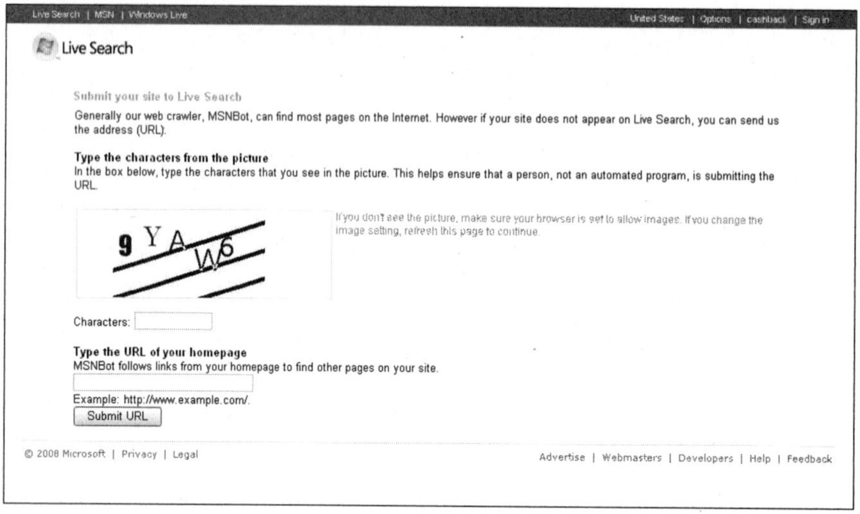

Figure 12-3:
Submitting
your blog to
MSN Live
Search.

Technorati

http://technorati.com/account/signup

Submitting your blog to Technorati, a blog search engine, is a multistep process. First, complete the online form to become a Technorati member, as shown in Figure 12-4, and select the I Have a Blog and Would Like to Claim It Now check box. You can then enter your blog's URL to claim it as yours. Note that Technorati membership is free.

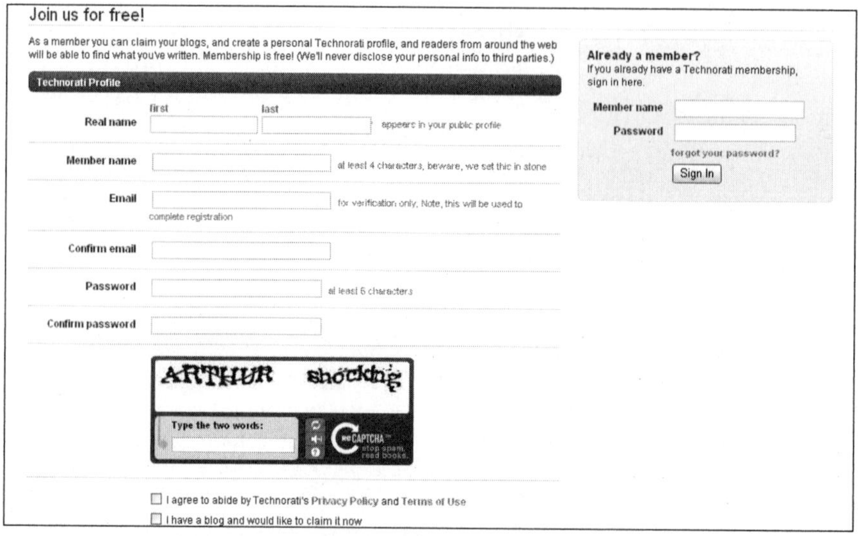

Figure 12-4:
Creating a
Technorati
account.

Submitting your blog to search engines isn't critical, but it can speed up the process of having your blog included in search engine results. To find out whether your blog is already included in search engine results, visit each search engine and type your blog's URL in the Search box. If your blog is included in the returned results, it has already been indexed by that search engine.

Navigating the Social Web

With the start of the 21st century came a new generation of the Internet: Web 2.0, or the *social Web*. At this time, Web content moved away from being one-sided, where Web sites typically provided information and transaction processing but little more. Web 2.0 ushered in a new type of Internet: Rather than have content pushed to users, they jumped on-board and began creating content of their own. The Internet went from being a passive medium to an active one and user participation began to control the online world.

More and more people now join the social Web by starting blogs, participating in online forums and chat groups, listening to online radio, watching and sharing videos, joining social networking sites, and participating in social bookmarking activities. The opportunities to join the conversation and share information are seemingly endless, and people and businesses are still just in the beginning stages of discovering how best to use the social Web.

Web 2.0 is still in its infancy, despite long strides having been made in a relatively short length of time. Throughout the brief evolution of the social Web, however, blogging has become an icon of what it's all about — sharing and actively discussing and participating.

Blogs become most successful when the bloggers behind them understand and maximize the opportunities that the social Web provides. It isn't a place to simply post information and walk away. Rather, it's a place to publish information and then encourage other people to comment, react, share, and discuss. The tools of the social Web can help bloggers promote their blogs and gain awareness and recognition for them, but it's the bloggers' efforts at building a community around the blog that can make or break their blogs' success.

Building a blog community

Most successful bloggers give the same answer when asked to identify the most important thing that helped them become successful — their communities of readers. The people who visit your blog enjoy what you have to say and return to read more. They can become your most loyal readers if you engage them and make them feel welcome and valued. These people get to know each other and develop online relationships with each other over time, and all have a few things in common: They share an interest in your blog's topic, they like what you have to say, and they feel comfortable visiting and discussing the topic at hand. That comfort level comes from the atmosphere you create on your blog.

Here are some ideas for how you can create a sense of community on your blog:

- ✔ Encourage visitors to leave comments. Ask questions in your blog posts, and encourage readers to leave comments with their opinions.
- ✔ Conduct a poll or host a contest to move lurkers to action.
- ✔ Request guest posts or content submission suggestions from your readers.
- ✔ Start an ongoing question-and-answer post series where you ask readers to submit questions and then you publish posts with the answers.
- ✔ When readers leave comments on your blog, take the time to respond to them. Leave comments in return to show readers that you value their contributions and to show other readers that each comment and reader is important to you.

Over time, your loyal readers will even step up to the plate and begin responding to comments before you have a chance to do so! Your job as the blogger is to spark the conversations on your blog, encourage them to continue and flourish, and reign in side conversations or inappropriate comments.

Publish a blog comment policy to protect your readers and your blog's reputation from the inevitable inappropriate comments that someone will leave on your blog someday.

Commenting on other blogs

Just as you want people to leave comments on your blog and start a conversation, other bloggers want the same thing on their blogs. An important part of being a member of the social Web is actively participating in it by venturing outside your blog and forming relationships with other bloggers. An easy way to start is to visit other blogs, particularly other blogs within your topic niche, and leave comments on posts you enjoy.

Leaving comments on other blogs not only makes those blog authors aware of who you are but also — when you include your URL with your comment — makes it more likely that the blog's author or readers will click your URL to find out more about you and read more of what you have to say. This statement is especially true if you leave relevant, thought-provoking comments.

Don't leave useless comments on other blogs, such as "Nice post." Instead, take the time to truly add to the conversation.

Tracking back

Although the Blogger software doesn't accept or send traditional trackbacks, you can use the backlinks function within Blogger to see who else links to your blog posts. Alternatively, you can link to other blog posts within your own posts, and those links are seen in the other bloggers' traffic statistics reports as referrals. Here are a couple of tips for using backlinks:

- ✔ When you link to another blog post, always click that link in your live post to ensure that it's working.
- ✔ Make sure that the backlinks function is set to allow backlinks on your blog posts. When Google Blog Search identifies blogs that link to yours, a backlink is published beneath the comments section in your blog posts. The backlink includes a snippet from the post that linked to yours and a live link to that post.

Bloggers like trackbacks and backlinks because those elements give them an opportunity to leave a link to their own blogs on another blog, which can drive traffic. Trackbacks and backlinks also notify other bloggers that you're interested in their content and you're sharing it, which gives them more exposure and more opportunities for increased traffic and incoming links.

When you find a blog post idea in another blogger's post, always link to the original source in your own post, to give that blogger credit for writing about it first. Doing so not only keeps you in line with the unwritten rules of the blogosphere but can also help you build a relationship with another blogger and drive traffic to your blog over time as your name and blog become more recognizable.

Introducing Social Networking

Social networking is just like traditional face-to-face networking, but rather than meet and talk to people in person, you do it by using the social Web. A variety of Web sites allow people to register for memberships, interact with other members, share content, and develop relationships. Some of those Web sites are discussed later in this chapter, but you also have ways to network online without using a specific membership Web site. In other words, don't think that social networking occurs on specific sites created solely for that purpose. Use any opportunity to network online to promote your blog just as you would if you were networking and promoting a business or yourself for a new career in face-to-face situations.

Promoting your blog by using social networking

As discussed earlier in this chapter, responding to comments left on your blog, leaving comments on other blogs, and linking to other blogs in your own posts are a few simple ways to meet other bloggers and develop relationships with them as well as potential new readers to your blog. All these activities can be considered forms of social networking.

Additionally, you can join one of the many online forums available on just about any topic you can think of and become an active participant. This strategy works best when the forums you're involved with are directly related to your blog's topic. You can also include a link to your blog in your e-mail signature, which gives every person who receives an e-mail from you the opportunity to discover your blog and possibly become a new networking connection related to your blog's topic.

Checking out popular social networking sites

Social networking can take a variety of forms and purposes, and a wide variety of social networking Web sites are available. Names such as MySpace, Facebook, LinkedIn, Friendster, and Orkut are just a few of the big players in the online social networking realm. Where should you start to build a profile, connect with people, and promote your blog? To get you going, the following sections provide an overview of three of the most popular social networking Web sites.

MySpace

www.MySpace.com

In terms of organized social networking, MySpace can be considered a viable option. If the truth is told, however, MySpace is more than a social networking tool because it provides far more options than social networking functionality, such as the ability to create individual blogs. It also allows anyone to create a MySpace page for any purpose. That means MySpace may not be useful for all blog topics.

MySpace has a reputation of being the place to be for teenagers and bands looking to make a break into show business. Although it's possible for anyone to set up a MySpace profile and build an online presence from it, some bloggers (think of a business blog or a highly technical blog) don't want their profile to be mixed with their 12-year-old daughter's page dedicated to the teen idol of the moment. It's up to you to determine whether MySpace is the right place for you to spend your time networking and building relationships.

Invest your time in networking at sites visited by people who might be interested in your blog topic. Look for like-minded people and begin developing relationships with them by sharing content, ideas, and links they might be interested in.

To join MySpace, follow these steps:

1. **Visit the MySpace home page.**

2. **Click the Sign Up link on the right side of the top navigation bar, shown in Figure 12-5.**

3. **Complete and submit the online application.**

4. **Set up your profile.**

The key to successfully using your MySpace page to drive traffic to your blog is to make friends with other MySpace users and get to know them by leaving comments on their profiles and starting conversations. You can learn all the details about using MySpace in *MySpace For Dummies,* 2nd Edition, by Ryan Hupfer, Mitch Maxson, and Ryan Williams (Wiley).

The Sign Up link

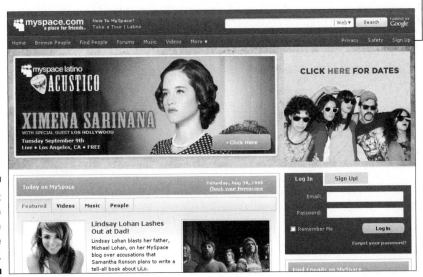

Figure 12-5:
The Sign Up link on the MySpace home page.

Facebook

www.Facebook.com

When you're looking at sites specifically designed for social networking, remember that Facebook is one of the most popular options. Facebook is different from MySpace in that you can view complete profiles of only the people who are in your network, which means that Facebook is better for targeted networking and protected from spam. Although Facebook was originally created for college students, it has grown to become a popular social networking tool for people from around the world and from all walks of life, regardless of age or organization.

Here are some ways you can use Facebook to drive readers to your blog:

✔ Add your blog's feed to your Facebook profile.

✔ Post personal notes and updates to keep people within your network apprised of what you're working on and news you want to share. For example, if you just wrote an excellent blog post that you think is worthy of other bloggers linking to, you can send a message or publish an update about it on your Facebook profile to spread the word.

✔ Use the Facebook Groups function to create a group for just about anything you want and invite people to join it. Then you can send messages, share information, and converse with the members of that group.

To join Facebook, simply complete the signup form on the right side of the Facebook home page and click the Sign Up button, shown in Figure 12-6. Make sure that you take the time to create a comprehensive profile and start making friends!

Figure 12-6:
Facebook offers a wealth of networking opportunities for bloggers.

Bloggers can use Facebook in many ways to promote and grow their blogs, businesses, or themselves. For more ideas and tips, read *Facebook For Dummies,* by Carolyn Abram and Leah Pearlman (Wiley).

LinkedIn

www.LinkedIn.com

LinkedIn has a reputation of being the go-to place for business and career-related social networking. It has a stripped-down interface that's intended to be free of spam and irrelevant content. Rather than add "friends," LinkedIn users make *connections.* Similar to Facebook, you cannot view another member's profile unless you have been introduced to that person and are connected to him. Finding another person on LinkedIn can be difficult, which is a common complaint.

Your LinkedIn profile acts similarly to an online résumé. In it, you upload your business and career accomplishments. Then you can add your blog information. If your blog is related to your career or business in any way, your LinkedIn profile can be another tool to help you drive traffic to it. The more connections you make, questions you answer, and relationships you build, the more potential you have for blog traffic.

You can join LinkedIn by visiting the LinkedIn home page and completing the Join LinkedIn Today form on the right side of the page, shown in Figure 12-7. When your account is activated, be sure to take the time to create a comprehensive profile and then start making connections.

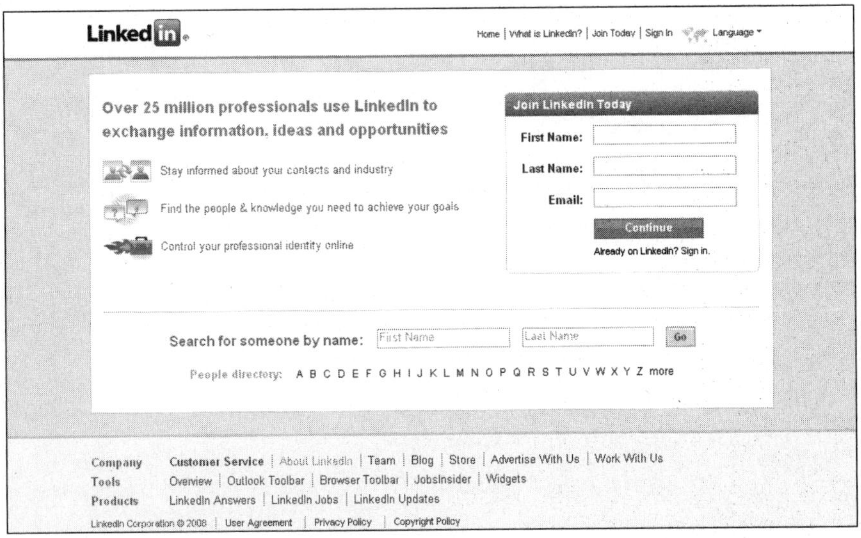

Figure 12-7: LinkedIn is the social network for career and business development.

You can read about other popular social networking sites in Chapter 17.

Understanding Social Bookmarking

Social bookmarking is basically having an online list of your favorite Web links that you can share with others. Rather than save a Web page you like by using your Web browser's Favorites or Bookmarks function, you can save those pages online using a social bookmarking site for access from any computer at any time.

Have you ever been using a computer that doesn't belong to you and tried to find a page that you saved in your home computer's Favorites menu? The problem is solved when you use a social bookmarking site to save your favorite Web pages because, rather than save them on your hard drive, they're saved online. You simply log in to your account at the social bookmarking site and — voilà — all your saved Web pages are available to you. You can easily find your saved pages by using a social bookmarking site because you can save them using *tags* — keywords to help you categorize your saved links that make it easy to find them later.

Social bookmarking becomes social when you share your bookmarks with other users. Most social bookmarking sites are set up so that saved links are automatically available for other users to find when they search for content using specific tags. Furthermore, many social bookmarking sites use some kind of voting mechanism that lets users drive links to the home page of the site for the world to see by simply adding them to their own bookmarks, which "votes them up." Alternatively, some social bookmarking sites let users bury links by "voting them down."

Promoting your blog by using social bookmarking

The social aspect of social bookmarking helps bloggers promote their blogs. If you find a blog post or article online that you think other people will enjoy, add it to a social bookmarking site. Be sure to

✔ **Include a helpful description:** To encourage people to click through to read your entire submission

✔ **Use relevant keywords:** To help people find your submission

The more outstanding content you submit, the better your reputation becomes on that site. That means more users get to know you, which creates more relationships that can turn into blog traffic.

Following the rules

Even social bookmarking sites have rules. Keep in mind that these rules are most important to follow if you're using social bookmarking sites as a way to promote your blog and build relationships to that end. If you're simply using social bookmarking for your own, personal purposes, you might not have to be as concerned with these rules. However, you never know how your blog or online activities can grow and change. One day, you might want to use social bookmarking sites for more than online storage of personal favorites. Again, read the rules for each site you use and follow them to ensure your long-term success.

Following are a couple of rules that are common among social bookmarking sites:

- ✔ **Do not submit your own content:** Some social bookmarking sites don't like users to submit their own content and penalizes users who do so. Be sure to read the policies and restrictions related to each social book-marking site you join so you don't waste time submitting content that might be buried immediately. On social bookmarking sites with restrictions related to submitting your own content, ask your friends or colleagues to submit your content for you, or post a message in your social networking profiles to ask your friends and connections to submit your content for you. That's just one more way that social networking can help you to promote your blog!

- ✔ **Do not submit content from the same site repeatedly:** Make sure that you submit content from a variety of sites, and always submit the original article source rather than a recap article that merely links to the original source. In other words, give credit where credit is due. Unless a post adds a significant contribution to the original article (for example, a helpful analysis, additional information, or an opinionated review), always submit the source.

Getting to know the popular social bookmarking sites

No matter which social bookmarking sites you decide to use, the basic methodologies behind how they work are similar. Some of the most popular social bookmarking sites are discussed in this chapter. You can find out about other commonly used social bookmarking sites in Chapter 17.

Digg

`www.Digg.com`

Digg is one of the most popular social bookmarking sites. In fact, it's viewed more as a social news site because its primary purpose is to share links to content more so than to bookmark content for personal use. Users submit content (or "digg" content) by entering the URL, description, and title for the specific Web page they want to share. They must also select a category that the content fits into from an automated list, so other users can find it easily. Recent submissions appear on Digg on an Upcoming page. As other users find the same content, they can either digg the content if they like it or bury it if they don't like it. Doing so can help the content either rise to the home page of Digg, where millions of people can see it, or fall to a deep page, where fewer people can find it.

Most bloggers want to see their content appear on the home page of Digg — which means lots of traffic! However, it's quite difficult for average users to find their content rise to the home page of Digg. Much of a user's success on Digg comes from the social aspect of the site, where users do the following:

- ✔ Make friends with other users.
- ✔ Share content.
- ✔ Help promote each other's content.
- ✔ Comment on each other's content.
- ✔ Gain increased authority.

If you want to succeed with Digg, you need to be an active user and follow the rules outlined in the Terms of Use document, found on the Digg Web site, as well as the Frequently Asked Questions (FAQ) list, which provides the most current information.

You can get started on Digg by clicking the Join Digg link in the top navigation bar on the Digg home page. Just complete and submit the application to create your account and then begin submitting content, by following these steps:

1. **Log in to your Digg account and click the Submit New button from the top navigation bar.**

   This step opens the Submit a New Link page, as shown in Figure 12-8.

2. **Enter the URL for the page you want to submit and then click the News Article, Video, or Image radio button, depending on the type of content you're submitting.**

   Digg automatically digs through your submission as it processes before an expanded Submit a New Link window opens, as shown in Figure 12-9.

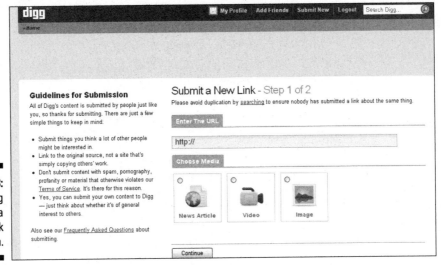

Figure 12-8:
The Digg
Submit a
New Link
form.

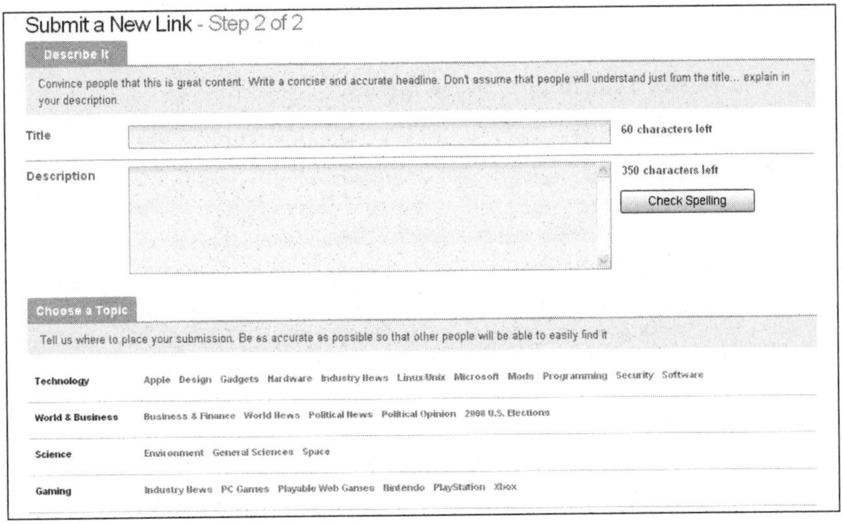

Figure 12-9:
The
expanded
Submit a
New Link
window.

3. **In the Submit a New Link window, enter a title for your submission in the Title text box.**

   Make sure that the title you enter is relevant and compelling and fewer than 60 characters.

4. **Enter a description for your submission in the Description text box.**

   Take a few minutes to write a good description that helps people understand what the submitted content is about.

5. **Click the radio button next to the thumbnail image that you want to appear with your submission.**

   Choose the most appropriate thumbnail. If none of them is appropriate, click the radio button next to the No Thumbnail image.

6. **Select the best category that your submission falls into by clicking the appropriate link in the Choose a Topic section of the form.**

   Take a moment to pick the most relevant category for your submission.

7. **Look at the information in the Preview section of the form to ensure that your submission looks correct.**

   Scroll up and make any changes, if necessary.

8. **Type the spam-blocker text that's displayed in the box under the Are You Human heading.**

   This step is used to prevent spambots from automatically submitting content.

9. **Click the Submit Story button.**

   The Are You Sure It's Not a Duplicate window opens.

10. **Scroll through the submissions on the Are You Sure It's Not a Duplicate page, to ensure that the content you're submitting hasn't already been submitted to Digg.**

11. **If your submission is on the list of links already submitted to Digg, simply click the appropriate link to add your vote. If your submission is new to Digg, click the Totally Original, I Swear! button at the bottom of the page.**

    The Success! Your Story Has Been Submitted! window opens, and you're done!

StumbleUpon

www.StumbleUpon.com

StumbleUpon is another popular social bookmarking site where users submit (or "stumble") and share links to content they like. The site uses a voting system that's fairly similar to the one at Digg. Users stumble content, and other users vote on the content, giving it a thumbs-up or a thumbs-down. Content that receives a lot of thumbs-ups can make it to the front page of StumbleUpon and drive a lot of traffic to that site.

To join StumbleUpon, simply click the Join StumbleUpon button on the site's home page and complete the online form. After you join, you can add the StumbleUpon toolbar to your Web browser, which makes it easy to stumble content with the click of a mouse.

Also similar to the Digg system, StumbleUpon users can add friends to their networks and use their networks to promote and share specific content. One of the keys to StumbleUpon success is making many friends and submitting a lot of excellent content to build your reputation. Although it isn't against the rules to submit your own content to StumbleUpon, there's an unwritten rule to submit more content that *is not* yours than content that *is* yours.

This strategy is easy to follow by using the StumbleUpon toolbar, which works in popular Web browsers. When you stumble upon a Web page that you want to share, simply select the thumbs-up icon on your StumbleUpon toolbar. If the content is new to StumbleUpon, a window automatically opens, where you can enter details about the submission. If the content has already been submitted to StumbleUpon, one click of the thumbs-up button (or thumbs-down button, as the case may be) is all it takes to share the content you like.

Follow these steps to submit new content to StumbleUpon:

1. **When you find a page you want to stumble, simply click the thumbs-up icon from the StumbleUpon toolbar in your browser window.**

    This step opens the StumbleUpon content submission window, shown in Figure 12-10.

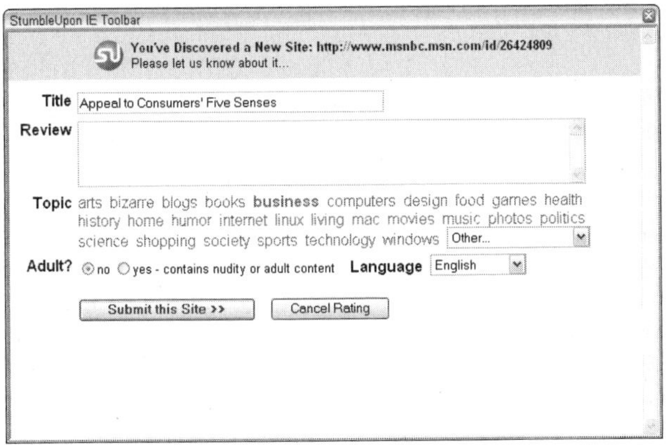

Figure 12-10: Complete the submission form to stumble content.

2. **If text automatically populates the Title text box, check to ensure that it's accurate.**

   Be sure to check punctuation marks as well as the text in this box.

3. **In the Review text box, enter a description of the content on the page you're submitting.**

   Make sure that the description you enter is relevant and useful.

4. **In the Topic section, click the link for the category that's most appropriate for your submission.**

   If you don't see an appropriate category in the list, use the drop-down menu to find more categories to choose from.

5. **Click the appropriate radio button on the Adult line to identify whether the submission contains content that's appropriate only for adults.**

   You can't submit your content unless you click the Yes or No radio button in the Adult section of the submission form.

6. **Use the drop-down menu to select the language that the content is written in.**

   The default is English, but a wide variety of language options are available to choose from.

7. **Click the Submit This Site button.**

   A Rating Submitted message appears, and the window closes automatically. That's it. You're done!

Delicious

www.delicious.com

Delicious is a popular social bookmarking site that works slightly differently from Digg and StumbleUpon. Rather than submissions being based on topics and categories, they're based on keyword tags. The power of Delicious, therefore, in terms of driving traffic to your blog, comes from the quality of the keywords chosen to tag your content.

Similar to the social aspect of Digg and StumbleUpon, users submit content and share it with their networks of friends in order to promote it and drive traffic to it. The chances of your content making it to the front page of Delicious, where it can be discovered by the highest number of people, often depends on the size of your network of Delicious user connections that promote your submissions.

To sign up for an account with Delicious, click the Join Now link in the upper-right corner of the Delicious home page and complete the online registration form. After your account is created, you can download Delicious toolbar buttons so that you can submit content with the click of a mouse. Follow these steps:

1. **When you find a page that you want to bookmark with Delicious, click the Delicious Tag button from your browser toolbar.**

   This step opens the Save Bookmark window with the URL field already populated for the page you want to bookmark, as shown in Figure 12-11.

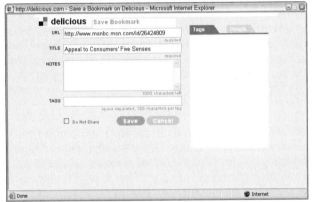

Figure 12-11:
Submitting content to Delicious.

2. **In the Title text box, ensure that the title reads correctly.**

   If the title field automatically populates with a title for the page you're submitting, make sure that it's accurate. If necessary, correct the title or enter a new one that's appropriate.

3. **In the Notes text box, enter a description of the content you're submitting.**

   Take the time to write a relevant, useful description.

4. **In the Tags field, enter a series of relevant keywords that describe your submission.**

   Separate each tag with a space, and take the time to enter keywords that people would use to search for the type of content you're submitting.

5. **If you're submitting a piece of content that you don't want to share with other people, select the Do Not Share check box.**

   This feature is useful if you use Delicious to save content for personal use as well as public use.

6. **Click the Save button.**

The Save Bookmark window closes and your content is saved to your Delicious account.

Social bookmarking is unlikely to bring floods of traffic to your blog immediately. It takes time, practice, networking, and commitment to grow your blog through social bookmarking, but social bookmarking is one more tool in your promotional toolbox that you can use to slowly create a well-trafficked blog.

Microblogging for Blog Traffic

Microblogging, a relatively new tool of the social Web, allows users to publish short blog posts or messages, typically fewer than 140 characters, through their computers and mobile phones It's a helpful way to keep your name in front of people and to announce and highlight new blog posts, upcoming events (such as blog contests or carnivals), and more. The possibilities are virtually limitless! Think of it as free publicity.

When you begin microblogging, you create an account and start publishing content. You can even include some microblogging feeds in your social networking profiles, such as in your Facebook account. Microbloggers sign up to "follow" other microbloggers they like. That's what makes microblogging social. When users sign up to follow each other's content, microblogging becomes a tool for sharing, networking, and relationship building.

The best part about microblogging is the quick and easy way it allows users to share news, information, and content. It's this type of sharing that can make a post go *viral* (spread across the Web). The potential exists, at the least, for news and information to travel quickly online. Microblogging really just began in 2007, but already millions of people have joined through Web sites such as Twitter and Plurk.

Twitter

www.twitter.com

You can join Twitter by visiting its home page and clicking the Get Started — Join button, shown in Figure 12-12. Complete the online form to create a free Twitter account and then you can start "tweeting!"

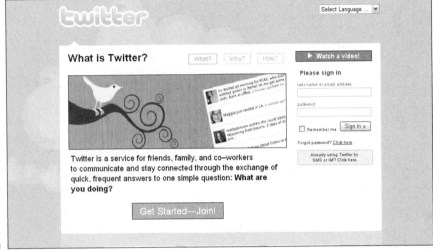

Figure 12-12:
Visit the
Twitter site
to start a
free Twitter
account.

Plurk

www.plurk.com

To join Plurk, simply visit the Plurk home page and click the Sign Up for Free button, shown in Figure 12-13. Complete the online signup form, and you're ready to go!

Figure 12-13:
Sign up for
a free Plurk
account.

Use microblogging to supplement your blogging efforts by writing short updates and messages and sharing links, videos, and more. The choice is yours!

Chapter 13

Boosting Your Search Engine Ranking

In This Chapter

▶ Understanding the basic concepts of search engine optimization

▶ Increasing your search engine ranking

▶ Looking up your page rank and links

*O*ne statistic that you as a blogger are likely to be interested in during the course of your blogging endeavors is how people find your site. You're likely to learn over time that the vast amount of traffic to your blog comes from search engines. Popular search engines include Google, Yahoo!, MSN, AOL, and Ask, but many others are also available to Web surfers. The key to blogging success is to find ways to help those Web surfers find your blog as a result of their search engine queries. That's where search engine optimization comes into play.

This chapter isn't meant to provide a comprehensive look at search engine optimization but rather, an overview of how you can begin thinking about search engine optimization as you develop your blog. When you're ready to dive into search engine optimization, I recommend that you read *Search Engine Optimization For Dummies,* Third Edition, by Peter Kent (Wiley), and spend some time reading Web sites dedicated to the topic, such as www. SeoMoz.com.

Understanding Search Engine Optimization

Search engine optimization (SEO) is the process of creating or modifying your Web pages to increase their rankings in search engine queries. You might think of it this way: If you write a blog about parenting, for example, would people find your blog if they type the word *parenting* into their preferred search engines? Unfortunately, the answer is probably not. Why? It's simple, really. Millions of Web sites and Web pages discuss parenting. A Google search using the search term *parenting* returns nearly 92 million results, as shown in Figure 13-1. With all that competition, how can you make your blog posts rise to the top? One answer is search engine optimization.

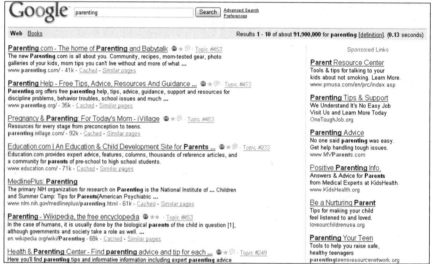

Figure 13-1: A Google search using the keyword "parenting" returns 91.9 million results.

Implementing SEO tactics on your blog is just one key to the search success model — you also need to work on increasing your blog's page rank by writing useful content, networking, and generating lots of incoming links, particularly from popular sites. Post frequently to provide numerous entry points to your blog, and keep learning, tweaking, and testing to find what works best for you, your blog, and your visitors. In other words, there's no quick solution and no simple answer to blogging success. It takes time, patience, and effort to develop a popular blog. However, you can take steps to reach your blogging goals, and SEO is one of those steps.

Driving traffic to your blog

The vast majority of search engine-related blog traffic comes from Google and Yahoo! followed by MSN, AOL, and Ask. Google and Yahoo control more than 50 percent of the online search market, so it's safe to say that in the beginning stages of your SEO efforts, focusing on those two search engines is a less intimidating route to follow. Search engines use proprietary criteria to crawl (or search through), rate, and index pages then match those pages to keyword queries based on a variety of factors. No one truly knows the factors used to rank search results, and just when someone thinks that he has figured it out, the algorithms undoubtedly change. A few elements seem to be standard. Results are typically delivered based on three primary factors: links that help to define the site's overall popularity, content that helps to determine what the page is about, and frequency of updating which shows the site is active.

So how can you optimize your blog posts for search if no one knows search engine criteria used to rank pages? Of course, you can always hire a professional SEO expert to help you, but that's not usually in the beginner blogger's budget. Instead, the average blogger usually does some research and tries to implement a handful of tactics to give her blog a boost in overall search engine rankings for targeted keywords.

Using keyword analysis

To find information they're interested in, people enter keywords and keyword phrases into search engine query fields. The search engine returns relevant results and ranks them for users to scroll through and select results that appeal to them. Most people don't look beyond the first few pages of search results, which typically place ten results on a page. Unless your blog appears within the first 30 or so results for a specific keyword search, therefore, people are unlikely to find your blog by using engines.

Not all the news is bad, however. With each new blog post you write, you create a new entry point for your blog. You can optimize each post for search engines in order to exponentially boost your chances of people finding your blog by way of search engines. In other words, each blog post gives you a new opportunity to create content that focuses on keywords your audience uses to find content. Your goal is to write useful content on your blog so that when a person finds it by using a search engine, she's compelled to click through and visit additional posts. The ultimate goal is to convert that search traffic into loyal readers.

Of course, keyword-targeted posts can drive traffic, but unless those keywords are relevant to your overall blog content, don't expect visitors who find your blog by searching for those irrelevant keywords to stay for long, and they certainly won't become loyal readers. When people who want to find the type of content you publish on your blog open their preferred search engines and type their queries, they use certain keywords. Your goal is to write posts that contain those keywords.

It pays to be specific. Using the example mentioned earlier in this chapter, if your blog is about parenting, you need to determine your overall niche or the niches of your individual blog posts. Rising to the top ten in a Google search for the keyword *parenting* is nearly impossible because so much competition exists, including competition from some of the top Web sites now online that have deep pockets and phenomenal reputations.

Many bloggers use keyword analysis tools to determine which keywords to focus on in their blog posts in order to boost search engine traffic to their blogs. An easy and free way to determine the popularity of keywords is to create a Google AdWords account and pretend that you're an advertiser. AdWords pay-per-click advertisers have to determine which keywords people are searching for, so they can bid on them to maximize the success of their ads. You can do the same thing and search for keywords related to your blog's content that are driving high bids. Then use those words within your blog posts.

It isn't necessary to bid on keywords to use AdWords for your keyword analysis.

To create a Google AdWords account, visit `http://adwords.google.com` and click the Start Now button shown in Figure 13-2.

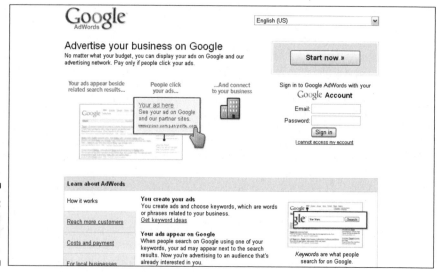

Figure 13-2:
Determining keyword popularity.

If you prefer, you can use a version of the Google AdWords Keywords tool without creating a Google AdWords account: Visit `https://adwords.google.com/select/KeywordToolExternal`, as shown in Figure 13-3.

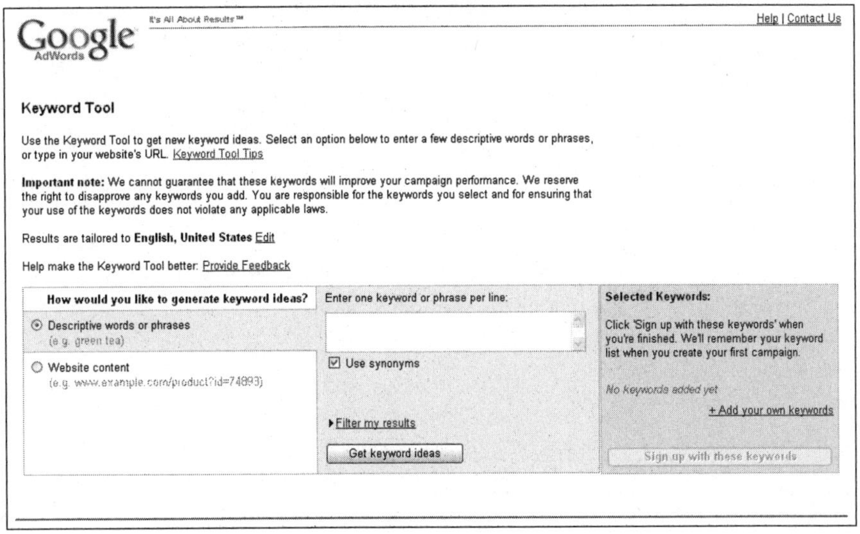

Figure 13-3: Use the free Keywords tool to find popular keyword suggestions.

Simply enter a keyword and click the Get Keyword Ideas button, and a list of keyword suggestions is displayed with average search volume statistics and search volume statistics for previous months, as shown in Figure 13-4.

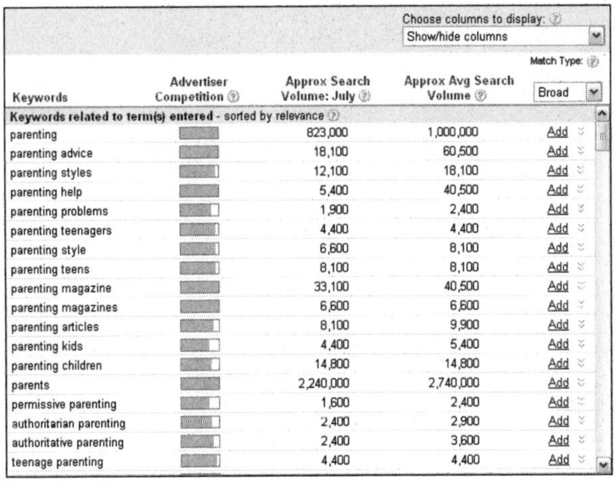

Keywords	Advertiser Competition	Approx Search Volume: July	Approx Avg Search Volume	
parenting		823,000	1,000,000	Add
parenting advice		18,100	60,500	Add
parenting styles		12,100	18,100	Add
parenting help		5,400	40,500	Add
parenting problems		1,900	2,400	Add
parenting teenagers		4,400	4,400	Add
parenting style		6,600	8,100	Add
parenting teens		8,100	8,100	Add
parenting magazine		33,100	40,500	Add
parenting magazines		6,600	6,600	Add
parenting articles		8,100	9,900	Add
parenting kids		4,400	5,400	Add
parenting children		14,800	14,800	Add
parents		2,240,000	2,740,000	Add
permissive parenting		1,600	2,400	Add
authoritarian parenting		2,400	2,900	Add
authoritative parenting		2,400	3,600	Add
teenage parenting		4,400	4,400	Add

Figure 13-4: A search for *parenting* using the Keywords tool returns 50 relevant results.

Use the Choose Columns to Display drop-down menu to see as many as seven columns of data, as shown in Figure 13-5. You can also use the Match Type drop-down menu to display broad, phrase, or negative results, and you can scroll to the bottom of the list of related keywords to find links that let you save the results as a text, Microsoft Excel, or CSV file.

Keywords	Estimated Ad Position	Estimated Avg. CPC	Approx Search Volume: July	Approx Avg Search Volume	Search Volume Trends	Highest Volume Occurred In	
parenting	1 - 3	$2.58	823,000	1,000,000		May	Add
parenting advice	1 - 3	$2.92	18,100	60,500		May	Add
parenting styles	1 - 3	$0.96	12,100	18,100		Nov	Add
parenting help	1 - 3	$4.19	5,400	40,500		May	Add
parenting problems	1 - 3	$1.69	1,900	2,400		Nov	Add
parenting teenagers	1 - 3	$1.04	4,400	4,400		Nov	Add
parenting style	1 - 3	$0.53	6,600	8,100		Nov	Add
parenting teens	1 - 3	$1.42	8,100	8,100		Apr	Add
parenting magazine	1 - 3	$1.01	33,100	40,500		Jan	Add
parenting magazines	1 - 3	$1.36	6,600	6,600		Oct	Add
parenting articles	1 - 3	$1.03	8,100	9,900		Nov	Add
parenting kids	1 - 3	$1.17	4,400	5,400		Apr	Add
parenting	1 - 3	$0.98	14,800	14,800		Apr	Add

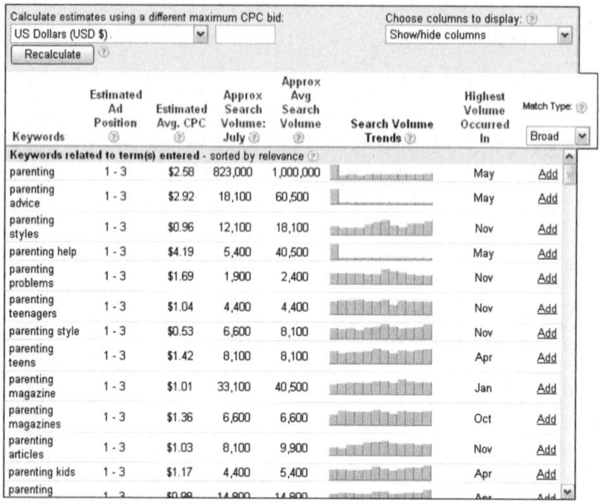

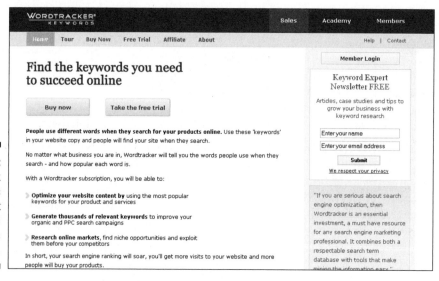

Figure 13-5: The Keywords tool provides seven types of data.

If you're serious about search engine optimization and prepared to invest some money into keyword analysis, you can open an account with a keyword research Web site like Wordtracker (`www.Wordtracker.com`). Simply go to the Wordtracker home page and click the Buy Now link (see Figure 13-6).

Figure 13-6: Check out this excellent keyword analysis tool.

Wordtracker offers a wide variety of tools and reports to help you narrow the list of which keywords you should focus on in your blog posts to maximize potential traffic. Other options similar to Wordtracker include the ones at www.Wordze.com and www.KeywordDiscovery.com. Like Wordtracker, each of these sites requires paying a fee, but free trials are available so you can test drive-them before you pay anything out of your pocket.

Boosting popularity by using links

Another critical component to search engine optimization success is link building — particularly, attracting incoming links from popular Web sites. Search engines rank sites with many incoming links higher than those with few incoming links. The reason is that search engines are programmed to assume that sites with many incoming links contain useful content that people want to link to. In other words, if the content on a site is terrible, no one wants to link to it, but useful content attracts many links. Your goal in search engine optimization is to attract incoming links, particularly incoming links from popular, authoritative blogs and Web sites.

The best way to attract incoming links is to write excellent blog posts that people want to share. Other bloggers are a likely source for incoming links, but even online news and media outlets such as the _Wall Street Journal_ and _New York Times_ have been known to link to individual blog posts. Those links are valuable to beginner bloggers!

You can increase your incoming links by making the most of your online relationships in the following ways:

- ✔ Use social bookmarking, social networking, and microblogging to share links to useful posts, as described in detail in Chapter 12.
- ✔ Write content for multiple Web sites and interlink them.
- ✔ Write articles for online publications related to your blog's topic.
- ✔ E-mail top bloggers or news organizations who might be interested in sharing your posts.
- ✔ Don't be afraid to "toot your own horn" when you think you have something interesting to share.

Outgoing links are also important to search engine optimization. Search engines value linked text, and as far as Google is concerned, the links within your blog posts as well as the text _around_ the links within your blog posts are rated as more important than the other text within your blog posts. Use relevant keywords in your links whenever possible to make sure search engines see them and weight them accordingly. Search engine optimization tips are discussed in more detail later in this chapter.

A key component to SEO success is building relationships with other bloggers and Web site authors who are likely to link to, share, and promote your content.

Using SEO to Increase Your Search Engine Ranking

You can use a variety of activities and tactics both on and off your blog to boost your search engine rankings. Similarly, you can do things that hurt your search engine rankings. Google, the most popular search engine, might even drop your blog from its search results entirely for certain actions you might take. The following sections provide some tips for things you can do, and can avoid doing, if you want to generate more traffic from search engines.

Using SEO tips and tricks

Search engine optimization can seem daunting, but you can take a number of simple actions to boost your rankings. Try the suggestions described in the following list on your own blog and start driving search traffic to your posts:

- **Use your keyword or keyword phrase in your blog post titles.** Search engines weigh titles more heavily than other text, so do your best to include your keywords in your post titles.

- **Use your keyword or keyword phrase within the first paragraph of your blog post.** Search engines value the text within the first few hundred characters of your post more heavily than other text, so be sure to repeat your keywords in this part of your post.

- **Use your keyword or keyword phrase as hyperlinks within your blog posts.** Make sure that the hyperlinks within your blog posts include your keywords when it's appropriate. For example, rather than write "Read more here," with the word *here* as the hyperlink, write "Follow the link to read more about parenting tips," with *parenting tips* as the hyperlink. Search engines value linked text higher than normal text, so use that concept to your advantage by using keywords in your links.

- **Use heading tags and include your keywords within them.** Rather than simply make headings and subheads boldface, apply the HTML H1, H2, and H3 tags to that text. These tags are valued higher by search engines than normal or bolded text is.

✔ **Use your keyword or keyword phrase around links in your posts.** Search engines value the text surrounding links within your posts higher than normal text, so if you can't use your keywords within a link, try to use them in the text surrounding the links.

✔ **Use your keyword or keyword phrase to name images used in your posts.** Take a moment to rename images used in your blog posts to include your keywords when those keywords are relevant to the image. Enter a descriptor using your keywords in the `alt` tag (the alternative text if the image doesn't appear in the person's Web browser) of your post's HTML.

✔ **Include your keyword phrase in your blog's URL.** If you can get a domain name that includes your keywords, you hit the jackpot. When possible, try to include keywords in some part of each blog post's URL.

✔ **Ask for incoming links from similar sites.** Leverage your online relationships, as described earlier in this chapter, to boost incoming links to your blogs. Links from topically similar blogs and Web sites are weighted more heavily than those from irrelevant sites. Similarly, links from popular blogs and Web sites are weighted more heavily than links from blogs and Web sites that have little traffic and lower page ranks.

✔ **Use variations of your keyword or keyword phrase.** Don't feel tied down to a specific keyword or keyword phrase. Search engine algorithms are intelligent, and they accordingly understand and rank variations of a word or phrase used within your blog posts.

✔ **Intralink your blog posts.** Although links within your own blog aren't valued as highly as external links by search engines are, they're still important. Internal links are given some weight in search engine rankings, but more importantly, they lead visitors to more content, which can provide more opportunities for visitors to find content of interest that they want to link to from their own blogs or Web sites.

✔ **Post frequently.** Your posting frequency has an indirect effect on your search engine traffic. With each new keyword-optimized blog post, you increase the chances that someone will find your blog, enjoy the content and link to it, and generate more incoming links, which search engines value highly.

✔ **Comment on other blogs and in online forums and groups.** Commenting is useful in terms of indirect search engine optimization because it can lead new visitors to your blog who might enjoy what they read there and link to it from their own blogs and Web sites — thereby boosting your search rankings.

✔ **Build relationships.** With each new relationship you build online, you develop another portal for sharing information and potential incoming links.

✔ **Write useful content.** The bottom line is that you should write posts that people want to link to.

Hurting your ranking by making simple mistakes

As you begin driving traffic from search engines to your blog, you can easily fall into traps that can have the opposite effect on your blog. Search engines such as Google don't typically give Web sites or blogs a second chance after they're caught doing something that the search engine doesn't like. Often, you have no recourse. The difficult part of search engine optimization is that sites such as Google don't tell people what they did wrong to end up being blacklisted. With that in mind, heed some of the following warnings to stay on Google's good side.

- ✔ **Don't keyword stuff.** Use a keyword or keyword phrase, but don't plaster it all over your blog. *Keyword stuffing* is a big no-no as far as search engines are concerned. If you're found keyword stuffing, your blog is flagged as spam and is likely to be removed from Google searches entirely.

- ✔ **Don't hide keywords.** Don't try to hide keyword stuffing by including your keywords at the bottom of your pages in an extremely small font or in a color that matches your blog's background. Search engines find them and punish you for it.

- ✔ **Don't buy links or publish links that are paid for.** Search engines don't like text link ads that don't use the NoFollow tag because they give the purchaser an unnaturally inflated number of incoming links. Both the purchaser and the publisher are then penalized harshly.

- ✔ **Don't publish sponsored posts without using the NoFollow tag.** Just as search engines don't tolerate link buying in the form of text link ads, they also don't like it in the form of sponsored posts. If you're caught writing posts for payment that include specific keyword links without the NoFollow tag, your blog can be removed from search engine rankings.

- ✔ **Don't go link-trading-crazy.** You may be tempted to try to trade links with as many other blogs and Web sites as possible, but this strategy doesn't boost your search engine rankings. Instead, invest your time in building relationships with key bloggers and Web site authors who publish content similar to yours. These links are far more valuable to your search engine optimization efforts.

Think quality, not quantity.

- ✔ **Don't include a high quantity of irrelevant links to external pages within your blog posts.** Again, quality wins over quantity. Linking to sites related to yours that offer high-quality content groups your blog with those other sites as far as search engines are concerned and gives your blog better rankings.

✔ **Avoid companies that offer pie-in-the-sky search engine optimization claims.** Always research a search engine optimization company before you pay for any services. Many companies that claim immediate, drastic results simply operate link farms that have exactly the opposite effect on your blog's search engine results than you want.

✔ **Never copy content from another page or Web site.** Search engines don't tolerate copying content from another page within your own blog (an entire page of content), but they tolerate it even less if they catch you copying *someone else's* content. Copying content from another site *(scraping)* is not only a spam technique but also a violation of copyright laws. Instead, create original, compelling content.

✔ **Don't limit your search engine optimization efforts to Google.** Sure, Google is the world's largest search engine, but it can also be the most competitive for boosting your rankings and traffic. Take some time to invest your search engine optimization efforts in search engines such as Yahoo! and MSN. Spend time tracking your success on those sites as well as on Google.

✔ **Don't give up.** Keep search engine optimization in mind every time you write a blog post. You never know which post might be the one that will drive lots of traffic to your blog!

The do's and don'ts listed in this chapter refer primarily to blog posts, but don't forget to apply these techniques to other parts of your blog, including your sidebar elements.

No one knows the criteria used by search engines to deliver keyword search results. If you're serious about implementing search engine optimization techniques on your blog, research SEO online and stay current with the changes and opinions of the experts.

Checking Your Page Rank and Links

An important part of search engine optimization success is tracking the results of your efforts. Two simple ways to track your ongoing success include checking your page rank and checking the number of incoming links to your blog. A variety of Web sites offer free page rank and link checker tools. The following list describes some of the most common ways to check both your blog's page rank and incoming links:

✔ **Incoming links according to Google Web search:** Visit www.google. com and enter the text **link:www.yourblogname.com** in the search box. The returned results show you the pages that link to your blog.

✔ **Incoming links according to Google Blog Search:** Visit `www.blog search.google.com` and enter **link:www.yourblogname.com** in the search box. The returned results show you a list of blogs that link to yours.

✔ **Comprehensive information from Google Webmaster Tools:** Visit `www.google.com/webmasters/tools` and set up an account to get comprehensive information about your blog.

✔ **Incoming links according to Yahoo!:** Visit `www.yahoo.com` and enter **linkdomain:www.yourblogname.com** in the search box. The returned results show you pages that link to your blog according to the comprehensive Yahoo! Site Explorer tools.

✔ **Incoming links according to Technorati:** Visit `www.technorati.com/blogs/`*yourblogname.com*`?reactions?` (replace the italics with your blog name). The returned results show you blogs that link to yours.

✔ **Incoming links according to Marketleap:** Visit `www.marketleap.com/services/freetools/default.htm` and click the link for the free Link Popularity Check tool. Complete the online form to find a wealth of information about incoming links to your blog. Marketleap also offers a free keyword verification tool and a free search engine saturation tool. Take some time to experiment with these tools to see how they can help you analyze your blog's performance.

✔ **Incoming links according to PRChecker.info:** Many Web sites offer free tools for checking your page rank. Simply enter **page rank checker** into the Google search box, and a variety of results is returned. PRChecker. info is a commonly used tool: Visit `www.prchecker.info/check_page_rank.php` and enter your blog's URL in the text box. Click the Check PR button, and your Google page rank is automatically returned. You can also add Google Page Rank buttons to your blog's sidebar by using PRChecker.info.

Alternatively, you can set up a Google Alert so that each time another blog or Web site links to yours, you receive an e-mail notification message. To do so, follow these steps:

1. **Visit Google Alerts at `www.google.com/alerts`.**

   This step opens the Google Alerts page, shown in Figure 13-7.

2. **Enter** link:www.yourblogname.com **in the Search Terms text box.**

   This step tells Google Alerts that you want to be notified anytime a blog or Web site links to your blog.

3. **From the Type drop-down menu, choose the Comprehensive option.**

   This step configures your alert to notify you of all results from multiple sources (news, Web, and blogs, for example) rather than just specific types of results.

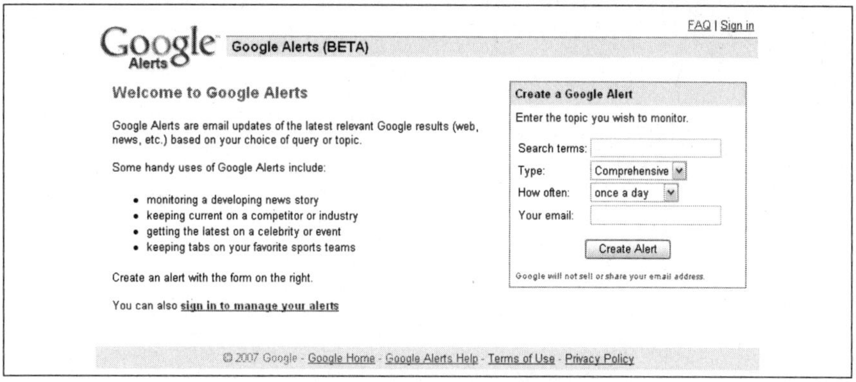

Figure 13-7:
The Google
Alerts page.

4. **From the How Often drop-down menu, specify how often you want to receive updates.**

   You can choose to receive updates as they happen, once per day, or once per week.

5. **Enter your e-mail address in the Your Email field.**

   The e-mail address entered in this box is where your Google alerts are sent.

Although each of these tools provides results that you can use for analysis, keep in mind that none of them is 100 percent accurate. If you use more than one tool, you're likely to notice that your results differ from one tool to the next. A variety of reasons lurk behind the scenes, but the important thing to remember is that these tools can give you a basic idea of your blog's popularity and position within the blogosphere.

Part V
Extending Your Blog

The 5th Wave   By Rich Tennant

"Our customer survey indicates 30% of our customers think our service is inconsistent, 40% would like a change in procedures, and 50% think it would be real cute if we all wore matching colored vests."

In this part . . .

Many options are available to Blogger users to extend their blogs. Chapter 14 shows you how to add and delete blogs and set up multiuser blogs.

Chapter 15 deciphers the nuances of moblogging, vlogging, and podcasting, and Chapter 16 tells you all about how to take your blog to the next level by redirecting it to your own domain and hosting it through a third party.

Never fear: Chapter 16 also shows you where to get help if you need it!

Chapter 14

Growing or Downsizing Your Blog

. . . .

In This Chapter

▶ Creating another blog or getting rid of one

▶ Creating multiuser blogs

. . . .

Considering that a wide world of opportunity is open to bloggers and Blogger users, you may want to prepare yourself for future success by finding out how to grow or downsize your blog.

As you spend time blogging and become more familiar with Blogger and the overall blogosphere, you might find yourself in a position to add blogs to your Blogger account — or even to delete a blog. The day might also come when you want to cancel your entire Blogger account. This chapter shows you how to accomplish these tasks.

As your blogging experience and know-how increases, you may decide to start a team blog. Setting up multiuser blogs is easy in Blogger, and this chapter shows you how to do it. You can even find out how to join and leave other people's team blogs.

Adding and Deleting Blogs

Over time, your blogging goals inevitably change. What began as a fun personal blog can grow into a blogging career. Your success comes from the time and effort you put into your blogging. With this concept in mind, you should understand how to add and delete blogs from your Blogger account.

Adding a blog

The process for adding a new blog to your Blogger account is simple: Just sign in to your Blogger account and follow these steps to add another blog to your existing account:

1. **After logging in to your account, click the Create a Blog link in the upper-right corner of your Blogger dashboard.**

   This step opens the Name Your Blog page, where you can enter the details for your new blog (see Figure 14-1).

Figure 14-1:
The Name
Your Blog
page.

2. **On the Name Your Blog page, enter a title for your blog in the Blog Title text box.**

   This title appears in the header of your new blog. You can change the title later, if you want.

3. **In the Blog Address (URL) text box, enter the name you want to use in your blog's URL.**

4. **Click the Check Availability link to ensure that the name you enter isn't already taken.**

   A message appears telling you if the name is available. If the name isn't available, repeat Steps 3 and 4 until you find an available name that you like.

5. **Enter the text that's displayed in the Word Verification box.**

   If you can't read the text, turn on your computer speakers and click the wheelchair icon to hear a series of numbers, which you can enter in the Word Verification box rather than the displayed text string.

In the Advanced Options section is an area where you can designate where you want to host your blog. Third-party hosting is described in detail in Chapter 16.

If you want to host your new blog at Blogger, simply skip this section of the Name Your Blog page.

6. Click the Continue button.

The Choose a Template page opens, as shown in Figure 14-2.

Figure 14-2: Choose a template for your new blog from the ones provided by Blogger.

7. Scroll through the template options to find the one you want to use on your new blog.

Click the radio button next to your template of choice.

8. Click the Continue button at the bottom of the screen.

The Your Blog Has Been Created page opens (see Figure 14-3).

9. Click the Start Blogging button to write your first post on your new blog.

Click the Dashboard link in the upper-right corner of your screen to see your new blog listed on your Blogger dashboard (see Figure 14-4).

Deleting a blog

You can easily delete a blog from your Blogger account, but because doing so is so easy — and permanent — you must be careful not to inadvertently delete a blog that you want to keep. Follow these steps to delete a blog from your Blogger account — but always make certain that the blog you choose to delete is the correct one!

1. **From the Blogger dashboard (refer to Figure 14-4), click the Settings link under the blog you want to delete.**

   In this example, the Growing and Downsizing Blogs blog is chosen for deletion.

   This step opens the Settings page in your Blogger account with the Basic tab automatically selected, as shown in Figure 14-5.

Figure 14-5:
You can delete a blog from the Basic Settings page within your Blogger account.

2. **Scroll to the bottom of the Basic Settings page to the Delete Your Blog section, shown in Figure 14-6.**

   Click the Delete This Blog button.

   A dialog box opens and asks, "Permanently delete this blog and all entries? Note: This will not delete any files that were transferred to your server."

3. **If you're certain that you want to delete your blog, click the OK button.**

4. **When you visit your Blogger dashboard, the blog you deleted no longer appears in your list of blogs, as shown in Figure 14-7.**

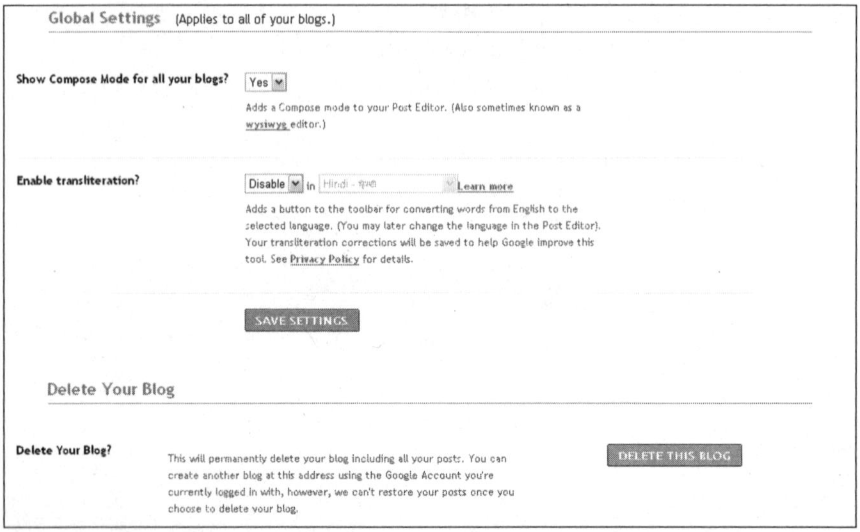

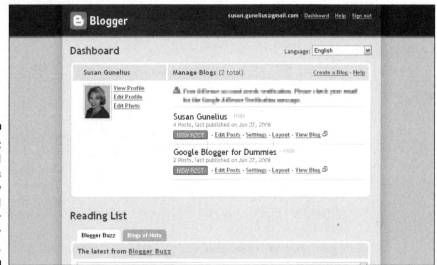

Figure 14-6:
Deleting a
blog is as
easy as
clicking a
mouse
button.

Figure 14-7:
A deleted
blog is
immediately
removed
from your
Blogger
dashboard.

You cannot restore a blog after you delete it. Make sure, therefore, that you're 100 percent sure you want to delete a blog and that you're deleting the correct one before you click that final OK button.

Canceling a Blogger account

Although there's no way to completely cancel your Blogger account, you can take a couple of actions to make your Blogger account invisible to the online community.

✔ Delete any blogs in your Blogger account.

✔ Remove all personal information from your Blogger profile. Replace information in required fields with nonsensical information.

Do not delete your e-mail address from your Blogger account unless you are 100 percent certain you will never want to use your account again. Without your e-mail address, Blogger cannot provide your username and password to you if you request it later.

Setting Up Multiuser Team Blogs

As your blog grows, you might find that you want to invite additional bloggers to write posts on your blog with their own bylines. There are many reasons to start a team blog, such as to

✔ Add different voices to a topic

✔ Increase post frequency

✔ Increase exposure

Luckily, Blogger makes it quite easy to add team members to your blog, set permissions for each member, and even remove members later, if necessary.

Adding team members

Adding a team member to a Blogger blog is as simple as sending an e-mail through an online form and clicking your mouse button a few times. Follow these steps to add a team member to your blog:

1. **From your Blogger dashboard (refer to Figure 14-4), click the Settings link for the appropriate blog.**

   This step opens the Basic Settings page (refer to Figure 14-5).

2. **Select the Permissions tab from the top navigation bar.**

   The Permissions Settings page opens, as shown in Figure 14-8.

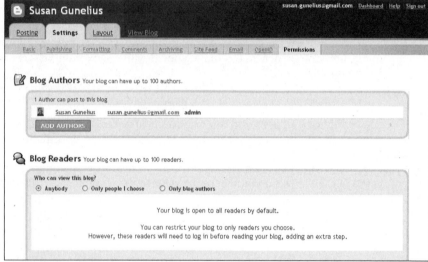

Figure 14-8:
The
Permissions
Settings
page.

3. Click the Add Authors button in the Blog Authors section.

A text box appears in which you can type the e-mail addresses of people you want to invite to become authors on your blog, as shown in Figure 14-9. Be sure to separate each e-mail address with a comma if you're entering more than one.

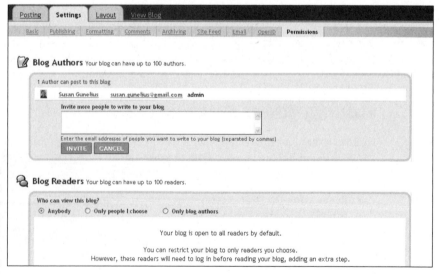

Figure 14-9:
Inviting
people to
write on
your blog.

4. Click the Invite button.

An e-mail is automatically sent to each person whose e-mail address you entered in the invitation field (see Figure 14-10). Each individual's e-mail address to which an invitation was sent appears on your Blogger dashboard with the date the invitation was sent on the right side of the page (see Figure 14-11). Each person invited to become an author on your blog receives an e-mailed invitation that she must respond to in order to gain access to your blog.

Figure 14-10:
An e-mail invitation to become an author on a blog.

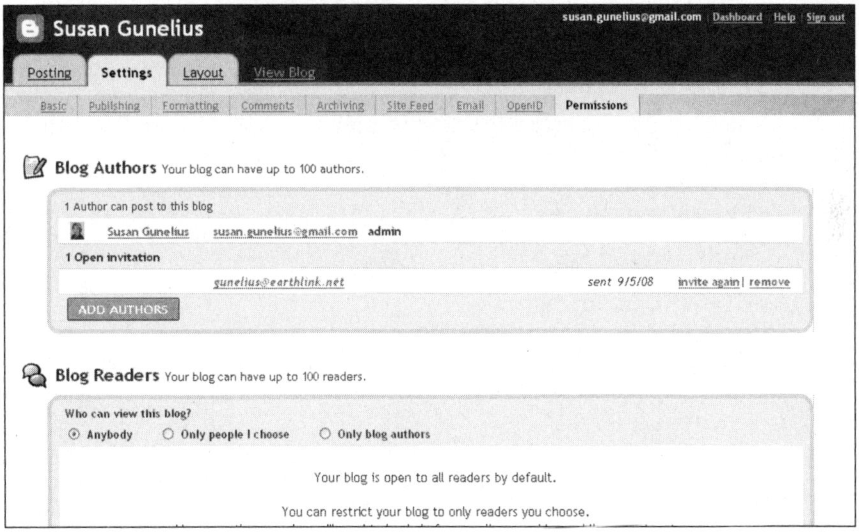

The Blogger user Susan Gunelius has invited you to contribute to the blog: Susan Gunelius.

To contribute to this blog, visit:
http://www.blogger.com/i.g?inviteID=1883443909372857097&blogID=4625758504806348540

You'll need to sign in with a Google Account to confirm the invitation and start posting to this blog. If you don't have a Google Account yet, we'll show you how to get one in minutes.

To learn more about Blogger and starting your own free blog visit http://www.blogger.com.

Figure 14-11:
As team members are added to your blog, their statuses will change on the Permissions page of your Blogger dashboard.

An Invite Again link is also included, which you can click to resend your invitation. A Remove button is also included, which is discussed in greater detail in the section, "Leaving a Team Blog," later in this chapter.

When the invited author responds to the e-mail invitation that was sent to him by clicking the link in the e-mail and signing in with his Google Account username and password, the status on the Permissions page for that member changes to Author.

A Grant Admin Privileges link appears next to each author. This link is discussed in detail in the following section.

If the link within an e-mail invitation to join a team blog doesn't work, the recipient can try to copy and paste the link into her browser window rather than simply select it with her mouse. Not all links always work in an e-mail program.

The link included in a team blog invitation works one time only. If a recipient clicks the link but doesn't complete the login process to accept the invitation, the link is no longer valid and a new invitation must be sent to that person.

Establishing the blog administrator and permissions

On any team blog, at least one person must have access to all the features and functionalities of the blog and be able to make necessary changes to it. That person is the blog *administrator* (or *admin*), and he controls all the blog's settings, including being able to

✔ Modify the template

✔ Add and remove team members

✔ Edit or delete posts

You can have more than one blog administrator for a blog, but *at least one* must be defined within the blog's settings.

You can change blog administrator settings by visiting the Permissions page within your Blogger dashboard. As team members accept your invitations to join your blog, their statuses change to Author. Authors are allowed to write, publish, and edit posts, but nothing else.

A Grant Admin Privileges link is included next to each author's name and e-mail address . If you want to give a specific author access to the various settings of your Blogger account for this blog, click the Grant Admin Privileges link next to that author's name and e-mail address. Her status changes to Admin. Similarly, you can remove that person's administrator privileges by clicking the Remove Admin Privileges link next to that admin's name and e-mail address. It's that easy!

Joining and leaving team blogs

Although you might want to add or remove team members from your own blog, you might also be invited to write for other blogs. If so, you should understand how to join (and leave) another blogger's team blog.

Accepting Blogger author invitations

When you're invited to join a team blog, you receive an e-mail like the one shown in Figure 14-10. To join the blog as an author, simply click the link provided in the e-mail and log in as instructed using your Google Account username and password. That's all there is to it. You can now create and edit posts for that blog. The blog also appears on your Blogger dashboard login screen and in your Blogger profile.

Leaving a team blog

Leaving a team blog is even easier than joining a team blog. Simply visit the Permissions Settings page of the Blogger dashboard. If you're an administrator of that blog, you can simply click the Remove link next to your name and e-mail address. If your status is set as Author, a Remove Yourself from This Blog link appears. Simply click that link, and you're done. Your posts still appear on the blog, but you can no longer access the dashboard to write or edit posts, and the blog is removed from your Blogger login dashboard and profile.

Chapter 15

Blogging from Different Media

. . . .

. . . .

As you become more comfortable with blogging, you might want to branch out and try new methods of creating content and new technology to add interest to your blog. Using Blogger, you can blog on the go, publish audio and video blogs, and more. It's up to your creativity and the technology you want to invest in. Remember that it's your blog, and you decide what you publish on it.

With those creative opportunities in mind, this chapter introduces you to some of the different media available to help you create and publish content to your blog. Although some of the techniques discussed in this chapter require you to purchase additional equipment, remember that none of these options is essential. (They're just options.) You might want to try some of these techniques right away, or you may never use any of them. Again, it's your blog, so you run the show.

Blogging on the Go: Mobile Blogging

Blogger users can publish blog posts using their cellular phones with Blogger Mobile. You simply create a message — which can consist of text, video, or a photo — and send it to go@blogger.com. A new blog is automatically created to publish your mobile blog posts, and you receive a return a message that provides you with the address for your new mobile blog — or *mo-blog*.

You also receive a "token" (sort of like a digital code) that lets you claim your new mobile blog from your existing Blogger account. Just log in to www.go.blogger.com, enter the token in the Claim Token text box (see Figure 15-1), claim your new mobile blog, and follow the instructions that are provided to merge the blog with your existing Blogger blog. You can modify your mobile settings at any time by clicking the Mobile Devices link that appears on your Blogger dashboard after the initial setup is completed.

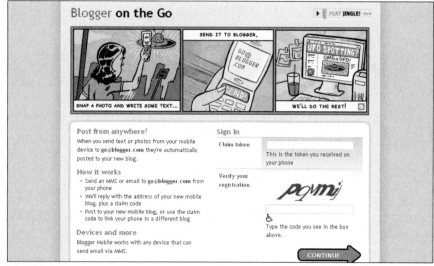

Figure 15-1:
Follow the
instructions
to claim
your mobile
blog.

To create a mobile blog, you need to use a participating carrier and have a service plan that includes multimedia messaging and text messaging. (Also, your phone must be able to send and receive text messages.)

Imagine that you're on vacation and see an amazing sight that you want to share with your blog readers. Using Blogger Mobile, you can — within minutes — snap a picture with your cellular phone and send it to publish on your blog.

Podcasting with Audio

A *podcast* is an audio or video blog post. It can be about any subject you want, and it can be as long (or short) as you want. A variety of tools are available online and offline to help you create an audio file, upload it to the Web, and then publish it on your blog. This section focuses on audio, and the "Podcasting with Video" section focuses on video.

After your podcast is published in one of your blog posts, your readers can listen to it and comment on it. The reader experience is exactly the same as in a traditional written blog post, but rather than read, visitors listen as if they're listening to a radio broadcast. The comment, conversation, and linking process works the same as it does with traditional written blog posts.

If you're truly interested in knowing all the tricks and tools to become a top podcaster, read *Expert Podcasting Practices For Dummies* by Tee Morris, Evo Terra, and Ryan Williams (Wiley).

Making the case for podcasts

It has been said that podcasts have drawn a completely new audience to the blogosphere over the course of the past several years. A medium that was once enjoyed primarily by people who liked reading became a medium that now attracts people who enjoy *listening*, too. In fact, podcasting has grown in popularity so quickly that Web sites dedicated entirely to sharing bloggers' podcasts have popped up, and some have even turned podcasts into online radio shows, such as the one at www.BlogTalkRadio.com.

No single format for podcasting success exists. If you search the Internet, you can find podcasts on just about every subject imaginable. From cooking to sports, music to gardening, and everything in between, people are creating podcasts about it. The key to podcasting success comes not from the topic you're talking about, but, rather, from what you're saying. The same recipes for successful blogging can be applied to successful podcasting.

Say something interesting, and people will come.

You can also promote your podcast just as you promote your written blog posts. Additionally, a number of podcast directories are available online, such as the one at www.Podcast.com, that allow you to post your podcast link and drive traffic to it.

Just as podcasts can attract a completely new audience to your blog, they can also alienate (or at least confuse) your current readers. Test the waters with your audience to ensure that they're receptive to podcasts. If necessary, provide detailed instructions to help your current readers understand how to listen to your podcasts.

Ensuring that you have the right podcasting tools

Unfortunately, to create a podcast, you probably need to buy some equipment. It's essential that your podcasts are recorded clearly, or else no one will listen to them. Make sure that your microphone works well and has excellent sound quality, and record your podcast when there's no chance that background noise will interrupt the recording.

Podcasting also requires the use of sound recording and editing software. Luckily, some free options are available online, such as http://audacity.sourceforge.net. You also need a place to store your podcasts online. You can use a hosting or storage site, such as BlueHost (www.bluehost.com) or Box (www.box.net). Alternatively, you can use a service such as Gabcast (www.gabcast.com) or Hipcast (wwwHipcast.com), both of which offer methods for you to easily create podcasts and publish them to your blog.

Be certain to check the fees and restrictions for hosting or storage providers to ensure that the offerings and price meet your needs.

As you research sound recording, editing, hosting, and storage providers, look for free trial offers so you can take a test drive before you commit to paying for anything.

As podcasting becomes more popular, people are continually branching out and trying new methods and tools. For example, Skype users (www.skype. com) can talk to each other over the Internet for free. The conversation can even be recorded, saved, and published on your blog as a podcast interview!

Creating and publishing a podcast

Creating a podcast can seem intimidating the first time you do it, but after you try it, you're likely to fall in love with it. Follow these directions to get started:

1. **Record your audio file and save it as an MP3 file.**

   MP3 files are commonly used for audio files, and they play on most computers and audio players. Imagine someone downloading your podcast and listening to it on his iPod during a morning jog!

2. **Upload your podcast file to your host or online storage provider.**

   No one can hear your podcast unless it's available somewhere online for them to access. That's where the host or storage provider enters the picture.

3. **Copy the URL for your podcast and keep it handy. Then open your Blogger dashboard and click the Settings link.**

   The Basic Settings page opens.

4. **From the Basic Settings page, select the Formatting tab in the top navigation bar.**

   The Formatting Settings page opens.

5. **On the Formatting Settings page, shown in Figure 15-2, scroll down to the Show Link Fields option.**

   You use the Show Link Fields option to set your blog to enable enclosure links. Once allowed, you can link to your podcast file from directly within the blog post editor in your Blogger dashboard.

6. **Select Yes from the Show Link Fields drop-down menu, shown in Figure 15-3. Then click the Save Settings button.**

   This step adds the appropriate enclosure link field to your blog post editor.

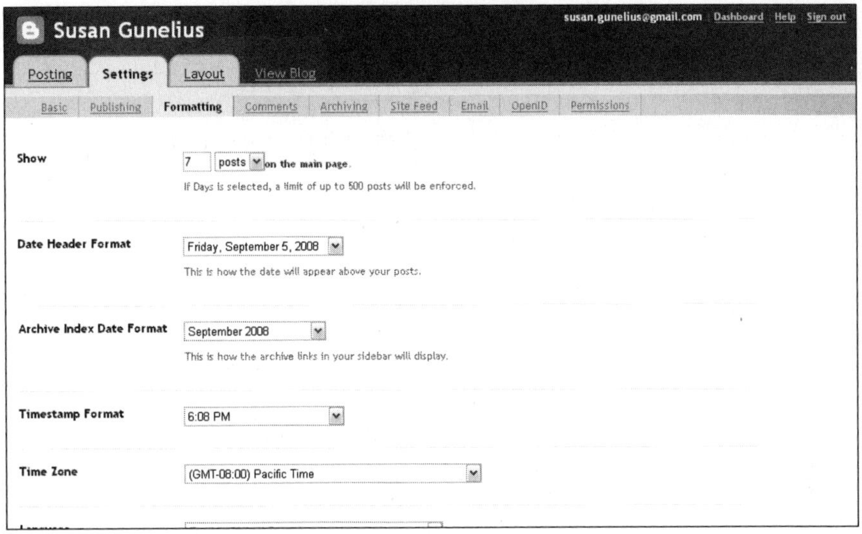

Figure 15-2:
The
Formatting
Settings
page.

Figure 15-3:
Adding an
enclosure
link.

7. **Select the Posting tab from the top navigation bar, shown in Figure 15-4, to open your blog post editor.**

   You now see, under the Title text box, a Link text box, where you can enter a URL that you want your title to link to. For podcasting, however, you want the link labeled Add Enclosure Link, which appears under the Link box.

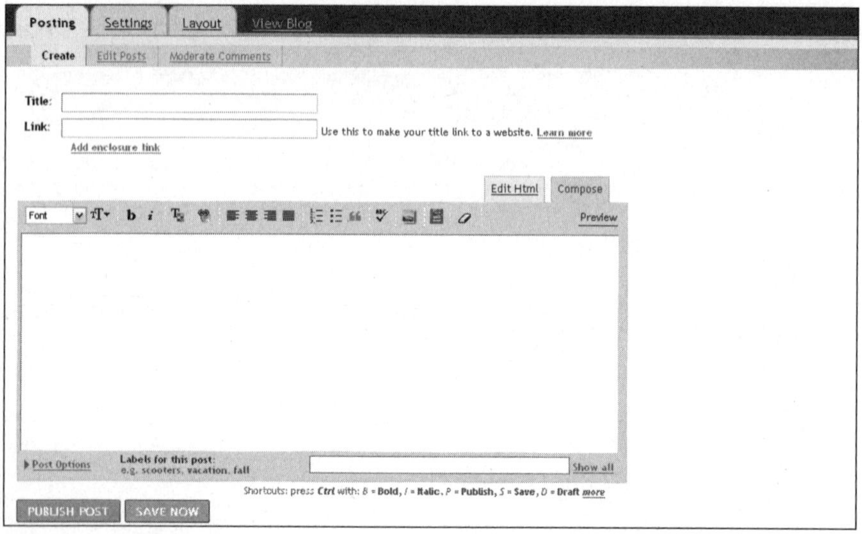

Figure 15-4:
The Add
Enclosure
Link in the
blog post
editor.

8. Click the Add Enclosure Link.

A new section of the page opens, as shown in Figure 15-5.

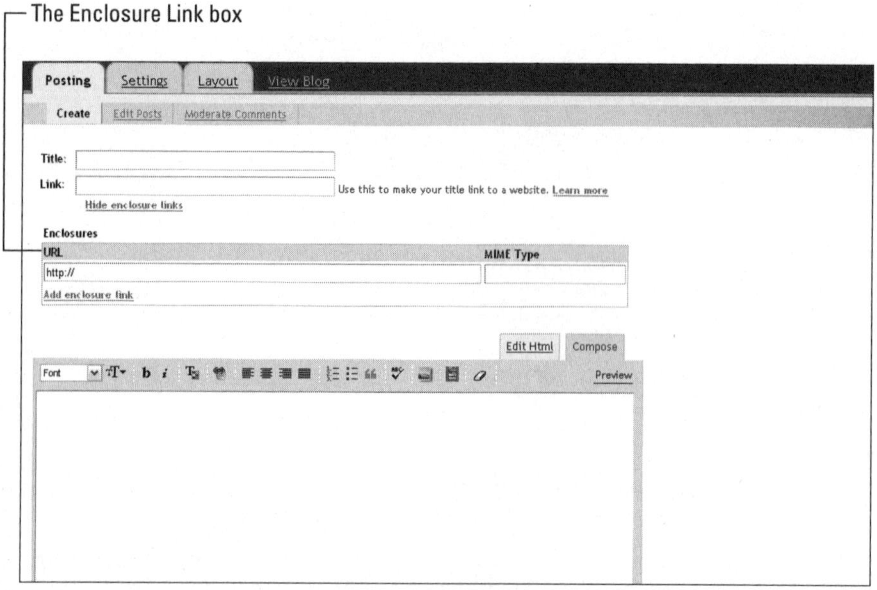

The Enclosure Link box

Figure 15-5:
The
Enclosure
Link box.

9. Enter the URL of your podcast under the URL heading in the Enclosures section.

Blogger autodetects the mime type of your podcast file, so just leave the Mime Type field blank.

10. **To add more podcasts to your blog post, click the link labeled Add Enclosure Link again.**

Another text box appears, as shown in Figure 15-6 where you can add another podcast link URL. Continue adding enclosure links until all the podcast links you want to add to your post are included.

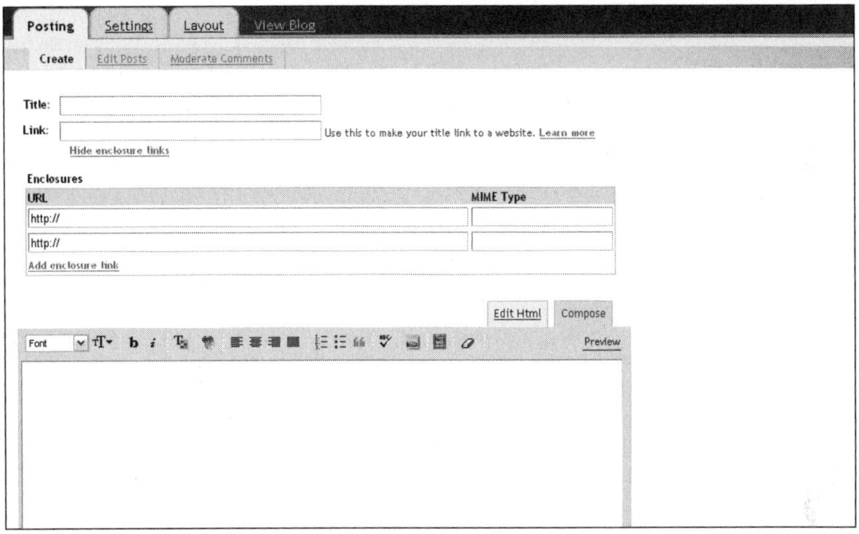

Figure 15-6:
Adding
multiple
podcasts.

When your blog visitors view your blog post that includes your podcast, they can listen to it by just clicking the mouse!

If you burned an RSS feed for your blog by using FeedBurner, you can also burn a feed for your podcasts that can be recognized and played in various feed readers, such as Google Reader, and by sites such as iTunes, Juice (formerly iPodder), and NetNewsWire. You can also monetize your podcast feed through FeedBurner.

Podcasting with Video

A video blog (or *vlog*) contains videos rather than written posts. Vlogging is becoming more popular everyday as bloggers try to find ways to reach new audiences and inject more personality into their blogs. Of course, you can include an occasional video post — or even frequent video posts — on your blog, although a true vlog is made up entirely of video posts.

Before the term *vlog* became popular, people referred to video blog posts as *video podcasts* and to audio blog posts as *audio podcasts*. Blogging vernacular has changed to differentiate between these types of posts, but you may still hear the term *podcast* to refer to both video and audio posts.

Using vlogging equipment

Vlogging is a fun way to share information and elicit comments from visitors, but it requires special equipment and considerations. First, you need a camcorder (or webcam) in order to upload videos to your computer's hard drive, and you need to take the time to understand how to use video editing software. Luckily, a variety of video editing software programs and applications are available. Some are even available for free. Determine your ultimate vlogging goals, and then do some research to find the video editing program that best meets your needs. Popular video editing programs include Final Cut Pro, iMovie (Mac), Vlog It (Adobe), and Windows Movie Maker.

After you set up your camcorder and video editing program, make sure that you have a high-speed Internet connection — online videos are nearly unwatchable unless you have high-speed Internet access. This concept applies to your audience, too: If the majority of your readers (or potential new audience members who are driven by your video content) don't have high-speed Internet access, they may not be able to watch your video posts.

You can learn more about vlogging in *Video Blogging For Dummies,* by Stephanie Cottrell Bryant (Wiley).

Creating a vlog with Blogger

After you create a video and store it on your computer's hard drive, you can upload it to Google Video directly from your blog post editor in Blogger. The following steps walk you through the process of adding a video to your blog:

1. **Click the New Post button on your Blogger dashboard.**

   This step opens the blog post editor.

2. **In the blog post editor, click the Add Video icon on the post editor toolbar, shown in Figure 15-7.**

   It's the second icon from the right and looks like a filmstrip. The Add a Video to Your Blog Post dialog box opens.

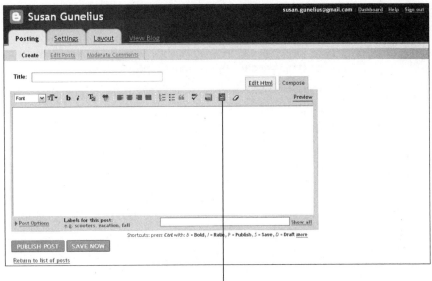

Figure 15-7:
The Add
Video icon.

Click to add video to your post.

3. **In the Add a Video to Your Blog Post dialog box, click the Browse button to find your video on your computer's hard drive (see Figure 15-8).**

   You can upload videos in AVI, MPEG, QuickTime, Real, and Windows Media formats. The maximum file size that's allowed is 100 MB.

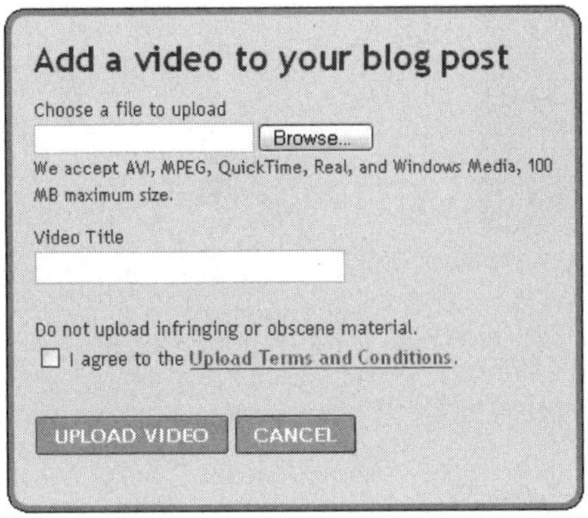

Figure 15-8:
Uploading a
video from
your com-
puter.

4. **In the Video Title text box, enter a title for your video.**

   This title is used to store your uploaded video in Google Video, which can be accessed at anytime at `http://video.google.com`.

The videos you upload by way of Blogger are stored in Google Video, which features videos uploaded from people around the world. However, the videos you upload by using the Blogger post editor are stored as private videos on Google Search, which means that they don't show up in searches on Google Video.

5. **Click the Upload Video button in the upper-right corner of the screen.**

   Your video is automatically uploaded to your blog post.

   The process of uploading your video can take several minutes. Be patient and let the process complete before you navigate away from your blog post editor.

   The speed of your video upload can be affected by the file size, resolution, and your Internet connection speed.

6. **Add a title to your post by typing it in the Title text box and then click the Publish Post button. That's all there is to it!**

   You can view your post live online to see how it looks. Figure 15-9 provides an example of how a vlog post looks.

Figure 15-9:
A vlog post looks just like a written blog post but with a video rather than text.

Visitors can click the Play button, located beneath the video, to watch your vlog post. By using vlogging, your visitors can see and hear what you have to say, making the experience on your blog seem even more interactive than written blog posts can provide.

Chapter 16

Moving Beyond Blogger

· ·

In This Chapter

▶ Assigning your own domain

▶ Redirecting readers to a new domain

▶ Exploring third-party hosting

▶ Using FTP to publish your blog

▶ Finding help

· ·

The longer you publish a blog, the more it grows and the more often opportunities arise for you to enhance and expand your blog and your overall online presence. In fact, the time may come when you want to remove the `.blogspot` segment of your blog's URL, which is automatically included in all free blogs hosted by Blogger.com. Many people perceive that section of a blog address as amateurish. Whether they're correct is open for debate; there's something to be said, however, for investing in a domain name of your own that typically costs very little but helps you create an online brand and credibility for yourself and your blog.

As your blog grows, you might want to pursue the option of hosting it by way of a third party other than Blogger, to allow maximum flexibility and growth. Keep in mind that obtaining your own domain name and third-party hosting is an added expense that you have to continually pay for. Making the decision to switch from a completely free blog to one that requires a monetary investment shouldn't be taken lightly or be done hastily.

This chapter explains some of the pros and cons of using your own domain and a third-party host to help you make informed decisions and get started after you make the decision to venture out into the world of domain name registration and third-party hosting.

Using Your Own Domain

One of the first issues that bloggers consider as their blogs grow is whether they need to have their own domain names. Free blogs from Blogger.com always include the `.blogspot.com` extension. For example, if your blog's URL is `www.MyGreatBlog.blogspot.com`, you might want to obtain your own domain name that doesn't include the `.blogspot.com` segment of the URL. You can search available domain names through Blogger or a third-party domain name registrar, such as GoDaddy or BlueHost. In this example, you might find that `www.MyGreatBlog.com` or `www.MyGreatBlog.net` is available. You can purchase one of these domain names and then redirect your Blogger blog to it. That way, rather than have users type `www.MyGreatBlog.blogspot.com` to access your blog, they can simply type `www.MyGreatBlog.com`.

Having your own domain name not only streamlines your URL but can also give your blog a credibility boost simply because a custom domain name can symbolize a long-term investment in your blog. Many free blogs that are published simply to generate money from advertising provide little in terms of valuable content. Of course, you can find many fantastic free blogs as well, but the number of spam blogs seems to grow faster every day. Branding your blog with a custom domain name can help your blog stand out from the crowds of spam blogs that blanket the Internet.

Obtaining a domain from Blogger

A helpful Blogger feature is that you can use your own domain name and Blogger will still host your blog for free! You have to pay for your domain name, but Blogger makes it easy to obtain your new domain and redirect your blog to it directly from your Blogger dashboard. All you have to do is follow these steps:

1. **Click the Settings link for the appropriate blog from the home page of your Blogger dashboard, as shown in Figure 16-1.**

   This step opens the main Settings page within your dashboard.

2. **Select the Publishing tab from the top navigation bar on the Settings page, as shown in Figure 16-2.**

   The Publishing page opens, where you can obtain your custom domain from Blogger.

3. **Select the Custom Domain link, shown in Figure 16-3.**

   A new section of the page opens, labeled Buy a Domain for Your Blog.

The Settings link

The Publishing tab

4. **In the Buy a Domain for Your Blog section of the Publishing page, shown in Figure 16-4, enter the domain name you want to purchase in the box labeled What Address Would You Like Your Blog to Have, and then click the Check Availability button.**

   Blogger responds and tells you whether the requested domain name is available. When you find an available domain you like, select the appropriate Google Checkout button to purchase the domain.

Click here to buy a custom domain.

| Posting | Settings | Layout | View Blog |

| Basic | Publishing | Formatting | Comments | Archiving | Site Feed | Email | OpenID | Permissions |

You're publishing on blogspot.com

Switch to: • Custom Domain (Point your own registered domain name to your blog)

Hint: If you want to publish to an external FTP server, you will need to Set 'Blog Readers' to 'Anybody' and use a Classic Template.

Blog*Spot Address   http:// susangunelius .blogspot.com

Subject to availability.

Word Verification

Type the characters you see in the picture.

Figure 16-3:
The Custom
Domain link.

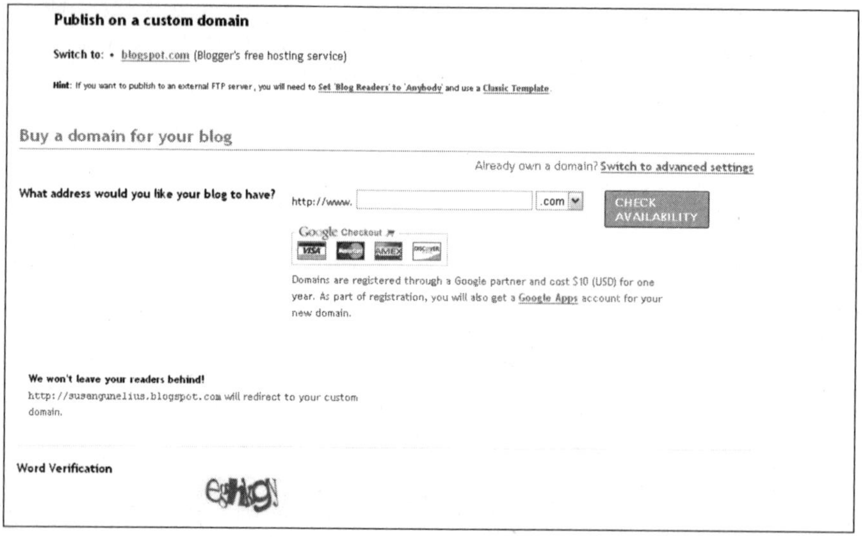

Publish on a custom domain

Switch to: • blogspot.com (Blogger's free hosting service)

Hint: If you want to publish to an external FTP server, you will need to Set 'Blog Readers' to 'Anybody' and use a Classic Template.

Buy a domain for your blog

Already own a domain? Switch to advanced settings

What address would you like your blog to have?   http://www. _____ .com ▾   CHECK AVAILABILITY

Google Checkout
VISA MasterCard AMEX DISCOVER

Domains are registered through a Google partner and cost $10 (USD) for one year. As part of registration, you will also get a Google Apps account for your new domain.

We won't leave your readers behind!
http://susangunelius.blogspot.com will redirect to your custom domain.

Word Verification

Figure 16-4:
Buying a
domain for
your blog.

You have to pay a fee to obtain a custom domain name. Blogger charges you $10 to register a domain name through a Google partner for one year. You must renew your registration when the one-year registration period is over.

When you obtain a new domain name through Blogger, you must sign up for a Google Apps account (for free) during the registration process. This account facilitates the domain name registration process. You can learn more about Google Apps in *Google Apps For Dummies* by Ryan Teeter and Karl Barksdale (Wiley).

When you switch to a custom domain, your old URL, which included the `.blogspot.com` extension, is automatically redirected to your new domain, so visitors who bookmarked your blog can still find it.

Buying a domain from a third party

If you purchase your new domain by way of a company other than Blogger, click the Switch to Advanced Settings link (refer to Figure 16-4). A new Advanced Settings page opens, as shown in Figure 16-5.

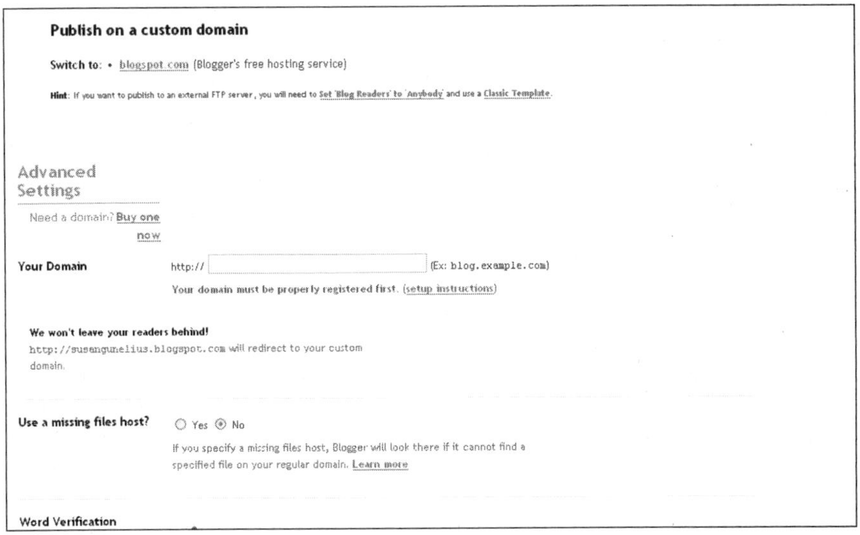

Figure 16-5:
Use the
Advanced
Settings
page to
redirect
your blog
to a domain
purchased
by way of a
third party.

> **Publish on a custom domain**
>
> Switch to: • blogspot.com (Blogger's free hosting service)
>
> **Hint:** If you want to publish to an external FTP server, you will need to Set 'Blog Readers' to 'Anybody' and use a Classic Template.
>
> Advanced
> Settings
>
> Need a domain? Buy one now
>
> **Your Domain**   http:// [   ]   (Ex: blog.example.com)
>
> Your domain must be properly registered first. (setup instructions)
>
> **We won't leave your readers behind!**
> http://susangunelius.blogspot.com will redirect to your custom domain.
>
> **Use a missing files host?**   ○ Yes ⦿ No
>
> If you specify a missing files host, Blogger will look there if it cannot find a specified file on your regular domain. Learn more
>
> **Word Verification**

In the text box labeled Your Domain, enter the new domain name you registered. Note that when you register your new domain this way, you have to update the Domain Name System (DNS) settings for it so that the Internet knows that it exists. The steps you follow vary among domain name registrars, so check with yours for specific instructions on how to update the DNS settings for your new domain. Also, be aware that it can take several days for DNS settings to finish updating and for your new domain to start working.

Overall, redirecting your blog to a new domain is fairly easy and causes few problems. It's definitely something to consider early in your blogging career to make the transition process as easy and painless as possible for you and your readers.

Using a Third-Party Host

The process of using a third-party (or an *external*) host other than Blogger to store and deliver your blog is more complex than redirecting your domain name. Blogger wasn't originally created as a blogging platform to be used through third-party hosts, but in recent years a work-around has been created to make Blogger more competitive with applications such as WordPress that work seamlessly with third-party hosts. Although the work-around isn't perfect, it gets the job done.

A *third-party host* is a company that stores your blog's content and makes it available to visitors online. Two primary advantages to using a third-party host are flexibility and control. With a third-party host, you can add any feature that you want to your blog and grow it as big as you want as long as you're willing to pay for the space that's needed. You can choose from a wide variety of blog hosts, including BlueHost, GoDaddy, 1and1, Network Solutions, and more. Be sure to research several blog hosts before deciding on the one that will work best for meeting your needs at an acceptable price.

Even if you host your Blogger blog by using a third party, you're still required to adhere to the Blogger and Google terms of use and policies.

Although using a third-party host gives you maximum flexibility and control, it requires more technical knowledge, effort, and time to make everything work correctly, and of course, it requires that you pay hosting fees. It's up to you to weigh the pros and cons of using a third-party host or sticking with Blogger as your host. Whatever you do, don't make a decision without fully thinking through the process as well as the benefits and downsides of making the switch.

Publishing via FTP

The longer you blog, the more courageous you're likely to be about tackling new tools, particularly those that allow you to expand and enhance your blog. Using a third-party host is one of those options you might want to use one day. When you use a third-party host, you must publish posts to your blog using an FTP (File Transfer Protocol) connection.

In other words, you need to connect your Blogger account to your third-party hosting account to upload your files to your blog. To do so, you have to

✔ Follow the directions provided by your external host to configure your account with that host to be able to receive, store, and publish your blog correctly.

✔ Configure your Blogger account to correctly send your blog files to your third-party host.

The following steps walk you through the process of configuring the settings in your Blogger dashboard to begin publishing by way of FTP to your third-party blog host:

1. **Obtain your FTP path from your third-party host account.**

   The FTP path tells Blogger where to put your files on the third-party host's server when you transmit them through your FTP connection.

2. **Open the Publishing page from the Settings tab of your Blogger dashboard and select the FTP link to switch to FTP publishing through a third-party blog host.**

   A new section of the page opens, where you can enter your FTP settings.

3. **Enter your FTP server (typically, your domain, such as yourdomain. com), your blog URL, your FTP path (from Step 1), and your blog filename (obtained from your third-party blog host). Then select the Save Settings button.**

   Your blog is now configured to use FTP publishing.

4. **Go to the Posting tab in your Blogger dashboard and select the newly available Status tab.**

   This step opens a page where you can republish your blog in order to reflect the updates you just made.

5. **Select the Republish Entire Blog button.**

   Your entire blog is automatically republished using the FTP settings you just configured. Be patient. If your blog is large, this process can take several minutes to complete.

After you set up the FTP settings for your blog, you also need to change the path for your blog archives on the Archive Settings tab of your Blogger dashboard. You also have to redirect your blog's feed to your new feed files on the Site Feed Settings tab of your Blogger dashboard.

Much of the work to set up your blog using a third-party host is done within your hosting account. Each blog host works a bit differently, so you must work directly with your host to ensure that your account is configured correctly to work with your Blogger account.

Don't be afraid to call and ask your host for help in setting up your blog. Most are quite familiar with the challenges bloggers face in trying to move their blogs to their own hosts and are happy to help you successfully make the move.

Getting Help

Configuring your Blogger blog to work with your own domain and a third-party host can be confusing and challenging. Luckily, you can find help in a variety of places as you work your way through the process.

Blogger Help

```
http://help.blogger.com
```

The official Blogger.com help site provides a wealth of information to help you start your blog, including information about custom domains and external hosts.

Blogger Buzz

```
http://buzz.blogger.com
```

The official Blogger.com blog provides updates about new features and enhancements that can make your blogging life easier.

Blogger Help Group

```
http://groups.google.com/group/blogger-help
```

The official Google Group dedicated to providing Blogger.com help is a useful resource where users help each other find answers to questions and solve problems. You can join the group and post your questions to find help from people around the world.

BloggerHelp channel on YouTube

```
http://www.youtube.com/BloggerHelp
```

The BloggerHelp channel on YouTube has several useful video tutorials to help you use a variety of Blogger features, including a video that shows you how to set up a custom domain: www.youtube.com/watch?v=2X8RMLsN61I.

Blogger Buster

www.BloggerBuster.com

The Blogger Buster blog is written by Amanda Fazani, a freelance blogger and a Web and blog designer. She writes clear and easy-to-follow posts on her blog, which is all about using Blogger.com. Her blog also includes a forum where visitors can further discuss questions and problems.

Part VI
The Part of Tens

The 5th Wave   By Rich Tennant

CAUTION LIVE SNAKES

So old Dave's presentations are boring? They're dull, huh? "Add some dynamic content," they said. I'll give you dynamic content...

In this part . . .

*E*veryone loves lists. The Part of Tens gives you lists of places to find Blogger templates, solutions to common problems, useful social networking and social bookmarking sites, and more. In time, you'll undoubtedly find more resources to add to these lists to make them your own!

Chapter 17

Ten Useful Social Networking and Social Bookmarking Sites

A powerful strategy for building your blog is to take advantage of social networking and social bookmarking sites. Chapter 12 provides a wealth of details to help you find out how to use these tools, including some of the most popular social networking sites (such as MySpace, Facebook, and LinkedIn) and social bookmarking sites (such as Digg, StumbleUpon, and Delicious), but you have *many* more options to choose from. That's where this chapter comes into play.

Don't rely solely on the heavy hitters of the social Web, described in Chapter 12, to network and share content online. A variety of niche and growing social networking and social bookmarking sites can help you build an audience for your blog. In fact, new sites pop up every day. Take the time to research the networking and bookmarking sites and find ones that will help you the most, and then focus your efforts on those sites. The ones you choose are the ones where people like you (and the people who would want to read your blog) are spending their time.

Friendster

www.Friendster.com

The popular Friendster site is very similar to other popular social networking sites such as Facebook and LinkedIn. Friendster (shown in Figure 17-1), which is open to anyone over the age of 16, invites its more than 75 million members from around the world to connect, share information, and communicate in a common space. The site offers a variety of applications to users to customize their experiences, including a mobile application. The clean design of Friendster helps you easily find friends and try applications.

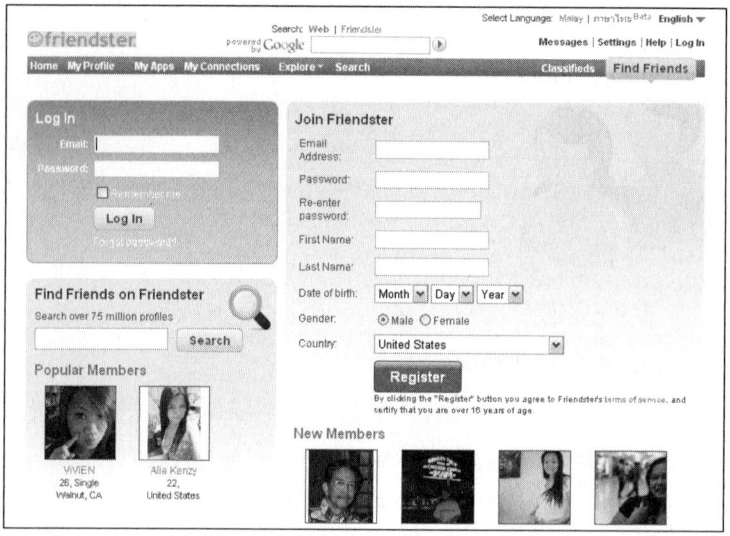

Figure 17-1: The clean design of Friendster makes it easy to find friends and try applications.

BlogHer

www.BlogHer.com

The BlogHer social networking site is unique in that its intended audience is women bloggers. BlogHer (shown in Figure 17-2) offers a directory of female bloggers, advertising, forums, and conferences. Additionally, members can create their own blogs on BlogHer to share thoughts, ideas, and news so female bloggers can communicate, network, and grow.

Figure 17-2: BlogHer provides easy navigation to blogs, a blog directory, conferences, ads, and more.

Orkut

`www.Orkut.com`

Members of Orkut, a social networking site owned by Google, can communicate, connect, and share information, pictures, and videos. Although Orkut isn't one of the most popular social networking sites, it has a strong Brazilian user base. You can sign in to Orkut by using the Google Account information you set up when you created your Blogger blog (see Figure 17-3), so it's easy to get started.

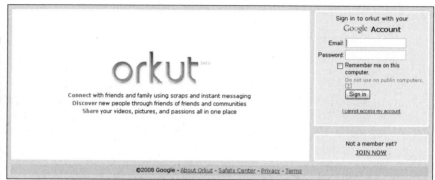

Figure 17-3:
You can sign in to Orkut with your existing Google Account information.

Reddit

www.Reddit.com

Reddit (shown in Figure 17-4) is a popular social bookmarking site known for its "no frills" appearance. To use Reddit, you create a free account and begin submitting content by clicking the Submit button on the Reddit site. As users vote content up and down, the most popular content makes it to the home page of Reddit and drives a lot of traffic to that blog or Web site. Reddit has a reputation of focusing on offbeat news and unique commentary on current news.

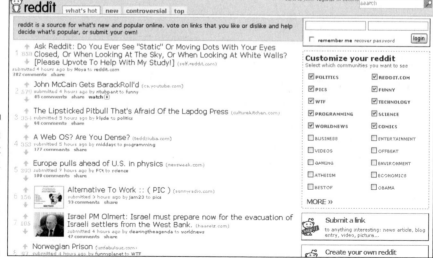

Figure 17-4:
Reddit might not look like much, but it's jam-packed with user submissions.

Furl

www.Furl.net

Furl (see Figure 17-5) is a unique social bookmarking site because it lets users save, for later access, a copy of any page online as it appears at that moment. Each member can store as much as 5 gigabytes of data. Users can also search and share saved pages with each other.

Figure 17-5: Furl lets users find, save, and share content.

Slashdot

www.Slashdot.com

The Slashdot slogan says it all: "News for nerds and stuff that matters." Slashdot (shown in Figure 17-6) has a reputation for being an outstanding social bookmarking site for people looking to find and share content related to technology, science, or science fiction. Slashdot works slightly differently from other social bookmarking sites in that submissions are reviewed by editors before they're available for the Slashdot community to view.

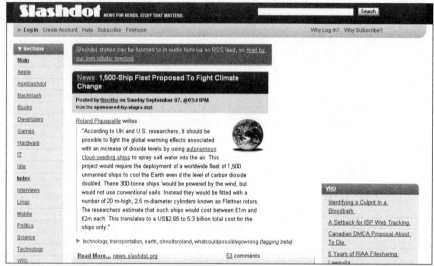

Figure 17-6:
News for
nerds and
stuff that
matters.

Newsvine

www.Newsvine.com

The Newsvine social bookmarking site (shown in Figure 17-7) weighs submissions by popularity, freshness of content, and reputation of the user who submitted the content. The site is popular for finding serious business or news content. The community rates submissions, and highly rated submissions can drive a lot of traffic to the original site or blog.

Figure 17-7:
Newsvine
caters to
news and
business
niches.

Magnolia

www.Ma.gnolia.com

The growing social bookmarking site Magnolia lets users save Web pages
with tags, search other people's tags, make friends, and share content.
Magnolia's reputation relies more on its strong focus on joining communities and discussions rather than on finding content. From the Magnolia home
page (shown in Figure 17-8), for example, users can easily enter tags in the
Search field at the bottom of the page to find content of interest.

Figure 17-8:
Magnolia focuses on helping users join communities and discussions.

Kirtsy

www.kirtsy.com

Although Kirtsy (see Figure 17-9), a newer social bookmarking site, focuses on content of interest to a female audience, it's open to anyone to join and use. Members share content, make friends, and communicate with each other. Additionally, a group of editors provides content that's featured on the Kirtsy home page.

Figure 17-9:
The Kirtsy home page prominently displays links to popular content and editor picks.

Propeller

www.Propeller.com

Propeller (shown in Figure 17-10) is offered through AOL and works similarly to other popular social bookmarking sites, such as Digg. The interface looks good, and it works well too. Users submit and vote on content, search by using user-defined tags, communicate, and share information in a social atmosphere. Propeller has a reputation of focusing on news and political content.

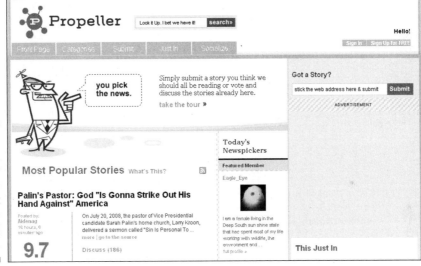

Figure 17-10: The sleek Propeller design makes it easy to find useful content.

Chapter 18

Ten Common Blogger Problems and Possible Solutions

In This Chapter

▶ Keeping your Blogger account accessible

▶ Avoiding spam problems

▶ Making all your blog elements show up properly

▶ Ensuring that strange characters don't show up

As you work with Blogger, you're likely to encounter questions or problems. Unfortunately, as with most computer and Internet applications, Blogger doesn't always work perfectly. Known bugs and fixes are frequently posted on the Blogger Buzz blog (at `http://buzz.blogger.com`), but solutions to common problems such as recovering a forgotten password or publishing your profile can be found in this chapter or by visiting the Blogger Help Web site at `http://help.blogger.com`.

If you encounter a problem with Blogger, don't panic. Take some time to read through this chapter, visit the Blogger blog and the Blogger Help Web site, or post a question in the Blogger Help Group (`http://groups.google.com/group/blogger-help`). Chances are good that someone else has struggled through the same problem you're having, and the answer can be found with a bit of research.

You Have Trouble Signing In to Your Blogger Account

You might have trouble signing in to your Blogger account for many reasons, such as

▮ ✔ You're using an incorrect username.

✔ You're using an incorrect password.

✔ You're having browser problems.

Username problems

The first thing to check when you try to log in to your Blogger account without success is your username. Make sure that the one you enter into the login box is correct. Your username is the same as the e-mail address you used to set up your original Google account. If you can't remember the e-mail address you used then, visit the Google Accounts Password Assistance page at https://www.google.com/accounts/ForgotPasswd, shown in Figure 18-1.

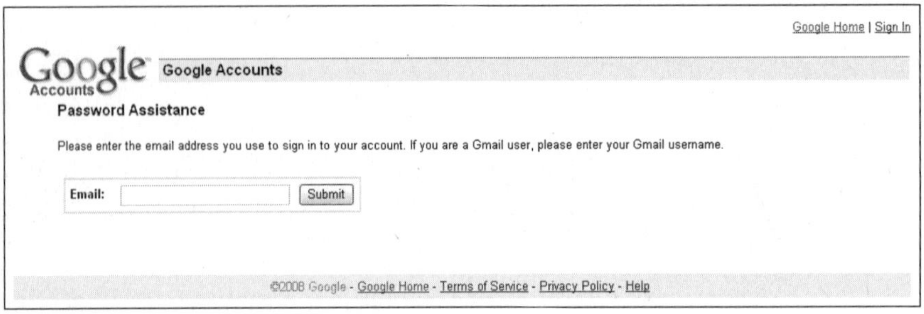

Figure 18-1:
Accessing
your
Blogger
username.

Google Home | Sign In

Google Accounts

Password Assistance

Please enter the email address you use to sign in to your account. If you are a Gmail user, please enter your Gmail username.

Email: [   ] [Submit]

©2008 Google - Google Home - Terms of Service - Privacy Policy - Help

One at a time, enter into the Email text box each possible address that you could have used to set up your Google account, and click the Submit button each time. A message is returned after each submission stating that either an account doesn't exist for that e-mail address or an e-mail has been sent to that address with a link for you to click to reset your password. Follow the link in the e-mail message to reset your password. Going forward, use that e-mail address as your Blogger account username and use your new password to log in to your account.

You can also look up your username by filling out the Forgot Your Username or Password form, described in the following section.

Password problems

If you can't remember your Blogger account password, simply click the question mark symbol in the Password (?) link. It's in the upper-right corner of the Blogger home page (www.blogger.com), shown in Figure 18-2. The Forgot Your Username or Password form opens, as shown in Figure 18-3. Complete this form to access your account information. Your password is automatically e-mailed to the e-mail address associated with your Blogger account.

Figure 18-2: Click the question mark (?) link to retrieve your password.

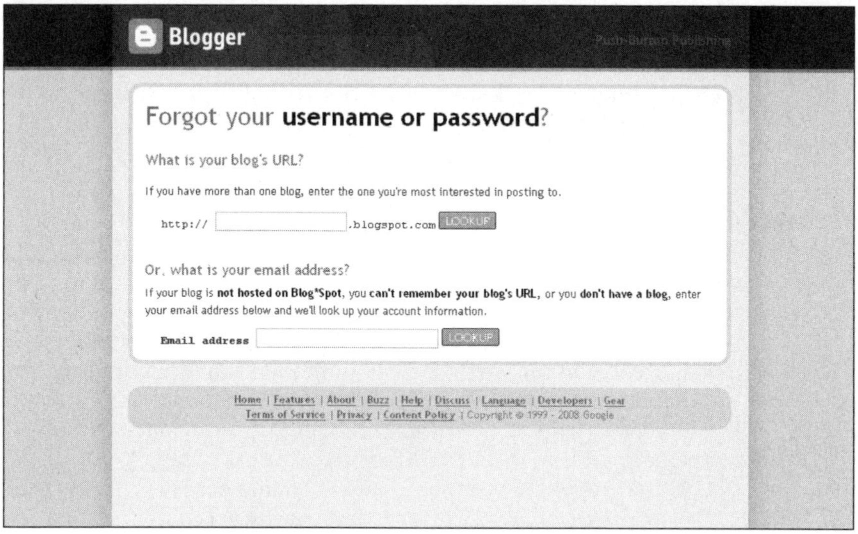

Figure 18-3: Complete the recovery form to access your forgotten username or password.

Browser problems

Your browser settings can make it difficult for you to log in to your Blogger account. Your first step to fix a browser problem is to clear your browser's cache and cookies. Also make sure that your computer's antivirus software and firewall are configured correctly to accept Blogger's cookies and enable JavaScript, both of which are required for Blogger to work properly.

You Cannot Access Your Blogger Account

Although Google tries to ensure that Blogger is accessible at all times, sometimes when you try to log in to your Blogger account, you see a browser error page telling you that the page isn't available. If this happens, check to make sure that your internet connection is working. If possible, try to access your account from another computer. If you still can't access your blog, visit `http://status.blogger.com`, where you can find updates on current Blogger status issues.

You Discover the Case of the Disappearing Blog

Unfortunately, sometimes a blogger is faced with a blank dashboard after logging in to a Blogger account. Alternatively, bloggers and readers sometimes type known URLs into their browsers only to find that the blogs are no longer available. Two primary reasons explain the mystery of the disappearing blog:

- **The blogger logged in to his Blogger account with the wrong username and password.**

  This situation happens frequently to people who maintain more than one Blogger account.

- **The blogger violated the Blogger or Google terms of service.**

  This problem happens to bloggers who didn't adhere to the policies they agreed to abide by when they created their Google and Blogger accounts. For example, a blog that publishes pornographic, violent, or hateful content would be in violation of the Blogger content policy.

If your blog is truly gone, contact Blogger for assistance by submitting the online help form at `www.blogger.com/problem.g`.

Your Blog Is Identified As Spam

The most common reason a blog might be identified as spam is when it includes ads with no (or very little) original content, which is a violation of the Blogger and Google terms of service. Google uses an automated process to identify blogs as spam. Unfortunately, that means some blogs that aren't spam can be erroneously identified as spam and disabled. If this happens to your blog, it appears on your Blogger dashboard, but you cannot access it. Luckily, Blogger users can follow a review process to request that Google reactivate their blogs.

Typically, when a blog is locked after being detected as potential spam, an e-mail is sent to the e-mail address used to set up the original Google account. The message notifies the blogger that

✔ An automated system determined the blog to be spam.

✔ The account has been locked.

The e-mail also provides a link that the blogger can follow to complete a form requesting manual review and unlocking of the blog. In the e-mail, the blogger is given a specific timeframe to submit a review request.

Some blogs identified as potential spam are modified by Google and a word-verification step is added to the post editor. To publish a new post, the blogger must enter the word-verification text. The blogger can click the question mark icon next to the word-verification form and fill out a form to request to have the blog reviewed and the word-verification step removed.

You Don't' Know Why Changes Aren't Being Published

Sometimes, you can make changes to your blog, click the Save or Publish button, and nothing happens. The changes you made appear within your Blogger dashboard, but your live blog looks exactly the way it did before you made any changes. What's going on? This common problem is most often caused by your browser's cookies and cache settings.

Web browsers store copies of pages that you visit as you're surfing the Web. When you load a page online (for example, a page you just published on your blog), the saved version stored in your blog's cache sometimes appears rather than the newest version. If your recent changes don't appear on your blog, use your browser tools to clear your cache and delete your cookies, and then refresh the page in your browser window.

If a single blog post doesn't publish, check to make sure that you didn't save it as a draft rather than publish it.

You Have Profile Problems

Although Chapter 5 shows you how to create a complete profile, sometimes you can have trouble publishing certain elements of your profile. If your profile picture, blogs, interests, and favorites don't appear correctly online, you can try some of these suggestions to fix the problem:

✔ **Your profile picture doesn't publish.**

Make sure that the image was correctly uploaded to the Web using Picasa, Flickr, or your preferred method, and then ensure that you entered the correct URL for the image. The URL must be fewer than 64 characters, and the file size must be smaller than 50KB. Additionally, you should use a Web-friendly format, such as JPG, GIF, or PNG.

✔ **One or more of your blogs doesn't appear on your list of blogs in your profile.**

Click the Edit Profile link on the Blogger dashboard. The Edit User Profile window opens. In the Show My Blogs section, click the Select Blogs to Display link and select the check boxes next to the blogs you want to display on your profile, as shown in Figure 18-4. Remember to click the Save button.

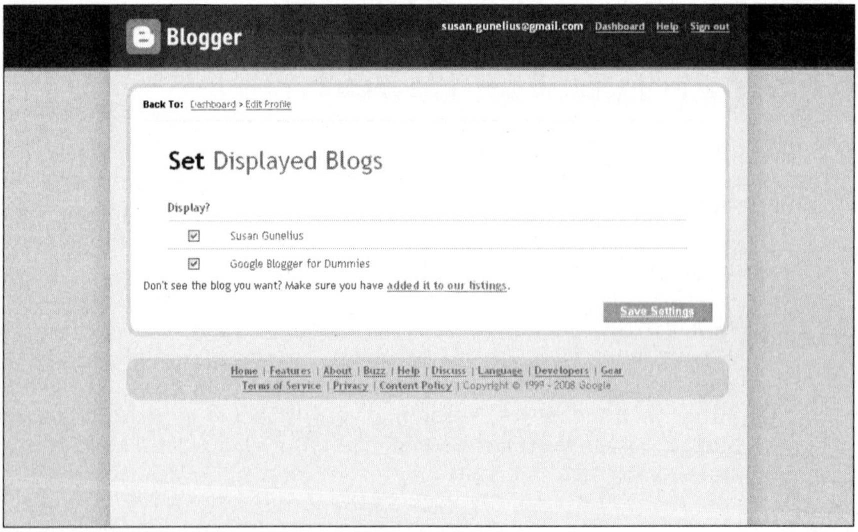

Figure 18-4:
Only the blogs you select appear in your profile.

✔ **Interests and favorites don't publish.**

Each of the Interests and Favorites sections of your blog profile must be fewer than 2,000 characters or else they don't publish.

Your Text Formatting Buttons Are Missing

The Blogger post editor allows users to type blog posts using HTML code or a WYSIWYG (What You See Is What You Get) post editor. Using the WYSIWYG post editor, referred to as working in *Compose* mode, provides users with a toolbar of useful icons to make blog post writing similar to writing a document in word processing software.

If the formatting icons don't appear in your post editor, visit the Settings page within your Blogger dashboard and select the Basics tab. Scroll down to the Compose Mode for All Your Blogs option and choose Yes from the drop-down menu. Remember to click the Save button to save your changes. After this setting is configured, you can use the Compose mode with the formatting buttons visible to write your blog posts.

Many features of Blogger use JavaScript, including the text formatting buttons. If your browser doesn't support JavaScript, the text formatting buttons don't work.

Your Post Labels Are Missing

If you enter labels into your posts but they don't publish on your blog, make sure that they're configured to be displayed. From the Blogger dashboard, click the Layout link and then the Page Elements tab. In the Blog Posts box, click the Edit link to change your blog post configuration settings. The Configure Blog Posts window opens. Select the check box next to Labels, and then click the Save button. After you save your change, labels automatically appear on your blog.

You See Strange Characters, Blank Pages, or Undecipherable Code

If you copy and paste text from Microsoft Word or another program that uses encoding that's different from Blogger's, the published text might look strange. A simple way to correct this problem is to copy and paste the text into Notepad or a similar program to remove all encoding. Then copy it again from Notepad and paste it into your Blogger post editor.

You Have a Floating Sidebar

If you include an element in one of your blog's columns that's wider than the width of that column, the sidebar moves to the bottom of the page. It's important to note that the sidebar might float to the bottom of the page on your computer, but not on your friend's computer. Similarly, the sidebar might float to the bottom of the page when you view your blog in one browser, but not in another.

Each browser and computer is set up differently, but if your sidebar is floating in one, you have to find out what's causing the problem. Check the width of the various elements included in your blog's columns, and find the one that's too wide for the column it's in. Make the necessary changes to the element that's causing the problem. Refresh your browser, and your blog should display correctly.

Chapter 19

Ten Places to Find Free Blogger Themes and Templates

In This Chapter

▶ Creating a unique look and feel for your blog with third-party templates

▶ Finding free Blogger themes and templates

*I*f you want your blog to have a more distinctive look and feel than the commonly used Blogger templates provide, you can look into having a custom Blogger template created for your blog. Of course, custom design work doesn't come without a price tag, so if you want to keep expenses down and still have a distinctive blog design, you can download a free template from a wide variety of Web sites.

Many blog designers create Blogger templates and share them with Blogger users for free. Although another person is likely to choose the same free template you choose, it will certainly be more distinctive than if you simply use one of the templates from your Blogger dashboard. Chapter 7 provides details on how to switch from a free template from Blogger to one that you download from another Web site. This chapter provides ten resources where you can find free Blogger templates to use on your blog.

eBlogTemplates

www.eblogtemplates.com

The eblog templates site provides a huge directory of Blogger templates that you can download for free. Each free template is listed along with reviews, live demos, statistics, download instructions, creation dates, and designer information. You can sort the free Blogger templates by review rating or download frequency. Chances are good that even the pickiest bloggers can find templates they like from the more than 140 free Blogger templates.

To find the free templates, shown in Figure 19-1, just select the Blogger tab from the top navigation bar. You can then click through the various pages listing the free Blogger templates that are available for immediate download to use on your blog.

Figure 19-1:
A site that even picky bloggers can love.

BTemplates

http://btemplates.com

BTemplates offers more than 450 free Blogger templates for download and use without restrictions. The site is dedicated solely to providing Blogger templates, so you aren't bogged down by wading through WordPress or other blogging platform templates. In the right sidebar of the BTemplates Web site (see Figure 19-2), you can choose from a variety of categories to narrow your search. For example, you can filter the Blogger templates by number of columns or colors.

The free templates available at BTemplates are displayed with review information and the creation date and number of downloads. Overall, the site is easy to navigate and gives you lots of choices for free Blogger templates.

BlogFlux

http://themes.BlogFlux.com

BlogFlux offers a blog theme directory with more than 130 free Blogger templates available for download. Each template is displayed with a review rating and an online demo, and the creation date is listed. You also see a link to view the BlogFlux profile for the template designer.

To view the free Blogger templates available from BlogFlux, click the Blogger link in the left column under the Blog Software heading, shown in Figure 19-3. Then click through the Blogger template designs to find one you want to download.

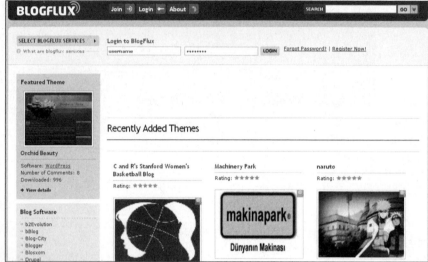

Figure 19-3:
Check out
the review
ratings of
free Blogger
templates.

BloggerBuster

www.bloggerbuster.com

The Blogger Buster blog, written by Blogger user and designer Amanda Fazani, also includes a list of free Blogger themes that she created. A long-time Blogger user, Amanda creates templates from the fun and quirky design to the serious and professional layout. You can also view demos of each of Amanda's Blogger template designs and find instructions to use each one.

To find free templates on Blogger Buster, simply select Templates from the top navigation bar, as shown in Figure 19-4.

Figure 19-4:
Find templates from the fun and quirky to the serious and professional.

Pyzam

www.Pyzam.com

Pyzam.com offers a wide variety of blog template designs, MySpace layouts, graphics, widgets, pictures, and much more, including free Blogger templates. Prepare to spend some time searching the site because it offers more than 1,000 free Blogger templates. Fortunately, you can search using the handy categories available in the left sidebar. Thousands of keywords are used to create categories on Pyzam.

To search the free Blogger templates offered on this site, shown in Figure 19-5, click the Blogger Templates link in the left sidebar. The sidebar expands to reveal a variety of Blogger template categories to choose from. Select More Categories from that list to display an alphabetical listing of all the keywords used to categorize the Blogger templates available on the site.

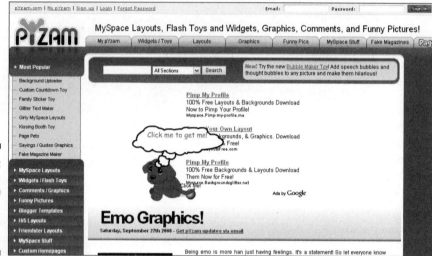

Figure 19-5:
Find more
than 1,000
free tem-
plates at the
Pyzam site.

All Blog Tools

> http://www.allblogtools.com/category/blogger-templates/

All Blog Tools has a goal to be the largest online source for free Blogger templates. All designs are credited to the original designers, and the site makes finding just the type of template you want very easy.

To view the free Blogger templates on this site, visit www.allblogtools. com, and select Blogger Templates from the top navigation bar. Then simply use the Browse by Category and Browse by Layout links in the sidebar shown in Figure 19-6 to narrow your search, scroll through the design thumbnails, and select each one to view a larger example, a demo, and design details.

Figure 19-6:
AllBlog
Tools.com
provides
free Blogger
templates
from a
variety of
designers.

Blogger-Templates.Blogspot

www.Blogger-Templates.blogspot.com

The popular Blogger-Templates site lets you find free Blogger templates, even though it can be cumbersome to navigate and search. You can use the links in the Browse Templates section of the right sidebar, shown in Figure 19-7, to narrow your search, and you have a wide variety of designs to choose from.

Figure 19-7:
This site is
somewhat
cumber-
some but
popular and
useful.

JackBook

www.jackbook.com/category/blogger-templates-gallery

The popular and well-known site JackBook is helpful for finding free Blogger templates. Its downside is that it takes a while to navigate the list of templates to find one you like, because you have to click each template listing to view it. However, JackBook is also known for providing some of the most popular Blogger templates, so it's definitely a site that's worth taking some time to explore.

To find free Blogger templates on JackBook (shown in Figure 19-8), simply visit the URL listed here, and then scroll through the list of links to find available Blogger templates.

Figure 19-8: JackBook provides popular, free Blogger templates.

BlogCrowds

www.blogcrowds.com/resources/blogger_template.php

The Blogcrowds site offers nearly 100 free Blogger templates. You can find simple download instructions and demos, and the site's categorization helps you easily find the type of template you're looking for. To find free Blogger templates, click the Resources link from the top navigation page. Then click the Blogger Templates link on the Resources page, shown in Figure 19-9, to open the directory of Blogger templates.

Figure 19-9:
This well-known and well-established site offers a variety of templates.

BloggerBlogTemplates

www.BloggerBlogTemplates.blogspot.com

The Blogger Blog Templates blog is written by Blogger users, who provide a useful compilation of some of the best free Blogger templates available online. You use the simple links at the top of every page to filter templates by number of columns, by selected colors, or by a variety of other criteria. The site is easy to navigate and use, and each template includes a commentary from the site's authors.

To find free templates at the Blogger Templates site, shown in Figure 19-10, scroll through the blog posts. Alternatively, you can use the navigation tabs at the top of the page or the tags in the tag cloud (the series of keywords) at the top of the page to narrow your search.

Always save and back up your existing template code before you replace it. Read Chapter 7 for complete details on changing your Blogger template.

Figure 19-10: Author commentary is included in the templates on this easy-to-use site.

Glossary

affiliate advertising: A process in which bloggers display ads for advertisers as affiliates for those advertisers, and the advertisers pay the bloggers every time blog visitors follow those ad links and make purchases or perform specified actions. Popular affiliate advertising programs include Amazon Associates, LinkShare, and Commission Junction.

archive: The location on a blog where posts that aren't current are stored for easy access by visitors.

Atom: A type of syndication format used to deliver feeds. *See also* feed, feed reader, RSS.

attribution: The citing of the source of a story, a quote, or an image used within a blog post.

audio blog: *See* podcast.

backlink: A reference link (or "shoulder tap") used to notify one Blogger.com blog when another Blogger.com blog has linked to that site. Backlinks appear as links within the comments section of blog posts

blog: An online diary with entries listed in reverse chronological order, one of the first methods of bringing user-generated content to the mainstream. It's a shorter version of the original term *weblog,* a fusion of the words *Web* and *log.* As blogging grew in popularity, individuals, groups, and businesses joined the blogosphere. Blogs uniquely provide a two-way conversation between author and visitor by using the commenting feature.

blog carnival: A blogging promotional event in which a group of bloggers gathers virtually to write about a predetermined topic. All participants submit the links to their posts, and all links are published in a single carnival round-up post. All participants promote the carnival on their blogs with the intention of driving traffic to all blogs involved.

blog contest: A blogging promotional event in which a giveaway is raffled in order to drive traffic to the hosting blog.

blog host: A company that provides space (for free or for a fee) on its servers to store and maintain blogs.

blog marketing: The process of promoting your blog to drive traffic to it. Examples of blog promotion tactics include leaving comments on other blogs with links back to your blog; linking to blogs within your blog posts and sending backlinks or trackbacks to those blogs; adding blogs to your blogroll; and participating in social bookmarking and networking. Also called *blog promotion.*

blog post: An individual entry written by a blogger and published on a blog.

blog promotion: See *blog marketing.*

blog statistics: The data used to track the performance of a blog.

blogger: A person who writes content for a blog.

Blogger: An online software program, owned by Google, that helps users create and maintain blogs.

blogging: The act of writing and publishing blog posts or entries.

blogging software: The program used by bloggers to create and maintain blogs, such as Blogger, LiveJournal, Moveable Type, TypePad, and WordPress. Also called *blog platform.*

blogosphere: The online blogging community, made up of bloggers from around the world creating user-generated content as part of the social Web.

blogroll: A list of links created by a blogger and published on her blog. Links in a blogroll are typically related to the blog topic or other sites that the blogger enjoys or recommends.

bounce rate: The percentage of people who leave a blog immediately after finding it.

browser: A software application used to surf the Internet, including Internet Explorer, Firefox, Opera, Safari, Google Chrome, and others. Also called *Web browser.*

comment: An opinion or a reaction, written by a blog reader, to a specific post. Comments can be submitted at the end of blog posts when the blogger has chosen to allow them.

comment moderation: The process of holding comments for review before publishing them on a blog so spam and offensive comments aren't published.

comment policy: A set of rules and restrictions published on a blog to set visitor expectations about which types of comments are allowed and which types are likely to be deleted.

contextual advertising: A type of ad that's based on the content found on the page where the ad appears. Popular contextual advertising programs include Google AdSense and Kontera.

CSS: The acronym for *Cascading Style Sheets*, which is used by Web designers to create blog layouts. CSS coding directs the look and feel of a blog.

dashboard: The primary account management page of an online software program, such as Blogger or Google AdSense, where users can access the tools and functionality to modify settings and create content, for example.

domain name: The part of a URL that represents a specific Web site. Domain names are typically preceded by the letters www. and end with an extension, such as .com or .net.

feed: The syndicated content of a blog. *See also* feed reader, RSS.

feed reader: A tool used to receive feeds from blogs and deliver them to subscribers in aggregated format for quick and easy viewing in one place.

flame: A message, a comment, a blog post, or another online published submission intended to attack or undermine another person.

flame war: The process of exchanging blog posts, comments, or online content between two people in an ongoing, back-and-forth manner for the purpose of attacking or undermining one another.

flash: Streaming animation that appears on Web pages.

footer: The area spanning the bottom of a blog page, which typically includes copyright information and may include other elements, such as a contact link or ads.

forum: An online message board where participants post messages in predetermined categories, creating an online conversation between a potentially large group of people.

FTP: The acronym for File Transfer Protocol, a process used to transfer files from one computer to another across the Internet.

Google: A company based in California that produces software, programs, tools, and utilities to help people use the Internet to accomplish tasks.

Popular Google programs include Google AdSense, Google AdWords, Google Docs, Google Groups, and Google Search.

guest blogging: The process of writing free posts to appear on another person's blog, or accepting free posts from another blogger to publish on your blog, with the purpose of networking and driving blog traffic.

header: The area spanning the top of a blog page where the blog title, graphics, and, possibly, navigational links or ads appear.

hit: A blog statistic that's counted every time a file is downloaded from your blog. Each page in a blog or Web site typically contains multiple files.

home page: The first page visitors see when they enter a root domain name.

HTML: The acronym for Hypertext Markup Language, a programming language made up of tags used to create Web sites and blogs.

HTML editor: The section of the blog post editor within a blogging software application, such as Blogger, in which the blogger must enter HTML code to create the post rather than typing text in a WYSIWIG (What You See is What You Get) post editor. *See also* WYSWIG.

hyperlink: *See* link.

impression-based advertising: An ad model in which bloggers publish ads for advertisers and are paid based on the number of times visitors see those ads. Popular impression-based advertising programs include Tribal Fusion and ValueClick.

keyword: A word or phrase used to help index a Web page by topic so that search engines can find it.

label: A keyword used in Blogger to categorize a blog post.

link: A connection between two Web sites that, when selected, opens another Web page in the user's browser. Also called *hyperlink*.

link bait: A post written for the primary purpose of attracting traffic and links. Link bait posts are typically related to popular topics that might have nothing to do with the topic of the blog on which the post is published.

lurker: A person who frequently reads blogs but doesn't leave comments or make his presence known.

message board: *See* forum.

microblogging: A method of publishing short snippets (typically 140 characters or fewer) by using a site such as Twitter or Plurk.

moblogging: The process of writing and publishing blog posts using mobile technology, such as cellular phones. A fusion of the words *mobile* and *blogging,* it's also called *mobile blogging.*

multiuser blog: A blog authored by more than one person that can be edited by multiple people using blogging software.

newbie: A person who is new to blogging or forum participation or another online activity. Also called *noob.*

niche: A specific and highly targeted segment of an audience or market. A niche blog appeals to a specific group of people.

page rank: A ranking used to determine a blog's popularity, typically based on traffic and incoming links.

page view: A blog statistic that tracks the number of times a Web page is viewed independent of who is viewing the page.

permalink: A link to a specific page in a blog that remains unchanged over time. It's a fusion of the words *permanent* and *link.*

ping: A signal sent from one Web site to another to ensure that the other site exists. Pings are also used to notify sites that receive information from ping servers of updates to a blog or Web site.

podcast: An audio file that's recorded digitally for playback online. Bloggers use podcasts to create audio blog posts. Also called *audio blogging.*

post: An entry on a blog, typically published in reverse chronological order.

post editor: The blogging software function that a blogger uses for typing the content of a blog post. *See also* HTML editor, visual editor.

professional blogger: A person who writes blogs as a career.

profile: A blogger's About Me page, which describes who the blogger is and why she's qualified to write the blog.

referrer: A Web site, blog, or search engine that leads visitors to a blog.

RSS: The acronym for Really Simple Syndication, the technology that collects Web content. Users subscribe to Web sites and blogs. The updates to those Web sites and blogs are collected together, and subscribers receive new content from those sites in one place within a feed reader. *See also* feed, feed reader.

search engine: A Web site used to find Web pages related to specific keywords or keyword phrases. Search engines use proprietary criteria to examine the Internet and return results relevant to submitted keywords. Results are typically presented in a ranked order determined by the aforementioned proprietary criteria. Google, Yahoo! and MSN Search are popular search engines.

search engine optimization: The process of writing Web content, designing Web pages, and promoting online content to boost rankings within search engine keyword searches. Also called *SEO.*

SEO: *See* search engine optimization.

sidebar: A column on a blog to the right or left or flanking the largest, main column. Sidebars typically include ancillary content, such as a blogroll, archives, and ads.

social bookmarking: A method of saving, storing, and sharing Web pages for reference. Popular social bookmarking sites include Delicious, Digg, Reddit, and StumbleUpon.

social networking: The act of communicating and building relationships with other people online. Popular social networking sites include Facebook, Friendster, and LinkedIn.

social Web: The second generation of the World Wide Web, which focuses on interaction, user-generated content, communities, and building relationships. Also called *Web 2.0.*

spam: A type of comment submitted on a blog for no reason other than to drive traffic to another Web site. Spam can also come in e-mail form.

sponsored review: A blog post written for the purpose of being paid by an advertiser who solicits it. Popular sponsored review networks include PayPerPost.com, ReviewMe.com, and SponsoredReviews.com.

subscribe: To sign up to receive a blog's feed in a feed reader or by e-mail.

tag: A keyword used to identify and categorize a blog post. Tags are also read by blog search engines to provide search results to users.

Technorati: A popular blog search engine.

template: A predesigned blog layout created to make it easy for people with little to no computer knowledge to start and maintain a blog. Also called *theme.*

text link ad: A type of ads that appears as a simple text link on blogs and Web sites. Text link ads are typically used to drive business and to boost the number of incoming links for the advertiser's Web site, thereby boosting the advertiser's page rank.

third-party host: A company other than a blogger's blogging software provider that stores blogs on its server for a fee.

trackback: A reference link (or "shoulder tap") used to notify a blog when another blog has linked to that site. Trackbacks appear as links within the comments section of blog posts. Blogger.com does not accept trackbacks from other blogs.

troll: A person who posts comments intended to detract from the ongoing conversation on a blog.

unique visitor: A person who visits a Web page and is counted one time regardless of how many times he visits it. *See also* visitor.

URL: The unique address of a specific page on the Internet consisting of an access protocol (for example, `http`), a domain name (for example, `www.sitename.com`), and an extension identifying the specific page within a Web site or blog (for example, `/specificpage.htm`). It's the acronym for Uniform Resource Locator.

visit: The occurrence of accessing a page on your blog.

visitor: A person who views a page (or multiple pages) on your blog.

visual editor: The blog post composition function that bloggers use to type posts by using an interface similar to common word processing. *See also* WYSIWYG.

vlogging: The process of publishing videos rather than written blog posts. A fusion of the words *video* and *blog;* also called *video blogging.*

Web log: *See* blog.

Web 2.0: *See* social Web.

WYSIWYG: The acronym for What You See Is What You Get. The visual editor provided by most blogging software programs allows users to type blog post content in a form similar to traditional word processing software, so they can see how a post will look online as they type it.

Index

• *C* •

• N •

• O •

• P •

• •

• •

BUSINESS, CAREERS & PERSONAL FINANCE

Accounting For Dummies, 4th Edition*
978-0-470-24600-9

Bookkeeping Workbook For Dummies†
978-0-470-16983-4

Commodities For Dummies
978-0-470-04928-0

Doing Business in China For Dummies
978-0-470-04929-7

E-Mail Marketing For Dummies
978-0-470-19087-6

Job Interviews For Dummies, 3rd Edition*†
978-0-470-17748-8

Personal Finance Workbook For Dummies*†
978-0-470-09933-9

Real Estate License Exams For Dummies
978-0-7645-7623-2

Six Sigma For Dummies
978-0-7645-6798-8

Small Business Kit For Dummies,
2nd Edition*†
978-0-7645-5984-6

Telephone Sales For Dummies
978-0-470-16836-3

BUSINESS PRODUCTIVITY & MICROSOFT OFFICE

Access 2007 For Dummies
978-0-470-03649-5

Excel 2007 For Dummies
978-0-470-03737-9

Office 2007 For Dummies
978-0-470-00923-9

Outlook 2007 For Dummies
978-0-470-03830-7

PowerPoint 2007 For Dummies
978-0-470-04059-1

Project 2007 For Dummies
978-0-470-03651-8

QuickBooks 2008 For Dummies
978-0-470-18470-7

Quicken 2008 For Dummies
978-0-470-17473-9

Salesforce.com For Dummies,
2nd Edition
978-0-470-04893-1

Word 2007 For Dummies
978-0-470-03658-7

EDUCATION, HISTORY, REFERENCE & TEST PREPARATION

American American History For Dummies
978-0-7645-5469-8

Algebra For Dummies
978-0-7645-5325-7

Algebra Workbook For Dummies
978-0-7645-8467-1

Art History For Dummies
978-0-470-09910-0

ASVAB For Dummies, 2nd Edition
978-0-470-10671-6

British Military History For Dummies
978-0-470-03213-8

Calculus For Dummies
978-0-7645-2498-1

Canadian History For Dummies, 2nd Edition
978-0-470-83656-9

Geometry Workbook For Dummies
978-0-471-79940-5

The SAT I For Dummies, 6th Edition
978-0-7645-7193-0

Series 7 Exam For Dummies
978-0-470-09932-2

World History For Dummies
978-0-7645-5242-7

FOOD, GARDEN, HOBBIES & HOME

Bridge For Dummies, 2nd Edition
978-0-471-92426-5

Coin Collecting For Dummies, 2nd Edition
978-0-470-22275-1

Cooking Basics For Dummies, 3rd Edition
978-0-7645-7206-7

Drawing For Dummies
978-0-7645-5476-6

Etiquette For Dummies, 2nd Edition
978-0-470-10672-3

Gardening Basics For Dummies*†
978-0-470-03749-2

Knitting Patterns For Dummies
978-0-470-04556-5

Living Gluten-Free For Dummies†
978-0-471-77383-2

Painting Do-It-Yourself For Dummies
978-0-470-17533-0

HEALTH, SELF HELP, PARENTING & PETS

Anger Management For Dummies
978-0-470-03715-7

Anxiety & Depression Workbook
For Dummies
978-0-7645-9793-0

Dieting For Dummies, 2nd Edition
978-0-7645-4149-0

Dog Training For Dummies, 2nd Edition
978-0-7645-8418-3

Horseback Riding For Dummies
978-0-470-09719-9

Infertility For Dummies†
978-0-470-11518-3

Meditation For Dummies with CD-ROM,
2nd Edition
978-0-471-77774-8

Post-Traumatic Stress Disorder For Dummies
978-0-470-04922-8

Puppies For Dummies, 2nd Edition
978-0-470-03717-1

Thyroid For Dummies, 2nd Edition†
978-0-471-78755-6

Type 1 Diabetes For Dummies*†
978-0-470-17811-9

INTERNET & DIGITAL MEDIA

AdWords For Dummies
978-0-470-15252-2

Blogging For Dummies, 2nd Edition
978-0-470-23017-6

Digital Photography All-in-One Desk Reference For Dummies, 3rd Edition
978-0-470-03743-0

Digital Photography For Dummies, 5th Edition
978-0-7645-9802-9

Digital SLR Cameras & Photography For Dummies, 2nd Edition
978-0-470-14927-0

eBay Business All-in-One Desk Reference For Dummies
978-0-7645-8438-1

eBay For Dummies, 5th Edition*
978-0-470-04529-9

eBay Listings That Sell For Dummies
978-0-471-78912-3

Facebook For Dummies
978-0-470-26273-3

The Internet For Dummies, 11th Edition
978-0-470-12174-0

Investing Online For Dummies, 5th Edition
978-0-7645-8456-5

iPod & iTunes For Dummies, 5th Editi
978-0-470-17474-6

MySpace For Dummies
978-0-470-09529-4

Podcasting For Dummies
978-0-471-74898-4

Search Engine Optimization For Dummies, 2nd Edition
978-0-471-97998-2

Second Life For Dummies
978-0-470-18025-9

Starting an eBay Business For Dummi 3rd Edition†
978-0-470-14924-9

GRAPHICS, DESIGN & WEB DEVELOPMENT

Adobe Creative Suite 3 Design Premium All-in-One Desk Reference For Dummies
978-0-470-11724-8

Adobe Web Suite CS3 All-in-One Desk Reference For Dummies
978-0-470-12099-6

AutoCAD 2008 For Dummies
978-0-470-11650-0

Building a Web Site For Dummies, 3rd Edition
978-0-470-14928-7

Creating Web Pages All-in-One Desk Reference For Dummies, 3rd Edition
978-0-470-09629-1

Creating Web Pages For Dummies, 8th Edition
978-0-470-08030-6

Dreamweaver CS3 For Dummies
978-0-470-11490-2

Flash CS3 For Dummies
978-0-470-12100-9

Google SketchUp For Dummies
978-0-470-13744-4

InDesign CS3 For Dummies
978-0-470-11865-8

Photoshop CS3 All-in-One Desk Reference For Dummies
978-0-470-11195-6

Photoshop CS3 For Dummies
978-0-470-11193-2

Photoshop Elements 5 For Dummie
978-0-470-09810-3

SolidWorks For Dummies
978-0-7645-9555-4

Visio 2007 For Dummies
978-0-470-08983-5

Web Design For Dummies, 2nd Editi
978-0-471-78117-2

Web Sites Do-It-Yourself For Dummi
978-0-470-16903-2

Web Stores Do-It-Yourself For Dummi
978-0-470-17443-2

LANGUAGES, RELIGION & SPIRITUALITY

Arabic For Dummies
978-0-471-77270-5

Chinese For Dummies, Audio Set
978-0-470-12766-7

French For Dummies
978-0-7645-5193-2

German For Dummies
978-0-7645-5195-6

Hebrew For Dummies
978-0-7645-5489-6

Ingles Para Dummies
978-0-7645-5427-8

Italian For Dummies, Audio Set
978-0-470-09586-7

Italian Verbs For Dummies
978-0-471-77389-4

Japanese For Dummies
978-0-7645-5429-2

Latin For Dummies
978-0-7645-5431-5

Portuguese For Dummies
978-0-471-78738-9

Russian For Dummies
978-0-471-78001-4

Spanish Phrases For Dummies
978-0-7645-7204-3

Spanish For Dummies
978-0-7645-5194-9

Spanish For Dummies, Audio Set
978-0-470-09585-0

The Bible For Dummies
978-0-7645-5296-0

Catholicism For Dummies
978-0-7645-5391-2

The Historical Jesus For Dummies
978-0-470-16785-4

Islam For Dummies
978-0-7645-5503-9

Spirituality For Dummies, 2nd Edition
978-0-470-19142-2

NETWORKING AND PROGRAMMING

ASP.NET 3.5 For Dummies
978-0-470-19592-5

C# 2008 For Dummies
978-0-470-19109-5

Hacking For Dummies, 2nd Edition
978-0-470-05235-8

Home Networking For Dummies, 4th Edition
978-0-470-11806-1

Java For Dummies, 4th Edition
978-0-470-08716-9

Microsoft® SQL Server™ 2008 All-in-One Desk Reference For Dummies
978-0-470-17954-3

Networking All-in-One Desk Reference For Dummies, 2nd Edition
978-0-7645-9939-2

Networking For Dummies, 8th Edition
978-0-470-05620-2

SharePoint 2007 For Dummies
978-0-470-09941-4

Wireless Home Networking For Dummies, 2nd Edition
978-0-471-74940-0

OPERATING SYSTEMS & COMPUTER BASICS

Mac For Dummies, 5th Edition
-0-7645-8458-9

Laptops For Dummies, 2nd Edition
-0-470-05432-1

Linux For Dummies, 8th Edition
8-0-470-11649-4

MacBook For Dummies
8-0-470-04859-7

Mac OS X Leopard All-in-One Desk Reference For Dummies
8-0-470-05434-5

Mac OS X Leopard For Dummies
978-0-470-05433-8

Macs For Dummies, 9th Edition
978-0-470-04849-8

PCs For Dummies, 11th Edition
978-0-470-13728-4

Windows® Home Server For Dummies
978-0-470-18592-6

Windows Server 2008 For Dummies
978-0-470-18043-3

Windows Vista All-in-One Desk Reference For Dummies
978-0-471-74941-7

Windows Vista For Dummies
978-0-471-75421-3

Windows Vista Security For Dummies
978-0-470-11805-4

SPORTS, FITNESS & MUSIC

Coaching Hockey For Dummies
8-0-470-83685-9

Coaching Soccer For Dummies
8-0-471-77381-8

Fitness For Dummies, 3rd Edition
8-0-7645-7851-9

Football For Dummies, 3rd Edition
8-0-470-12536-6

GarageBand For Dummies
978-0-7645-7323-1

Golf For Dummies, 3rd Edition
978-0-471-76871-5

Guitar For Dummies, 2nd Edition
978-0-7645-9904-0

Home Recording For Musicians For Dummies, 2nd Edition
978-0-7645-8884-6

iPod & iTunes For Dummies, 5th Edition
978-0-470-17474-6

Music Theory For Dummies
978-0-7645-7838-0

Stretching For Dummies
978-0-470-06741-3

Get smart @ dummies.com®

- Find a full list of Dummies titles
- Look into loads of FREE on-site articles
- Sign up for FREE eTips e-mailed to you weekly
- See what other products carry the Dummies name
- Shop directly from the Dummies bookstore
- Enter to win new prizes every month!

Separate Canadian edition also available
Separate U.K. edition also available

Available wherever books are sold. For more information or to order direct: U.S. customers visit www.dummies.com or call 1-877-762-2974.
U.K. customers visit www.wileyeurope.com or call (0) 1243 843291. Canadian customers visit www.wiley.ca or call 1-800-567-4797.

Good ✓

HAIR

Good
HAIR

NEW
HOLLAND

LIBBY PEACOCK

First published in 2005 by
New Holland Publishers
London • Cape Town • Sydney • Auckland
www.newhollandpublishers.com

86 Edgware Rd
London W2 2EA
United Kingdom

80 McKenzie Street
Cape Town 8001
South Africa

14 Aquatic Drive
Frenchs Forest, NSW 2086
Australia

218 Lake Road
Northcote, Auckland
New Zealand

Publisher: Mariëlle Renssen
Publishing managers: Claudia Dos Santos, Simon Pooley
Commissioning editor: Alfred LeMaitre
Studio manager: Richard MacArthur
Editor: Katja Splettstoesser
Designer: Elmari Kuyler
Illustrator: James Berrangé
Proofreader: Leizel Brown
Picture researchers: Karla Kik, Tamlyn McGeean
Production: Myrna Collins
Consultant: Beryl Barnard FSBTh. M.PHYS. ATT, Education
   Director, The London School of Beauty and Make-up

ISBN 1 84330 763 4 (HB); 1 84330 764 2 (PB)

Reproduction by Hirt & Carter (Cape) Pty Ltd
Printed and bound in Malaysia by Times Offset (M) Sdn. Bhd.

10 9 8 7 6 5 4 3 2

DEDICATION

This book is dedicated to all my wonderful friends. Thank you for helpin
me through the bad hair days!

DISCLAIMER

The author and publishers have made every effort to ensure that th
information contained in this book was accurate at the time of going
press, and accept no responsibility for any injury or inconvenience sustaine
by any person using this book or following the advice provided herein.

ACKNOWLEDGEMENTS

With special thanks to: Dr Sue Jessop (senior specialist and lecturer, division of Dermatology, Groote Schuur Hospital and University of Cape Town), for advising on and checking the medical sections in *Good Hair*. Dr Larry Gershowitz and the Medical Hair Restoration Clinic in Cape Town for up-to-date information on hair transplants. Dermatologist Dr Ian Webster for information on hair-removal methods and the pros and cons of laser hair removal in particular. Julia Lovely, dietician in private practice in Cape Town, for information on the impact of diet on hair. Tony Martin of Yazo4Hair salon, for parting with expert tips on hairstyling for men and women, and for top colouring advice. Dima Tsobanopulos of D&D Designers for Hair for styling tips, and information on face shapes and the latest straightening techniques. Carlton Skincare Centre, Constantia, Cape. Skincare therapist Gerda van Rooyen for the latest on hair removal and Ellen Nwenesongole of Procter & Gamble SA (Pty) Ltd, for reference material on hair and hair products.

contents

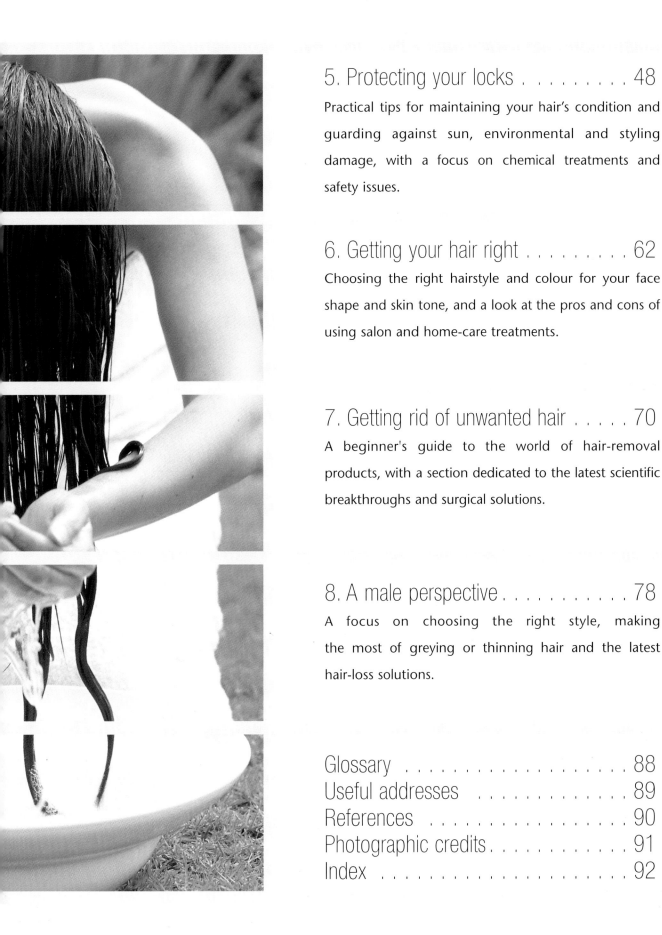

Hair as we know it

The English language is rich in hair-related expressions, for good reason: our hair is not only useful, it also reflects who we are. So, when we nitpick about small things, we split hairs; when we have a narrow escape, we escape by a hair's breadth; and when we have a good time, we let our hair down.

Hair gives away clues about our personalities and carries cultural connotations. Pious Christian nuns cover their hair. Muslim women wear headscarves to hide theirs from the eyes of all men but their husbands and immediate family. In India, hair is regarded as one of the most important aspects of feminine beauty. In some faiths, hair is cut during mourning. Several ancestral cultures still believe hair has magical powers; even in modern European countries some parents keep locks of their babies' hair.

Legends abound about hair: when Biblical hero Samson's long hair was cut, he lost his power; and, while blondes have more fun, redheads are believed to have a fiery temperament. Thankfully, many of these perceptions are not scientifically supported!

> *Assuming about 80 per cent of scalp hairs are in the active growth phase at any given time, a human produces about 9km (5.6 miles) of hair every year.*

8

Your hair's structure

Given that healthy hair is a reflection of one's general health, it is ironic that the visible part of a hair – the hair shaft – is physiologically speaking, dead, with only the tiny part underneath the scalp (the root or dermal papilla) consisting of living hair-forming cells known as trichocytes and keratinocytes. The dermal papilla, nourished by a network of blood vessels and nerves, is nestled in a tubelike hair follicle and surrounded by what is known as the bulb. The bulb is embedded about 4mm (0.2in) in the subcutaneous fat of the scalp. The outer layers of the hair bulb are known as the outer and inner root sheaths. It is in the dermal papilla that most hair growth takes place. In order for hair to grow, cells have to reproduce. This takes place around the dermal papilla in what scientists call the zone of proliferation.

Each hair has a protective outer cuticle, made up of tiny overlapping scales, often compared to miniature roof tiles, and a thick cortex that lies under the cuticle and consists of the protein keratin. Keratin is also found in human skin and nails, as well as in the feathers, claws, hooves and wool of birds and animals.

Hair also contains the elements carbon, oxygen, nitrogen and sulphur and a tiny percentage of the trace elements zinc, iron, copper and iodine. Other components include fats, and water, which makes up about 12 per cent of a hair's weight.

Some types of hair – particularly thick, dark hair – also have a central medulla, which when inspected under an optical microscope, looks a little like a central canal. Some scientists believe it enhances the thermal-insulation properties of hair. Others speculate that the medulla carries nutrients to the cuticle and cortex, while yet another theory is that it contributes to the shine of hair.

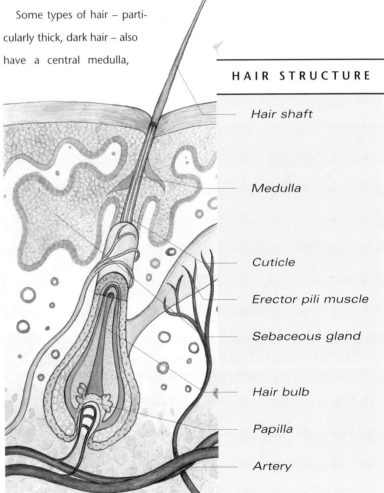

HAIR STRUCTURE

- Hair shaft
- Medulla
- Cuticle
- Erector pili muscle
- Sebaceous gland
- Hair bulb
- Papilla
- Artery

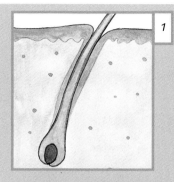

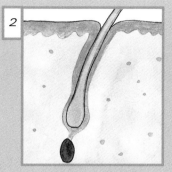

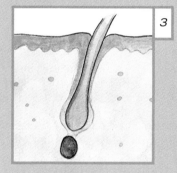

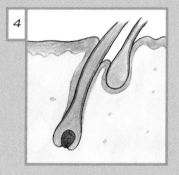

The anagen phase: Active growth takes place in the hair bulb. This phase can last for years, often between three and seven years.

The catagen phase: This is a relatively short phase, during which the follicle stops producing hair and the hair bulb starts to break down.

The telogen phase: A resting phase during which there is no growth and the hair is ready to be shed.

A new anagen phase: The old 'club hair' is ready to fall or be pushed out.

THE GROWTH CYCLE OF HAIR

Hair passes through a growth cycle broken up into three main phases: an active growth phase known as the anagen phase; a short, transitional catagen phase during which the hair stops growing and the hair bulb begins to break down (but there is still cellular activity in the papilla); and a resting telogen phase when no growth takes place and the hair is ready to be shed. The duration of the different phases varies from person to person, but the anagen phase can last anything from three to seven years, and in some cases even up to nine years. The catagen phase lasts roughly two to four weeks, while the telogen phase is estimated to last three to four months.

Function of the cortex and cuticle

The cortex cells give hair its strength and elasticity, while the cuticle reflects its condition.

If the protective scales of the cuticle are undamaged and lie flat, hair appears shiny and healthy, and is soft and manageable, but if they have been broken or damaged through straightening or colouring, hair looks dull and unhealthy. Environmental factors, including sunlight, air pollution and wind, can also damage the cuticle. The more damaged it is, the more tangled hair becomes and the more difficult it is to brush. Hair with smooth cuticle surfaces, on the other hand, reflects more light than hair with rough cuticle surfaces, which is why straight hair appears glossier than curly hair.

Different types of human hair

- **Lanugo hair** is the first hair to be produced by the hair follicles of a developing foetus. It normally covers the foetus until the seventh or eighth month of gestation, is fine and soft and contains no medulla and no pigment. After it has been shed, it is replaced by vellus hair and terminal hair.

- Newborn babies' bodies are covered with **vellus hair**, although they have terminal hair on their heads and eyebrows. The fine hair on parts of some adults' bodies is also vellus hair. These hairs are short, just a centimetre or two long, and they are soft, with no medulla. Occasionally, they contain pigment.

- **Terminal hair**, which grows on the head and also makes up beards, eyelashes and armpit hair, replaces vellus hair. These hairs are longer and coarser than vellus hair, often have a medulla and are usually pigmented.

A touch of colour

Melanin, found in the cortex, gives hair its colour. Pigment makes up only about one per cent of a hair, and although there is a wide range of human hair colours, they all derive from only two melanin pigments: eumelanin, a dark pigment predominating in black and brown hair, and phaeomelanin, a light pigment predominating in blonde and red hair. Many people's hair contains a mixture of the two pigments: the more eumelanin, the darker the hair.

Each hair has a tiny muscle – the erector pili – attached to it. This muscle contracts when it is cold, pulls the hair erect and causes goose flesh. Sebum, an oily substance secreted by the sebaceous glands in the skin, lubricates the hair, making it waterproof and shiny. As all teenagers discover sooner or later, an excess of sebum leads to greasy hair. Too little of it causes dry hair.

Thick or thin

We are all born with a set number of hair follicles and the thickness of our hair is determined by the size of these follicles: thick hair grows out of large follicles, while fine hair grows out of small follicles. So, unfortunately, there is no product on earth that can make your hair thicker or increase the number of hair follicles on your head! A single hair might appear thin and fragile, but according to international cosmetics giant L'Oréal, tests have shown that a healthy hair can carry a weight of about 100g (0.2 lb). If you multiply this by 120 000 – the average number of hairs on the human head – you can deduce that a head of hair could, theoretically, support 12 tonnes (in reality, of course, the scalp is not strong enough to make this possible).

The growth factor

Just like there are changes to the body and skin, your hair's structure and its appearance also change as you grow older.

■ Babies are born with a specific, genetically determined number of hair follicles. Yet some babies have hardly any hair at birth, while others have quite a bit. This is no indication of what the state of their hair will be later in life!

■ Small children's hair often has characteristics that are lost later in life. For example, blonde hair may darken as they grow older and curls may disappear. The thickness of children's hair increases fast until the age of three or four. The diameter continues to increase more slowly until the age of 10 or 11, when the hair should be at its thickest.

■ In puberty, the body undergoes a number of metabolic changes. These also affect the hair. The sebaceous glands are stimulated, often secreting an excess of oil and resulting in oily hair. Dandruff can also appear at this stage, the result of oil secretion and hormonal changes.

▲

This baby's sparse hair is no indication of what her hair might look like in future, and her sister may still find her blonde hair darkening.

■ Around the age of 25, the diameter of hair starts to decrease. In the next 15 years the hair-growth cycle changes, with fewer hairs in the anagen phase and more in the resting phase. Hair growth thus slows down.

■ The age at which grey hairs start appearing is genetically determined. Hair turns white when melanin is no longer produced. Individual hairs become thinner. Many men start losing their hair, and a percentage of women experiences some thinning.

Defining your ethnic hair type

Human hair – which grows everywhere on the body except the palms of the hands, soles of the feet, eyelids and lips – can differ markedly in texture and colour. Yet all human hair has similar functions. Scalp and body hair is believed to keep us warm by preserving heat. It cushions our heads, giving some protection against injury. The hair inside our nose and ears and around our eyes protects against dust and germs, while eyebrows and eyelashes protect our eyes against sweat, harsh light and tiny particles. Armpit hair helps to reduce friction.

Unlike other mammals, humans do not moult, because our hair follicles are all at different stages of the growth cycle at any given time. (If they had all been synchronized, everybody would have gone bald from time to time.) Nevertheless, we do shed our hair at a rate of 50 to 80 scalp hairs a day (the figure of 100 hairs a day, often quoted as the average daily hair loss, is now believed to be exaggerated). As we'll see later, factors like changing hormone levels, diet and medication can influence the hair-loss rate quite drastically.

Your hair type is determined by your genetic make-up; you can change your look, but not your hair's inherent characteristics.

In a class of its own

Human hair can be coarse and black, fair and fine, straight and thick, wavy or kinky, but despite the different variations in colour and texture, it is generally classified into three ethnic types: Caucasian, Asian and African.

Although the hair of most Scandinavians differs markedly from that of a South American or Spaniard, they all have hair that can be classified as Caucasian. The same goes for Indonesian and Japanese hair – both are Asian hair types. Typical Caribbean hair is classified as African hair. Even though there are variations within hair types, the three main ethnic classifications have very distinctive characteristics.

Your hair type is determined by your genetic make-up and although there are ways to temporarily change its look, you can never change its inherent characteristics.

CHANGING YOUR LOOK

Unlike facial features or body shape, hair is relatively easy to change, and the hair products industry is booming, with industry players spending millions on research each year. A crucial element to offering consumers what they want and need is a thorough understanding of hair types.

The chemical compositions of the three ethnic hair types, and the molecular structure of the keratin therein, are all similar, but the hair shafts differ. While there is some understanding of the reasons for this, research into the differences continues.

African hair is dark and tightly curled; Asian hair tends to be straight, coarse, dark and thick, while Caucasian hair ranges from fine and straight to relatively thick and wavy, and has the greatest variation in colour. The differences between the hair types, according to international hair products company Wella, centre on its longitudinal and cross-sectional shape, thickness, ellipticity (whether the hair is 'round' or 'flat') and colour.

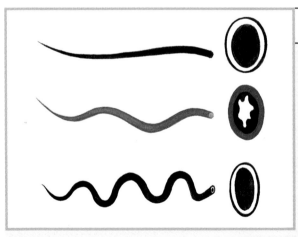

Axial shapes   Ellipticity

HOW HAIR TYPES DIFFER IN SHAPE

◀ *Asian hair: This hair type has an approximately round shape.*

◀ *Caucasian: This hair type has an oval shape.*

◀ *African: This hair type is extremely oval, almost flat.*

Texture

A strand of Caucasian hair has an average thickness of 0.07mm (3in) and, seen in cross section, has an oval shape. Coarser Asian hair, about 0.09mm (3.5in) thick, has an approximately round shape, while African hair, ranging between 0.04 (1.6in) and 0.12mm (5in) in thickness, is extremely oval (nearly 'flat').

It is generally no longer believed that the shape of a curly hair is caused by a curved hair follicle. The follicles of curly hair are, in fact, straight. Further evidence that follicle shape has nothing to do with the curliness or straightness of hair is that some types of medication may cause curly hair to suddenly go straight, without any change to the follicle. All hair – even straight Asian hair – twists as it grows, but the more it twists, the curlier it is. African hair is the most fragile of the three hair types.

Hair product company L'Oréal's institute for ethnic hair and skin research considers the particular structure of African hair to be the reason for this. As mentioned, each African hair shaft has a distinct oval – almost flat – shape. The outer cuticle scales protecting each hair are thinner in the areas where the oval-shaped hair shaft is thinnest. As a result, these thin parts of the cuticle

An example of typical Caucasian, African and Asian hair types. Caucasian hair has the greatest variation in texture and colour.

break easily, exposing the inner cortex of the hair. Once the more vulnerable cortex is no longer protected it then also breaks easily. In addition, the chemical composition of a part of the cuticle, prone to microscopic cracks, causes African hair to have weak mechanical resistance, according to L'Oréal scientists.

The weak points along the hair shaft and the spiral twists make African hair quite difficult to groom, and certainly more difficult to comb than straight Caucasian hair. It is also more brittle, splits more easily and has a lower moisture content. To straighten such hair, heavy-duty chemicals are needed, and damage is bound to occur to the hair structure.

Asian hair is thicker than Caucasian hair and has about 10 layers of cuticle cells, making it stronger and stiffer with more body. Asian hair contains a medulla filled with plenty of dark pigment, thought to contribute to their shine and high moisture content. Asian hair also tends to grow longer than African and Caucasian hair as it has the longest growth cycle of the three hair types: up to nine years. In addition it grows faster than African and Caucasian hair – about 1.3cm (0.5in) per month, compared to the

The characteristics of hair

Whatever your hair type, all hair shares certain properties:

■ It is elastic because of the coiled structure of the keratin, and this elasticity increases when hair is wet. Because of its elasticity, a healthy hair can stretch up to 20 or 30 per cent of its length before it breaks.

■ Hair swells (gets thicker) if it is soaked in water, as the water enters the air spaces between the fibres of the cortex. A hair in good condition can, in fact, absorb about 30 per cent of its own weight in water.

■ Hair is porous, and liquids can pass between the outer cuticle scales into the cortex. Porosity increases if the cuticle is damaged or if the cuticle scales are lifted through heat, steam or chemical treatments. Sebum and certain conditioning creams or lacquers can decrease the porosity.

■ Hair is hygroscopic and absorbs moisture from the air. This explains why the same head of hair can behave very differently in dry and humid conditions. When it is humid, hair absorbs a lot more moisture and tends to become frizzy, whereas it tends to be straight in a dry climate. The normal moisture content of hair is about 10 per cent of its weight, but this can increase to 30 per cent.

1.2cm (0.4in) and 0.9cm (3.5in) of the two other hair types respectively. On average, Asians also shed fewer hairs a day than Africans or Caucasians, and Asian men tend to experience less balding (Caucasians have the highest incidence of male-pattern baldness).

Greying also starts later. However, there is evidence that Asian women over 45 tend to experience more overall thinning of hair than their Caucasian and African coun-terparts, and because Asian hair is thicker and often longer than other hair types it tends to lose more moisture, which leads to dryness and split ends.

About 70 per cent of Caucasians have finely textured hair, and 30 per cent have medium-textured or coarse hair. Colour and texture appear to be linked: blondes tend to have the finest hair, while redheads tend to have the coarsest. Although Asian hair is thicker, Caucasian hair has the highest density of the three hair types.

Hair can be fine, medium-textured or coarse. Fine hair always tends to lack volume, while medium hair is often quite easy to handle, strong and elastic. Coarse hair brings its own problems: it is abundant, but can be heavy, frizzy and difficult to control. You may find that you have fine hair in your hairline and on your temples, while the rest of your hair is medium or coarse.

A QUESTION OF OIL AND MOISTURE

Whether you have dry, oily, normal or combination hair depends on how much oil your sebaceous glands produce, and how you treat your hair. It is impossible to stop your sebaceous glands producing grease, and it is also an old wives' tale that oil production is very much affected by your diet. Eating too many choco-lates or greasy food may well lead to weight gain, but it will not make your hair oilier! While you cannot change your genetics, understanding your hair type and treating it accordingly can help you have a healthy, good-looking head of hair.

Oily hair

If your sebaceous glands produce too much sebum, your scalp and hair tend to be oily and your hair may even become lank and greasy only a few hours after you have washed it. You will therefore need to wash it more often than someone with normal hair. Contrary to popular belief, frequent washing does not exacerbate the oil problem. If you tend to have greasy hair, do not touch it often or run your fingers through it constantly, as this can make hair appear greasy quicker. Too much brushing also helps to distribute oil. While some experts advise using a shampoo formulated for oily hair, others believe that it's better to wash your hair often with a mild shampoo. Apply conditioner only to the ends. A good tip is to use hairspray after you have styled your hair. This keeps it out of your face and stops you from touching it frequently.

Dry hair

Dry hair – which literally contains too little moisture – can be caused by a variety of factors: naturally it is the result of sebaceous glands producing too little sebum, but chemical treatments, frequent washing, harsh sunlight, wind, overuse of hair-dryers and hair age (hair that has not been cut for a long time) can also cause dry, brittle hair. This hair type can lack shine, feel rough and break, and

◄ *Heat from a hair-dryer can be damaging to hair. Try to cut down on blow-drying, particularly if your hair tends to be dry and brittle.*

tangle easily. Use a shampoo for dry hair and always follow a wash with conditioner. Try to cut down on blow-drying and avoid chemical treatments such as bleaching, straightening and perming. A regular hot-oil treatment may help, but the better solution for dry and split ends is to cut them off.

Normal hair

Normal hair is neither too dry nor too oily, feels soft and healthy and does not tangle easily. This type of hair is easy to manage and style, and usually has not been coloured, straightened or permed. The sebaceous glands tend to produce just the right amount of oil, but a healthy lifestyle, good grooming habits and sensible treatment of your hair also help. Wash your hair regularly, but not every day, and use a light conditioner.

Combination hair

If your roots and scalp are oily, but your hair ends are dry, you have combination hair. This can be the result of treatments which strip the hair of moisture. Harsh sunlight and long hair that has not been cut for some time can also lead to combination hair. When washing your hair, concentrate

on the scalp area and always use moisturizing conditioner on the ends. Bear in mind the guidelines for both oily and dry hair if you have combination hair: do not touch your hair too much, and go easy on the hair-dryer and styling tools.

▲

The only cure for split ends is to cut them off, but conditioner can help to prevent further damage and improve the feel of your hair.

Hair and scalp problems

Although the visible part of each hair on your body is, technically speaking, dead your hair is still one of the best barometers of your general health and one of the quickest indicators that something is wrong. This is because hair-forming cells in the dermal papilla are some of the fastest dividing cells in the human body. Baldness and thinning hair affect millions of people and can be hereditary, or caused by a variety of factors.

A loss in the condition of your hair can be an early warning sign of an underlying problem. See a doctor if you notice flaking, itching or crusting of the scalp, a sudden increased hair loss – particularly if accompanied by other symptoms – and irritated skin patches on the scalp. Unfortunately, not all remedies on the market are based on scientific principles, so make sure you get an authoritative medical view before trying a new treatment. Also, not all hair problems make sense – sometimes even the most experienced specialist will not be able to pinpoint the reason for hair loss, for example.

> *Be aware that a loss in the condition of your hair can be an early warning sign of an underlying problem.*

Hair loss

Hair loss (alopecia) can affect anyone – man, woman or child – at any time, but male-pattern hair loss or male androgenetic alopecia is the most common form.

It is normal to lose between 50 and 80 hairs daily but when the hairs you are losing start to outnumber the new hairs appearing, your hair will start thinning; if this continues, you will start balding. There are a number of treatments available, but their efficacy depends on the type of hair loss you are experiencing.

MALE- AND FEMALE-PATTERN HAIR LOSS

Male-pattern hair loss is the most common type of hair loss in men and is usually hereditary – a history of androgenetic alopecia on either side of the family increases a man's risk of balding. Heredity also affects the age at which men begin to lose hair, as well as the speed and extent of the loss.

Male-pattern baldness usually starts with a receding hairline, leading to baldness on the top of the head, which then spreads. Hair loss can start any time after puberty. Caucasian men are more likely to lose hair than African or Asian men – it is estimated that 96 per cent of mature Caucasian men experience some recession in their hairline, even if they are not destined to lose all their hair. Male-pattern hair loss is discussed in more detail in Chapter 8.

Although androgenetic alopecia mostly affects men, some women also get it. It is then called female-pattern hair loss, or female-pattern androgenetic alopecia. The pattern differs from the male hair-loss pattern in that the woman's hairline does not recede, rather the hair

Stress and hair loss

It is believed that there is a link between stress and depression, and hair loss. There are documented cases of people starting to lose hair, anything from a few weeks to a few months after a stressful episode in their lives. Of course, hair loss itself is stressful, so it is not always clear which came first, hair loss or stress.

According to the American Academy of Dermatology, men and women with androgenetic alopecia have a higher incidence of personality disorders. According to the academy, women with hair loss experience a lack of self-esteem, are introverted, feel less attractive, and are tense in public places.

becomes thin over the entire scalp. Women suffering from female-pattern hair loss are likely to first notice it somewhere between their late 20s and early 40s. They are particularly prone to some hair loss at times of hormonal change, for example when they start or stop taking the contraceptive pill, after having a baby and during early menopause.

Handle thinning hair gently: avoid overbrushing and steer clear of appliances or hair tools that pull the hair. Granny's advice was well meant, but 100 strokes a day will do more bad than good.

Alopecia areata

Alopecia areata – which can cause all, or much, of the hair on the head or body to fall out – is thought to affect about two per cent of the population in some form, at some point in their lives. Some people only experience one small patch of hair loss, while others may have many large patches.

Alopecia areata is classified as an autoimmune disease – the result of the immune system's white blood cells attacking the fast-growing hair cells in the follicles. No-one knows what causes the white blood cells to do this. As a result, the follicles

▲

Always handle your hair gently. Use a quality hairbrush and do not over-brush or pull on your tresses.

become smaller and hair production slows down. The hairs that are produced are fragile and break off even before they reach the skin's surface. Alopecia areata is a very distressing condition, but fortunately often disappears as suddenly as it appears. Alopecia areata does not cause follicles to lose the potential to form new hair, but hair may take years to grow back. Some scientists believe certain people may be genetically predisposed to it.

There are different types of alopecia areata: if all your scalp hair, as well as your eyebrows and eyelashes fall out, this condition is known as alopecia areata totalis. When all the hair on your head, face, and body is lost, the condition is known as alopecia areata universalis.

There is no cure for alopecia areata, but certain treatments – including cortisone injections or pills – may alleviate the condition. Tarlike ointments, commonly used to treat the skin disease psoriasis, may stimulate new hair growth.

Disease

If your thyroid gland is overactive or underactive, your hair may fall out. When the thyroid disease is treated, the hair-loss problem is usually also solved. An overactive thyroid (hyperthyroidism) may lead to scalp hair becoming fine and soft with some hair loss, while an underactive thyroid (hypothyroidism) can lead to dry, coarse head and body hair, and partial hair loss.

Many chronic illnesses, including bowel disorders involving malabsorption, endocrine abnormalities, renal and hepatic disease and cancer (even without chemotherapy) are also associated with hair loss. Conditions like diabetes and the autoimmune disease lupus may also cause hair loss.

Hormone imbalance and childbirth

If male hormones (androgens) or female hormones (oestrogens) are out of balance, it can lead to hair loss. Correcting the imbalance may stop your hair loss. Some types of birth-control pills – particularly the older types – may also lead to hair loss for some women.

Many women shed quite a lot of hair for several months after having a baby. This commonly starts about three months after the birth and is nothing to worry about. It is also related to hormonal changes in

It is a myth that...

■ shampoos and conditioners can cause abnormal hair loss. This is rarely, if ever, the case.

■ hair can turn white overnight. In fact, the greying process is gradual. (Sufferers of alopecia areata, however, may find that their regrowing hairs are white, which may have led to this myth.)

■ dandruff is infectious, or the result of bad hygiene or stress. Not true.

■ baldness is inherited from the mother's family. It can be inherited from your mother or father's side of the family, but sometimes there is no history of baldness on either side of the family, and you are simply unlucky!

■ vitamins and proteins can be absorbed into hair. This is impossible; the only way they can benefit your hair is through a healthy diet.

the body. During pregnancy, the hair-growth cycle changes and far fewer hairs are shed than normally, the result of high oestrogen levels that keep hairs in the active growing phase. Following the baby's birth, oestrogen levels return to pre-pregnancy levels, more hairs go into the resting telogen phase and are shed as the growth cycle returns to normal.

Medication and medical treatment

Certain drugs may cause hair loss. These include particular medications for gout, arthritis, depression, heart problems and high blood pressure. If you stop the medication, your hair should grow back, or the doctor may be able to prescribe an alternative that does not have this side effect.

Chemotherapy often causes hair loss, because it targets fast-growing cancer cells and, as a consequence, also affects fast-growing hair cells. Hair loss – which does not always start immediately – can occur on all parts of the body. The hair usually grows back after the treatments are over. Sometimes, hair may grow back a different colour or texture. Special ice caps, to be worn during chemotherapy sessions, may improve your chances of keeping your hair.

Many women lose quite a lot of hair in the months following the birth of a baby, but the situation normally rectifies itself without medical intervention.

Fever or surgery

You may find yourself losing more hair than normal two to five months after an illness accompanied by a prolonged fever. Scientists believe the cause is hair entering its telogen phase early. The situation normally rectifies itself. You may also lose some hair after an operation, although the reason for this has not been established.

Scalp disorders

The scalp differs from the skin on your body in that it has an abundant supply of oil from the sebaceous glands and has hair follicles that produce long terminal hair. Most scalp problems are easy to solve, others are chronic and more problematic.

DANDRUFF

Dandruff (*pityriasis simplex* or *furfuracea*) is more of an aesthetic concern than a medical problem. It has been associated with a tiny yeast cell (*Pityrosporum ovale*) found on all scalps, but which seems to grow more rapidly on the heads of dandruff sufferers. Dandruff has a social stigma, and sufferers dread the sight of the characteristic small white scales – tiny pieces of skin shed from the scalp. Dandruff is more common in men than women, suggesting there is some link with male androgens.

By the age of 20, about half of all Caucasians are affected by dandruff to some degree, and the condition often clears spontaneously by 50 or 60 years of age. There are many effective antidandruff shampoos on the market, but the scales normally

Common scalp infections

Even in First World countries, infections by fungi, bacteria and lice – collectively known as dermatophytes – are fairly common. These organisms are transferred quite easily through personal contact and shared towels, bedding and clothing.

One of the most common scalp infections is scalp ringworm, or *tinea capitis*. This fungal infection causes itchy, circular patches on the skin and can lead to some hair loss. It is easily spread – not only on combs or brushes but even on furniture. Ringworm, which mostly affects children, can be treated with antifungals and lost hair generally grows back once the infection is under control.

Head lice (*pediculosis capitis* or *pediculosis*) – identified by an itchy scalp and eggs attached to hair roots – are transmitted through contact with clothes and grooming tools. Infection has nothing to do with hygiene, dirty hair or personal grooming habits. In fact, lice love long, clean hair! Although treatments are available, studies suggest lice are becoming resistant to the products. Experts believe that removal using a nit comb is still the most effective.

form again within four to seven days. It's a good idea to alternate a dandruff shampoo with a regular shampoo (although antidandruff shampoos are generally not harsher on hair than other shampoos). Effective antidandruff ingredients include zinc pyrithione, salicylic acid compounds, selenium sulfide or coal tar (in small concentrations).

SEBORRHOEA

Seborrhoea is characterized by a very greasy scalp and greasy hair. It has also been linked with hirsutism (excessive facial and body hair). The condition can quite effectively be controlled with specially formulated shampoos.

Seborrhoeic dermatitis is more serious. It is a form of chronic eczema resembling psoriasis and is characterized by large, greasy yellow scales. It is not known what causes it. Seborrhoeic dermatitis can be treated with corticosteroid lotions and antifungal shampoos.

PSORIASIS

This disorder is often not confined to the scalp, but its effects on the scalp include silvery scales and tender, sometimes itchy, skin. Treatments include tar-based shampoos, salicylic acid, cortisone and ultraviolet light.

ECZEMA

Eczema affects different parts of the body, including sometimes the scalp, and causes itching and soreness. There is no cure for it, although some treatments alleviate the symptoms.

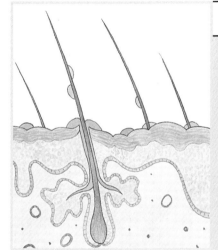

CONTACT DERMATITIS

As the name suggests, this condition flares up on contact with a product – such as a hair colourant or straightening solution – that the scalp is sensitive or allergic to. If your skin flares up after using a certain product, switch to another, preferably with less colouring or perfume.

SEBORRHOEA

Seborrhoea, characterized by abnormal secretions of the sebaceous glands, can be controlled with medicated shampoo.

DANDRUFF

Dandruff is a common condition leading to small white scales (tiny pieces of skin) being shed from the scalp.

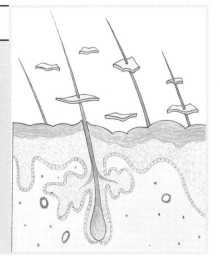

Treatment for hair loss

Treatment depends on the cause and extent of your hair loss, and contrary to claims by many marketers keen to exploit those desperate to reverse their natural hair loss, there simply is no magic cure.

One of the most well-known treatments for hair loss, approved by the United States Food and Drug Administration and other regulatory bodies, is the drug **minoxidil** (available over the counter as Rogaine™ or Regaine™).

A side effect of minoxidil, which was originally used to treat hypertension, is increased hair growth. It is available in two and five per cent solutions and is rubbed topically on to the scalp. Some users do seem to experience some regrowth, but the new hair is often thinner and lighter and dryness or irritation of the scalp may be experienced. Unfortunately, minoxidil does not work for everybody and commonly appears only to slow down the rate of hair loss.

Another drawback is that new growth ceases as soon as users stop taking the drug – and its prolonged use could get very expensive.

Another drug that has been shown to slow hair loss and bring about some new hair growth is **finasteride**, marketed as Propecia™.

Modern hair-implant methods – using mini and micro grafts – yield better results than older methods and also give a more natural regrowth pattern. ▶

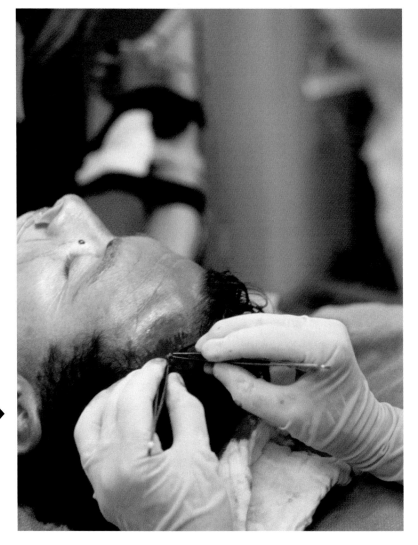

This medication, taken in tablet form, is only used for male-pattern baldness and is not approved for use by women as its suitability during pregnancy has not been established.

The drug works in men by inhibiting the conversion of testosterone into dihydrotestosterone, a hormone significant in male hair loss, as it shrinks hair follicles. Side effects are rare, but research suggests it can temporarily affect sexual function or libido in about two per cent of users. Again, benefits cease once the drug is stopped.

Neither minoxidil nor finasteride should be used for hair loss due to illness.

Hair-implantation methods have improved in recent years, with mini and micro hair grafts yielding better results than the older punch-biopsy methods that often failed. Modern hair grafts also give a more natural regrowth pattern. (*See* Chapter 8 for more about surgical solutions to hair loss.)

Hair-loss fact file

- By the age of 50, half of all men will have some obvious hair loss.
- Hair loss starts an average of 10 years later in women than in men.
- Humans are not the only mammals to suffer from baldness. Chimpanzees and orang-utans often also show signs of baldness when they reach sexual maturity.
- Women's hairlines tend to remain unchanged throughout life even though they may experience general thinning, but about half of all men can expect their hairline to recede to some extent as they get older.
- Many alcoholics experience poor hair growth, or even hair loss, as their illness can lead to malnutrition.
- Trichotillomania is a compulsive desire to pull out one's own hair. This habit can lead to damage of the hair root (if the hairs are pulled out during the active anagen growth phase). Trichotillomania seems to be more common in women than in men, and children can also suffer from it.

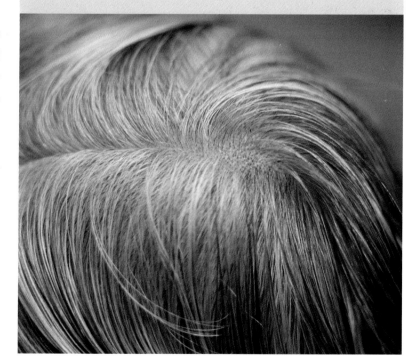

The impact of diet

Growing hair receives nourishment by means of the bloodstream and, contrary to claims by some manufacturers, products applied to the hair externally cannot nourish it, although they may improve the hair's condition.

A healthy diet is therefore important for hair health.

Protein is vital for building hair but increasing the amount of protein in the diet does not necessarily increase hair growth. Malnutrition, or a serious lack of protein in your diet, can lead to hair loss. The condition known as Protein Energy Malnutrition not only leads to hair loss but also causes dry, brittle hair.

According to the American Academy of Dermatology, calorie and/or protein malnutrition forces the body to save protein by shifting growing hairs into the resting phase. This causes shedding of the hair spread out over the entire scalp. This type of hair loss, known as telogen effluvium, is slow and often not noticeable until nearly half the hair is lost. Body hair, on the other hand, may increase at the same time. By returning to a balanced diet, the hair loss can be reversed.

While it is well known that one of the noticeable manifestations of the eating disorder anorexia nervosa is hair loss, dieters often do not realize that

◄ *Fresh fruit contains Vitamin C, which helps with the absorption of iron (and iron deficiency and anaemia can lead to hair loss).*

HAIR AND SCALP PROBLEMS

Hair analysis - a far-fetched fad?

Hair analysis involves the testing of hair strands to confirm the presence or absence of specific substances. Practitioners promoting hair analysis claim that the levels of minerals in the hair correlate with the levels in the body, and that by testing hair they can check for deficiencies (or abnormally high quantities) of minerals in the body. Many then offer supplements to address these deficiencies.

Scientists tend to be sceptical about these claims, however, and many believe them to be unreliable. Scientific studies have concluded that analysis is not particularly useful for assessing levels of minerals such as sodium, magnesium, phosphorus, potassium, calcium, iron and iodine in the body. Researchers have also pointed out that dyes, chemical treatments, age, season and hair length, may affect the results. It is, therefore, unlikely that nutritional therapy based on hair analysis is of any benefit, and it is more than likely a waste of your money. What's more, instances have been recorded where different laboratories came to different conclusions after testing identical hair samples!

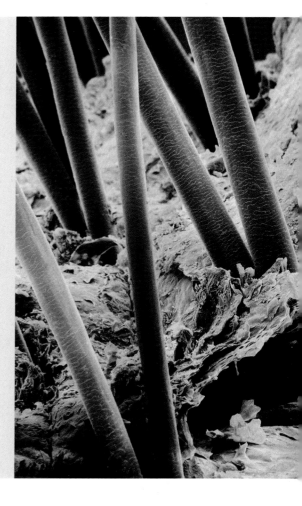

they do not have to be noticeably underweight, or suffer from an eating disorder to start losing hair. In fact, dieticians have noticed that a loss of a mere five kilograms (11 lb) can lead to some hair loss, particularly if you cut down drastically on protein and/or fats.

As a diet high in fat poses health risks, try to choose mainly low-fat proteins such as fish, chicken, lean red meat, eggs, milk and pulses. Make sure you eat enough food containing vitamins and minerals. It is important to eat enough sources of Vitamin C (available from fresh fruit and vegetables) and Vitamin B (found in oily fish, peas, eggs, milk and wholegrain cereals) on a daily basis. The Vitamin B complex, and particularly biotin, is important to keep hair follicles in good health. It appears that a lack of biotin (found in nuts and eggs) may lead to a reduction in activity in hair follicles. Vitamin B1 is also believed to be important for healthy hair. (Even so, there is no proof that taking Vitamin-B supplements actually prevents hair loss.)

Although Vitamin C cannot be directly linked to healthy hair, it does help with absorption of iron (iron deficiency and anaemia can lead to

A grey matter

Greying is not a medical problem, but a natural process. Cells in the dermal papilla manufacture hair pigment (melanin). As you grow older these cells make less pigment. The result is grey hair that still contains some pigment and, ultimately, white hair that has none at all. The age at which you start greying and the rate at which grey hairs appear depend on genetic factors.

hair loss). Telogen effluvium which results from an iron deficiency is relatively common in young women who menstruate. Doctors do not always pick this up, since they may test for aneamia and the result may come back negative. Make sure that your iron stores, in particular, are checked if you suspect that your levels are low. Also ensure that your diet contains enough iron-rich foods, including green leafy vegetables, eggs, dates, raisins and liver (but avoid liver if you are pregnant, as it contains very high concentrations of Vitamin A, which can harm the developing foetus).

In large doses, Vitamin A causes hair loss, and some drugs that contain

Save your hair

Do an Internet search, or visit health shops and pharmacies, and you will find many products claiming to combat hair loss. In truth, very few of these can promote hair growth or stop hair loss.

In 1980, an advisory panel to the US Food and Drug Administration studied a number of substances that are used in hair-growth products. They found them to be ineffective and proposed that they be removed from the market.

The substances included jojoba oil, lanolin and wheatgerm oil, which are often said to combat alopecia. Others on the list were amino acids, amino-benzoic acid, ascorbic acid, benzoic acid, B vitamins, hormones, sulphanilamide and tetracaine hydrochloride, as well as urea.

Scalp massage, changes in diet (unless you had an eating disorder or were seriously malnourished), electrical stimulation and Chinese herbal extracts are not effective tools to treat androgenetic alopecia either. Similarly, vasodilators – products that you rub into the scalp, supposedly to increase and stimulate blood supply and hair growth – are also a waste of money.

Vitamin A derivatives are also associated with this problem. Such drugs inhibit cell division and slow down keratinization, thereby slowing down activity in the hair follicles.

Hereditary or acquired zinc deficiency is also known to lead to hair loss, so make sure you have enough zinc in your diet (found in shellfish, red meat and pumpkin seeds). Zinc can improve thyroid function (and an underactive thyroid, as mentioned, may lead to thinning hair).

Supplements that can improve the condition of your hair in the long term include those containing essential fatty acids such as flaxseed and evening primrose oil. Essential fatty acids are also found in oily fish and nuts.

It makes sense that a well-balanced diet, which is good for your body, is also good for your hair. Drink at least eight glasses of water a day. Finally, since your hair follicles need a good supply of oxygen and nutrients from the blood, it cannot hurt to boost your circulation with exercise! However, it has to be stressed that boosting your circulation alone will unfortunately not lead to your hair growing faster or thicker.

Plenty of water and exercise is good for your general health and thus for your hair.

THE IMPACT OF DIET

Treatments, tools & tackle

A bottle of shampoo might be the most basic hair grooming product in any bathroom today, but this has not always been the case: in the 17th and 18th centuries, most people did not wash their hair more than once or twice a year. Marie Antoinette, the self-indulgent last queen of France, and her peers are said to have used perfumes, potpourri and perfumed candles in a desperate attempt to disguise the resultant odours. To compound the problem, high-society ladies wore such elaborate hairstyles that many would spend nights sleeping sitting up rather than risk ruining their crowning glories. Elaborate hair constructions built over wire cages were decorated not only with feathers and jewels, but even fruit, vegetables and animal menageries, attracting rats and other vermin.

Fortunately we no longer need smelling salts to cope with our lack of sensible hair hygiene. The menageries are out of fashion, but our hairstyle choices still say a lot about who we are, and the myriad treatments and products on the market bear testimony to this.

> *You should wash your hair as often as needed. Washing it daily will not trigger your sebaceous glands to produce more oil.*

Back to basics

Shampoo is the most basic of haircare products, designed to clean your hair and scalp. (The word shampoo, interestingly, has its origin in the Hindi word *champi*, which means 'head massage with oil'.) Most shampoos are classified as detergents, with the exception of dry, powder shampoos that are less effective and tend to leave hair dull-looking. These can be useful, however, when you are not able to use normal shampoo because of your location or lack of time. Some shampoos contain soap, but most, these days, are soap-free and contain agents known as surfactants, otherwise known as surface-active agents, that lather well in all types of water. (Soap shampoo forms a scum with hard water.) Most modern shampoos also contain conditioning agents to make it easier to comb your hair after washing it.

A good shampoo should spread easily over the hair, rinse out, not irritate your skin or eyes and leave your hair manageable. The lather is not actually essential to clean your hair efficiently, but it does offer a guide to how much detergent you are using.

There is a wide range of shampoos for different hair types. If you wash your hair frequently or have

◀ *Shampoo is the most basic haircare product. A good one should spread easily over your hair, rinse out easily and leave your hair manageable.*

What's in shampoo?

■ Cleansing agents (surfactants). The two most common are ammonium lauryl sulphate and ammonium laureth sulphate, the milder of the two.

■ Conditioning agents.

■ Additives to control pH and thickness of the shampoo (if it is too runny, it would be messy to apply; if it is too thick, it would be hard to spread). Shampoos are usually slightly acidic, with a pH between 3.5 and 4.5.

■ Preservatives to prevent the shampoo from going off or ingredients from decomposing, which could lead to bacteria multiplying, and pose a health risk.

■ Colourants, perfumes and other ingredients to make the shampoo enjoyable to use.

■ Some shampoos such as antidandruff preparations contain zinc pyrithione.

a sensitive skin, choose a gentle formula. For colour-treated, permed or dry and brittle hair, a moisturizing shampoo may help. There are also special shampoos available for coloured hair but in truth they cannot really prevent colour fade, although they do moisturize the hair and help to maintain its condition. There is ongoing debate about the benefits of clarifying shampoos, which are used (normally about once a month) to remove so-called product build-up on the hair. Some hair experts dismiss them, saying that a good regular shampoo should be able to remove all build-up of dirt and products on the hair anyway.

There are also many special formulations for greasy, dry and normal hair as well as shampoos for blonde hair that are designed to help it appear brighter.

Wash your hair as often as you need to – daily if necessary – but do not use too much shampoo, as it won't make your hair cleaner! Brush your hair before you wash it – this loosens dead skin cells and any dirt sticking to your scalp.

Harsh sunlight, wind and other environmental hazards, as well as styling and chemical treatments, can damage the outer cuticle cells of your hair leaving it dull, dry and tangled. Unfortunately, conditioner cannot repair such damage but it can improve the appearance of the hair by coating the shaft, smoothing rough cuticle scales as a result, and making the hair easy to comb. Once the cuticle scales are flattened your hair also appears shinier. Whatever a manufacturer may claim, no conditioner can be absorbed into the hair shaft.

Always apply conditioner to freshly washed hair that has been patted dry with a towel. You need about a tablespoon of conditioner for short hair; double that for long hair. You can also massage conditioner into the scalp if the skin is dry and needs nourishment. Thereafter, comb it through the hair, concentrating on the ends. Rinse your hair very well after conditioning, as it can end up looking dull or even a little oily if you don't. After patting your hair dry detangle it gently with a comb.

Light conditioners are ideal for normal, healthy hair, and make it easy to detangle with a comb after washing. Intensive conditioners do the same job as regular ones, but are specially designed for dry, difficult to manage hair. Creamy, oil-based conditioners can improve the appearance and feel of dry hair. Volumizing conditioners can help fine hair to appear fuller. Very curly African hair needs to be particularly well-conditioned, as it tends to be dry and fragile. A gentle shampoo should be coupled with a rich conditioner.

Leave-in conditioners are less time-consuming than the types that have to be rinsed out and are designed to protect hair against heat damage and reduce static. To protect your hair from harsh sunlight, try a leave-in conditioner containing zinc oxide.

While nothing, except for a haircut, can cure split ends (the result of the outer, protective cuticle being stripped away or damaged) protein conditioners can smooth them temporarily, making them less obvious.

Types of conditioning treatments include: sprays, used before you style your hair to protect it against heat damage and to banish static electricity; and hot-oil treatments to deep condition dry and damaged hair. Regular hot-oil treatments are recommended for African hair.

Two-in-one shampoos – containing both cleansers and a high percentage of conditioners – were first introduced to the hair-cosmetics market in the 1980s, by pharmaceutical company Procter & Gamble. Their benefits, or lack thereof, were at first rather hotly debated, but these days about a fifth of all shampoos sold are two-in-one formulations that make use of silicones to carry out their dual task.

Tools of the trade

There is an array of styling products on the market. Here are some guidelines to help you choose.

CURL-DEFINING SPRAYS

As the name suggests, these are products for curly hair – they help to define your curls so that they do not go frizzy.

HAIR GEL

Gel comes as a transparent jelly or spray and can be used to mould damp or dry hair. It also gives lift to roots and structure to curls. The key is to use it sparingly: if you use too much you may end up with messy, sticky hair and have to wash and style it again.

Gel works better on coarse than on fine hair. It is good to control frizz and combat static electricity.

Mousse gives body and volume to hair – apply it from the roots to the ends. ▶

HAIRSPRAY

Hairsprays, quick-drying solutions containing polymers, are used to hold your hairstyle in place. They can also be used to reduce static electricity and give lift to your hair roots.

Look for the spray to suit your needs; options range from light to firm hold. Take care not to use too much or your hair could end up looking stiff and unnatural.

MOUSSE

Mousse is foam that gives body and volume to hair and is, therefore, particularly good to use on fine hair.

Choose a mousse to suit your purposes; some formulations offer firmer hold than others. Put the mousse on your hair from the roots to the ends before, or while you style your hair. It works especially well on curls and with diffuser drying or scrunching.

SERUMS, GLOSSES AND SHINE SPRAYS

Serums, glosses and shine sprays contain silicone or oils that form a microscopic film on the surface of the hair, boosting shine.

Use them on dry hair as the final step in your styling routine. They achieve the best results on sleek, straight hair. Some of the heavy serums can feel quite oily, so they should be used sparingly. Serums can help to fight frizz and make split ends less obvious.

STRAIGHTENING BALM

Straightening balms are used to protect your hair while using straightening irons or blow-drying frizzy hair straight.

STYLING LOTIONS

Styling lotions are designed to help your hair set into a particular shape. They are applied to wet hair, before you start styling. Some of them also protect hair against heat damage.

VOLUME ENHANCERS

Volume enhancers are specifically designed to add volume to limp, fine hair by coating the hair shafts.

WAXES AND POMADES

These products are great on African, thick and dry hair. Skip them if you have fine hair. They also help to control curly, unruly strands and are useful in humid climates, where moisture in the atmosphere tends to make hair frizz despite your best efforts to control it.

Rather than fight your natural kinks and curls, use wax or pomade to sculpt them into something spectacular. Waxes and pomades must be used sparingly, as too much can make your hair look dull. They come in different strengths – gentler pomades generally provide a more natural look.

The right tackle

A regular grooming and beauty routine is unthinkable without all the right tools. Just pick your preference.

BRUSHES

If you are serious about styling your hair, invest in a number of hairbrushes with different purposes. Large paddle brushes are great for detangling long hair. For straightforward brushing, flat brushes are the best, but you need a round brush for effective blow-drying. If you have short hair, it is easy to use a thin brush, while a brush with a larger diameter achieves the best results with long hair. If blow-drying is part of your grooming ritual, invest in a vent brush with a hollow centre. This allows hot air to flow through and assists with the process. The longer your hair, the larger the brush should be.

Also consider the bristles, which can be either natural (hog bristle) or synthetic (nylon, plastic or metal). Natural bristles are less damaging, but often too soft to brush through thick hair. Brushes with rubber balls on the tips of the bristles are kinder to your hair and scalp than those without. A hairbrush and curly hair are not compatible – use a wide-toothed comb instead. If you are losing your hair or have very fine and soft hair, stick to a soft natural-bristle brush.

▲

There is a hairbrush for every purpose – from round brushes for blow-drying to paddle brushes for grooming.

COMBS

Grooming combs come in many shapes and sizes, with fine or wide teeth.

Long, widely spaced teeth are great for African, permed or very thick and curly hair, while regular wide-toothed combs are good to comb fragile wet hair or to detangle curly or permed hair. A tail-comb (with fine teeth and a long, thin tail) is used to make partings or to section off hair for blow-drying.

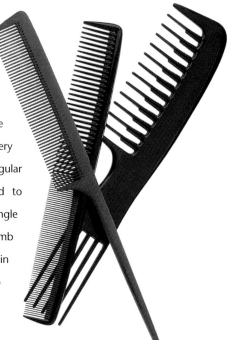

Use a tail-comb to create partings, a wide-toothed comb for curls and a regular comb to detangle knotted hair.

Do not use electrical hair appliances on chemically treated hair. The heat can damage the hair further and cause split ends.

Getting a head start

There is probably little truth to the claim that head massage aids hair growth but it does help blood circulation – and it is blood that brings nutrients to the hair-forming cells in the hair follicle. It can also help to relax your scalp and, in effect, release tension in your entire body.

Many salons provide scalp massages. If you want to try it at home: after you have applied conditioner, use your fingertips to gently rotate sections of your scalp, starting at the forehead and moving on to the sides, crown and finally the neck. Then place your fingertips on a section of the scalp and knead without moving your fingers. Do this for a short while and then move on to the next section, and so on.

Hair extensions

Hair extensions are nothing new. In the late 1800s, fashionable upper-class women in Europe regularly used false hair to enhance their own. The hair came from young nuns whose heads were shorn upon entering convents, from prisoners and from poverty stricken young women who sold their hair for income. Modern-day extensions consist of real human hair or acrylic strands that get glued onto your own hair.

Professionally done extensions can add volume, length and colour to your own tresses, and change your image. They can easily be removed with solvent when they need replacing (after three months), or when you tire of them, but are not a long-term solution. Extensions attached by a qualified hairdresser should not damage your own hair or scalp and you can wash your hair as you normally would. If glued-on extensions seem too drastic, you can always experiment with temporary ones that clip onto your own hair. Just remember to hide the clips under your hair.

CRIMPERS AND STRAIGHTENERS

Like curls, crimping goes in and out of fashion. Crimping devices that consist of two ridged plates to produce ripples in the hair can be tough on hair, so limit their use and do not use them on damp, bleached or damaged hair.

Chances are, if you have naturally curly hair, you will yearn for rod-straight tresses. Blow-drying is the most common way of achieving this, but straightening irons – resembling crimpers with flat plates instead of ridged ones – have also become popular in recent years. To do their job well, straighteners need to be very hot, so make sure you protect your scalp (and your ears!) while using them. Even if fashion calls for poker-straight hair, try not to use straighteners every day. Crimpers and straighteners should always be used with heat-protective styling sprays.

Most hair-dryers have nozzle attachments concentrating the hot air on small sections of hair. Use these for the sleekest results.

HAIR-DRYERS

It is worth investing in a quality hair-dryer if you blow-dry your hair regularly. A good blow-dryer has several heat settings: high heat for fast drying (but limit the use of this setting, as it is most harmful to your hair), medium heat to finish off your style and cool air to set it.

Hair-dryers come in different strengths, but 1200 watts should suit most people's requirements. Use a diffuser – which comes as a separate attachment – for curly or permed hair. The diffuser fits on the dryer's nozzle to gently spread the airflow so that your curls keep their shape.

To protect your hair, do not blow-dry it when it is sopping wet. Instead, remove the excess water by blotting it with a towel. Apply the styling product of your choice (preferably one offering some heat protection) and blow-dry your hair section by section. Most hair-dryers have a nozzle attachment that concentrates the hot air on a small section of hair – use this attachment for a straight and sleek result.

Always blow-dry down the hair shaft, so that the outer cuticle cells are pushed flat (which makes hair look healthy and shiny). Do not continue until your hair is bone dry; this is a sure way of damaging the hair shafts as removing too much moisture can lead to brittleness and breakage.

HOT BRUSHES AND HOT TONGS

Hot brushes and hot tongs should be used only on dry hair – both for safety's sake and to protect your hair.

A hot brush has bristles and, essentially, works like a standard brush combined with heat to help with styling. Take care when you wind your hair onto the hot brush, particularly if it is long, as it can easily get tangled.

A question of styling...

Hairstyling that does not involve chemical processes such as perming or highlighting is temporary, and sadly lasts only until the next shampoo. The reason is that, while your hair's keratin structure is permanently changed when you have it chemically treated, you can only alter it for a short period when you blow-dry your hair, or use hot curling or straightening irons.

Hot tongs – which do not have bristles and are used primarily to create curls – come in different diameters. They can get very hot, so always make sure you protect your scalp when using them.

ROLLERS

If you often use conventional rollers choose smooth or foam-covered ones, which are less hazardous to your hair. The type with Velcro covering may be easy to use as they stay in your hair without clips, but they are almost inevitably difficult to remove, pulling out and breaking some of your hairs in the process. Thin curlers give tight curls, while thick ones create wavy hair.

Heated rollers – which come in sets and are heated on metal posts – work like conventional rollers and are good for giving volume while

Even if fashion calls for straight hair, do not use straighteners every day and always use heat-protective styling sprays.

creating curls. They work in a fraction of the time taken by conventional rollers. Choose the new types, which do not have potentially hair-damaging spikes. Use them on dry hair and remove them once they are cold, which can be in as little as 10 minutes.

Smooth or foam-covered rollers are less hazardous to your hair than Velcro-covered ones.

Protecting your locks

The multilayered structure of hair makes it strong and resilient, but your hair can only take so much before it will inevitably start to show signs of damage or weathering.

Obviously, chemicals used in solutions to straighten, perm or colour hair are some of the biggest culprits when it comes to hair damage. In addition, dermatologists worldwide have warned against the dangers of plaits that are made too tightly, particularly where fragile African hair is concerned – as these very often lead to scarring and hair loss. It is important to note that this is not only an adult problem: children may look very cute with tightly braided hair, but such styles may not be good for their future hair and scalp health.

The chemicals used to straighten, perm or colour hair are some of the biggest culprits when it comes to hair damage.

The age of individual hairs naturally plays a major role when it comes to health and shine; the longer your hair, the more years it has been exposed to all sorts of hazards and the more difficult it is to maintain, and to keep split ends at bay.

The great outdoors

Just as the weather and your lifestyle impact on your general health, these factors also affect your hair. The sun can bleach your hair, strip it of moisture and weaken its protein structure, while wind knots and tangles it, causing split ends and damaged cuticles.

Protect your locks by wearing a hat or bandanna when you are out on a hot, sunny day. When it is windy, tie up long hair to keep it from knotting.

Many hair products these days contain sun-protection ingredients. Unfortunately, many are not effective as their contact with the hair is too short to make a real difference, but if you can find a leave-in conditioner containing sunscreen, use it liberally on the beach or at the poolside.

◀ *Wear a wide-brimmed hat to protect your tresses against harsh sunlight, which can bleach your hair, weaken its protein structure and strip it of moisture.*

Alarmingly, blonde or highlighted hair tends to turn a shade of green after prolonged exposure to swimming-pool water, the result of a chemical reaction with the chlorine. Experienced hairdressers advise using tomato sauce as a solution for green hair. Just apply, wait a while and rinse off.

To prevent this from occurring, renowned trichologist Philip Kingsley's advice is to comb a water-resistant product through your hair before you go swimming. You can make your own by mixing together some high-factor sun protection oil and hair conditioner. This protects your tresses from the harmful effects of chlorine as well as salt water, and

Bad hairdressing methods are a common cause of hair loss and hair damage, particularly when it comes to fragile African hair.

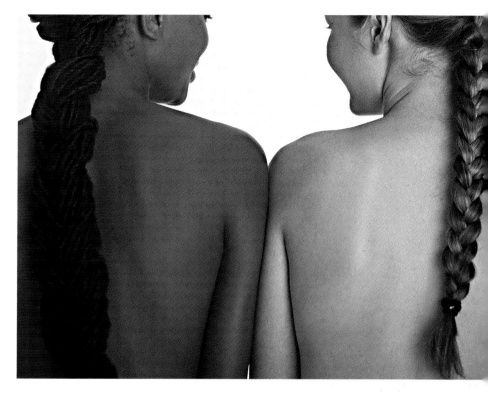

helps to maintain the moisture levels and condition of your hair. Also, remember to rinse your hair well with clean, clear water after swimming to get rid of chemical or sea-salt build up, or better still, wear a swimming cap.

Lastly, air conditioning not only dries the air, it also has a drying effect on your hair. Use a humidifier. Alternatively, a do-it-yourself option is to place a bowl of water near the air conditioner to replace the moisture that is taken out of the air.

▲

Tying up long hair in windy conditions protects it against knotting.

Styling sense and healthy hair

Bad hairdressing methods are a common cause of hair loss and damage, and devastating results are particularly widespread when it comes to fragile African hair. Tight braids, comprising your own hair or hair extensions, the misuse or overuse of chemical hair products, and constant pulling on the hair can all cause a condition known as traction hair loss or traction alopecia, prevalent among African and African-American women.

Traction hair loss often starts with the hair thinning at the front hairline, and then spreads. Balding can also occur in a band around the scalp, known as banded traction alopecia.

Chemicals used for straightening or 'relaxing' hair are potent and if not used properly – or overused – can burn the scalp. Serious burns can even destroy hair-follicle cells. Known as scarring traction alopecia, this condition in itself not only leads to hair loss, but also to inflammation and swelling of affected areas on the scalp.

Scarring traction alopecia is common and a much-discussed issue in dermatological circles. The consensus is that early diagnosis and a change in hairstyling habits are crucial to combating this problem.

◀ *Tight ponytails can cause traction alopecia. Never pull your hair back so tightly that your scalp hurts.*

All this does not mean you should never consider braiding or relaxing your hair. If your hair is in good condition, a skilled hairdresser using good products can get excellent results.

Alarm bells should ring, however, if you notice hair damage or loss. In this case, reconsider your styling methods immediately. Remove tight braids or stop straightening your hair, and take preventive and restorative action (otherwise you may well be on the road to permanent hair damage, hair loss or scalp problems). Remember to condition your hair often to combat brittleness, brush relaxed hair with a natural-bristle brush, and never use unprotected and thin, elastic hair bands that can cut into your hair, damaging it and sometimes even intertwining with it. Thicker, fabric-covered bands are far better to gather your hair.

Sleeping in rollers, and repeatedly using heated rollers and electrical hot brushes, straightening devices and other appliances can also lead to hair damage and patchy hair loss. They are also known to lead to the phenomenon known as 'bubble hair'. This is caused by using the hair-dryer on too high a setting, or overusing other heated appliances. The heat causes the water inside the hair to boil, and results in the formation of little bubbles. The hair eventually breaks off at, or near, the bubble.

▲

When towel drying your hair, do not rub it vigorously. Blot it with a towel instead.

A question of chemicals

Let's face it, it is better not to perm your hair, but since perming also has its cosmetic benefits (such as giving volume to fine, thin hair and making hair more manageable), there will always be a need – and a case – for it, if it is done professionally. Modern products, while doing the same job as their predecessors, are gentler on your hair and less likely to damage it.

The strong and flexible keratin protein structure of hair makes it possible to style it in a variety of ways. Temporary styling – such as blow-drying and the use of electrical styling appliances – works on weak bonds between atoms in the long chains of amino acids that make up keratin. These weak bonds – mainly of hydrogen – can be temporarily broken by water or even humidity. As they break apart when hair gets wet, and form again during the drying process, these bonds give hair flexibility, because the bonds tend to form again in different places, changing its shape. For example, wet hair left to dry naturally ends up looking different from hair wound onto a brush and blow-dried.

(This is why your hair looks a mess if it gets wet in the rain or if you don't control the drying process!) If you want to permanently alter the structure of your hair, however, you need to

▲

New straightening methods, such as thermal restructuring, are much easier on the hair than traditional chemical straighteners.

tackle the strong bonds of hydrogen in your hair, which can only be broken through the use of chemical compounds. These bonds – which are, in fact, some of the strongest found in nature – are disulphide bonds (or disulphide linkages or bridges). By breaking them, you make straight hair curly (by means of a perm) and curly hair straight by means of chemical straightening.

PERMS

Perming works as follows: a hairdresser applies a slightly alkaline liquid – a curling fluid which contains reducing agents – to the hair to break down the strong disulphide bonds. The most commonly used reducing agent is ammonium thioglycollate. The hairdresser winds the hair around curlers to create the curls, which are then fixed with an acidic oxidizing solution, normally containing hydrogen peroxide (a neutralizing agent that fixes the chemical bonds in their new positions). The degree of curliness depends on the diameter of the curlers.

Perms are best done professionally so choose a reputable salon. A skilled stylist who applies the neutralizer at exactly the right point so that the perm is fixed with as little hair damage as possible can save you a lot of anguish!

One of the reasons care has to be taken during perming is that the scalp is vulnerable while, and after, the chemical solution is applied to the hair. Perming damage can also be minimized by using a quality product. (The scalp is even more vulnerable during straightening.)

To get the best out of a perm, make sure your hair is in the best possible health, and deep-condition it several times in the weeks preceding the perm. Do not use chemicals on your hair if you have a scalp condition or any sores on your head. Importantly, once it has been permed, do not wash, vigorously brush or blow-dry your hair for two days to make sure the keratin has properly hardened into its new shape. Use conditioner after every wash. If you want to get a home perm, follow the instructions carefully – it is important that every step is carried out as indicated. Remember, the temperature of the room can increase the speed at which the chemicals work, so be careful with them and do not keep them on your hair too long.

Do not perm and colour your hair on the same day as this will most certainly damage your hair. If you really need to perm and colour your hair, do the perm first, at least a week or two before the colour. A good salon should always do a patch test before perming or colouring your hair to assess whether there will be any serious hair damage, or allergic reactions to the dye.

Among the perms available are body perms, using large curlers to produce soft curls and volume; root perms, designed to give volume only to the hair-root area; spiral perms, creating masses of spiral curls (best on long hair) and spot perms, targeting only certain areas, for example the crown or areas around the face.

A relatively new development is the semipermanent perm that gives volume to hair but does not last long. Modern products are gentler on the hair than those used a few decades ago, but do step up on deep-conditioning treatments, use a diffuser on your hair-dryer and never brush your permed hair – use a wide-toothed comb instead.

STRAIGHTENERS

The permanent straightening or 'relaxing' of curly hair works on the same principles as a perm and the reduction and oxidation process is similar but instead of winding hair on curlers, hairdressers comb it out straight from root to tip to uncurl it and then apply the neutralizer.

To straighten frizzy or kinky hair – such as African hair – alkaline products (like sodium or potassium hydroxide) are used. As they can harm the scalp, they are suspended in thick creams. Sodium and potassium hydroxide definitely have a weakening effect on hair and make it far less elastic than untreated hair. There is also the danger that the traction of combing the hair can pull it out or break it off.

If you're having your hair straightened, go to an experienced professional. Also consider thermal restructuring, also known as Japanese hair straightening, thermal reconditioning or bio-ionic therapy (marketed as delivering negative ions to the hair).

▲

This woman has had a successful body perm, which has given her lovely hair volume and has produced soft, loose curls.

To colour or not to colour?

Certain types of hair colouring, such as temporary tints, are not damaging to your hair, but bleaching and high-lighting can adversely affect its condition. This is because chemical treatments alter the hair's cortex and affect its elasticity, which means that the hair stretches only to a limited extent and breaks easily when groomed.

Permanent colouring normally makes use of two solutions – one is the bleach to remove existing colour and the other is the new colouring agent. Bleach, commonly an ammonia or hydrogen peroxide solution, strips colour from your hair. When applied, it damages the hair's protein structure, giving it a characteristic brittle texture. It is thus recommended not to bleach or highlight your hair too often. Similarly, the more drastic your colour change the worse the brittleness will be.

Bleaching also makes hair more porous and vulnerable to other chemical

▲

A change in hair colour can really lift your spirits, but make sure you use a good product and follow the instructions carefully.

processes. This may cause irregular colouring as dry, porous hair absorbs colour too quickly.

Ensure your hair is in very good condition before you apply permanent colour to it, and thereafter, remember to condition it after every wash.

HIGHLIGHTS

Highlighting is a process during which small sections of hair are bleached. The old-fashioned way to do this was to pull strands of hair through a pierced cap. These days, sections of hair are normally wrapped in foil. Only a portion of the hair is bleached, so the process is less harmful than bleaching a whole head of hair, and it doesn't need to be done as often. However, repeated highlighting can still lead to damaged and dry hair.

Highlighting used to consist of two processes: the application of bleach, followed by rinsing, and the application of the required colour. Nowadays the two processes are combined using products containing both bleach and colour.

With permanent tints and highlighting, make sure you only have your roots touched up when necessary, so that the same hair does not get repeatedly blasted by drying chemicals.

On the upside, expertly done colouring can not only give you a fresh new look, it can also combat greasiness and make fine hair look thicker, as it swells the hair shaft.

Permanent solutions through the years

■ The first perms were done at the start of the 20th century, when chemicals, combined with high heat, produced 'permanent' curls. The early experiments led to scalp burns and hair breakage.

Fortunately for us, 'cold permanent waving', which did not require heat, was introduced in the 1940s. It is still the basic process used today.

■ Hair damage through styling is not a modern phenomenon. In the 1970s, L'Oréal, in collaboration with the Judiciary Identity Laboratories, studied 33-centuries-old hair taken from the mummy of the Egyptian pharaoh Ramses II.

They found that his hair – unsurprisingly – had been badly damaged. Although the passage of time was partly responsible, some of the damage was attributed without much doubt to his rudimentary combs.

■ Thick hair is easier to perm than thin hair. Perming solutions developed for Caucasian hair are diluted for use on Asian hair.

*During highlighting, small sections of
hair are wrapped in foil
and bleached.*

A natural alternative

Henna, the most well-known natural hair dye, extracted from the Egyptian privet (*Lawsonia inermis*), is widely used in India and the Middle East. It comes as a powder that is mixed with water to form a paste, and works much like a semipermanent colour, staining the outside of the hair shaft.

While it does not have the damaging effects of chemical dyes, it can be difficult to predict the colour you will get. It is definitely best used on dark brown and black hair, to which it imparts a red glow. The longer you leave henna on your hair, the more intense the resulting colour will be.

Never be tempted to use henna on blonde, grey or highlighted hair – unless you don't mind a scary orange! Other natural dyes are chamomile and tea leaves.

Although henna is regarded as very safe, people who suffer from asthma and allergies should take care when using it.

▲

Henna, a natural hair dye regarded as very safe, is widely used in India and the Middle East.

Is it safe?

While some doctors advocate that you wait until the first trimester of your pregnancy has passed before you dye your hair, authorities such as the UK-based Oxford Hair Foundation conclude that dyeing your hair during pregnancy is safe.

Sceptics point out that – while there is no proof that chemicals in hair dyes are dangerous during pregnancy – there are also no reliable studies proving them to be safe. If you're worried, avoid dying your hair during the first trimester.

Highlighting hair is considered safer than colouring your whole head (particularly when using a dark colour). Vegetable-based products, such as henna, are also considered safer.

Concern about a possible link between dark hair-colouring products and cancer is nothing new. In fact, the hair dye industry has, in recent years, stopped using several ingredients that have been found to cause cancer in animals. There is, however, little concern that some of these dangerous compounds have now been replaced by chemicals with very similar structures.

Adding to the debate is a new scientific study conducted by Yale University researchers and published in the American Journal of Epidemiology at the beginning of 2004, which indicates that women who have been colouring their hair for some 24 years or more, starting before 1980, are a third more likely to develop non-Hodgkin lymphoma.

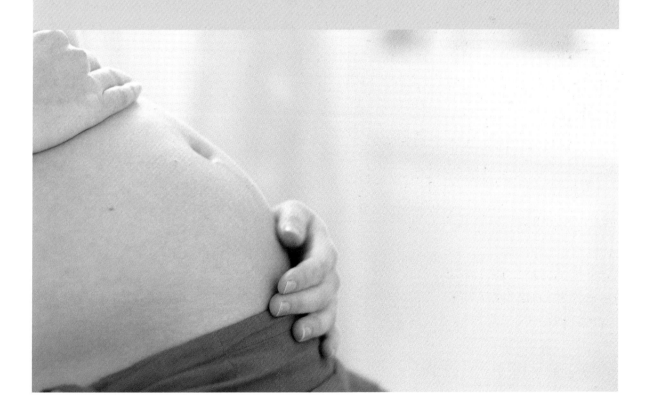

Getting your hair right

One of the most exciting things about hair is that you can change it so easily. Up to a point, you can play around creatively with what nature has given you; but not every style and colour is ideal.

The following guidelines should help you decide whether a certain style or shade would suit you but there are really no hard and fast rules. While your particular facial shape may call for a short cut, you may in fact detest short hair and feel more confident with long tresses. In that case, there is no point in chopping off your crowning glory. Your personality also plays an important role: that trendy cut and bright colour may theoretically suit you, but if you generally prefer not to draw too much attention to yourself, anything too wild may make your life a misery.

If you are planning a major change, talk it through with a hair-stylist, who should be able to advise you on what will complement you and whether it will actually be possible to achieve a certain look with your hair type.

Up to a point, you can play around creatively with what nature has given you but not every style and colour suits everyone.

Your face the canvas

Hairstylists mainly distinguish between curved and angled faces. Curved or contoured shapes include oval, round, pear-shaped and heart-shaped faces. Angular face shapes include diamond-shaped, square, rectangular (long) and triangular faces.

If you are not sure what your facial shape is, tie back your hair, look straight into a mirror and trace the outline of your face on the mirror. Hopefully the shape will become clear to you. Remember, though, that how you see yourself is not exactly how other people see you – your side profiles and three-quarter profile are as important (prominent features being your nose and chin) as the full-frontal view.

The most desirable facial shape – from a hairstyle point of view – is the oval face. If you are lucky enough to have been born with an oval-shaped face, you are likely to be able to wear any hairstyle of your choice. In fact, stylists like to create the illusion of an oval face, for example, by 'broadening' and 'shortening' a rectangular (or long) face.

If you have a long face, the idea is to optically shorten it by wearing a fringe and/or layers. Preferably avoid long, straight hair, as this can accentuate the length of your face.

A heart-shaped face tends to be wide at the forehead, with a narrower jaw line. A hairstyle that narrows the forehead, but widens the

DIFFERENT FACE SHAPES

There are basic guidelines that can help you to choose the most flattering style for your facial shape, but do remember: side and three-quarter profile are also important.

Square face

Oval face

Pear-shaped face

Long face

'A'-triangular face

Heart-shaped face

jaw line – with curls or waves, for example – should be a good choice. In this case, hair no longer than shoulder-length should be flattering. (The same goes for a diamond-shaped face.)

A pear-shaped face is just the opposite of the heart shape. In this case, you should attempt to widen your forehead and narrow your jaw line. Hair that is fuller around the forehead, with a narrowing effect at the jaw, should create good balance.

For both a round and square face, stylists recommend a style that will lengthen and narrow your face shape. This you can do by creating height with your hairstyle. A round, curly style will let your face seem even rounder – instead keep the sides short or long, sleek and close to the face. For a square face, try a side parting to draw the eye away from the square-ness of your face. Soft waves can create softness for a square face. Avoid severe hairstyles, such as a straight bob, which can make your look hard.

There are two types of triangular faces – the V-triangle and the A-triangle. The 'V' is widest at the forehead and thus needs less hair in that area and more around the chin (a round bob could work well), while the 'A' needs a style that is fuller at the forehead, for a widening effect. You may also have a combination of facial shapes, so use your common sense. A simple guideline to remem-ber is that where your face is at its widest, avoid bulk or volume. (Keep your hair straight or tucked behind your ears, for example.) Where your face is narrow, use volume or layers to create width. Also, bear in mind that there should be a balance between the shape of your face and the rest of your body. (Masses of long hair are unlikely to suit someone who is short and petite.)

A question of colour

Just like no two faces are the same (except for those of identical twins), no-one else has exactly the same hair colour as you. Even black has subtle shade differences – determined by the type and amount of melanin in your hair. Changing your hair colour is a great way of reinventing yourself, but, again, there are some guidelines to bear in mind, the most important of which is your basic skin tone, which can be warm ('yellow') or cool ('blue').

If you are pale-skinned, a good way of determining whether your skin tone is warm or cool is to inspect the freckles on your arm. If they appear to have a charcoal colour, you are likely to have a cool skin tone. If they look honey-coloured or orange, your tone is warm. If you have dark Mediterranean skin or black skin, you are also likely to have dark eyes and dark hair, but you, too, can have a yellow (golden) or blue undertone in your skin.

Generally, you should go for warm hair colour if your skin tone is warm (with golden or reddish tones) while a cool colour should suit you if you have a cool skin tone (with a bluish undertone). Also remember that, while a certain shade of blonde, red or brown may not suit your complexion at all, another may do wonders for it.

Lastly, it is not only your skin colour that should act as a guide, your eye colour is also important. If you have dark eyes and skin, dark

◄ *When it comes to hair colour, you have a wide choice, but do make sure you choose a tint that suits your natural colouring.*

Salon products vs. store purchases

This is a thorny issue. Many – if not most – salon owners swear that the expensive salon products on their shelves are far superior to their supermarket counterparts.

Is this really the case though, or should you save your money? Several dermatologists believe salon products are not necessarily superior in any way, apart from the more expensive and exclusive packaging. Many contain simple ingredients, such as salicylic acid, and products with a similar make-up can be bought less expensively elsewhere. Even when it comes to medicated shampoos, you are able to find products that are as effective as their salon counterparts on the supermarket shelf.

As stated earlier, the cleansing agent sodium laureth sulfate is gentler than sodium laurel sulfate, so a product containing the former may be a better choice. You will find plenty of supermarket products containing sodium laureth sulfate. Some manufacturers use natural ingredients or honey as a selling point. This may sound nice, but does not necessarily have anything to do with the effect of the product on your hair.

hair looks fabulous. Light eyes with dark skin? Then keep your options wide open, but light eyes combined with light skin generally calls for a lighter hair colour.

■ If you want to go red, but have a cool skin tone, burgundy, mahogany and similar shades will work for you. If your skin tone is warm, choose oranges, Titian or pure red.

■ If you want to go blonde, choose a gold or honey-blonde for a warm skin tone. Ash-blonde, Nordic blonde or beige are good options for a cool skin tone.

■ If you don't have a dark complexion or naturally dark hair, it is generally a bad idea to dye your hair pitch black, as it is likely to make you look older and paler. There are always exceptions, though. Typical pale Irish skin is very well complemented by very dark hair, for example. Not everyone can go very fair either

– particularly if you have very pale eyes you may end up looking rather washed out. (However, good make-up may solve this problem.)

■. Solid colours that are very blonde, or dark, are generally not flattering unless you have very clear skin. They can also look unnatural, particularly if you are using it to disguise grey.

■ Highlights are a great option if you don't want to dye your whole head, but are not suitable for everyone.

Highlights look best if you have fair or medium brown hair, but steer clear if your hair is dark brown, black, or grey. (Lowlights – dark streaks, as opposed to light ones – work well with grey, particularly for men).

■ If you want to cover grey hair, don't choose a dye too similar to your natural hair colour. As you grow older, lighter colours may do more for your complexion. Temporary colour won't cover grey successfully; demi-permanent or permanent dye will.

Of course, the more radical the change, the more time-consuming it is likely to be to keep up your new colour, so consider your lifestyle and willingness to spend a fair amount of time at the hairdresser. (As an indication, if you choose a permanent colour that is far from your natural one, you may need to have your roots tinted every four to six weeks.) Also bear in mind the harmful effects the chemicals can have on your hair (therefore, only the roots that have not been in contact with dye before should be touched up).

Water-based temporary colours coat only the outside of your hair and are easily washed away. They contain no chemicals and do not harm the hair shafts. Temporary colours carry relatively fewer risks of allergic reaction than permanent colours do.

Semipermanent colours penetrate the outer cuticle scales of the hair and cover the inner cortex, but also wash away after six to 12 shampoos. You can only go darker or redder, as this type of dye cannot lighten hair (it does not contain hydrogen peroxide or ammonia).

Demipermanent colour lasts longer than semipermanent colour (up to 26 washes). It does not contain ammonia, so you cannot lighten your hair using demi-colour. It does contain a small amount of peroxide,

If you are a natural blonde, add a few golden highlights.

If you find your red hair dull, get some copper streaks.

To brighten up your black hair, consider a few highlights.

▲

*Modern permanent colouring
methods tend to be gentler on the
hair than the older two-step process.*

however, which opens up the cuticle scales so that the colour can penetrate the cortex to a certain extent. Demipermanent colour is very good to cover grey and, as it washes away, regrowth is not nearly as obvious as with permanent colour.

Permanent colour enters the hair's inner cortex, and a chemical reaction – brought about by ammonia and peroxide – results in a permanent change to the colour (until it grows out). The benefit of permanent colour is that it can make hair darker or lighter. It does not fade like semi-permanent colour.

Modern permanent colouring methods tend to be gentler on the hair than the older two-step process, during which hair was first stripped of all its melanin, and then dyed to a new colour using another chemical process. These days, a less concentrated bleach solution (containing about 20 per cent hydrogen peroxide) is used, in conjunction with a dye and cleansing agent, to achieve the new colour in one single step.

Getting rid of unwanted hair

Hair removal for cosmetic reasons is nothing new – the ancient Egyptians are believed to have used sugar and beeswax to remove superfluous body hair. The threading method of removing excess facial hair – which is still used today, particularly in the Arabian Gulf and India – is believed to be many centuries old. Archaeologists have also found instruments like sharpened rocks, suggesting that men shaved their beards many thousands of years ago.

In Elizabethan times it was considered extremely desirable for fashionable women to have high foreheads – this resulted in women plucking their front hairlines to make their foreheads appear higher.

The threading method of removing excess hair - used particularly in the Arabian Gulf and India - is believed to be centuries old.

As your choice of hairstyle gives some indication of your personality; so too, your decision on whether or not to remove body hair makes a personal statement. And this does not only apply to women as an increasing number of spas and beauty clinics now cater for men. In particular, waxes and laser hair-removal treatments have become a unisex pursuit.

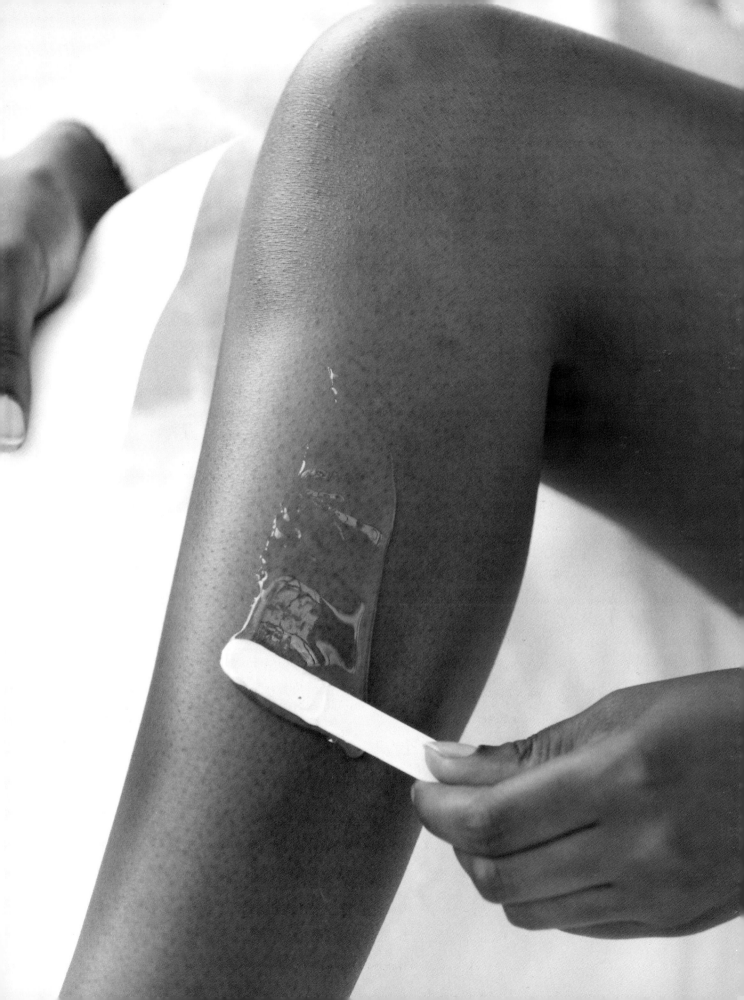

A guide to hair removal

Hair can be removed temporarily through depilation (the removal of the part of the hair that is visible, for example by shaving or using depilatory creams) or epilation (removing the entire hair by plucking or waxing).

SHAVING

This is the most common and straightforward way of hair removal; particularly useful in getting rid of unwanted hair on legs or under the arms. Make sure you use a sharp blade and sufficient lather. Shaving can irritate the skin or lead to ingrown hairs on sensitive areas, such as the bikini line for women.

Contrary to popular myth, shaving does not make hair grow out darker or thicker and it does not stimulate hair growth. The hairs may feel prickly while they are growing out, but they are unchanged in every way once they are fully grown.

◀ *Use a sharp blade and sufficient lather when you shave your legs, as shaving can irritate the skin or lead to ingrown hairs.*

DEPILATORY CREAMS AND LOTIONS

These contain chemicals that easily dissolve the protein that makes up unwanted hairs. They work well for some people, but are not recommended if you have a very sensitive skin or are prone to skin pigmentation, as they can cause inflammation. If it is possible, limit the use of depilatory creams to your legs. Keep them far away from your face as even a mild chemical burn could cause hyper-pigmentation. (You could end up with a hairless but unsightly, pigmented moustache area, for example.) It is a very good idea to first test a patch of skin for possible irritation.

EPILATORS

Because rotary epilators pull hair out this process of depilation is very painful. Aside from the benefit that no chemicals are used, there are no advantages to using epilators. They are known to be ineffective in pulling out fine and short hairs, because the tweezers cannot grasp them, and those hairs that are seized tend to be broken.

Plucking is an effective way of pulling out stray eyebrow hairs. Refrain from tweezing your chin or upper lip, however, as this can cause a distortion of the papillae, which can lead to branching and increased growth. Similarly, never pluck any hairs growing from pigmented moles – they have a tendency to turn cancerous.

PLUCKING

Plucking (tweezing) is an effective way of pulling out individual stray hairs on the eyebrow area, and can be painful. (Never tweeze the hairs on the upper lip or chin, or those on a pigmented mole.) Always use a good quality pair of tweezers; an inferior one could break off hairs or tweeze your skin along with the hair. A benefit of this method is that, if tweezing is done correctly, it does not damage the skin and, like threading gets rid of stray hairs for two to four weeks.

Rubbing some ice over the area that you plan to pluck before you start may help to slightly numb the site, making it less painful.

THREADING

This is a very quick and effective, traditionally Indian and Middle Eastern, way of getting rid of rows of unwanted hair, but it is catching on in the West too. The therapist uses a piece of taut twisted thread to pull out the hair. It is no more painful than tweezing and is faster.

WAXING

Waxing – during which strips of hair are plucked out by their roots – is one of the most popular ways of salon hair removal (it can be done at home, too, but is better left to the professionals). It is known to be painful but effective, and many women – and men – keep going back for more! However, waxing can inflame sensitive skin and should not be used if you are prone to broken capillaries.

There are two types of waxes: 'hot' and 'cold' (although cold wax is also slightly hot to the touch when applied). Hot wax is a thick substance, generally used on sensitive areas, such as the face, bikini line and under the arms, while cold wax is much thinner and runnier, like syrup, and is usually used on body areas where the skin is less sensitive, such as the legs and arms. Ingredients include beeswax and paraffin.

As waxing plucks out the hair, regrowth is slower than with shaving. Side effects may include allergic contact dermatitis due to the colophony (a substance used in wax obtained from the sap of pine trees). Do not wax when you are on the drug Roaccutane (used to treat acne), as

the waxing does not only remove the hair, but also a layer of skin. When you choose a beauty salon, make sure that the therapists are qualified and that hygienic practices are followed (some salons still recycle their hot wax after use, although this practice has been strictly outlawed).

ELECTROLYSIS

Electrolysis is a process during which the hair follicle is targeted by an electrical current from a very thin needle, causing localized damage to the dermal papilla. The hair is then simply removed with a pair of tweezers.

Electrolysis can be a very good tool to get rid of unwanted hair. However, make sure you choose a qualified and skilled practitioner, as the procedure can produce little white scars if not done properly. Also, it is a time-consuming process during which individual hairs are targeted and is only useful for small areas. (Since the arrival of laser hair removal, electrolysis has shifted into the background somewhat.) However, unlike lasers, electrolysis is effective for both dark and fair hair.

Take care to stay out of the sun – or use a very good sunscreen – for about

If you are considering laser hair removal :

■   See a dermatologist for an initial consultation to make sure you don't have an underlying medical condition.

■   Avoid fly-by-night clinics, or clinics not attached to certified medical facilities. It is best to be referred by a dermatologist.

■   Preferably have the treatment during winter, when your skin is paler than in summer.

■   For a month before laser treatment, stay out of the sun, use a high-factor sunscreen, and do not use self-tan lotions or sunbeds.

■   As laser treatment targets anagen hair (hair in their active growth phase), you should not wax, bleach or tweeze for six weeks before a treatment, and do not use any hair-removal creams either.

two days after having electrolysis, and keep perfume and chemicals away from the treated area. While having the treatment, you feel a tingling sensation in your hair follicle. The discomfort is more acute in sensitive areas. You repeat the treatments every six to 10 weeks.

It is safe to have hair removed from most parts of your body using electrolysis, as long as the skin is undamaged. Exceptions are the hairs inside your nose and ears, and those on pigmented moles.

LASER HAIR REMOVAL

The most revolutionary method of successful modern hair removal is, without a doubt, laser hair removal, and this technology is continually being fine-tuned and improved.

During the treatment, a laser, consisting of one wavelength and a pulse width of monochromatic light, targets the melanin in the hair (the darker the hair, the better). The aim is for the laser to destroy the hair follicle without harming surrounding tissue or causing hypopigmentation of the skin (areas of lighter pigmentation).

Laser hair removal is sometimes marketed as being permanent – although this is not the case, even though it can remove some hairs permanently in instances where the hair follicles are completely destroyed. (This is also the case with electrolysis). Unfortunately, not all hair follicles are targeted accurately enough to achieve permanent removal of all the hair. So, at most, you can expect hair reduction. You will also need multiple treatments over several months – how many, depends on the part of your body that you are having treated, and this

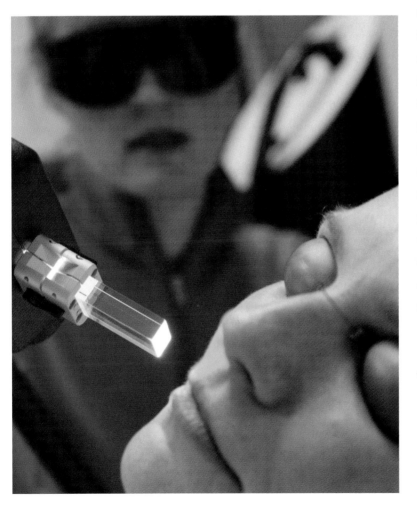

◀   *This woman is having laser treatment to remove unwanted hair from her face. Both she and the laser operator are wearing goggles to protect their eyes.*

also varies from person to person. The good news, however, is that laser treatment does delay hair growth, and scientific studies have shown that this may lead to temporary hair loss for about three months.

Because the laser targets the melanin, the treatment works best for people with dark hair (containing lots of melanin) and fair skin (containing little melanin), but as the technology improves, good results are also being achieved on darker skin (however, if you have very dark or black skin, laser treatment is definitely not for you). As you have to have pigment in your hair for laser hair removal to work, you are also not a candidate if you have blonde or grey hair.

One of the major benefits of laser treatment is that when it is done professionally, it is a safe procedure and can treat large parts of the body in a short period of time (as opposed to electrolysis where each hair is targeted individually). There are a number of excellent lasers for laser hair removal. The one best suited to you depends on your skin type and the part of the body that is to be treated. These days, dermatologists seem to prefer lasers with a slightly longer wavelength, such as the normal mode alexandrite laser, the pulsed diode laser and the YAG laser.

You have to wear eye protection during the treatment to prevent any possible damage to your retinas. Depending on your pain threshold, there is minimal pain. (Generally, you do not need anaesthesia, but for larger or more sensitive body areas, a topical anaesthetic, applied as a cream, should do the trick.) If you have dark skin, you may have some temporary hypopigmentation (lighter areas of pigmentation) following the treatment.

There is a risk of scarring if the laser practitioner uses too powerful a laser during the treatment – another reason to choose the best clinic you can find. Opting for a less reputable establishment offering inexpensive treatments may not save you money in the long run.

STICK TO THE TRIED AND TESTED

The treatments mentioned are established and medically approved methods of hair removal. However, if you do an Internet search – or scan the classified advertisements in certain publications – you may come across a number of other hair-removal methods, some not approved by medical bodies or scientifically tested.

Stick to the tried-and-tested techniques, and do not waste your money – or compromise your health – on bogus treatments. Some of these include electric tweezers (using electrified tweezers to apply an electric current to the hair), dietary supplements and 'hair growth inhibitors'.

Non-laser light hair removal

Non-laser light sources (also known as Intense Pulsed Light Source) produce a multiwavelength light and have been scientifically shown to effectively remove hair. (The technology has been marketed as EpiLight.) A specific wavelength can be chosen to suit your hair colour and skin type. Studies have shown about 60 per cent hair removal 12 weeks after a single treatment, but long-term studies are continuing.

Silky-smooth, hair-free legs can be achieved in a number of ways – from shaving and waxing to using depilatory creams and lotions.

A male perspective

Human beings, according to the UK-based Oxford Hair Foundation, have more hair on their heads than any other species of primate, but researchers continue to debate its function and the reasons for men losing their hair in the case of genetic male-pattern baldness. The question is whether the hair on your head and face really serves a purpose in temperature regulation and sun protection (the counter-argument here is that humans have not kept the hair on their noses, which are particularly vulnerable to sun damage), or whether, in fact, it has more to do with sexual signals and attracting a mate.

Whatever the reason, men these days have a myriad options when it comes to styling, colouring and combating greying. Even when it comes to balding, you have safe avenues that could take years off your age and boost your self-confidence. Fortunately, a neat style is no longer limited to short back and sides – partly thanks to style icons like British footballer David Beckham modern men have been freed to literally let their hair down.

> *Men these days have a myriad options when it comes to styling, colouring and combating greying.*

The best style for you

It is not only women who should consider their facial shapes when choosing a hairstyle – the same goes for men. However, where women have to make do with the hair on their heads, men can use beards or goatees, or even a moustache, to make the most of their features, or to conceal features considered less flattering. Just remember that a beard or moustache does not suit everyone, and that facial hair can be ageing. Your side and three-quarter profiles, as well as features such as a prominent chin, nose or ears, play a role when choosing a hairstyle. Longer hair at the sides can conceal ears that are large or stick out, while a big nose could be balanced by hair that is a little longer at the back.

As with women, an oval face is the ideal. If you have this facial shape, you are spoilt for choice. If you have a square face, most hairstyles will suit you – just keep your hair relatively short around the ears, so that the square look is maintained. If you have a long (rectangular or oblong) face, choose a style with a shortening effect. A fringe or layers could work wonders. A round face looks thinner when offset by a well-styled beard. Slightly longer hair could have a lengthening effect.

Hair that is a little longer at the back could work well to balance out a V-triangular face with a pointy chin. (Alternatively, a goatee could camouflage the chin.) If you have an A-triangular face, try a fringe or layers to create some bulk around your forehead.

You can have the best cut in the world, but not be able to maintain it if you are unsure of what products to use: a hair serum is best for a sleek style, for example, while a wax is good to control curly or frizzy hair.

◀ *Your hairstyle should suit your facial shape and hair type, but it is equally important to consider your personality, lifestyle and profession. This businessman's hairstyle helps to give him a professional and distinguished look.*

Style sense

There is no need to despair if you find your hair thinning or greying. Apart from the fact that these changes are completely natural, there are a number of ways that you can make the best of what you have.

IF YOUR HAIR IS THINNING:

If you are balding, the golden rule is to keep your hair short and neat – stylists advise that any hairstyle requiring you to comb long strands of hair over balding areas is a strict no-no. Have your hair cut by an experienced and professional hairdresser.

Not everyone can carry off the shaved-head look. Unless you are nearly bald, extremely handsome or a sporty type of man, you should probably steer clear of this. A good tip is that colouring thinning hair just one shade darker tends to make it seem fuller. Products that take the sheen off your scalp are a variation on this theme – they are based on the premise that your hair seems thicker if less of your scalp is visible. Some gels and sprays may make your hair seem thicker and fuller. A beard could give you a whole new look.

However, being bald or balding can be stylish these days – Hollywood superstars like Jack Nicholson and sport legends such as Andre Agassi are leading the way. Flaunt your pate by donning stylish eyewear, dressing well or sporting a trendy bandanna.

Male-pattern baldness starts with a receding hairline at the temples. Eventually only the hair at the sides and back may remain.

IF YOUR HAIR IS GREYING:

Greying hair is a natural part of growing older. Like balding, it is genetically determined. Caucasian hair tends to grey quickest – by the age of 50, 50 per cent of Caucasians find that half the hair on their heads is grey. Greying starts near the temples, the result of a gradual decline in melanin production.

Fortunately, most men look distinguished with a little grey in their hair. However, a good way of camouflaging your grey is by getting lowlights (darker streaks, the opposite of highlights). The result is often more natural than if you tint your whole head, and you need to have it done less often. This is because regrowth is less obvious, and blends in with the rest of the hair. If you know from the outset that you want to disguise your grey, do not wait until you are noticeably grey before doing something about it.

Although mainly aimed at women, there are a few home-colouring ranges for men. Remember, temporary colour doesn't cover grey; demipermanent and permanent colour does. (Permanent colouring is best done at a salon.)

Male hair-loss myths

■ The degree of baldness corresponds with the density of hair on the body.

■ There is no basis to believe that any link exists between male baldness and libido.

■ Male-pattern alopecia is caused by poor blood circulation. (Many bogus products marketed as combating hair loss are based on ingredients that would supposedly improve blood circulation and thereby stimulate hair growth or regrowth. Save your money.)

■ While it is true that starving or extremely malnourished people do tend to lose some hair, natural hair loss experienced by a healthy person on a reasonably good diet cannot be linked to diet. Hair-loss products containing amino acids, vitamins and zinc will therefore not stop your hair from falling out.

■ Hair loss cannot be caused by clogged pores, frequent hair washing or tight hats and helmets.

■ Laser treatment cannot cure baldness and does not result in regrowth. When lasers are used in conjunction with approved drugs some regrowth may occur – but most dermatologists tell you that this is thanks to the drugs and not the laser (practitioners at centres that promote the use of lasers to remedy hair loss may disagree).

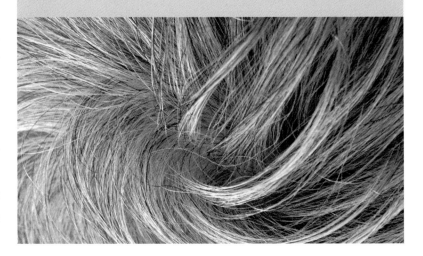

LOSING YOUR HAIR?

There are numerous possible reasons for hair loss (*see* Chapter 3), but by far the most common cause of thinning hair in men is male-pattern baldness (androgenetic alopecia). This starts with a receding hairline at the temples, followed by hair loss on the front of the head. In time, the bald patch enlarges, and eventually only hair at the sides and back of the head may remain. Eventually this hair, too, may fall out.

If your hair is thinning, bear in mind that this is such a common phenomenon that it is highly unlikely to bother anyone but yourself. Natural hair loss – even when premature – is not a medical problem and is entirely due to genetics. However, if you are one of many men who are willing to try almost anything to restore your locks to their former glory, the good news is that there are two drugs that may work wonders – minoxidil and finasteride – but only as long as you are having active treatment. A hair transplant may also be an option. Be under no illusion though – the vast majority of hair-loss remedies, including the much-touted laser therapy, are completely useless.

In case you have wondered, hanging upside down to improve blood flow to your head, rubbing your scalp with hot chillis and consuming vast amounts of vitamin and mineral supplements will not help.

Caucasians appear to be more prone to hair loss than Africans or Asians. It is estimated that up to 96 per cent of Caucasian men lose hair to some degree. According to research published in the Annual New York Academic Science, 30 per cent of them have androgenetic

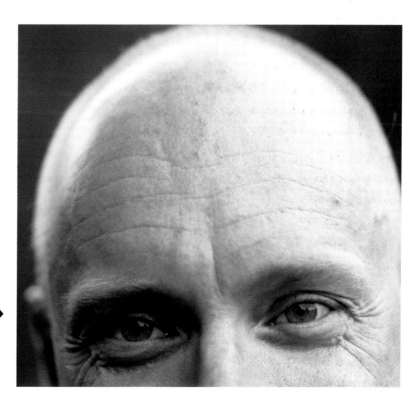

Some men lose all their hair within five years, but mostly it takes between 15 and 20 years. ▶

alopecia by the age of 30, and 50 per cent have it by the age of 50.

Male hair loss can start anytime after puberty, and some men bald much faster than others (again, this is genetically determined). Some lose all their hair within five years, but mostly it takes between 15 and 20 years.

How does it happen? Balding is partly the result of changes in the growth cycle of hair. The number of hairs in the active growth phase (anagen) starts decreasing, while more hair goes into the resting (telogen) phase. Also, long, dark, terminal hairs start to be replaced by short, unpigmented, vellus hairs. At the same time, 'miniaturization' of the hair follicles (reduction in follicle size) takes place. These events lead to increased shedding of hair and finer hair with less pigment being produced.

Male androgenetic alopecia is a progressive condition. You cannot stop it, although the two approved drugs minoxidil and finasteride may temporarily stop the process and result in some regrowth. Interestingly, not only humans tend to lose their hair. Orang-utans and chimpanzees reportedly also show some signs of balding after sexual maturity.

HAIR TRANSPLANTS

Hair loss as a result of male-pattern baldness is linked to the effect of the androgen dihydrotestosterone otherwise known as DHT, on susceptible hair follicles in men (and on those of a very small percentage of women) who are genetically predisposed to it.

Testosterone is changed to DHT by increased levels of a hormone known as 5(alpha)-reductase. (This interaction causes miniaturization.) The typical pattern of this type of hair loss clearly shows susceptible follicles to be concentrated at the top and front of the head, while the ones on the sides and back appear to be more resistant. Surprisingly, when hair from a part of the head that is not balding is transplanted to an area that is balding, the transplanted hair remains resistant to androgenetic alopecia. It is this characteristic that makes hair-transplant surgery possible.

The first hair transplants were carried out about 40 years ago. Up until the late 1980s, these transplants resulted in a look that became known as the 'corn-row' effect, whereby implanted hair was transplanted in neat rows using the now out of favour punch-biopsy method. The result was unnatural and accounts for a lot of the bad press that implants have received. Since then, techniques have improved

Top transplant tips

■ When choosing a hair-transplant clinic, thoroughly check the practitioners' credentials. Only consider the treatment if it is to be carried out by a skilled surgeon after an extensive consultation.

■ Ask to meet patients who have had the treatment and see results before you make up your mind.

■ Do not choose a clinic just because it offers less expensive treatments than others – you may pay dearly for your choice.

■ After the transplant, do not exercise for 10 days and avoid other activities that lead to sweating. Do not wash your hair for three days, to protect the implanted grafts.

vastly, and better results are obtained today. If done by a skilled surgeon, the modern way of implanting hair, by means of grafts, eliminates the 'corn-row' effect and leads to a natural-looking hairline.

How does it work? At the start of the process, a thin strip of skin with hair is taken from the area behind your ear. This donor skin contains follicles with hair that is not genetically programmed to be shed. The strip of skin is then dissected into tiny micrografts (containing one to three hairs) or minigrafts (three to five hairs). This is known as donor harvesting.

The donor area behind the ear is immediately stitched closed and covered by your existing hair. The harvested grafts are then painstakingly implanted into the skin in the bald area of the scalp or area where the hair is thinning.

A hair transplant, usually done ▶
under local anaesthesia, is a lengthy
process that can take several hours,
as thousands of grafts may need to
be implanted.

The transplanted hairs or hair units are planted into the skin less than 1mm (0.03in) apart. Depending on your degree of baldness, the process may be repeated a few times to achieve the required hair density. The transplant is usually done under local anaesthestic and is not painful. It is a lengthy process, however, that can take up to six hours, as several thousand grafts may need to be implanted.

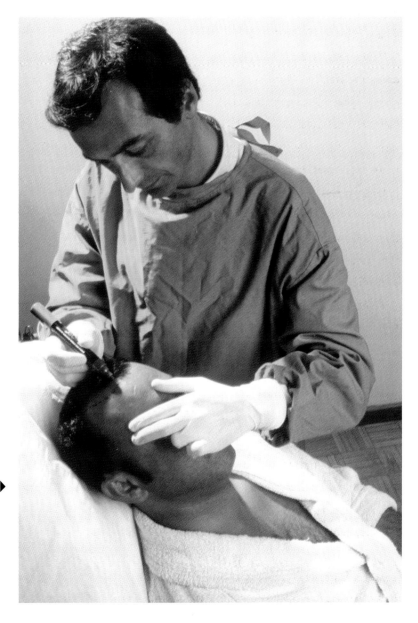

A hair-transplant surgeon painstakingly implants hair grafts into a patient's scalp.

The healing process takes about 10 days, during which there is some redness and scabs form where the hairs have been implanted. Once the graft sites have healed, there should be no visible scars. Do not be alarmed when the hairs in the grafts fall out within 10 days to two weeks after the transplant – this is normal. In the following eight to 20 weeks, the implanted follicles recuperate and generate new hair, which starts growing normally, with hair cells actively dividing.

Bear in mind that your expectations should be realistic. During a hair transplant, no more hair is created, but the existing hair is simply spread around. So, the coverage depends on how many healthy hair follicles you still have. If you are totally bald, you are unlikely to be a candidate for a transplant. If you have little remaining hair, a transplant is not

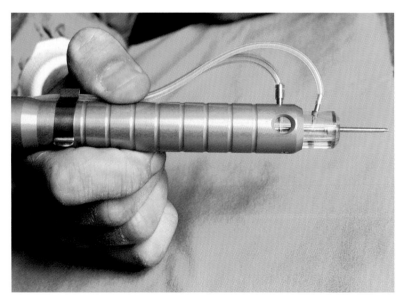

During a hair transplant, this device is used to implant the hair grafts.

going to provide you with a luxurious full head of hair but – if your hair is thinning or you have a small bald patch – the transformation could be quite spectacular. The key is to have enough remaining hair so that it can be transplanted to bald areas of the scalp.

Only consider a hair transplant if your hair loss is natural or the result of other non-reversible causes such as traction alopecia or burns. If the loss is reversible and caused by factors such as thyroid disease, high fever, medication or infection, the answer is not a transplant: you need to have the cause established and treated. You don't have to wait until you reach a certain age to have a hair transplant. If you address the issue early, your balding will be less visible.

The non-surgical option

Wigs and toupees have had bad press in the past, but modern hair systems – as they are known these days – should not be scorned. Made with human hair or quality synthetic strands, a good system can achieve a natural look. Fibres are usually implanted into a polymer material that looks like skin. (The older method involved the hair being tied into mesh bases.) The latest hair systems can be custom-made to match the client's natural hair colour and texture. The downside is that wigs and hairpieces are not permanent. Good ones are expensive, need a fair amount of maintenance and also need to be to be replaced regularly.

When considering a hair transplant, ▶ *it is important to be realistic, as you are not creating more hair, but simply spreading the hair you still have over a greater surface area.*

Glossary

Alopecia: Hair loss.

Amino acids: Basic components of proteins.

Anagen: The growing phase of hair with constant cell production.

Androgens: Male hormones.

Catagen: The transitional phase of the hair-growth cycle, when the follicle stops producing hair.

Club hair: Hair in the resting stage which is ready to fall out.

Cortex: The central part of the hair which is packed with keratin.

Cuticle: The outer layer of cells protecting the cortex of the hair.

Dermal papilla: The part of the hair follicle where growth takes place.

Dihydrotestosterone: A derivative of the hormone testosterone.

Eumelanin: The dark pigment predominating in dark hair.

Hair bulb: The part of the hair cylinder surrounding the dermal papilla.

Hair shaft: The visible part of the hair.

Highlights: The lightening of fine sections of hair with bleach.

Follicle: A depression in the skin containing the dermal papilla where a new hair originates.

Keratin: The protein that makes up the consistency of hair.

Keratinocytes: The cells that form the keratin that makes up the consistency of hair.

Lanugo hair: The hair on an unborn baby.

Medulla: A central hollow core in some hairs.

Melanin: Hair pigment.

Oestrogen: Female hormone.

Phaeomelanin: The light pigment predominating in blonde and red hair.

Sebum: An oily substance produced by the sebaceous glands in the skin.

Surfactants: 'Surface-active agents' found in shampoos.

Telogen: The shedding phase of the hair-growth cycle.

Telogen effluvium: General hair loss from the scalp.

Terminal hair: Long, thick hairs that grow on the head and parts of the body.

Testosterone: Male hormone.

Traction alopecia: Hair loss as a result of strong traction (pulling) caused, for example, by braiding or ponytails.

Trichocytes: Cells in the hair follicle that divide to form hair.

Trichologist: An expert in trichology, the branch of medicine that deals with the scientific study of the hair and scalp (and their diseases).

Trichotillomania: A compulsion to pull out one's own hair.

Vellus hair: Short, unpigmented hairs.

Useful Addresses

CONTACTS

UNITED KINGDOM

- Oxford Hair Foundation
- Department of Dermatology,

Churchill Hospital, Old Road, Headington,

Oxford, OXS 7LJ, United Kingdom

- Website: www.oxfordhairfoundation.org

- L'Oréal (UK) Ltd

255 Hammersmith Road,

London W6 8AZ

- Tel: +44 20 8762 4000
- Website: www.loreal.com

UNITED STATES

- American Hair Loss Council
- 125 Seventh Street, Suite 625,

Pittsburgh, PA, 15222,

United States

- Tel: +1 412 765 3666
- Fax +1 412 765 3669

- National Alopecia Areata Foundation
- PO Box 150760, San Rafael,

CA 94915-076, United States

- Tel: +1 415 472 3780
- Fax: +1 415 472 5343
- Email: info@naaf.org
- Website: www.alopeciaareata.com

ONLINE CONTACTS

CANADA
- The Canadian Hair Research Council
- www.hairinfo.org/en/learning/disorders.html

EUROPE
- European Hair Research Society
- www.ehrs.org

INTERNATIONAL
- Keratin.com hair information source
- www.keratin.com

- Wella
- www.wella.com

UNITED KINGDOM
- Philip Kingsley
- www.philipkingsley.co.uk

UNITED STATES
- North American Hair Research Society
- www.nahrs.org

- Proctor & Gamble
- www.pg.com/science/haircare

GENERAL WEBSITES
- www.thehairstyler.com
- http://hairdos.net
- www.hairboutique.com
- www.worldofhair.com

References

The following books and journals were consulted as sources of reference:

Alora, M., Arndt, K., Dover, J., and Geronemus, R., *Illustrated Cutaneous & Aesthetic Laser Surgery*, Second edition. Appleton & Lange, 1999.

Dawber, R., and Dawber, R.P, *Diseases of the Hair and Scalp*, Third edition. Blackwell Science, 1997.

Gray, J., and Dawber, R., *A Pocketbook of Hair and Scalp Disorders*, Blackwell Science Ltd, 1999.

Grey, J., *World of Hair: A Scientific Companion*, Palgrave Macmillan, 2001.

Jose, A., *Love Your Hair*, Thorsons, 2002.

Kingsley, P., *Hair – An Owner's Handbook*, Aurum Press Limited, 1995.

Openshaw, F., *Hairdressing Science*, Longman Scientific and Technical, 1986.

Reader's Digest, *Foods that Harm Foods that Heal: An A-Z guide to Safe and Healthy Eating*, Reader's Digest, 1997.

Rudiger, M., and von Samson, R., *388 Great Hairstyles*, Sterling Publishing Co., Inc., 1998.

Schwan-Jonczyk, A., *Hair Structure*, Wella AG, 1999.

Stoppard, M., *Woman's Body, A Manual for Life*, Dorling Kindersley, 1994.

Wadeson, J., *Hairstyles. Braiding & Haircare*, Lorenz Books, 1994.

Wingate, P., and Everett, F., *Hair & Makeup*, Usborne Publishing, 1999.

Photographic credits

All photographs by Micky Hoyle for New Holland Image Library (NHIL) with the exception of the following photographers and/or their agencies. Copyright rests with these individuals and/or their agencies.

(***Key to locations:** t = top; b = bottom.)

2–3	Digital Source		Warren Heath	65		Photo Access
4–5	Digital Source	33	Science Photo Library/	71		Ian Reeves/Shine Group
6	Photo Access		Susumu Nishinaga	72		Ian Reeves/Shine Group
9	Photo Access	34	Photo Access	75		Science Photo Library/
12	Digital Source	35	Photo Access			Michael Donne
13	Digital Source	40	Photo Access	77		Ian Reeves/Shine Group
15	Photo Access	50	Patrick Toselli	79		Photo Access
17	Photo Access	51	Photo Access	80		Photo Access
27	Photo Access	54	Patrick Toselli	82		Photo Access
28	Science Photo Library/	55	Digital source	85		Science Photo Library/
	Sue Baker	56	Ian Reeves/Shine Group			Mauro Fermariello
30	Science Photo Library/	60	Photo Access	86	t	Science Photo Library/
	Michelle Del Guercio	61	New Holland Image			Michelle Del Guercio/
31	Science Photo Library/		Library(NHIL)/		b	Science Photo Library/
	Lauren Shear		Ryno Reyneke			Mauro Fermariello
32	New Holland Image	63	Snapstock/Werner	87		Photo Access
	Library (NHIL)/		Bokelberg			

Acknowledgements

The publishers gratefully acknowledge the assistance of Marius Edgar of **FRONT COVER HAIR DESIGN** for giving us permission to use his beautiful facilities for the photo shoot as well as Karmen Lombard for the loan of her brushes and styling accessories.

Index

A

A-triangular face **64**, 65

African hair 16, **17**

air conditioning 51

alopecia 24 *see also* hair loss

alopecia areata 25, 26

alopecia areata totalis 26

alopecia areata universalis 26

ammonia 57

ammonium thioglycollate 55

androgenetic alopecia 24

androgens 26 *see also* male

hormones

Asian hair 16, **17**

autoimmune disease 25

B

baldness 22, 24, 52, 78, 84

banded traction alopecia 52

basal layer **10**

biotin 33

black hair colour 67

bleach 57, 58

blonde hair colour 67

blow-drying 43, 45

brushes 43

bubble hair 53

C

cancer 61

Caucasian hair 16, **17**

central medulla 10

characteristics of hair 18

chemicals 54—56

chemotherapy 27

childbirth 26

chronic illnesses 26

coarse hair 19

cold wax 74

colour 12, 57—59, 66, 67,
68, 69

combination hair 21

combs 44

conditioners 40

contact dermatitis 29

corneal layer **10**

corn-row effect 84, 85

cortex 10, 18

   functions 11

cortisone injections 26

crimpers 45

curl-defining sprays 41

cuticle functions 11

cuticle **10**

D

dandruff 28, **29**

demipermanent colour 68, 82

dermal papilla 10

dermatophytes 28

diet 32—35

dihydrotestosterone 31, 84

disease 26

disulphide bonds 55

donor harvesting 85

dry hair 20

E

eczema 29

electrolysis 74

epilators 72

erector pili **10**, 12

eumelanin 12

F

facial shapes **64**, 80

female hormones 26 *see also*
   oestrogens

female-pattern hair loss 24

fever 27

finasteride 31, 83, 84

fine hair 19

flat brushes 43

furfuracea 28

G

glosses 42

grafts 86

grey hair 68

greying 19, 34, 82

growth cycle, anagen phase 11

   catagen phase 11

   telogen phase 11